THE ILLUSTRATED PROFESSIONAL
WOODWORKER

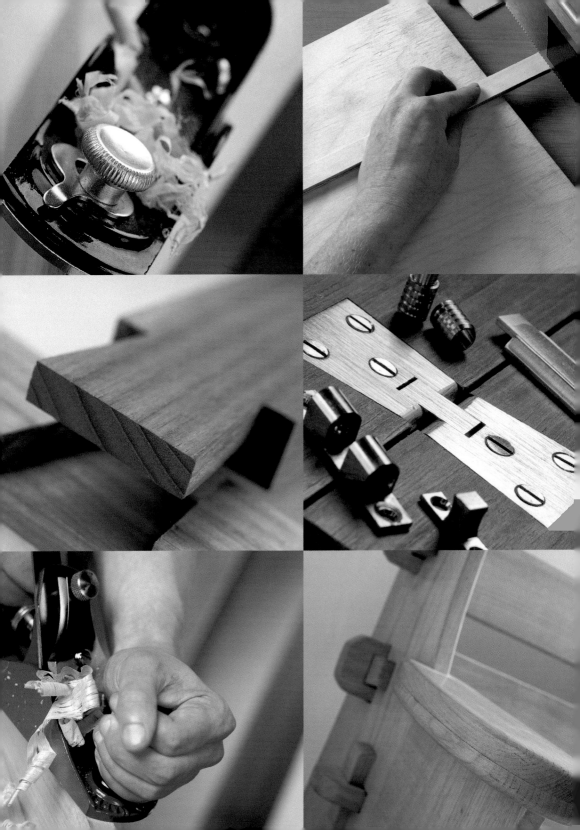

THE ILLUSTRATED PROFESSIONAL
WOODWORKER

TOOLS ▪ TECHNIQUES ▪ PROJECTS ▪ PICTURE FRAMING
JOINERY ▪ HOME MAINTENANCE ▪ FURNITURE REPAIR

a clear and comprehensive guide to woodworking of all types,
with expert advice and over 260 step-by-step techniques and
projects, illustrated with more than 2300 stunning photographs

Contributing Editor
Stephen Corbett

HERMES
HOUSE

This edition is published by Hermes House, an imprint of Anness Publishing Ltd
Hermes House, 88–89 Blackfriars Road, London SE1 8HA
tel. 020 7401 2077; fax 020 7633 9499

www.hermeshouse.com; www.annesspublishing.com

If you like the images in this book and would like to investigate using
them for publishing, promotions or advertising, please visit our website
www.practicalpictures.com for more information.

A CIP catalogue record for this book is available from the British Library.

Publisher: Joanna Lorenz
Editorial Director: Helen Sudell
Art manager: Clare Reynolds
Editors: Doreen Palamartschuk and Elizabeth Woodland
Contributors: Stephen Corbett (woodwork projects), Andrew Gillmore,
Bob Cleveland (woodworking techniques and carpentry projects),
John McGowan (Home Maintenance and DIY), Rian Kanduth
(Framing Projects), and William Cook (Furniture Repair and Restoration)
Text editor: Ian Penberthy
Designer: James Lawrence
Cover Designer: Jonathan Davidson
Illustrator: Julian Baker
Photographer: John Freeman
Stylist: Annie le Painter
Production controller: Claire Rae

ETHICAL TRADING POLICY
Because of our ongoing ecological investment programme, you, as our
customer, can have the pleasure and reassurance of knowing that a tree is
being cultivated on your behalf to naturally replace the materials used to make
the book you are holding. For further information about this scheme,
go to www.annesspublishing.com/trees

Bracketed terms are intended for American readers.

Previously published as part of four volumes, *The Practical Woodworker*,
The Complete Book of Picture Framing & Decorative Framework,
The Ultimate Do-It-Yourself Book, and *How to Repair & Restore Furniture*

PUBLISHER'S NOTE
The author and the publisher have made every effort to ensure that all
instructions contained in this book are accurate and that the safest methods
are recommended. The publisher and author cannot accept liability for any
resulting injury, damage or loss to persons or property as a result of using any
tools in this book or carrying out any of the projects. Before you begin any
woodworking task, you should know how to use all your tools and equipment
safely and that you are sure and confident about what you are doing.

Contents

INTRODUCTION

BY OPENING THIS BOOK, you have already displayed the first qualification to proceed further – a basic interest in wood and how it is used. Millions of people share this interest, and all of us benefit to some degree from its use. This book itself is made from paper, a universal product derived from the same raw material that goes into our houses, our furniture and many other items that we come into contact with daily. Despite the undoubted progress made by humankind in the development of metals, alloys, synthetic resins and plastics, wood, in its natural form, has been a part of our lives for thousands of years and will remain so.

Why wood?

Wood has a universal and appealing presence to every culture and country. As a constructional material it is invaluable and very strong for its weight. It can be used to create complex structures at relatively low cost. Properly looked after timber (lumber) will last for years, as an examination of your surroundings will confirm.

Centuries of woodworking tradition have refined the techniques and tools we currently use, allowing a multitude of uses and styles. Best of all, wood is a sustainable resource – well managed woodlands can produce an inexhaustible supply of raw material, as well as playing a vital part in a balanced environment. Imagine

Above Houses being constructed from timber (lumber).
Left Wood has been used for sculpture for centuries. Here is a showering couple in the Grizedale Forest, Hawkshead, UK.
Opposite Wood is strong, attractive and in furniture joints can be used as a decorative feature in a design.

asking modern technologists to invent a synthetic material with so many qualities. Then ask them to add other properties – to make it feel warm and alive to the touch, and to look attractive at the same time.

The secret of being a successful woodworker or furniture maker lies in understanding that wood, as an organic material, was once alive, and that it can live again when shaped and formed by the human hand. No two pieces of wood are ever the same, and appreciating the variation will allow you to make the most of the material's natural qualities. All the tools and techniques in the world will be of no use without this feel for the material, which every woodworker shares.

When you have made your first piece of work, try this simple test – show it to someone else and wait for them to reach out and touch it. Then you will know that you have become part of a tradition of craftsmanship that will always be with us, and that you have taken the first step on a rewarding journey that has no end.

How to use this book

The following pages provide an introduction to all the aspects of woodworking that will allow you to produce something that can be called your own work. From the recognition and selection of the right kind of timber (lumber) to the design and construction of the finished item, there is no area of understanding that a good craftsperson can ignore. The basics of every aspect of woodworking have been broken down into broad areas for easy reference.

The type and condition of the timber, the tools and techniques employed, the design principles and the basic safety rules that go with them all affect the finished

product. Taking short-cuts and making choices without exploring all the options can produce quicker results, but woodworking is not a race against time. Patience is one of the primary attributes of any good craftsperson. Take the trouble to consult each chapter in turn, using the information as the foundation of a thorough and sympathetic understanding of each task you approach. That way, you will always be learning something new and the benefits will be revealed in your work.

All the projects are suitable for the home woodworker, and range from simple, everyday household items to quite sophisticated pieces of furniture. They have been designed, made and photographed specifically and you will find all the information you need to recreate them. On the other hand, you can adapt the design and construction principles to suit your own ideas.

No two items made in wood are ever the same, and that is the way it should be. No woodworker is ever completely satisfied with the latest project, either – the next one will

always be better. There is no substitute for experience, and that is what you will find distilled in these pages. What you will not find is the reward that comes from your own efforts – the key to this lies in your own hands, and the understanding of the tools and materials you use.

Note on measurements

Making accurate measurements is one of the most important skills to acquire if you want to achieve good results. The task can be made more confusing by the fact that different countries and timber suppliers work to different standards, using either the metric or imperial system (or sometimes a combination of the two), when sizing the raw material.

The same applies to tool manufacturers and suppliers of fixings and hardware. The way through this maze is to develop an understanding of both systems until mental conversion becomes second nature. A pocket calculator will help, but actually can slow the process.

In this book, dimensions are given in both metric and imperial form, but you should always check that the accuracy of any conversion is sufficient for the task in hand. Fractions of an inch, or 1 or 2 millimetres, either way are less critical in gauging large quantities of timber than when setting out detail, and converted values are often rounded up or down to make life easier. The table shown below provides some useful conversion factors and short-cut methods for estimating larger quantities of wood.

Conversion table

Multiply	by	to obtain	short-cuts
inches	25.4	millimetres	divide by four and add two zeros (4in = 100mm)
feet	305	millimetres	multiply by three and add two zeros (1ft = 300mm)
square feet	0.093	square metres	divide by ten
cubic feet	0.028	cubic metres	divide by 35 (35cu ft = 1cu metre)
lb/cu ft	16.05	kg/cu m	add two zeros, divide by six
pounds	0.45	kilograms	divide by two and subtract 10% (2.2lb = 1kg)

1

WOOD

To most people, wood comes ready to use from a timber (lumber) yard or home improvement store, cut to standard lengths and planed to a smooth finish. Modern processing and marketing practices demand that the natural variation of the product is eliminated as far as possible. But wood is not a manufactured material, and its qualities are as varied as the trees from which it is derived.

As a discriminating woodworker, you will soon discover that the real pleasure of woodworking comes from exploring the potential of each species and using it to its best advantage. The knowledge and careful selection of the raw material is one of the most important steps to take in developing a feel for your craft. This chapter describes the immense variety and options available to you as the living tree is processed to arrive in usable form at your workbench.

THE RAW MATERIAL

Trees are arguably the most prominent members of the plant kingdom. They
have been around for millions of years, forming a vital part of the natural
biological cycle that keeps this planet alive. Like all plants, they depend on a
process called photosynthesis to harness the sun's energy, combine it with
carbon dioxide (CO_2) from the air and produce the nutrients they need to
grow. In return, oxygen is emitted to the atmosphere and vast quantities of
water evaporate from the leaves.

Tree trunks

The most useful and important part of
the tree is the trunk, or bole. This
performs three roles: it conducts
water, or sap, from the roots; it
supports the weight of the tree; and it
stores the nutrients produced in the
leaves to lay down new growth.
Different parts of the trunk are
adapted to each function, but all use
the same basic building blocks: the
cells, which have walls made of
cellulose, the raw material of wood.
When pulped and processed,
cellulose can be made into paper;
when it is left intact, it provides one of
the most versatile constructional
materials available.

Living cycle within the tree

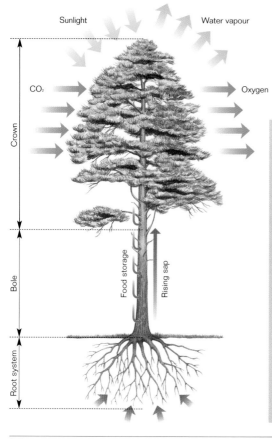

Sunlight

Water vapour

CO_2

Oxygen

Crown

Food storage

Rising sap

Bole

Root system

Above A western yellow pine (*Pinus
ponderosa*), a softwood species, in spring.
Opposite top A Californian redwood, a
softwood species, (*Sequoia sempervirens*).
Opposite below Mature oaks, a temperate
hardwood species, (*Quercus robur*), from a
post-Napoleonic-war plantation.

Timber properties

Softwoods	Hardwoods
low density: 400–600kg/cu m (25–37lb/cu ft)	high density: up to 1,000kg/cu m (65lb/cu ft)
great strength with lighter weight	heavier and sometimes more brittle
less durable in wet or damp conditions	more suitable for exterior use
less resistance to insect attack	more resistant to decay and rot
generally pale colouring	light to very dark colouring
generally more open grained	close-grained and harder to work
tendency to shrink or swell	more stable
low cost and more readily available	more expensive and harder to obtain

Softwoods and hardwoods
Depending on the species and conditions of growth, wood possesses a wide range of characteristics in varying degrees: strength, durability, flexibility, brittleness, and, of course, appearance. Understanding these qualities will help you select the best material for the job in hand. One of the first choices to make is not as straightforward as it may seem – softwood or hardwood?

Trees are divided into two botanical groups: *Gymnosperms* and *Angiosperms*, or conifers and broadleaves. These groups are popularly and respectively known as softwoods and hardwoods, but the terms can be misleading. Some so-called softwoods from coniferous trees, such as yew and pitch pine, are considerably harder than certain tropical hardwoods, not least balsa wood, which is the lightest of all.

The strength of timber (lumber) is determined by its density, which can vary within the same species according to its country of origin and rate of growth. Conifers are concentrated primarily in the cooler regions of the world, in both the northern and southern hemispheres, while tropical hardwoods, as the name implies, are found in the equatorial belt.

A third group, the temperate hardwoods, occupies the middle zone and is of special interest to woodworkers. Great variation can be found in the colour, distinctive grain figure and working properties of this group, and commercial supplies from sustainable sources are readily available at reasonable cost.

Whatever group timber belongs to, the woodworker will want to know its workability: how it behaves when worked by hand or machine tools, the quality of the grain, and how it takes to different adhesives and finishes. For most practical purposes, the more commonly available commercial softwoods all have certain similar features, with particular advantages and disadvantages as you can see in the table opposite.

STRUCTURE OF WOOD

A good woodworker does not have to be an expert in botany, or even dendrology (the study of trees), but it does help to have a basic knowledge of a tree's internal structure. This allows the selection of the best material for the job at hand and assists in spotting potential defects, which can show up and spoil the finished product.

Drying wood

An important part of the design process is knowing how wood behaves as it is worked and as it dries, which can vary depending on the part of the tree from which it originates. The cutaway section below of a tree trunk shows the principal elements that are common to most commercially available softwoods and temperate hardwoods.

The layers of a tree trunk

The outer layer is the *bark* of the tree, which protects it as it grows. Just beneath the bark is the *bast*, a vital part of the tree's make-up. It conducts the sugars manufactured in the leaves down toward the base of the tree for storage, while the narrow *cambium* alongside it is responsible for creating new growth each year. The outer

layers are attractive to pests in search of the food products they contain, so most of the seasoned timber (lumber) supplied for woodworking will have had them removed at an early stage.

In the *sapwood* layer, each year's new growth is laid down and the cells conduct the sap upward from the root system. In some species, the sapwood is distinct, being pale in colour, while in others there is no visible barrier between sapwood and *heartwood*. Sapwood has the same strength as heartwood, but is more vulnerable to attack by furniture beetle, so as a rule it should be cut away. It can develop unsightly greyish-blue stains and is porous, making good glued joints and smooth finishes difficult to obtain.

The heartwood makes up the bulk of the tree and is the most usable part.

Above Growth rings are clearly visible in the end grain of these boards.

The cells of the heartwood are not alive, but they provide all the strength of the tree. As the tree grows, sapwood becomes heartwood, which is more durable and often of a darker colour. Each year's new growth forms another layer, and these rings enable the age of the tree to be determined.

In many species, especially from temperate climates where there is a distinct growing season every year, the rings are clearly visible, giving rise to an attractive striped grain figure. When a board is cut radially, through the growth rings to the centre, the *rays* will be revealed in cross-section. These run horizontally through the tree, storing food deposits as it increases in girth. They are very visible in oak, producing a characteristic silvery band; in other species, they are barely detectable by the naked eye.

The *pith*, at the very core of the trunk, is the oldest part of the tree; however, it is not the strongest. It is the growth laid down when the tree is immature, and it is softer and less durable than the true heartwood. It can flake out when being worked, and is prone to decay and uneven shrinkage as the wood dries. Defects can arise at the centre of the pith, and often it is removed when the log is processed.

The structure of wood

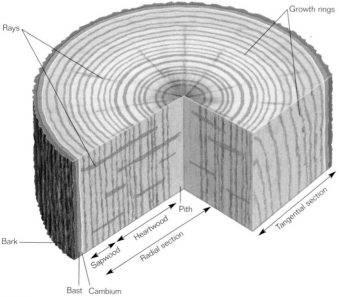

Rays

Growth rings

Bark

Bast Cambium

Sapwood

Heartwood

Radial section

Pith

Tangential section

Wood grain

Some species of timber (lumber) are termed straight-grained, where the growth rings are tight and concentric around the heart of the tree; they are a pleasure to work with.

Above These American white oak boards display the attractive striped grain figure common to woods with distinct growth rings. They have been cut tangentially – that is, cut across the face of the growth rings to reveal the cone-shaped formation.

Knots

A knot is simply the remains of a branch where it grew from the main trunk of the tree, but it should not always be regarded as a defect. Small knots can create interesting effects in an otherwise bland piece of timber.

Above This panel of black walnut contains a good example of a dead knot. The small "pin" knot lower down creates an attractive pattern, but the large dead knot above it is a defect to be avoided.

However, they do cause problems when working the wood, and joints and fine detail should be positioned away from them if possible. A dead knot, encased in a ring of bark where a dead branch has been absorbed by the growing tree, should be avoided. It is likely to shrink and fall out, and, in softwoods particularly, can be very resinous, causing problems when applying a finish.

Defects

Short- or cross-grain defects still occur, however, as a result of uneven growth or the grain being deformed around a knot. Very short or close grain is almost impossible to work successfully with hand tools without it tearing. It drastically weakens the material and should be avoided for constructional members and sections of wood close to joints. Certain species, particularly some tropical hardwoods, can always be expected to have difficult grain, growing naturally in spiral or interlocking patterns.

Above In this panel of European beech, the rays appear as small oval flecks distributed liberally across the face of the timber.

Shakes and checks

Heart shake

Ring shake

Surface checks

Reaction wood

This occurs where uneven growth in the trunk of the tree puts the fibres under great pressure. It can be identified by tight bands of growth rings that are much darker than their surroundings. These areas are much weaker, more difficult to work and subject to abnormal movement or shrinkage. Large areas of reaction wood should be cut out when selecting stock.

Above Sapele is an example of a hardwood with a difficult grain, the alternate formation of each band of cells producing a striped effect. The right-hand panel in this photograph not only shows unacceptable short grain, but also another defect known as reaction wood.

Shakes and checks

Small fissures, or *checks*, in the outer surface of a sample are not serious. Of greater concern are *shakes*, which arise within the tree due to decay or high stresses, or even old age. Star-shaped *heart shakes* can develop in the centre of a tree that has passed maturity. *Ring shakes* form between the growth rings and can be caused by the shock of being felled. A board with these defects should be rejected – it is unsound and will only deteriorate.

PRODUCTION AND CONVERSION

Imagine a tree with a trunk that is 610mm (2ft) in diameter, with a useful length of 12m (40ft) stretching up toward the crown. This represents a volume of timber (lumber) of 3.5cu m (124cu ft). Imagine a billion such trees and you will have an idea of worldwide timber consumption in a year. Not all of this is converted into useful wood products, however – in fact, more than half is burned for fuel. Much of the remainder is converted into wood pulp for the paper and packaging industries.

Above Resawing an oak board to remove the heart shake.

Tree felling

Timber production is a massive global industry, and the route taken by a piece of wood before it reaches your workbench is complex and varied. The home woodworker has a vast range of options available when specifying the correct quality and form of material to give the best results and reduce waste.

From the moment a tree is selected for felling, it is subjected to a continual process of evaluation to grade its quality and most useful content. When it reaches the sawmill, it will be allowed to "rest" for a period to allow the natural tensions within the trunk to equalize, before being converted into large slabs for seasoning. A skilled operator will know how to convert the log into the greatest quantity of usable timber with the minimum of waste.

As with most things, the higher the quality of product, the higher the cost, and the way in which the log is converted into convenient sizes can affect this dramatically.

Understanding the different methods and terminology will help you to specify the correct type of wood for your needs, and predict its behaviour under different conditions. The appearance of the cut surface, the amount of waste and the way in which the wood shrinks as it loses moisture are all affected by the conversion method.

The quickest and least wasteful method of converting the log, or baulk, of timber is to make a series of parallel cuts along its length. This process is known as through and through cutting, sometimes abbreviated to T/T.

Below A typical log storage yard.

Through and through cutting

This style of cutting is normal for most large-scale commercial sawmills. It produces large quantities of boards with a tangential figure, the cuts being made across the growth rings and producing the familiar cone-shaped pattern on the face of each board.

Such boards are described as plain sawn, flat sawn or slash sawn. Many species of wood with distinctive or contrasting growth rings are shown to their best advantage when converted in this way. To maximize the yield of highly figured boards, the entire baulk can be plain sawn.

Above Sawing a prime ash log on a bandmill.

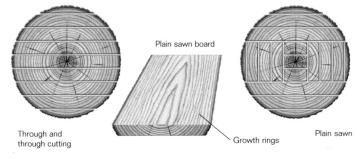

Plain sawn board

Through and through cutting

Growth rings

Plain sawn

Above Quarter sawing oak on a bandmill.

Quarter sawing

In contrast, when a log is cut into quarters, and sawn radially, at right-angles to the growth rings, with the cut passing through the centre, the figure displayed is markedly different.

The photograph on the right shows a good example of quarter-sawn oak, the silky blaze of the rays being clearly visible in cross-section and the growth rings reduced to fine parallel lines. As the diagram below shows, however, this method is wasteful of timber and time-consuming, since the log needs regular repositioning on the saw table. True quarter-sawn timber, with the cut surface intersecting the growth rings at a right angle, is only

produced when the quality or the decorative value of the timber warrants it.

Boards described as quarter sawn from the supplier will have been cut by one of several methods, as shown. These are a compromise and accept the rings running at any angle of more than 45 degrees from the face.

Another possibility is rift-sawn boards, where the log is split horizontally, then sawn through and through vertically to produce boards with a higher proportion of quartered grain. Sometimes this is described as one square edge and it can yield good-quality material at a much lower cost.

Above A fine example of black walnut, with a plain-sawn panel on the left, quarter-sawn on the right and rift-sawn in the centre. The changing angle of growth rings across the panel can be seen clearly.

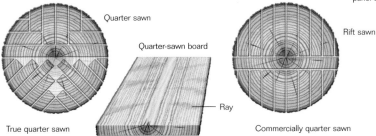

Quarter sawn

Quarter-sawn board

Rift sawn

True quarter sawn

Ray

Commercially quarter sawn

SEASONING WOOD

Newly felled timber (lumber) loses moisture rapidly at first as free water evaporates, then more slowly as water within the cell walls is given up. The woodworker should look for well-seasoned timber, which will have been dried at the sawmill under controlled conditions in two distinct stages.

Shrinkage

When newly felled, timber has a high water content and is termed "green". It is heavier and more vulnerable to decay than seasoned timber. However, it can be worked quite easily and is more flexible. As it dries, it will shrink slightly and can distort in shape.

The cherrywood bowl below shows how dramatic such changes can be. It is a section that was cut from the base of a cherry tree when it was felled. Note the deep colour of the heartwood in contrast to the sapwood. Without encouragement, within three months, the flat disc had formed a natural bowl shape. In this case, the result was turned to advantage, but such deformation would create havoc in a worked piece of furniture.

Right A cherrywood bowl. Note the contrast between heartwood and sapwood.

Below An air-dried timber (lumber) stack.

Air drying

Outdoors, timber will dry naturally to a certain extent. It must be stacked carefully to allow good ventilation. When treating hardwood, a sawmill will air dry the converted timber for a period of up to two years before further processing. The stack should be protected from the elements, and the layers separated by small sticks to encourage an even rate of drying and to reduce distortion. Some pale species of timber, such as sycamore, are prone to staining when very green, particularly where the sticks are laid. Initially, these may be *end-reared*, or stacked on end, to avoid this.

Above This shows how not to air dry timber. The boards have been piled in irregular fashion, unprotected from the heat of the sun. Rapid, uneven drying can split a board quite easily. Note the discolouration where the sticks were laid.

Stability and movement

Shrinkage describes the behaviour of timber as it dries, whereas *movement* is the tendency of wood to expand or shrink after it has been seasoned depending on its surroundings. Wood species with high stability are less likely to deform if the rates of tangential and radial movement are similar.

Certain species of wood, such as Douglas fir, teak, iroko and yellow pine behave much better than others and are preferable if this is an important consideration when choosing your wood.

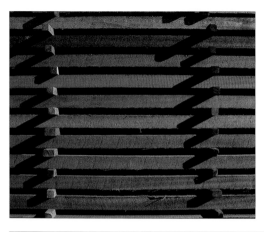

Wood species with low movement and good stability	
Softwoods	**Hardwoods**
Western red cedar	Muninga
Douglas fir	Teak
European spruce	Mahogany
Yellow pine	South American cedar
Western hemlock	Iroko

Kiln drying

Air drying is a lengthy process and can be unpredictable, as it is subject to varying weather conditions and seasonal changes. Kiln drying allows quicker production, while the quality and performance of the timber can be improved by careful control of the drying conditions. Today, nearly all commercially available timber is kiln dried, apart from beams of large section. Softwoods are normally kiln dried immediately after conversion, any preservative treatment also being applied at this stage. After drying, the timber may be cut into smaller sizes for distribution; it is in this condition that it usually reaches the home woodworker. Timber will produce disappointing results if it is worked before the seasoning process is over.

Moisture content

The moisture content of wood is measured as the percentage of its dry weight. A sample of fresh-sawn softwood weighing 10kg (22lb) might contain as much as 5kg (11lb) of water

Moisture content

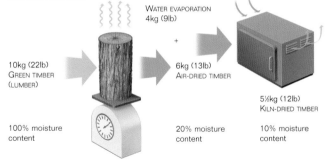

WATER EVAPORATION
4kg (9lb)

+

10kg (22lb)
GREEN TIMBER
(LUMBER)

6kg (13lb)
AIR-DRIED TIMBER

5½kg (12lb)
KILN-DRIED TIMBER

100% moisture content

20% moisture content

10% moisture content

and the same amount of dry wood. It would be described as having 100 per cent moisture content. In practice, wood is never dried completely to a zero per cent moisture content, but eventually it will reach a level consistent with its environment, which is called the *equilibrium moisture content* (emc). This can range from 18 to 20 per cent outdoors down to as low as 8 or 9 per cent in a warm, dry atmosphere. Kiln-dried timber is usually produced at a level of 10 to 12 per cent moisture content. It is essential to understand how changes in

the emc can affect the performance of a finished piece of woodwork, as the wood continues to absorb and lose moisture in response to changing levels of temperature and humidity. This is why doors and windows tend to stick during the cold months. A cabinet door that fits perfectly in the workshop can shrink or distort when installed in an air-conditioned, heated house. Consider storing the timber where it is to be used to allow it to acclimatize before being worked.

Moisture content can be estimated using a moisture meter. The meter must be suitably calibrated for the species concerned, and it will give only local values for moisture content, which will vary through the thickness of the wood. It provides a guide when monitoring timber as it dries.

Drying defects

As wood dries, it shrinks, and distortion can occur in the finished boards, partly because the shrinkage will be uneven. This is predictable to an extent, depending on how it is converted. It moves more readily in the direction of the growth rings, and a plain-sawn board can lose as much as ten per cent of its original width in drying. Quarter-sawn boards are more stable, and are often used for wide areas of panelling for this reason. Uneven grain and tensions within the timber can result in defects in a board as it dries, or when it is worked. Here are some of the common problems:

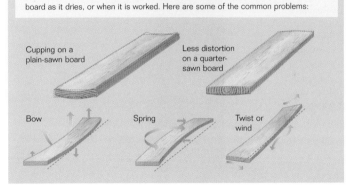

Cupping on a plain-sawn board

Less distortion on a quarter-sawn board

Bow

Spring

Twist or wind

Above Wood stacked high in a kiln.

SELECTING AND STORING WOOD

There are so many different species of timber (lumber) that it may seem difficult to decide where to start when making a selection. Your choice will depend on a number of factors, not least the cost and availability. It is well worth tracking down one or more suppliers who understand the needs of woodworkers, and striking up a good working relationship with them.

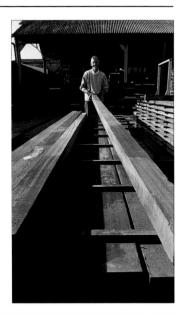

Choosing

Many stockists are set up to provide for the construction trade and do not take kindly to requests for small quantities of less common types. On the other hand, sometimes bargains are to be had from such companies, when they are left with short lengths of wood (sometimes sold as shorts or short ends) that are less useful to the trade. Also, bear in mind that boards with constructional defects, areas of sapwood or wild, knotty grain can be used to good decorative effect if selected carefully.

Although certain species of timber are specified for many of the projects in this book, the information should be used as a guide. Quite often, the first stage in the process of deciding what to make is to consider what timber is available and how its potential can be realized to the full, rather than sticking to fixed ideas. It is very rare that a substitute wood cannot be found that possesses the desired properties.

Right Stacking wood the correct way in a timber (lumber) yard.

Workability

Some timbers are noted for being easily worked, with a low cutting resistance and blunting effect on tools. They tend to be quite bland in appearance, but are ideal for making solid frameworks where accurate jointing and stability are important. Straight, even grain gives good glued joints and resistance to splitting when nailed or screwed. These timbers can be obtained at relatively low cost.

Finish

Not all species of timber will take a good finish – if the grain is very coarse, the surface can "pick up", requiring a lengthy process of filling the grain and rubbing down to produce a satisfactory result. Some species, such as teak, have a natural oily content that inhibits the bonding of the finish. Over the years, some woods have become highly prized for their lustrous qualities and their ability to take a high polish. Naturally they tend to be more expensive and hard to obtain.

Wood species with good working properties

Agba
Alder
Basswood
Obeche
Pine (most species)
Western red cedar

Left American basswood, or American lime, is fine grained, and easily worked without blunting your tools.

Wood species with good finishing qualities

Afrormosia
Ash
Cherry
Hemlock
Jarrah
Mahogany
Rosewood
Walnut

Left American black walnut, with its marked grain figure, is popular for high-quality cabinet-making and carving. It polishes to an excellent finish.

Durability

Timber (lumber) should be selected for durability if it will be exposed to moisture, not only outdoors, but also in areas of high humidity or condensation, such as kitchens and bathrooms. Sapwood is perishable and prone to staining in most timbers, but even the heartwood of some species is vulnerable. Many tropical hardwoods, and softwoods such as yew and cedar, are highly resistant to rot because of their oily nature.

Density

The density of wood (expressed as kilograms per cubic metre or pounds per cubic foot) is not only a measure of its relative weight, but is also linked to its strength and durability. Where these are important, your choice of species should reflect this. Bear in mind that most figures quoted are based on averages at a fixed moisture content, and the density of a single piece of wood can vary depending on its origin and growth conditions.

Storing

Many woodworkers will hoard timber (lumber). A piece of prime quality will be set aside until the right job comes along, or because it is "too good to use". There is nothing wrong with this, provided you have the space: the timber will come to no harm if stored in the correct manner and conditions, and may even improve with age. Do not let this hoarding instinct get out of control and keep track of your stock and manage it sensibly. Record the origin and date of purchase of each batch, and do not mix them in the same piece of work.

If you do not have enough space to keep all your stock in the workshop, it will survive perfectly well outdoors until it is needed. Bring it indoors well before working it though, to allow it to acclimatize to interior conditions.

Common durable wood species in order of durability

Less durable	Very durable
Alder	Teak
Birch	Iroko
Lime	Afrormosia
Ash	Jarrah
Poplar	Chestnut
Spruce	Oak
	Cedar

Above right Cedar of Lebanon (a true cedar), has a high resin content, and it is light and durable, one of the few softwoods suitable for exterior use without preservative treatment.

Common wood species in order of density

Softwood	Temperate hardwoods	Tropical hardwoods
Western red cedar	Basswood	Obeche
(least dense)	*(least dense)*	*(least dense)*
Spruce	Poplar	Agba
Hemlock	Alder	Meranti, Idigbo
Scots pine	Sycamore, Ash	Mahogany, Abura
Douglas fir	Elm, Chestnut	Iroko, Muninga
Larch	Walnut, Cherry	Utile, Sapele
Parana pine	Beech, Birch	Teak
Pitch pine	Oak, Rock maple	Afrormosia
Yew	Jarrah	Ebony
(most dense)	*(most dense)*	*(most dense)*

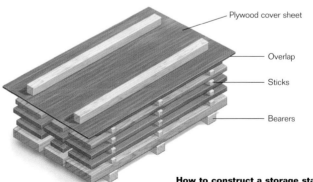

Plywood cover sheet

Overlap

Sticks

Bearers

How to construct a storage stack

Store long lengths of timber under cover, and ensure good ventilation. Warm, damp conditions encourage decay, and an attack of fungus in a wood store must be avoided at all costs. The spores that spread fungi are everywhere, and all they need are the right conditions to take hold.

BUYING WOOD

Over a quarter of the land area of the globe is occupied by forested regions, and we reduce it at our peril. Unlike many other materials that we consume, trees are a renewable resource – it makes no sense to ignore the potential for endless supply by not replacing them as we use them. Gradually, the timber (lumber) trade is becoming aware of this, and the responsible woodworker should encourage the attitude by seeking out suppliers who operate environmentally sound purchasing policies.

Above The country of origin of imported product is identified by distinctive shipping marks on the wood.

Timber awareness

There are organizations such as the Forestry Stewardship Council (FSC) and the American Forest and Paper Association (AF&PA) that are working worldwide to encourage certification schemes that promote the sustainable management of our forests.

Seek out the sources of timber available to you and satisfy yourself that your local supplier is aware of the issues involved.

The timber trade

The trade market has a great responsibility, not only in forestry management and purchasing policy, but in promoting the efficient use of the raw material. Poor-quality timber can be directed toward the mass needs of industry while the best is reserved for the most demanding use. Everyone in the chain of supply, from foresters down to individual woodworkers, has a part to play in grading and selecting the correct timber for its purpose. When

Above For a wood-product manufacturer, the use of wood from FSC sources shows a commitment to the conservation of the world's forests.

specifying and buying timber, be prepared to consider alternatives to avoid wasting a valuable resource. Already some species are endangered and no longer available commercially, such as Brazilian rosewood; others are in short supply or are best converted into veneers. There is nothing wrong with using sheet materials, manufactured from timber trimmings (wood scraps) too small to use as solid wood, to provide a stable base for veneered panels or to make the components that will not be seen in a finished piece of work.

There are real cost savings to be made, too, if timber of the correct size and quality is purchased. Buying timber that has been dimensioned, or re-sawn to a predetermined size, saves handling large boards if you do not have the facilities. If timber has been *prepared,* or planed all round with square edges and smooth faces, it is ready to use without further machining. Bear in mind that each stage of the preparation process adds more cost. In the long term, it may pay you to invest in the space and equipment to machine your own stock from rough-sawn boards, allowing you to use the stock more selectively.

Identifying timber

The timber trade has its own terminology for describing the different grades and appearance of the product. Some of the more common terms are specified in the accompanying panel; look out for them when specifying timber. There is a comprehensive range of common timbers suitable for practical woodworking. One of the first hazards to be aware of when selecting timber is that the common name for each species can be a pitfall. Many species are known by various names in different parts of the world, or even in the same country; just as often, the same name can be applied to more than one species.

The system of naming timbers is not deliberately intended to confuse, although it does seem that way sometimes. It came about because suppliers from different countries used their own systems of timber identification to suit their own market, sometimes for convenience, and even, it must be said, to give their product more value. "Mahogany", for example, is used to describe completely different species of timber from South and Central America, Africa, and Australia. "Douglas fir" is not a true fir, and although it is also known as "Oregon pine", it is not a true pine either. You have every right to be confused!

The best way through the maze is to refer to the botanical name of a species, which is unique to each one, and should always be checked with the supplier when specifying the product you wish to buy. The first half of the name describes the genus or botanical group; the second part is the particular species within that group.

Above Douglas fir, or Oregon pine, is a softwood with a distinguishing grain.

Timber trade terminology

Rough-sawn	Sawn on a bandmill or circular saw to approximate dimensions.
Prepared	Planed in a sawmill.
Surfaced	Only small areas of a board are planed to give the buyer an idea of the colour or grain figure of the timber.
PAR	Prepared all round: square-section timber with machined faces. Beware: exact finished sizes will vary (see below).
Nominal size	The original size of the stock before machining: "ex 50 x 100mm" ("ex 2 x 4in") describes the nominal size.
Finished size	The true size of prepared stock after machining. Approximately 3mm (⅛in) will be removed from each face during this process.
A/D	Air-dried timber. Expect it to be no less than 18% moisture content.
K/D	Kiln dried. Usually timber is dried in the kiln to around 12% moisture content.
T/T	Through and through. Boards converted by through-and-through cutting will be plain sawn.
1/SE	One square edge. Boards with one square edge and one waney (crooked) edge, likely to be rift sawn.
Waney edge	Board with the sapwood and uneven edge still present, although the bark will have been removed.
Unsorted	Surprisingly, this describes the best grade for joinery-quality softwoods. Also termed clears, or clear and better.
4ths & 5ths	Lower-grade softwood stock.
FAS	Firsts and seconds. The best grade to look for in hardwoods graded for good-quality work. At least 83% of each board will yield clear, defect-free usable timber in large sizes.
Commons	Second-grade hardwood, yielding between 67 and 83% clear timber in smaller lengths. Acceptable for cabinet-making and small projects.

Timber and the environment

Forests Forever is encouraging companies to adopt an Environmental Timber Purchasing Policy. Companies are encouraged to set environmental objectives and targets, and to internally audit their progress towards these targets. In particular, they are encouraged to implement a programme to assess and monitor the environmental and legal credentials of all their timber products suppliers, and to trace timber as far as possible to the forest of origin.

While you shouldn't boycott individual species, it is possible to play a positive environmental role by seeking to specify a wider range of timber species. The use of "lesser-known species" can assist certain countries, usually in the tropics, with the

implementation of their national sustainability programmes by taking pressure off those species which have, in the past, formed the mainstream of business. With a larger number of commercially valuable tree species, forestry departments have greater flexibility in planning harvesting regimes to ensure a better species balance in the future.

Bear in mind that in seeking to increase the range of species used, you shouldn't compromise on quality or performance. Your choice of species should always be governed by the need to ensure that it is technically suited to the application. However, keep an open mind to alternatives and don't be put off simply because a species name is unfamiliar.

SOFTWOODS

This type of wood is not necessarily soft, but all softwoods have in common the property of being conifers, or cone-bearing trees, and mostly evergreen, although the larch is a notable exception. Usually low in cost and readily available, most common softwoods are suitable for all forms of general carcassing and construction work.

Opposite left, centre and right
The storage chest is made from reclaimed pine floorboards; the magazine rack is pine; and the bar stool is constructed from Southern yellow pine.

   If better appearance and good finishing qualities are required, more careful selection is necessary. Softwoods are generally light in weight, less durable, and more susceptible to insect attack and fungal decay than most hardwoods. Pitch pine, cedar and yew are three notable exceptions.

	Common name	Other names	Botanical name	Origin
	Cedar of Lebanon	True cedar	*Cedrus libani*	Middle East, Europe
	Douglas fir	Oregon pine	*Pseudotsuga taxifolia*	USA, Canada
	Hoop pine	Queensland pine	*Araucaria cunninghamii*	Australia
	Kauri pine	Queensland kauri	*Agathis* spp.	Australia, NZ
	Larch	European larch	*Larix decidua*	Europe, Asia
	Parana pine		*Araucaria angustifolia*	S America
	Pitch pine	Longleaf pitch pine	*Pinus palustris*	USA, Central America
	Ponderosa pine	Bull pine	*Pinus ponderosa*	USA, Canada
	Rimu	Red pine	*Dacrydium cupressinum*	New Zealand
	Scots pine	European redwood	*Pinus sylvestris*	Europe, UK
	Sequoia	Californian redwood	*Sequoia sempervirens*	USA
	Silver fir	European whitewood	*Abies alba*	Europe
	Southern yellow pine	Carolina pine	*Pinus echinata, Pinus eliottii*	USA
	Spruce	European whitewood	*Picea excelsa, Picea abies*	Europe
	Western hemlock	Alaska pine	*Tsuga heterophylla*	USA, Canada
	Western red cedar	Shinglewood	*Thuja plicata*	USA, Canada
	Yellow pine	Quebec yellow pine	*Pinus strobus*	USA, Canada
	Yew		*Taxus baccata*	UK, Europe

Cedar of Lebanon

Larch

Southern yellow pine

Yellow pine

Description	Other properties	
Light brown heartwood, with distinctive growth rings	Very resinous, durable, easy to work, but low in strength	
Yellow to pinkish brown with marked growth rings	Slightly coarse, quite dense, durable with good workability	
Yellow brown heartwood, pale sapwood, as Parana pine	Not a true pine. Works and finishes well, very stable	
Fine, straight grained, creamy brown colour	Again not a true pine, but works well and is durable	
Resinous with pale sapwood and reddish heart	Heavier and more durable, but harder to work	
Attractive reddish brown heartwood with dark streaks	Straight grained and good workability, but poor stability	Douglas fir
Marked figure with yellowish to reddish heartwood	Coarse grained and resinous, but very durable	
Yellowish white, straight grained with delicate figure	Very stable, works well, excellent finishing	
Reddish brown heartwood with fine texture	Not a true pine, but equivalent working properties	
Pink to reddish heartwood with distinct growth rings	Resinous, good all-round working and performance	
Prominent growth rings, reddish brown heartwood	Similar to Western red cedar, but non-resinous	
Very similar to Spruce, sold generally as Whitewood	Soft and lightweight especially when fast grown	Scots pine
Yellow to reddish brown heart with marked growth rings	More durable and stable than Yellow pine	
Pale white with sapwood and heartwood very similar	Can be knotty and contain pockets of resin	
Fine, straight grain with dark red growth rings	Good workability and finish, but prone to movement	
Attractive heartwood varies from light pink to dark brown	Very stable and durable, but soft and low in strength	
Light tan to pinkish heartwood, good even texture	Good quality, stable, and slightly resinous	
Pale sapwood and reddish heart with colourful figure	Dense, oily wood works to a fine finish	Western hemlock

Yew

TEMPERATE HARDWOODS

There are thousands of species of hardwood to choose from, but those listed here have been selected because of their ready availability, cost and performance. Temperate hardwoods are grown away from the tropical belt, in Europe, Asia, North America and the Southern Hemisphere. They offer a vast range of different properties, making it possible to find a particular species to suit virtually any purpose.

Opposite left, centre and right
The occasional table is constructed from white ash; the picture frame from white oak; and the settle from sweet chestnut.

	Common name	Other names	Botanical name	Origin
Alder (American)	Alder (American)	Red alder	*Alnus rubra*	USA
	Ash	European ash	*Fraxinus excelsior*	USA, Europe
	Australian blackwood		*Acacia melanoxylon*	Australia
Basswood	Basswood	American lime	*Tilia americana*	USA, Canada
	Beech		*Fagus sylvatica*	Europe, Asia
	Birch (European)	White birch	*Betula alba*	Europe, Asia
	Boxwood		*Buxus sempervirens*	Europe
Birch (European)	Butternut	White walnut	*Juglans cinerea*	USA
	Cherry	American cherry	*Prunus serotina*	USA
	Chestnut	Sweet chestnut	*Castanea sativa*	UK, Europe
	Elm (European)	English elm	*Ulmus procera*	Europe
Chestnut	Hornbeam		*Carpinus betulus*	UK, Europe
	Jarrah	Australian mahogany	*Eucalyptus marginata*	Australia
	Maple (Hard)	Sugar maple	*Acer saccharum*	USA, Canada
	Maple (Soft)	Red maple	*Acer rubrum*	USA, Canada
Jarrah	Oak (American Red)		*Quercus rubra*	USA
	Oak (American White)		*Quercus alba*	USA
	Oak (European)		*Quercus robur*	Europe
	Sycamore (American)	Buttonwood, Lacewood	*Platanus occidentalis*	USA
Oak (European)	Sycamore (European)		*Acer pseuodplatanus*	Europe
	Walnut (Australian)	Queensland walnut	*Endiandra palmerstonii*	Australia
	Walnut (Black)	Virginia walnut	*Juglans nigra*	USA
	Walnut (European)		*Juglans regia*	Europe
Sycamore (American)	Yellow poplar	American whitewood	*Liriodendron tulipifera*	USA

Description	Other properties
Light brown, fine straight grain	Works well, but non-durable
Pale honey colour with marked growth ring figure	Good working and bending properties, excellent finish
Gold or red to dark brown with sometimes curly figure	Strong, works well and polishes to a high finish
Creamy white with close even grain	Low in strength and durability, works and carves very well
Pale brown with distinctive flecks	Hard, but good to work and finish
White or pale brown with little figure	Soft and easy to work
Pale yellow brown, fine even grain	Very dense and hard, good carving and turning wood
Light brown, straight coarse grain	Easily worked and very stable
Reddish brown with pale sapwood	Hard-wearing, but tough to work
Light brown, similar to oak, but without silvery ray figure	Bends well, easy to work and reasonably durable
Brown heartwood with twisted grain	Attractive, but hard to work
Uniform close grain, yellowish white	Very hard-wearing, but hard to work
Rich red heartwood, wavy figure	Strong, durable, but low in stability
Very close grain, creamy brown	Dense and hard wood, polishes well
Pinkish tinge to heartwood	Softer and lighter than above
Pinkish brown compared to *Q. robur*	Less obvious ray figure
Lighter, but similar to *Q. robur*	Less durable than European oak
Pale to dark brown; distinct growth rings and silvery rays	Strong and durable, bends well, harder to work
Light brown, straight even grain with wide rays	Ray figure produces attractive "lacewood" when rift sawn
Very pale, sometimes wavy grain	Stains and finishes well
Similar to European walnut	Interlocking grain, harder to work
Dark brown with purple tints	Coarse grain, but good to work
Greyish brown with rich dark streaks and wavy grain	Excellent finish, hard and durable
Pale sapwood, dark streaks in heartwood, straight grain	Good working properties and good finishing, stable

Ash

Beech

Cherry

Elm (European)

Maple (hard)

Oak (American red)

Walnut (black)

TROPICAL HARDWOODS

Tropical hardwoods have become a sensitive issue in recent times, as large areas of tropical rainforest around the world have been cleared by indiscriminate logging. This is not to say that some sources of tropical timber (lumber) are not managed responsibly. Indeed, where they are, they should be encouraged as a means of supporting local industries in the sustainable management of the resource. Identifying the species at risk (see chart) and using alternatives with similar properties is a responsible approach to the problem.

Opposite left and right The legs of the dining table are constructed from teak and the top is from elm. The conservatory bench is made from iroko.

	Common name	Other names	Botanical name	Origin
Afrormosia	Afrormosia		*Pericopsis elata*	W Africa
	Balsawood		*Ochroma lagopus*	S America
	Brazilian cedar		*Cedrela fissilis*	S America
	● Bubinga	African rosewood	*Guibourtia demeusei*	W Africa
Bubinga	● Cocobolo	Nicaragua rosewood	*Dalbergia retusa*	Central America
	● Ebony	Macassar ebony	*Diospyros macassar*	Indonesia
	Greenheart		*Ocotea rodiaei*	S America
	Idigbo		*Terminalia ivorensis*	W Africa
Idigbo	Iroko	African teak	*Chlorophora excelsa*	Central Africa
	Jelutong		*Dyera costulata*	Indonesia
	● Kingwood	Violetwood	*Dalbergia cearensis*	S America
	● Lignum vitae	Ironwood	*Guaiacum officinale*	C & S America
Iroko	Mahogany (African)		*Khaya ivorensis*	W Africa
	● Mahogany (Brazilian)		*Swietenia macrophylla*	C & S America
	Makore	African cherry	*Tieghemella heckelii*	W Africa
	Meranti	Lauan, Seraya	*Shorea* spp.	Indonesia, Philippines
Makore	Obeche	African whitewood	*Triplochiton scleroxylon*	W Africa
	Padauk	African or Indian padauk	*Pterocarpus* spp.	SE Asia, W Africa
	Ramin	Melawis	*Gonystylus macrophyllum*	Indonesia
	● Rosewood (Brazilian)	Rio rosewood, Jacaranda	*Dalbergia negra*	S America
Meranti	● Rosewood (Indian)		*Dalbergia latifolia*	India
	Sapele		*Entandophragma cylindricum*	W Africa
	● Satinwood		*Chloroxylon swietenia*	India, Sri Lanka
	● Teak		*Tectona grandis*	SE Asia
	Utile		*Entandrophragma utile*	W Africa
Teak	Wenge		*Milletia laurentii*	W Africa

● *Endangered species*

Description	Other properties	
Orange-brown, straight and fine-textured heartwood	Stable and durable, good alternative to teak and less oily	
Pale beige, porous and open-grained	Lightest and softest of all hardwoods	
Pink to mahogany coloured heartwood	Durable and good to work, resinous	
Reddish brown with dark figure	Hard and dense, coarse grained	Brazilian cedar
Dark brown with colourful streaks	Tough and dense with lustrous finish	
Dark brown with black stripes	Dense, used for turning and veneers in small quantities	
Yellowish to dark olive brown	Extremely durable, hard to work	
Pale yellowish with some figure	Stable and durable, poor finishing	Ebony
Yellowish to golden brown, with coarse striped grain	Durable with lustrous finish; hard to work and blunts tools	
Straight grained, pale creamy colour	Lightweight and stable, works well	
Even-textured with variegated figure from brown to violet	Lustrous and excellent finish, used for turning or veneers	
Olive to deep brown, interlocked grain and fine texture	Oily, hard and extremely dense, used mainly for turning	Mahogany (Brazilian)
Pale pinkish brown, with coarse or interlocking grain	Easy to work, reasonable substitute for true mahogany	
Light to dark reddish brown, straight and even grain	Stable with excellent working properties, good finishing	
Reddish brown, fine straight grain	Hard, dense and difficult to work	Obeche
Pink (White lauan) or reddish (Red lauan), coarse grain	Easy to work, often seen as Far Eastern plywood	
Creamy white to yellow, open grained	Light, but stable, easily worked	
Red to purplish brown; resinous and interlocking grain	Hard-wearing, very stable, hard to work and poor finish	
Straw to creamy brown with dark flecks, straight grained	Easy working, but poor stability, often used for mouldings	Ramin
Dark brown with variegated violet to dark bronze streaks	Attractive, but in short supply, used mainly for veneering	
More dull brown to purplish black	As for Brazilian rosewood	
Reddish brown; markedly striped quartered figure	Alternative to mahogany, easy to work, but less stable	Rosewood (Brazilian)
Golden brown with lustrous figure	Good to work, hard fine texture	
Honey coloured to dark brown with strong figure	Dense, oily, durable, attractive but hard to work	
Reddish brown, interlocking grain	Similar to sapele, but more stable	
Dark brown with black stripes	Hard and dense, attractive finish	Sapele

MANUFACTURED BOARDS

Manufactured boards in various forms are familiar and have revolutionized the principles of wooden construction. By processing solid timber (lumber) into sheets of stable material, glued together by various means, the suppliers have considerably increased their usable output and have improved the material's performance for many uses. Parts of the tree that otherwise would be pulped can be reformed to produce an economic building material. For the woodworker, the main advantage is the availability of large panels that are stable, easy to work and low in cost.

Above MDF is stable and easy to work, and ideal for making templates in the workshop.

Plywood

This consists of several thin layers of wood, usually with the grain at right angles in alternate layers (cross-ply). It is dimensionally stable and very strong. Useful thicknesses range from 3mm (⅛in) up to 25mm (1in).

Softwood ply is usually made from Douglas fir, and is coarse grained, but durable.

Birch ply has more laminations and is pre-sanded to give a smooth finish that is ideal for painting or varnishing.

Far Eastern ply is cheaper, but more open grained and more useful for structural work.

Exterior-grade ply uses a WBP (water- and boil-proof) adhesive and hardwood laminations.

Marine ply is the most durable of all and correspondingly expensive.

Flexiply has the grain running in the same direction on every layer and can be formed into tight curves. It also has no "voids" in its structure.

Decorative ply has a veneer of decorative hardwood bonded to one or both sides and is perfect for enclosed panels and carcass construction.

Blockboard

The core of blockboard is made from solid strips of softwood glued along their edges. It is faced with a layer of veneer on each side. Blockboard is lighter than plywood, resistant to bending, and is useful for large structures and shelving. Normally, it is available only in 19mm (¾in) and 25mm (1in) thicknesses.

Laminboard

Similar to blockboard, laminboard has an internal core made of much smaller strips of softwood. As a result, the board is more stable. It is ideal for a smooth, ripple-free finish.

Particle boards

In particle boards, no thin layers of solid wood are used at all. Instead, the board is made from small particles of processed timber bonded together with resin.

Chipboard is the most common type, being used as a base for laminated work or for utility shelving and carcassing. It has a smooth, hard surface and a softer core. Unlike plywood, it is prone to splitting when screws are driven into the edges.

OSB (oriented strand board) is similar to chipboard, but is made from larger, wafer-like particles and has uneven faces. Both types can be used to provide hard-wearing surfaces for bench tops and flooring, but they have poor moisture resistance and low integral strength. Chipboard shelving is prone to sagging unless well supported at close intervals.

Pineboard is like the core of blockboard, but without the outer layers. Small strips of pine are glued together on edge and sanded smooth,

Marine ply 6mm (¼in)

Far Eastern 5-ply 12mm (½in)

Hardboard

Chipboard

12mm (½in) medium-density fibreboard

19mm (¾in) medium-density fibreboard

Blockboard

Pineboard

making it ideal for instant shelving, carcassing and many home improvement projects.

Fibreboards

Wood is shredded into a fibrous form and bonded with resin under high pressure to manufacture various forms of fibreboard.

Softboard or *Insulating board* is extremely light and soft. It can be used as an insulating layer or as a pinboard.

Hardboard has one hard surface only, but is very stable and bends easily. It is useful for making templates.

Tempered hardboard is impregnated with resins to make it more water-resistant, but by no means is it completely waterproof.

MDF (medium-density fiberboard) is by far the most useful fibreboard product. It is dense, flat, stiff, has no knots and is easy to cut. It is very stable, and the fibres are compressed so finely that it can be cut and shaped without crumbling. It is best cut with carbide tools as steel cutting tools may dull easily. MDF makes an ideal substrate for veneer, and is available in decorative form with real hardwood veneers already bonded to both faces. Always wear a mask when working with MDF, as it creates fine dust particles which can be carcinogenic. Glues for MDF are also made with formaldehyde and are toxic.

Standard sizes

Nearly all manufactured boards have a standard size of 1220 x 2440mm (4 x 8ft). Some suppliers offer a metric size, which is smaller (1200 x 2400mm), so always check, as this can make a critical difference to your cutting list. Special sizes of plywood and MDF, up to 3m (10ft) in length, are available from some suppliers. Many stores will cut large sheets into smaller sizes if requested at the time of purchase.

Grain direction

The direction in which the grain runs on the outer layers is always given first when describing plywood. This can be important when planning your cutting list. With birch plywood, for example, 1220 x 2440mm (4 x 8ft) in a supplier's catalogue will indicate that the grain runs across the width of the board, not down its length.

Most veneered decorative boards are manufactured with the grain running across the length. In this case, the catalogue entry would read 2440 x 1220mm (8 x 4ft).

Common thicknesses of manufactured board

Type	3mm 1/8in	6mm 1/4in	9mm 3/8in	12mm 1/2in	16mm 5/8in	19mm 3/4in	22mm 7/8in	25mm 1in	32mm 1 1/4in
Plywood	X	X	X	X	X	X	X	X	
Plywood (D. fir)				X		X			
Blockboard						X		X	
Laminboard						X		X	
Chipboard				X	X	X	X	X	
OSB				X		X			
Hardboard	X	X							
MDF		X	X	X		X		X	X

Right An indication of the wide range of finishes that manufactured boards can offer.

Mouldings

This is the term used to describe any section of timber (lumber) that has been shaped, either by hand or by machinery, to alter the square profile of the original piece. This may range from rounding over the sharp edges of the finished work to adding more decorative detail. Ready-made mouldings, in a variety of different species, are sold by most timber suppliers and can be used to enhance your work. Alternatively, profiled cutters can be fitted in a router to make your own mouldings and create a range of decorative effects.

Parts of a moulding

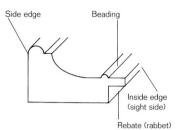

General-purpose mouldings

A range of commonly used profiles is available in standard lengths, usually 2.4m (8ft) and 1.8m (6ft), and to different sized sections. They are ideal for fitting in corners and along edges to break up sharp angles or for trimming the edges of manufactured boards to conceal their exposed cores.

A close-grained timber is normally used to form ready-made mouldings, reducing the risk of splitting when nails are driven through them, but even so small pilot holes may be needed, especially when fixing close to the ends.

Common species include pine and spruce, pale coloured hardwoods such as beech, ramin and poplar (ideal for staining or painting), and darker hardwoods such as mahogany, utile and meranti.

In former times, the woodworker would have had to hand a variety of moulding planes to produce a detail on a piece of work. Nowadays a power router can be used to achieve the same effect. If you cannot find a suitable ready-made profile, or would prefer to use the same material to match your project, you will find it just as easy to make your own with a profile cutter of the right shape.

Below A range of ready-made carved and embossed mouldings.

Common mouldings

Quadrant moulding A simple quarter-round moulding for breaking up the sharp edges of a corner.

Ovolo A stepped, convex profile that adds a visual break to a moulded edge.

Scotia (or cavetto) is a concave curve that works well on internal corners.

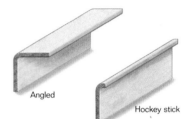

Angled

Hockey stick

Ogee moulding An S-shaped profile with reverse curve; often used as a panel moulding.

Astragal moulding Usually for small-section beading; suitable for dividing large panels into smaller areas, or as a cover strip.

Angled and hockey-stick mouldings These are commonly used for trimming edges.

TGV Cladding

TGB Cladding

Skirting torus moulding A half-round profile, one of several types often used for skirting (base) boards.

Chamfer skirting These may or may not have a rounded edge. Use them to remove the sharp edge, or arris, on the corner of a section.

Tongued-and-grooved mouldings can be used to make wide panels and wall cladding. Tongued, grooved and V-jointed (TGV) is the most common profile; tongued, grooved and beaded (TGB) incorporates a half-round bead along one edge. Also known as "bead board" in the United States.

DECORATIVE MOULDINGS

These can be fixed to walls or flush doors or cabinets to create a panelled or decorative effect and are available in a wide range of styles.

Panel mouldings

Ready-made sets of mouldings can be fixed to flat panels to create decorative effects. They may include curved sections for the top edges.

Carved mouldings

For intricate designs, small sections of decorative carved moulding with repeated patterns can be used to good effect. These are carved by machine, or sometimes "embossed" by stamping a relief into the surface of the wood.

Architectural mouldings

Certain mouldings are grouped together under the name "architectural" and are commonly used for interior joinery. However, they have many other uses, including adding decorative detail to cabinets and fitted furniture.

The wide range of sizes and profiles adds enormous potential to the woodworker's options when designing decorative pieces.

Architrave (trim) A moulded strip of wood that surrounds a door frame.

Pediments Pre-formed in fixed widths to suit standard door sizes, these can be used to good effect along the tops of bookcases and closets, matching the interior style of a room.

Plinth blocks and corner blocks A good method of producing a classical style, avoiding the need for mitred corners.

Skirting (base) boards Well-known features in any room and available in a useful range of profiles.

Above A variety of carved mouldings.

Above A variety of "egg and dart" style mouldings.

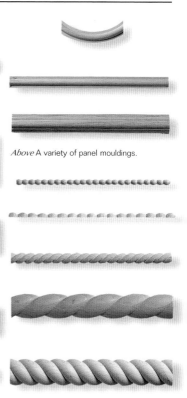

Above A variety of panel mouldings.

Above A variety of twist mouldings.

Architrave

Pediment

Joining mouldings

This is a typical layout showing how architectural mouldings are put to use. They are so called because they would be used to produce a certain effect in the interior of a room rather than for individual items of furniture.

Notice how they combine a decorative effect with good practical points: the plinth blocks and corner blocks around a door frame convey a classic formality, but they also avoid the need to form complex joints where two wooden components meet.

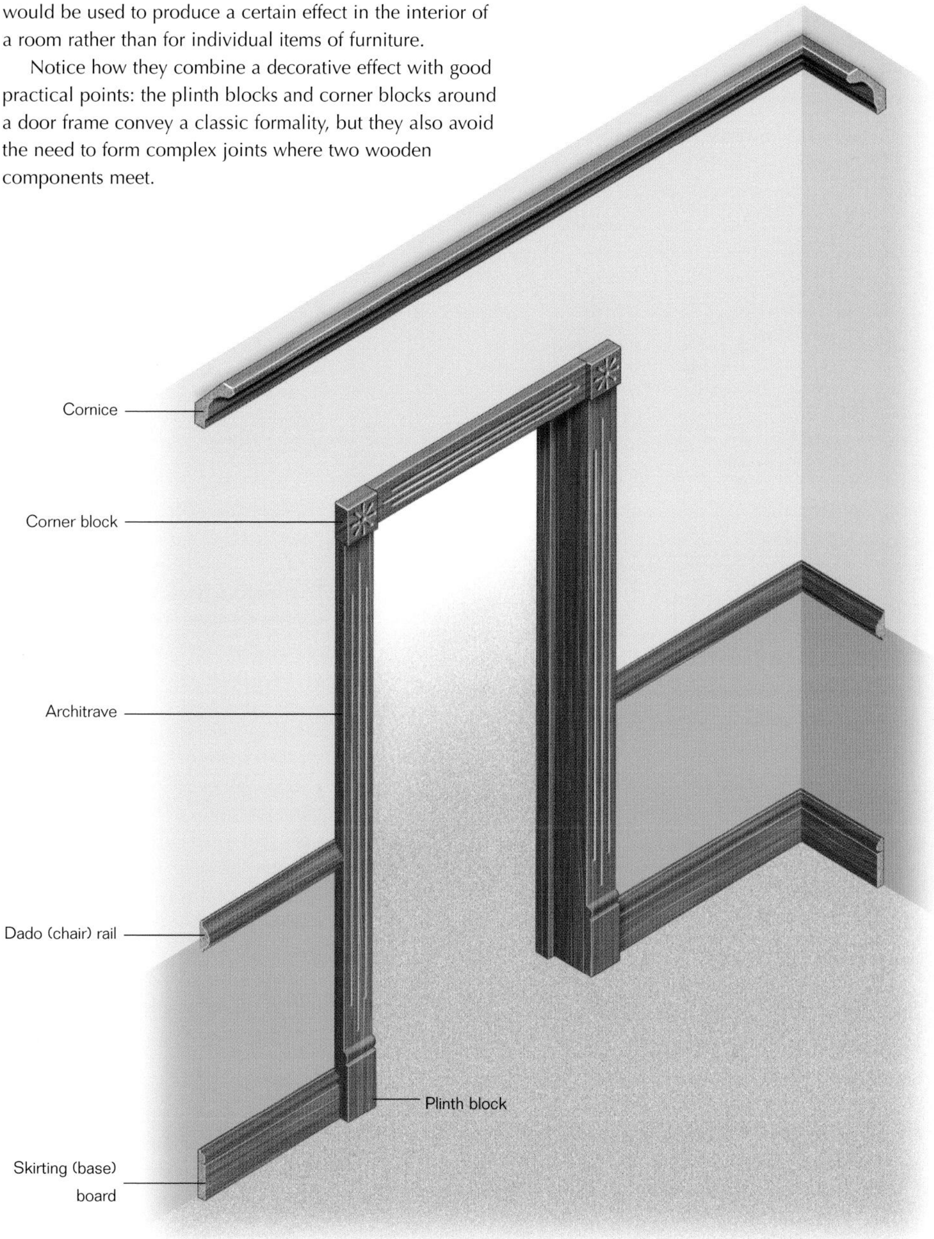

Cornice

Corner block

Architrave

Dado (chair) rail

Plinth block

Skirting (base) board

Veneers

Certain species of timber (lumber), which are expensive or have decorative properties (usually both), are frequently available as veneer forms. These are simply very thin sections of wood that have been peeled or sliced from the main trunk of the tree, allowing maximum use to be made of a valuable resource. When glued to a solid panel, they make all kinds of effects possible. As exotic timber from rare species becomes more difficult to obtain, the use of veneers is becoming more widespread. Decorative manufactured boards, already veneered with a range of hardwoods, are also commonly available.

Bird's eye maple

Fiddleback sycamore

Figured birch

Figured finegre

Cutting veneers

To slice veneers from a log, it is mounted in a frame that rotates or slides up and down against a razor-sharp blade. Depending on the way the log, or *flitch*, is mounted, different sections of the figure in the grain can be displayed to their best effect.

Figured sycamore

Pommelle

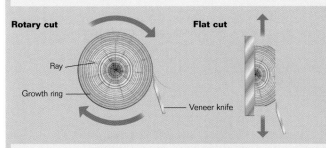

Rotary cut

Ray

Growth ring

Flat cut

Veneer knife

Rotary-cut veneers follow the growth rings in the log as it is "unpeeled" like a giant roll of paper. They are produced in large sizes. Commercially produced plywood is usually made from rotary-cut veneers.
Flat-cut, or *Crown-cut*, veneers are cut parallel to the centre line of the flitch, as in through and through conversion. Species with distinct growth rings are best sliced in this way.

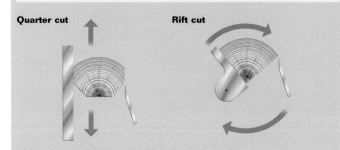

Quarter cut

Rift cut

Quarter cutting through the rings at right angles displays the rays in wide bands, as in quartered oak, where the silvery "flash" (rays) is distinctive. With the knife offset at a slight angle from the quarter position, a *rift* or *comb* cut is achieved. This produces a fine parallel grain figure and prevents the rays from flaking out of the thin slices of veneer.

Figured makore

Silky oak

Distinctive grains

Veneers are made from a wide range of wood species to produce various effects. Certain trees develop distinctive grain patterns and can be sliced into veneers to display these to maximum effect.

Bird's eye maple is a highly prized effect that arises in certain maple trees, and is selected for veneers wherever possible. The veneer is rotary cut to display the dimpled grain that resembles birds' eyes, hence the name. Sometimes a distinctive ripple arises in sycamore, known as fiddleback, so-called because sycamore was often used for making violins. Other species produce curious mottled and lustrous patterns. When a log is quartered to cut through the horizontal rays, the silvery pattern in some species is unmistakable, as in oak or silky oak (see above), which is not a true oak, but a similar-looking wood from Australia.

Burr veneers

Burr, or Burl, figure arises from an abnormal growth on the tree trunk, the grain becoming tortuous and disfigured. It can occur in many species and is sought after for veneering or turning.

Vavona (sometimes written vervona), is the name given to burr wood from the sequoia tree. Burr veneers need very careful handling as they are extremely fragile when sliced into thin sheets. They should also be well sealed and coated to prevent small fragments becoming separated.

Walnut burr

Oak burr

Elm burr

Ash burr

Vavona burr

Myrtle burr

Colour

Veneers are selected to display the striking colours of some species, from the bright orange of yew wood to the dark olive green sometimes found in the heartwood of ash.

Some wood tends to darken naturally when it is exposed to sunlight, as in the example of weathered sycamore. It should be well sealed to prevent further bleaching or discolouration. Other veneers are actually stained or tinted to produce a variety of coloured effects which can be quite striking.

Yew

Olive ash

Red elm

Walnut

Bolivor

Weathered sycamore

Exotic veneers

Rare species of wood are much more likely to be encountered in veneer form than any other.

Brazilian rosewood in its solid form has now been banned from international trade because of its scarcity. However, small quantities of veneer can still be obtained from specialist veneer suppliers. Even rare varieties of wood become available from time to time, and this is the most sensible and economical way of using a valuable resource.

Brazilian rosewood

Red gum

Santos rosewood

Madagascar rosewood

2

TOOLS

Woodworking requires a range of specific tools, which have been developed and become increasingly specialized to suit every conceivable task. Despite the introduction of power tools in recent years, few jobs can be done without using hand tools at some stage of the process, and every woodworker will gradually collect more of them as the need arises. The following pages include most of the tools in common use, but there is no end to the variety and different levels of quality and refinement available, as browsing through any tool catalogue will reveal.

Tools can be grouped into families according to each stage of the woodworking process – measuring and marking, cutting and shaping and finishing, for example. Only a few basic essentials from each group are needed to begin, but the serious craftsperson will soon find that learning new skills and acquiring the tools that go with them is a never-ending process, and part of the rewarding experience of fine woodworking.

THE BASIC TOOLKIT

"A bad craftsman always blames his tools." We have all heard this saying and understand what it means – you cannot expect a tool to do its job well if it is not handled correctly. This does not simply mean that you need to develop your woodworking skills; you also have to select the appropriate tool for the task at hand, understand how it functions and know how to keep it sharp and in good condition.

It will take some time and a little patience to gain confidence using hand tools, especially saws, chisels and planes but you will gain much satisfaction and increase your skills as a craftsperson.

Buying the best

A common mistake made by novices is to start out with a cheap "beginner's" toolkit. This can be a false economy – not only will the tools be made of poor-quality steel that will not hold a sharp edge, but also their overall quality and balance will make hard work of simple operations. As a result, you may become frustrated at your inability to achieve good results, no matter how much care you take, and lose interest in persevering.

There must be many people who think that they do not have what it takes for woodworking, when in fact all they need is the correct guidance and a little tuition in selecting the tools for the job.

Below Build your tool collection gradually by buying the best tools you can afford.

Starting a collection

	Basic toolkit	Next on the list
Measuring and marking:	Retractable tape Try square Marking knife Bradawl or awl	Steel rule Combination square Marking gauge Adjustable bevel gauge
Cutting:	Hardpoint saw Tenon saw	Professional hand saw Mitre saw
Shaping:	Bench plane Bevelled chisels	Block plane Firmer chisels
Assembling:	Screwdrivers Claw hammer Mallet G-cramps (C-clamps)	Cordless drill/driver Drill bits Pin hammer Sash cramps (Bar clamp)
Finishing:	Sandpaper/abrasive papers	Scraper

Getting the essentials

It is not easy to specify the tools that are essential for starting out, simply because the range of woodworking activities is so wide. A model maker needs different tools to a cabinet-maker; working with manufactured boards requires sharp, tungsten-carbide-tipped tools for best results, while softwoods can be worked easily with good-quality hand tools.

Nevertheless, most woodworking operations tend to have a definite sequence of work, and the basics will allow you to get started and explore further options as you progress. Included in the table are the tools that should form your "wish list" – the most useful items to save for.

Buying tools

Most large hardware and do-it-yourself stores stock a full range of tools and offer good value where the more basic items are concerned. For the best quality and a wider range of specialized tools, however, a professional tool shop is worth a visit. An expensive hand saw or plane must be handled and tested for balance before you buy.

A good tool supplier will understand this and should be able to offer a variety of different models so that you can choose the one that suits you best.

Spare parts and servicing are important, so try to develop a good working relationship with your supplier and discuss your needs. Remember that many expensive tools can be hired rather than purchased outright, if you need them only for the occasional project. This is also a good way of trying out different makes and models before buying a tool for yourself.

Browsing through tool catalogues is another habit that most woodworkers share. You cannot handle the tools or try them out, but a good mail-order supplier will offer a very wide range and can be a good source for really specialized items. Even second-hand tool shops are worth visiting if you get the chance. Examine the tools carefully to check that they are not damaged or incomplete; you may find a real bargain. Old tool steel was forged to a high quality and is definitely superior to some of today's cheap varieties.

Storing tools

Well-made tools are works of great craftsmanship in themselves. They should be chosen with care and looked after well. Most accomplished craftsmen still possess some of the first tools they ever acquired, even though they may be many years old. Always protect the cutting edges of tools. A good-quality hand saw needs a cover that clips over the blade – you can make one from thin strips of plywood or plastic tube if one was not supplied with the saw. Keep chisels in a leather tool roll, with divisions to separate the blades. Planes should always have their blades retracted when not in use and be stored on their sides to preserve the surface of the sole plate.

When buying power tools, the more professional models will usually be supplied in a carrying case, which should be considered a necessity rather than a luxury. As well as protecting the tool from dust, it will prevent damage to the power cord, and keep the accessories safe so that they are to hand when needed.

Power tools

Portable power tools represent a greater investment than hand tools and must be chosen carefully. They are listed in order of versatility and usefulness.

- Jigsaw (saber saw)
- Cordless drill
- Router
- Orbital sander
- Circular saw
- Power drill
- Power planer
- Belt sander
- Biscuit jointer
- Mitre saw

Below A good set of chisels, with high-quality steel blades that are kept sharp, will last for many years.

TOOLS FOR MEASURING AND MARKING

Accurate marking out is always the first step to a successful job. Poor-quality measuring and marking devices can lose their accuracy very quickly and spoil your work without you realizing until it is too late. Check them regularly for wear and damage, and if you think an item is suspect, put it to one side or dispose of it. A common mistake is to keep such a tool as a spare, but this is a false economy. A try square, for example, should form a perfect 90 degree angle – any variation makes it useless.

Units of measurement

When buying measuring and marking instruments, always check which units are used on the scale. Even though metrication of the woodworking trade has been in progress for many years, there are no signs of the imperial system dying out and certainly not in the United States. Suppliers, toolmakers and timber (lumber) yards seem to manage to work to both systems in parallel, and woodworkers need to be able to do the same. It is not as confusing as it seems, but there is always room for misunderstanding. Double check the specifications of the tools when you buy them.

Metric and imperial

A metric rule will be marked in millimetres or centimetres, or both; an imperial scale will be marked in feet and inches. Most useful of all might be a rule with both scales, on either side, but do remember to check that they are accurate. Some of the cheaper tools are poorly engraved or printed, and an inaccurate scale is not worth buying at any price.

T-square A combined straightedge and square for marking out.

Straightedge This is used as a measure and a guide for scoring and cutting. A large handle allows a firm grip and keeps fingers well away from the blade of a marking knife. A good straightedge will have thin friction pads on the underside to prevent it from slipping.

Steel rule For accurate setting out of joints and small dimensions, a steel rule with etched divisions is the best. It can be up to 1m or 36in long, but a 300mm (12in) rule will be more convenient for most marking-out tasks.

Combination square With a sliding scale and well-designed stock, this can be used as a try square, a mitre square and an adjustable depth gauge. This example even has a small spirit level mounted in the stock and a small pin for accurate marking.

Bench rule (*below*) A long wooden rule, less accurate for fine detail, but suitable for bench joinery and general cabinet-making. Brass-tipped versions prevent damage to the ends.

Mitre square (*above*) This is not a "square" at all, but an accurately machined blade and stock set at 45 degrees for gauging perfectly mitred corners.

Bradawl This is similar to an awl, but with a small flat end to the blade. It is used for marking hole positions and can be twisted into the wood without splitting the grain.

Adjustable bevel gauge or sliding bevel The hardened steel blade with locking lever can be adjusted quickly for measuring and transferring angles. A rosewood stock with brass strips ensures lasting accuracy.

Try square The classic carpenter's square, with a rosewood stock and brass facings for consistent accuracy. One of the first items for your toolbox.

Craft (utility) knife This has a multitude of uses, particularly for scribing and scoring the workpiece, as well as cutting. Choose a model with a retractable blade for safety.

Retractable tape An all-purpose measuring tape in a rigid case. Look for a good locking action, clear markings on the blade and a well-formed hooked end that allows both internal and external measurements.

Spirit level This is not vital for bench carpentry, but comes into its own when carrying out installation work. A small "torpedo" level can be kept in the toolbox.

Chalk line A quick method of marking out straight lines. Fill the reservoir with coloured chalk powder, clip the hook over one end of the work, pull the string tight and snap it lightly to leave a perfectly straight, temporary cutting line.

Vernier gauge Used for measuring both the inner and outer diameters of circular objects, or the widths of a mortise and tenon joint.

Profile gauge Small needles slide in the central stock, allowing the outline of any profile to be copied and transferred with ease.

Engineer's square An all-metal square, precision made with a hardened blade. Ideal for checking detail and can be obtained with a blade as short as 75mm (3in).

Awl A small pointed blade for starting holes or pricking out a mark accurately.

Mortise gauge This is used to mark out consistently accurate, parallel lines for cutting a mortise. The two brass pins are independently adjustable on accurate brass slides, while the sliding stock runs against the face of the work. There is a single pin on the opposite side of the shaft for marking a single scribed line.

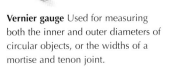

HAND SAWS

A well-balanced hand saw is an essential tool for any woodworker. Properly set and sharpened, it can produce a smooth, straight cut as quickly and even more accurately than a power saw. The performance of a saw depends on the size, shape and number of the teeth, which act as a series of miniature knives to slice through the wood. Each tooth is ground and sharpened individually, the quality of the steel determining how well it will perform.

Crosscut saw These are traditional saws. If they are well maintained, they will last a lifetime. Ideal specifications include a taper-ground blade, to prevent it from binding in the saw cut, with cross-ground teeth for splinter-free cutting across the grain. A 560mm (22in), 10- or 12-point saw is suitable for most tasks. A 10-point saw has ten tooth points for every 25mm (1in) of the blade.

Hardpoint saw Modern technology has produced saws with hardened teeth that remain sharp for longer, and have a specially ground profile for cutting along and across the grain with equal efficiency. However, hardpoint teeth cannot be resharpened.

Utility saw Consider using this "universal" saw for general-purpose use. It cannot be resharpened either, but can be considered as disposable when it has done its job. It is ideal for cutting manufactured materials, such as chipboard, which are less kind to traditional saws.

Tenon saws

This family of saws (*below*) was designed for small-scale, accurate work, such as making joints and so on. The blade is stiffened with a strip of steel or brass along the back, and consequently these saws may be described as "backsaws". They have smaller teeth, typically 15-point, for a finer cut.

Hardpoint tenon saw Like the larger hand saw, this cannot be resharpened, but is ideal for general-purpose use.

Classic tenon saw A good-quality tenon saw for the cabinet-maker.

Dovetail saw A smaller version for very fine joinery work, with 20-point teeth.

Special-purpose saws

Frame saws are designed for intricate work. The disposable blades are heat treated for hard wear and will cut wood, fibres or plastic. The frame allows the blade to be swivelled to any angle for cutting curves.

Piercing saw This has fine teeth (up to 80-point) for the finest modelling and engineering work. The quick-release facility allows the blade to be fed through the work and re-attached.

Coping saw Designed for quick adjustment, it allows curves to be cut by swivelling the blade within the frame.

Hardpoint padsaw This has a short, stiff blade that allows small cut-outs to be made in panels where access is restricted. Hardpoint teeth will cut fibre- or plasterboard with ease.

Pistol-grip padsaw This allows greater control of the blade with a pistol grip. Interchangeable blades, including hacksaw blades, can be used for cutting thin sheet metal.

Fret saw This can cut into the work as deep as 250mm (10in) from the edge before the frame impedes the cutting action. It works on the pull stroke for accurate control.

Mitre box and mitre block Useful sawing accessories without the expense of a mitre saw. To use them, insert a tenon saw blade into the pre-cut guide slots to make accurate square and mitre cuts. A mitre block has one slot, while a mitre box has two, to direct the saw blade.

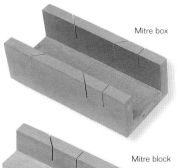

Mitre box

Mitre block

Mitre saw This makes short work of cutting accurate angles and offers fine adjustment. It is well worth the investment if working with delicate mouldings or making picture frames. The hardpoint blade slides in nylon bearings, which, in turn, guide the cutting action.

POWER SAWS

Power saws can save a lot of time and hard work, but they can also do a lot of damage if used incorrectly. Never force a saw through the work. If the blade is not sharp, or the motor is underpowered, not only will the cut be inaccurate, but also you'll be putting your safety at risk. Let the saw do the work, guiding it slowly, but surely, along the line. Use an adjustable fence if possible when making straight parallel cuts.

Jigsaw (saber saw)

The all-purpose power saw with a multitude of uses. As well as making curved cuts, a jigsaw is ideal for quickly roughing-out work before finishing by hand.

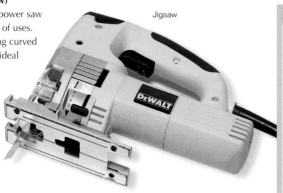

Jigsaw

Jigsaw key features:

- Pendulum action to reduce binding and increase the life of the blade.
- Variable speed for greater control to suit the thickness of material.
- A sawdust blower that directs the exhaust from the motor fan toward the cutting line to remove sawdust as you follow the line of the cut.
- An adjustable base plate to permit a variety of cutting angles.
- Scrolling action, allowing the blade itself to be swivelled for cutting curves of very small radius.

Reciprocating or sabre saw This is not really a common workshop tool, but it is useful for the rapid cutting of boards to length. Unless you do this frequently, a good, sharp hand saw will be just as effective.

Reciprocating saw

Saw blades

Jigsaw (saber saw) blades come in a variety for many purposes, but check that the model of jigsaw you buy will accept standard-fitting blades. There are many specialized blades available for cutting all kinds of material, such as wood, manufactured boards, metal, ceramics, plastics and laminates. A knife blade has no teeth, and is designed for cutting leather or rubber sheeting.

Bi-metal blades, though more expensive, will last longer and are less inclined to bend. Most blades are 100mm (4in) long, allowing a depth of cut of 50–65mm (2–2½in), but heavy-duty blades are available up to 150mm (6in) long. These should only be fitted to a machine with a powerful motor designed to accept the extra load.

Circular saw blades

Check that the bore of the blade (the diameter of the central hole that fits over the spindle) is compatible with the machine, as different makes vary. As with hand saws, the type of blade should suit the material and the cutting action, whether ripsawing along the grain, crosscutting, or making fine cuts in veneered or laminated panels.

Carbide teeth are cheaper for most general-purpose work; tungsten-carbide-tipped blades are sharper and much more hardwearing. They should be used when cutting composite materials and manufactured boards.

Powered mitre saws use special blades with teeth at a "negative rake" to suit the plunging action of the saw. They are not interchangeable with other machines.

Circular saw

Circular saw This is the best saw for cutting out large panels of plywood or similar manufactured materials. If it is used with a fence or purpose-made (custom-made) guide, it will make straight, smooth cuts with ease. The size of the machine and the diameter of blade determine the maximum depth of cut.

Circular saw key features:

- Tungsten-carbide-tipped (TCT) blade.
- Adjustable base plate or "shoe" for depth and angle of cut.
- Sliding fence for cutting parallel to the edge of the work.
- Good visibility in front of the blade to aid control when cutting freehand.
- Spindle and also electric brakes to stop the blade spinning as soon as the trigger is released.
- Spindle lock for fitting blades quickly and safely.

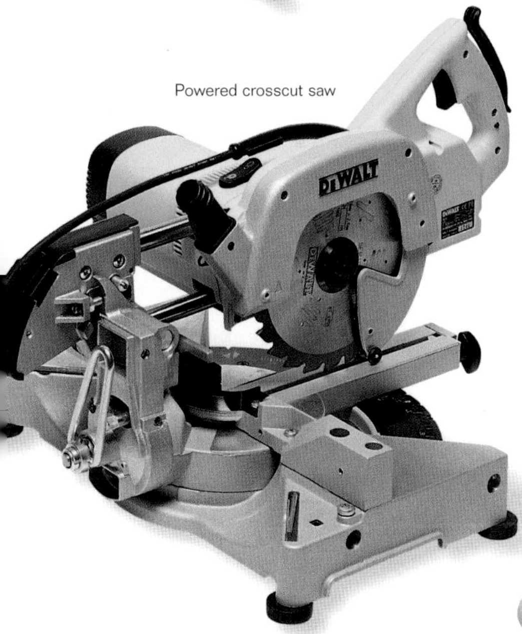

Powered crosscut saw

Powered crosscut saw Sometimes called a mitre saw, this is a more costly item, but a useful workshop tool. It makes quick work of cross cutting timber (lumber) accurately to length with perfectly square ends, or can be adjusted to make angled cuts up to 45 degrees. The best models allow the saw body to slide out on parallel bars for cutting extra-wide stock up to 250mm (10in) and have a swivel mount for cutting compound angles.

Cordless circular saw This version of the circular saw comes into its own when working outdoors away from a power source. It does have the added safety advantage of not having a vulnerable power cord, and can be used one-handed for light work. Note how on the model shown, the blade is mounted on the left-hand side of the body for better visibility.

Cordless circular saw

PLANES

Hand planes are among the most satisfying tools you can use. A finely set plane with a sharp blade will slice through the wood with an unmistakable sweet sound, leaving a smooth surface that scarcely needs any further treatment. As with other tools, different sizes and types of plane have been developed over the years to suit each particular task perfectly.

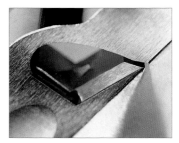

Bench planes

This is the standard family of planes for two-handed use on the workbench. Each type is designed for a specific function, depending on the length of the body and the angle, or set, of the blade. Try planes or jointer planes have bodies of up to 600mm (24in) in length and are used for "trying", or squaring up, perfectly straight edges. Fore planes are slightly shorter, at 460mm (18in), and are used for much the same purpose as the try plane.

Anatomy of a bench plane

The base of the plane is called the sole, or sole plate, and should be protected from damage to keep it perfectly straight and flat. The mouth in the sole allows the shavings to be cleared away as the plane is used. The frog is the machined block that receives the blade assembly; it can be adjusted to alter the width of the mouth. It is set to the ideal position during manufacture. Adjustment levers are mounted in the frog to control the depth of cut and to keep the blade perfectly straight. The blade assembly is removable for sharpening and maintenance, and consists of three parts: the blade itself, or plane iron, made of high-quality carbon steel for long life; the cap iron, which clamps over the iron to tension it and clear the shavings as they are produced; and the lever cap, which locates over a screw on the frog and clamps the whole assembly to the plane body.

A good-quality plane should be maintained whenever the blade is removed for sharpening. Clear all fragments of wood from the body, remove all dust and apply light machine oil to the moving parts.

Jack plane

At 300–380mm (12–15in), this is a convenient size for most workshops. It is ideal for flattening the faces and edges of boards, and for preparing sawn timber (lumber).

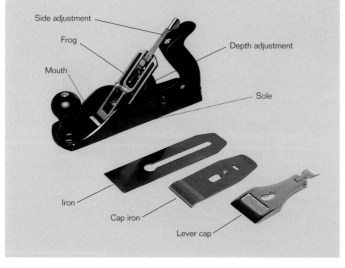

Side adjustment
Frog
Mouth
Depth adjustment
Sole
Iron
Cap iron
Lever cap

Smoothing plane

The most useful plane for fine finishing in all kinds of woodworking. It is usually 225–250mm (9–10in) long.

Block plane
This is not classed
as a true bench plane,
although the body has a similar
design. The blade has a much
shallower angle and can be set for the
removal of the finest shavings when
working across end grain. A versatile
tool, shaped to fit the palm of the
hand and often used one-handed.

Shoulder planes
(*above and right*) Each of these narrow
planes has its blade set at an acute
angle for the removal of fine shavings
when trimming joints. They are
essential tools when forming tenons or
cleaning-up small rebates (rabbets).

**Compass
plane** A very
specialized plane with a flexible sole
that can be formed into a shallow arc
for working on curved surfaces.

Rebate, or filister, plane (*right*)
The best plane for forming a rebate
(rabbet) along the edge of a length of
wood. Like the shoulder plane, its
blade spans the full width of
the body. Fitted with a
sliding fence to control
the width of the cut,
and a depth stop.

Plough plane (*below right*) A more
sophisticated version of the rebate
(rabbet) plane, having interchangeable
blades of different sizes. Can be used to
form grooves or rebates (rabbets) with
great accuracy. A combination plane
will accept other blades,
or cutters, of different
profiles to form beaded
and tongued mouldings.

Spokeshave This is a
two-handed tool for working on
rounded stock. Available with a flat
base or a rounded base for dealing
with convex or concave surfaces.
The name comes from the
days when wheelwrights
made spokes for
wooden wheels.

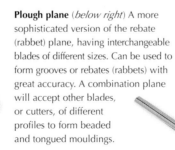

POWER PLANERS AND ROUTERS

These are quite different tools to power saws, but they have in common the use
of rapidly rotating cutter blades, which remove the stock very quickly and easily.
When used safely they can be a powerful aid to most shaping operations.
Tungsten-carbide-tipped blades make it possible to work with manufactured
materials that can be very hardwearing on the sharpest of hand tools.

Power planer key features:

- Reversible tungsten-carbide-tipped blades for longer life.
- Parallel fence for accurate rebating.
- Body design that allows a rebate (rabbet) depth up to 20mm (¾in).
- Dust extraction facility or collection bag for shavings.
- Automatic pivoting safety guard for cutter block.
- Safety switch and electronic speed control.
- V-groove in the sole plate to allow easy chamfering operations.

Power planer

Power planer This power tool is ideal for the rapid removal of large amounts of waste, but it should be handled with great care, as it is extremely easy to remove too much wood and ruin the work. The depth of cut in one pass ranges from 1.5 to 5mm (⅟₁₆ to ³⁄₁₆in) on more powerful models; 3mm (⅛in) is quite adequate for most general purposes.

The cutter block, in which the blades are mounted, rotates at very high speed and should be treated with great respect. Always make sure that the power cord is well out of the way when using a power planer, so that it does not impede the work. Keep your hands well away from the blades and wait for the cutter block to stop spinning before putting the tool down on the workbench.

Biscuit jointer A biscuit jointer is a handy tool for making quick work of all kinds of jointing operation. The "biscuits" are flat wooden dowels that fit into semicircular slots formed by the blade of the jointer. Its great advantage is the ease with which quick adjustments can be made to suit any thickness of wood. The best models have an adjustable carriage that can be tilted up to 45 degrees for dealing with mitred corners.

Biscuit jointer

Router A router is one of the most versatile and powerful tools a woodworker can have. It incorporates a rotary cutter mounted in an adjustable body, which removes small slices of wood with each rotation, allowing all kinds of profiling and shaping work.

The range of router cutters is huge, and a good way to begin is with a "starter" selection of ten or twelve cutters, which will cover a wide range of applications.

Router key features:

- Safety switch and "soft start" feature to prevent kick-back when starting.
- Variable speed control for different materials and delicate work.
- Stepped-adjustment depth gauge, allowing a series of passes at different depths.
- Dust extraction facility.
- Spindle lock for easy cutter changing.
- Range of collets to receive cutters of different shank sizes: 6–12mm (¼–½in).
- Parallel fence with fine tuning adjustment.
- Template follower for copying patterns and routing curves.

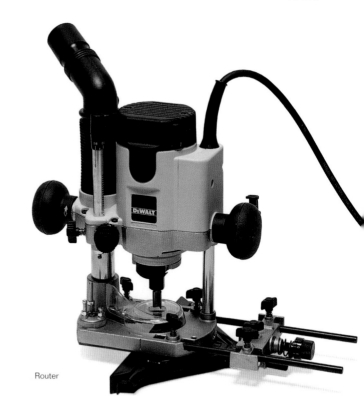

Router

Router table More powerful routers can be mounted upside-down in a work table, allowing very efficient machining operations. With a sliding fence and protective cutter guard, continuous profiling work will be accurate and safe. Large-diameter professional cutters make short work of mouldings and tongued-and-grooved panels.

Router table

CHISELS

A high-quality forged steel blade set in a tough handle are the qualities to look for in a good woodworking chisel. Traditional chisels with hardwood handles should only be struck with a wooden mallet; more modern versions with shatter-resistant polypropylene handles can withstand hammer blows equally well. Most chisels are available in matched sets, ranging in size from 6 to 38mm (¼ to 1½in) or more, but for a more modest outlay, a set of three, comprising the most useful sizes of 12, 19 and 25mm (½, ¾ and 1in), will suffice.

Bevelled chisels

Bevel-edge, or bevelled, chisels are the most versatile type you can buy for most woodworking tasks. They can be used for chopping out material when struck with a mallet, or for more gentle paring and shaping tasks when used freehand. A newly purchased chisel will have the main bevel ground on the end of its blade, but a secondary bevel will need adding to hone it ready for use.

| 32mm | 25mm | 19mm | 12mm | 10mm | 6mm |
| (1¼in) | (1in) | (¾in) | (½in) | (⅜in) | (¼in) |

Firmer chisels

A firmer chisel is just that: a stronger blade designed to accept heavier blows when chopping out a mortise or socket. The end bevel is designed for slicing across the end grain of wood, while the long edges are not bevelled, allowing the cutting of square, parallel-sided mortises. Usually, firmer chisels are sold only in four common sizes to suit the standard widths of mortise used in general joinery. Good quality steel is essential for these chisels, to give a good sharp edge, which can withstand heavy use.

| 25mm | 19mm | 12mm | 6mm |
| (1in) | (¾in) | (½in) | (¼in) |

Gouges

Although gouges are used principally for carving, most woodworkers will have one or two in their toolkits for dealing with curved mouldings and other shaping operations.

Gouges can be bevelled on the outer, convex surface of the cutting edge (out-cannel gouge), for most grooving actions, or on the concave surface (in-cannel gouge) for paring, trimming and carving.

25mm	19mm	12mm	6mm	25mm	19mm	12mm	6mm
(1in)	(¾in)	(½in)	(¼in)	(1in)	(¾in)	(½in)	(¼in)

Sharpening equipment

A good sharpening stone is a vital part of the toolkit. Without a sharp edge, a chisel will be not only difficult to work with, but also dangerous. The chisel will follow where the wood directs it, rather than where you want it to go, and can easily slip.

Chisels should be sharpened at the beginning and end of every session. If they are attended to regularly, just a few minutes' work will keep the honed edges in prime condition. Once in a while, a longer honing session might be necessary – if the bevel loses its original angle or if the edge is chipped.

Natural sharpening stones are quite expensive, and synthetic versions are commonly used. Japanese water stones are of natural stone and need water as a lubricant. They can produce a finely ground edge on the best-quality steel. For more general use, oilstones are sufficient.

A combination stone is the best buy, two stones of different grades being bonded together back to back.

The coarse stone is for regrinding to the correct bevel; the fine stone for delivering a keen honed edge. A honing guide is a useful accessory and will assist in maintaining the correct angle of a chisel or plane iron when being sharpened. By clamping the blade in the guide and moving it gently to and fro on the stone, you will be able to grind a constant angle without difficulty.

Conical and cylindrical slipstones and wedges are sometimes used to achieve the correct profile on the blades of curved and angled chisels.

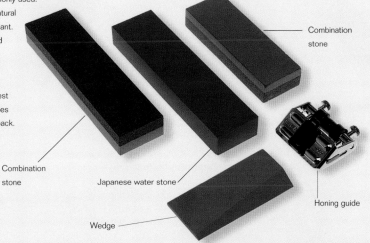

Combination stone

Combination stone

Japanese water stone

Honing guide

Wedge

HAND DRILLS

There are few woodworking projects that do not require drilling holes of some kind, if only for fixing screws. To insert a screw correctly, a clearance hole should be drilled in the piece to be fixed to match the size of the screw's shank and prevent the wood from splitting as the screw is tightened. A countersink or counterbore may also be needed to sink the head of the screw below the surface. Finally, a pilot hole is usually advisable, of the correct diameter to suit the tapered, threaded end of the screw. All these operations can be carried out easily with a hand drill.

Accurate drilling

This is an important woodworking technique, and it has been much simplified in recent years with powered hand drills and even more so with bench-mounted pillar drills. Hand drilling with a brace still has a place, however, especially in sites far removed from electric power. Even in the workshop, it is often quicker to reach for a small hand drill than to set up a power drill just for the few holes required before proceeding to the next stage of the job.

Hand drill A useful tool for quickly producing small holes when needed. Ideal for drilling pilot holes and countersinking. Its small size comes in handy in tight corners.

Practical tip

Never interfere with the centre point of a drill if it has one – this will almost certainly affect its concentricity.

Gimlet The screw thread is for starting a screw hole without fear of splitting the wood when the screw is inserted.

Carpenter's brace This is a powerful drilling tool, which provides ample leverage from the wide sweep of its handle. Look for a "universal" jaw – a chuck that accepts both tapered and parallel drill bits – and a reversible ratchet action.

Bradawl Sharp pointed shaft for scribing and piercing holes for pins and nails.

Drill bits

Great advances have also been made in the pattern of bits and there are now bits especially designed for setting dowels. This technique is often used in projects involving manufactured boards such as chipboard or ply and these produce flat-bottomed holes. There are also flat bits, which work with a scraping action and cut large holes very rapidly, although these are not as accurate as twist bits. For the home worker on a limited budget, an adjustable bit is a good investment but these can only be used in a hand brace and not in any powered tool. The ordinary twist bit is used for making small holes and for starting screws. Beware of buying cheap sets of drill bits. They can be made of poor-quality steel and can be easily blunted.

Standard twist drills (*left*) Sometimes described as HSS (high-speed steel), these bore holes easily in steel, but are equally suitable for woodworking. They are made in a wide range of sizes at small increments – 1mm (¹⁄₂in) – so there should be no difficulty in finding the correct size.

Spade, or flat, bits (*right*) These are the traditional woodworker's drill bit for larger holes up to 32mm (1¼in) in diameter. Drill vertically, using a brace, for best results.

Centre-point (brad point), or "lip and spur", bits (*right*) These should only be used for wood. The point centres the bit exactly, preventing slipping and helping to keep the hole straight as you work. Made in a smaller range of sizes than standard twist drills, but still adequate for most needs. They are also known as dowel drill bits, as certain diameters match the small wooden dowels used for aligning joints – 6, 8 and 10mm (¼, ⁵⁄₁₆ and ³⁄₈in).

POWER DRILLS

For any repetitive work, or removing large amounts of waste, a power drill is essential. Certain types of drill bit are designed specifically for use at high speeds and will not produce satisfactory results in a hand drill. Sometimes, a low speed with high torque, or turning force, is the best combination, and a power drill of the correct rating is ideal for this. The power source of the drill is all important – motors range in capacity from 300 watts (3 amp) for light duty to 1000 watts (10 amp) and above for really heavy work; a 600 watt (6 amp) motor is fine for general duties. A motor will soon burn out if the drill is overloaded.

Cordless drill

Cordless drill One of the first items in your toolkit should be a cordless drill. These are relatively recent products, but in the space of ten years or so they have been found to be so useful that there is now a vast range on the market. One of the advantages for the woodworker is that many cordless drills can be used as slow speed, powered screwdrivers.

The voltage of the battery determines the power of the drill and the length of time it can be used before recharging. Top-of-the-range models have 18 volt batteries – 9.6 or 12 volt is adequate for general use. Always check the manufacturer's instruction manual.

Cordless drill key features:

- Spare battery, allowing uninterrupted use without having to wait for recharging.
- Carrying case and rapid charger.
- 10mm (⅜in) keyless chuck, allowing quick changing of drill bits.
- Screwdriver bits, clipped to the body of the drill when not in use.
- Two-speed or variable-speed facility.
- Reversible action (essential for screwdriving).
- Adjustable torque control to prevent breaking screws.
- Electric brake that stops rotation instantly when the trigger is released.

Electric drill For more regular use, there is no substitute for a power drill operating on mains voltage. This will run continuously at higher speeds and is ideal for mounting in a drill stand. Many power drills have a percussion facility useful for drilling into masonry, stone or brick, but this can be switched off for normal use when working with wood. A depth gauge is useful, as is a variable-speed/reversible action. A side handle provides extra grip and makes it easier to hold the drill vertical when used freehand. Some drills even have a side handle containing a small spirit level for greater accuracy. The extra power means that a 13mm (½in) chuck can be fitted to accommodate the largest drill bits.

Electric drill

Percussion drill A hammer, or percussion, drill is only required for drilling into masonry, using specially hardened masonry bits. It will be useful for installing items that need fixing to plaster or brickwork, but unless you intend doing a lot of work of this kind it could be an expensive luxury. Consider renting one when necessary – do not be tempted to overload a smaller drill that is not designed for heavy duty use.

Percussion drill

Specialized drill bits

Plug cutters are a useful addition to any workshop, especially where quality work is undertaken. Another common accessory to drilling is the countersink. This allows the head of a screw to be sunk cleanly flush with the surface of the wood.

Forstner bits are designed to drill large flat-bottomed holes that do not go through the wood, such as might be needed to fit kitchen cabinet hinges. They are also accurate for drilling deep holes even in the end grain of timber.

Boring bit Used for boring holes for concealed hinges or other fittings of a standard size. Available in 25 and 35mm (1in and 1⅜in) diameters. Drills a shallow, flat-bottomed hole, with a centre point to keep it centred accurately.

Counterbore, or 3-in-1, bit This device will drill a pilot hole, clearance hole and counterbore for a screw in one operation. Obtainable in different sizes to suit a range of screws and usually sold with a plug cutter of the same gauge.

Plug cutter This makes small wooden plugs for concealing fixings. Ideally, it should be used in a drill stand, as it is not self-centring.

Countersink bit A "rosehead" countersink creates a recess for the screw head so that it is flush with the surface. Use with care, as it is very easy to spoil the work by drilling too deep.

Masonry bits Available in many different sizes. You will need to use this bit when attaching fittings for wooden cupboards, shelves and other types of furniture to masonry walls.

Circular hole cutter

This must be used in a fixed drill stand or a drill with an additional side-mounted handle for safety. Select a low drill speed with a high torque setting, as the teeth remove a large amount of waste. Various sizes are available and fit a common arbor, which contains a 6mm (¼in) pilot drill to centre the hole. Holes up to 100mm (4in) in diameter are possible.

Auger bit This will drill deep holes quickly, removing waste. If used with a power drill, the motor must have a reverse facility, otherwise you will not be able to remove it.

TOOLS FOR FIXING

No tool box is complete without a hammer and a screwdriver for straightforward assembly work. There are different types to suit every need. Even though they are familiar items, they should be selected and used carefully.

Hammers

The head, or poll, of a hammer should be of good quality steel, heat treated and hardened for a long life. Hammer sizes are ranged by weight measured in ounces, even in these days of metrication: from 4oz for a small pin hammer up to 20oz.

Cross pein, or pin, hammer The small cross pein opposite the striking face comes into its own when fixing small panel pins (brads). Hold each pin between finger and thumb, and the narrow blade will be small enough to slide between them to deliver a few gentle taps to start it.

Ball pein hammer
More of an engineer's tool; the most heavy-duty hammer in common use and not often called for in woodworking.

Rubber mallet A useful tool for assembly work, when a reasonably firm blow may be required to knock a component into position. The rubber head will not bruise the surface of the wood. You can also buy a dead-blow mallet, which is a synthetic hammer with a hollow head, which is filled with lead shot. It delivers a sharp blow with little effort and no bounce. It is useful for assembly work.

Carpenter's mallet A solid beech mallet is of the correct strength and density to deliver a sound blow to a chisel without jarring. An essential tool for any carpenter.

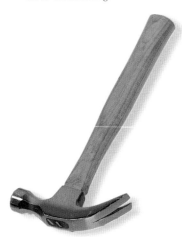

Claw hammer A good-quality traditional claw hammer has a handle made of hickory, selected for its great shock-resistant properties. The precision-ground head should be fixed firmly to the shaft with hardwood and iron wedges, and feel well balanced for driving nails straight.

Slotted screwdrivers (*left*) and cross-head (Phillips) screwdrivers (*right*)

Screwdrivers

Screws come in all shapes and sizes, with different types of head, and there are just as many types of screwdriver to suit them. The quickest way to strip the head of a screw is to use a screwdriver that does not match. Worse still, it can slip out of position and damage the work. Screwdrivers with interchangeable bits, which can be quickly inserted into a socket on the screwdriver shaft, make life easier, but there is still no substitute for the traditional cabinet-maker's tool.

Screw heads vary in size according to their gauge, common sizes ranging from a No.4 (the smallest) up to a No.12 or greater, and you will find a screwdriver to fit each perfectly. A longer shaft will provide more torque; a short screwdriver makes up for this with a larger handle for extra grip. Slotted screws are steadily being replaced by screws with cross-heads, which prevent the driver from slipping out of position, provided it is of the correct size. Make sure you have a set of screwdrivers handy to cover most needs. Never use a screwdriver blade as a lever to open a can of paint – the tip of the blade is tempered steel and can easily shatter if misused.

Screwdriver bits

Small bits with hexagonal shafts are designed for use in special socketed handles, but some can also be clamped into the chuck of a cordless power drill.

A selection of driver bits will take up far less space than a set of separate screwdrivers. They range from long bits for heavy-duty work to short, 25mm (1in) bits, which must be fitted in a holder. All have a standard 6mm (¼in) hexagonal shank. A magnetic bit holder makes quick work of changing bits and will hold a steel screw on the tip for one-handed operation. Cross-head screws are available in two

Above Screwdrivers range considerably in size, from large heavy-duty drivers with a flared tip to the smallest stubby screwdrivers. The tips are described according to the size of screw they are designed for: gauge sizes for slotted screws, and point sizes for cross-heads.

types, which require different screwdrivers. A Phillips head has a simple four-way cross design, while the Pozidriv version gives a more positive grip with four additional flutes between the main slots.

It is important to be able to recognize the difference and select the right bit to suit the screw, otherwise the head will strip as you tighten up the screw.

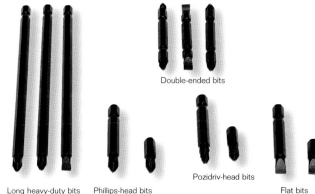

Double-ended bits

Pozidriv-head bits

Long heavy-duty bits   Phillips-head bits

Flat bits

ABRASIVE PAPERS AND SCRAPERS

"Sandpaper" has always been used to give a final finish for wood, although it is not made with sand. Small abrasive particles, glued to a backing paper, are graded according to their size: the finer the grit, the smoother the finish. Grades range from 40 grit up to 1200 grit, so fine that sometimes it is called flour paper in some countries.

Varieties of paper

Many different types of material are used to make abrasive papers. For the woodworker, the most useful include garnet paper, silicon carbide and aluminium oxide paper. Garnet paper is dark red in colour and fairly coarse. It is used for flattening rough-sawn surfaces. Glass paper is paler in colour and available in the full range of grit sizes. It tends to wear quite quickly, but is economical to use.

Silicon carbide paper is more hardwearing and quite efficient. Light grey silicon paper is self-lubricating, providing a smoother finish. Dark grey paper is sometimes called "wet and dry" paper and needs lubricating with water. It is available right up to 1200 grit and is used for fine finishing.

Aluminium oxide paper is sometimes called production paper. It is the hardest wearing material and is the best option for heavy-duty use. However, it is not generally available in much finer grades than 180 grit. For woodworkers, the grades of silicon carbide and aluminium oxide papers most used are 80, 100, 120, 150, 180, 240 and 320 grit.

Use a square of sandpaper wrapped around a cork or rubber sanding block for best results. A small wooden block can be used with some success, but using a more flexible material allows better control and reduces wear on the paper, making it last longer. Make sure the face of the block is free of defects to avoid scoring the surface of the work.

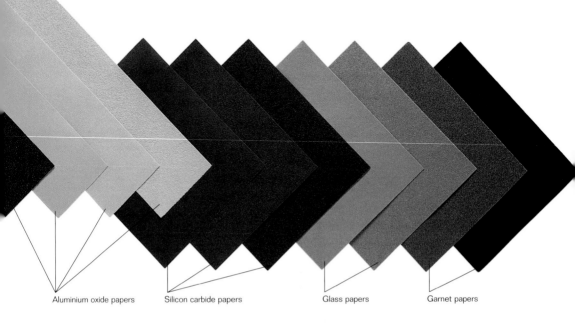

Aluminium oxide papers   Silicon carbide papers   Glass papers   Garnet papers

Scrapers

A cabinet scraper works by cutting the wood fibres rather than wearing them down through abrasion, but is capable of delivering a very smooth finish. It is well worth acquiring the knack of sharpening and using one. A set of scrapers of different profiles will allow the finishing of curved and moulded surfaces. Whereas sandpaper tends to round off sharp edges, the profile of a gooseneck scraper can be matched to almost any curved moulding, thus preserving fine details.

Gooseneck scraper

Flat cabinet scraper

Convex/concave scraper

Rasps

Rasps are useful for roughing out or smoothing the edges of wood when working freehand. A wood file can then be used to achieve a finer finish. Both tools come into their own if you are dealing with variable or uneven grain where using a plane produces poor results. They can be flat or round, and a half-round profile is the most versatile. The pointed end of the file is the tang, and is generally fitted into a separate wooden handle. A surform rasp has holes in its teeth and does not clog up as much as normal rasps.

Wire (steel) wool

This is useful for final finishing. It is available in nine grades and from 5 at the coarse end for stripping and 0000 at the fine end. It is clog resistant.

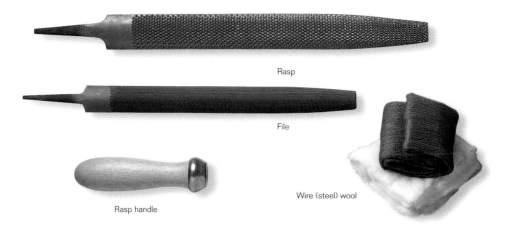

Rasp

File

Wire (steel) wool

Rasp handle

POWER SANDERS

These come in two main types. Belt sanders employ a cloth-backed sanding belt, usually of fairly coarse grade, for the rapid removal of stock. Orbital sanders have a backing pad that makes rapid circular movements and is capable of fine finishing work.

Belt sander This should be used with great care, as it can easily dig in to the surface, leaving deep scour marks. The most important feature to look for is efficient dust extraction, as large amounts of waste are produced. A dust collection bag is essential, but the facility for connecting to an extractor unit is even better.

Different models of belt sander use belts of varying sizes, and for some reason no common standard size has been adopted by manufacturers, so check that the belt size you need is widely available.

Belt sander key features:

- Two-speed or variable-speed motor to suit different surfaces.
- Automatic tracking control to keep the belt running smoothly.

Belt sander

Orbital sander More useful than a belt sander for general use. The sanding action is less severe, and by using progressively finer grades of paper, a fine finish can be achieved. Three common sizes of sander are available: half-sheet, one-third sheet and quarter-sheet. These denote the size of sandpaper that needs cutting from a standard sheet thus avoiding waste.

Orbital sander key features:

- Effective dust collection pouch.
- Perforated base and sanding sheets that prevent dust from collecting under the sander.
- Quick-release clips for changing sanding sheets.
- Variable speed for delicate work.

Orbital sander

Multi-function sanders

For intricate modelling and restoration work, a family of sanders with specially shaped sanding pads are worth considering. Delta sanders have a triangular base ideal for reaching into the corners of panels. Self-adhesive sanding sheets can be changed quickly without clips, but are more expensive.

Multi-function sanders

Palm sander This allows one-handed operation and is not suitable for heavy work, but it is ideal for a light touch to produce a fine finish. The sanding base vibrates at a higher speed than a large orbital sander. It takes quarter-sheet of standard sized sandpaper, and as with larger models, a dust-collection pouch is advisable.

Palm sander

Random orbit sander This is a versatile tool, combining two functions in one. Hold the sander lightly and the circular sanding disc spins in a circular motion for the rapid removal of rough surfaces. Apply more pressure and the action changes to a reciprocating orbital motion for finer finishing.

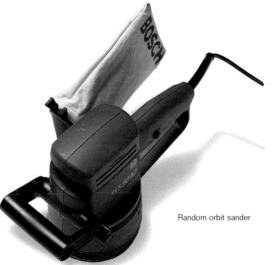

Random orbit sander

Clamps, Toolboxes and Workbenches

There are many varieties to meet the needs of different workshop tasks. Most woodworking adhesives depend on high pressure to form a solid bond and need to be clamped for long periods. Clamps, sometimes called cramps, have other uses, too, such as locating components temporarily when setting out and holding wood steady while working. Clamping the work firmly before any operation is a vital part of safe woodworking practice. The well-equipped workshop will have a collection of several types and sizes of clamp.

Sash clamp (*above*) Two clamp heads on a steel bar deliver firm parallel pressure, on which accurate joinery depends. Available in lengths up to 1.2m (4ft) and more, and most useful when employed in pairs.

G-clamp (*above*) The traditional woodworker's tool – you can never have too many G-clamps. Good-quality forged steel is essential; cheaper cast versions can shatter if overtightened.

Mitre clamp (*above*) A specialized tool that is ideal for frame making. Slide two components together to meet at the centre of the clamp, which guarantees a true right angle.

Web clamp (*below*) Useful for furniture making and assembling objects of irregular shape. The strong nylon webbing extends around the work and is tightened with a small spanner (US wrench), applying tension equally around the assembly.

F-clamps, or screw clamps (*above*) These versatile clamps are quickly adjustable. Slide the movable arm along the bar until it locks against the work, then tighten the screw.

Quick (spring) clamp (*above*) This only applies light pressure, but is useful for a temporary fixing, as it can be used one-handed, leaving the other hand free to locate the components.

Toolboxes

Good tools need to be well organized and protected from damage. In earlier times, the first task of the woodwork apprentice was to make his own toolchest or toolbox, designed for his own personal toolkit. A simple box made from a few pieces of plywood, with internal compartments to keep tools separated, is well worth making when time allows. Alternatively, there is a good range of ready-made items to choose from.

A robust steel engineer's toolbox is good for smaller hand tools, with easily accessible compartments in a compact form.

Cheaper versions in rigid plastic are useful for keeping screws and nails tidy and ready for use.

Larger tools, such as hand saws and planes, can be protected in a heavy-duty canvas toolbag, while a leather tool roll is ideal for chisels. When buying a power tool, a purpose-made carrying case is a good option to look for. It will keep the tool free of dust and protect the power cord.

Engineer's toolbox

Plastic toolbox with separate compartments

Workbenches

A good workbench will have a solid flat top with a vice fixed at one end. Even in the workshop a folding portable workbench comes into its own as a temporary support. The adjustable jaws are ideal for clamping lengths of timber (lumber).

A foldaway portable workbench

A permanent wooden workbench

MACHINE TOOLS

Equipping a professional workshop with heavy-duty machine tools is a costly process, but the serious woodworker can benefit from smaller versions, designed for semi-professional and home workshop use. For your own safety, these machines should not be used without proper training. Many local technical schools and colleges offer evening courses in woodworking, and this is a good way to learn the principles of operating powerful machinery and to expand your abilities. If your workshop space and budget allows, this overview of woodworking machinery will give you an idea of the most popular machines and their function.

Saw bench (Table saw) The heart of a workshop, allowing solid timber (lumber) and sheet materials to be cut to precise dimensions with ease. The saw motor is mounted beneath the table, having a rise-and-fall action to control the height of the blade and a tilting carriage for cutting angles up to 45 degrees. A parallel fence, which slides on a calibrated scale, allows quick adjustment.

Bandsaw (*right*) A continuous blade of flexible steel, running through an adjustable table, makes all kinds of woodworking operations possible. A bandsaw is less powerful than a circular saw, but capable of ripping wide boards lengthways to produce thinner stock, crosscutting, and cutting curves and angles.

Jointer surfacer A separate machine that produces straight, square stock, as with a planer thicknesser, but removes the necessity to reset the machinery for dual operation. It is ideal for producing square-edged boards for joining together in wide panels.

Radial saw (*right*) A circular saw body mounted overhead on a radial arm; ideal for continuous crosscutting work. The arm can also be swivelled through 90 degrees, permitting ripsawing and angled cuts.

Morticer (*above*) A real time-saver when making mortises. An auger revolves in a square chisel, removing waste and forming a perfectly square mortise. The key to accurate work is a solid table that keeps the work square to the direction of cut at all times.

Planer thicknesser (Combination jointer) (*right*) One of the most useful machines for the home workshop. Two sets of operations are possible. On the overhead table (jointer), a length of timber (lumber) is fed over the cutter block, which is exactly square to the side fence. This produces a perfectly square edge on rough stock as a first stage. Below the table, a length of timber is fed between an adjustable bed and the rotating cutter block to produce parallel, smooth faces to accurate dimensions.

Lathe (*left*) Unlike any other machine tool, the lathe makes possible a whole new dimension of woodworking, by turning the stock lengthways against the tool. Any cylindrical form can be produced, from spindles to bowls and goblets.

Spindle moulder (*left*) Similar to a powerful router. The spindle carries a set of steel cutters, revolving at high speed, for making mouldings and shaping wood. A high degree of precision is possible, allowing the production of large quantities of profiles with consistent accuracy.

Pillar drill (Drill press) (*above*) A heavy-duty drilling machine with an adjustable table; perfect for repetitive drilling work with consistent accuracy. Multi-speed for working with different materials, and controllable for drilling blind holes to an accurate fixed depth.

3

GETTING
STARTED

No one simply decides one day to become a woodworker. The introduction to the craft of woodworking is a gradual process, as one increasingly finds that handling and working with wood produces a feeling of satisfaction and reward.

A useful way to begin is to use ready-made plans to make something you need or that you find attractive, where the design and method of construction are already worked out. It will become more important to understand how and why things are done in a certain way, and to broaden your experience with other projects, different types of wood or new tools and techniques. From there, it is a small step to want to make variations, try out new ideas and develop your own designs.

There is no need to feel restricted by a fixed set of rules – the attraction of working with wood stems from the infinite possibilities that the material offers. Nevertheless, certain principles should be followed to avoid early disappointment. This chapter provides an introduction to the planning and design process, and gives a few pointers to safe and successful woodworking practice.

WORKSHOP PLANNING

The novice woodworker might start out by working on a portable workbench in the backyard, a garage or a spare room, only to discover the frustrations of limited space and lack of opportunity to tackle more elaborate projects. Defining a viable workspace, whatever its size, is the first step to working safely and efficiently. A workshop will often be expanded as one's skills and ambitions develop, but if this happens without forethought, confusion and inefficiency are inevitable.

Above Benchhook

Workbenches

The centre of operations for any woodworker is the workbench. Above all, it must be stable and able to resist the forces applied to the work when clamped to it. Also, it must have a perfectly flat top for accurate assembly tasks. If the surface of the workbench is not true, it cannot be relied on for setting out accurate joinery: anything you make on it will reflect the deformity when assembled.

Hardwood workbenches can be purchased in a kit form at fairly low cost, or you can make one yourself along the same lines. A good workbench will have a solid flat top

with a vice fixed at one end. For a right-handed woodworker, the left side of the bench is the best position for the vice. Holes at suitable intervals in the top of the bench act as locations for "dogs", or bench stops, against which a piece of wood can be wedged to hold it while planing or sawing. The traditional bench has a recessed well along the back edge to store tools while working.

A drawer for small items that otherwise may go astray is well worth having, while a stout lower shelf will help to stiffen the construction and keep it square. Strong legs provide support – when hammering or using a

mallet, the work should be positioned directly over one corner to avoid straining the top. Some woodworkers prefer to attach a "sacrificial" top of cheap plywood, which can be replaced from time to time as it wears.

Bench accessories

A vital piece of equipment is a bench vice, which should be of good quality as it is a precision instrument for holding your work squarely and securely. A woodworking vice can be obtained as a separate item from any tool shop and fitted to your own bench if required.

You can add a variety of useful accessories to a workbench, such as a simple tool rack made from a strip of plywood and a series of hardwood blocks screwed to the end of the bench. A bench hook is a square of plywood with a lip that hooks over the front of the bench, and a backstop to support the work.

Screw a board to the wall directly above the workbench for storing other tools and workshop items. Fit it with spring clips for holding chisels and screwdrivers, and wooden pegs for suspending hand saws.

Below Workbench — Bench dog — Bench hook

Well

Tool rack

Vice

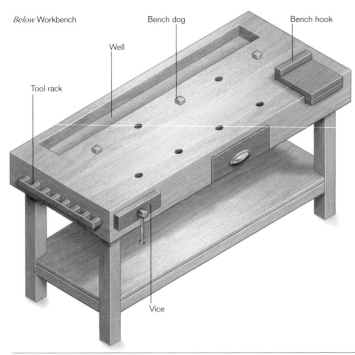

Practical tip

Spend time getting your bench at exactly the height that suits you. An incorrect height can prove to be tiring. Never shorten the legs of a bench if it is too high, work off a duckboard if necessary.

Workshop layout

If you have plenty of space at your disposal, give some thought to the overall layout of the workshop. Think of the route taken by the wood as it is worked into the finished article, and treat the workshop as a small production line, with separate areas for each stage of the operation.

Setting out your work needs a large flat area along one side. The workbench, with tool or wood storage above, should be alongside this, with a clear space in the centre for any tasks involving power or machine tools. Keep the finishing area separate from the work area and, if possible, behind a partition to keep dust to a minimum. Use a dust extractor when creating large quantities of shavings or fine sawdust.

If you have room for a saw bench (table saw) or other machinery, a central position with plenty of clear space around it will be required to accommodate large sheets of plywood and long lengths of timber. Build a table at the right height to support the work as it passes beyond the saw, and economize on space by using the same area for feeding planed timber back toward the saw in a circular route. The table can also act as an assembly area for large projects, with good access from all sides and room for timber storage below.

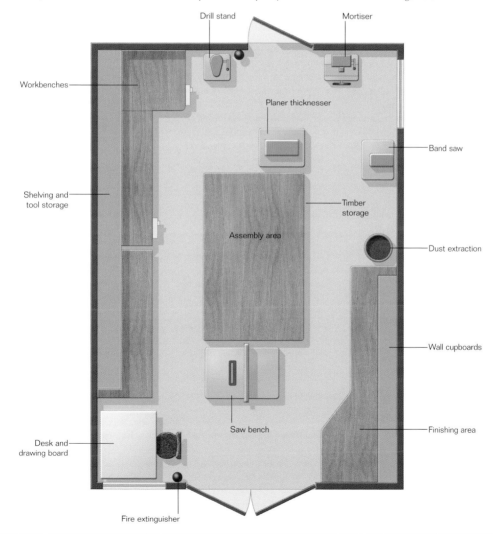

Drill stand

Mortiser

Workbenches

Planer thicknesser

Band saw

Shelving and tool storage

Timber storage

Assembly area

Dust extraction

Wall cupboards

Saw bench

Desk and drawing board

Finishing area

Fire extinguisher

HEALTH AND SAFETY

Your personal safety should underlie every stage of woodworking practice, including the layout of a workshop. It is better to plan your work to eliminate hazards rather than accommodate them – for example, using a dust extractor on a machine that creates a lot of dust is a better solution than wearing a dust mask. Because woodworking depends on the use of cutting tools, this may seem a risk that cannot be avoided, but any experienced craftsman will confirm that a sharp tool is actually less dangerous than a blunt one or a tool that is used incorrectly.

Fire extinguisher

Working practice

Working safely is largely a matter of common sense and awareness. More accidents occur as a result of losing concentration than for any other reason. Develop a sense of rhythm and routine when working, so that you are in tune with what you are doing. Never rush to finish a job, whatever the motivation. There is no advantage in quick results if you risk ruining the work, not to mention suffering injury.

If someone enters your workshop while you are working, finish the task and switch off any machinery before addressing them. They will soon learn to follow your work discipline. For obvious reasons, do not lock yourself in to avoid being disturbed when working alone. On the other hand, do keep the workshop locked in your absence for the safety of others.

Personal safety

Avoid wearing loose clothing and jewellery when working, especially with machinery and power tools. A stout pair of boots should be worn in case of accidents – a sheet of plywood will be painful if it slips and lands on your toe. You can prevent this by wearing a pair of leather or canvas gloves when handling timber. Always inspect a piece of wood for splinters and protruding nails before picking it up. Always have a first aid kit in the workshop for minor injuries. When you work on large machines, do not work alone in case of injury.

Workshop safety

Observe the following points to reduce the risk of accidents:

Keep the workshop tidy An obvious point, but at times it may be tempting to leave the chore of sweeping up until another day. Make a habit of tidying the workshop at the end of every session and dispose of dust and debris sensibly. Keep a check on small offcuts (scraps) that tend to collect wherever you are working and present a real hazard underfoot. Wood and sawdust are biodegradable, so they can be disposed of easily at a local recycling depot.

Treat chemical waste with care Many finishing products are inflammable or harmful to the environment and should be stored separately in a secure place, inaccessible to children and animals. Used chemicals should be collected in resealable containers and disposed of safely at an appropriate waste depot. This even applies to finishing cloths and wipes. Certain volatile products are highly inflammable in concentrated form; spread out contaminated rags so that solvents can evaporate before disposal.

Consider the fire risk Avoiding all naked flames can reduce the risk of fire and, it goes without saying, the workshop should be a non-smoking zone. Install a powder-filled fire extinguisher at every exit door, and fit a smoke alarm. A pile of sawdust can smoulder for hours before bursting into flame. A well-kept workshop has no piles of sawdust, of course, but a smoke alarm guarantees peace of mind.

Observe electrical safety Install a safe power circuit, protected by a circuit breaker to cut off the power in case of any wiring fault or accident. Make sure the circuit is adequate for the load of any machines likely to be used, and fit a master switch near the entrance to the workshop so that switching off all the power becomes routine at the end of every session.

Extension cords trailing across the floor are common causes of accidents, so keep them clipped out of harm's way if they have to be used. Examine all power cords regularly for wear, replacing any that have damaged outer sleeving. Make sure the workshop is well lit with bright fluorescent lighting.

Safety equipment

Even though a private workshop is not required to comply with health and safety legislation, which applies to commercial premises, it makes sense to observe the same safety disciplines and use the personal protection equipment that is recommended and readily available.

First aid kit Obtain the correct size of kit recommended for small workshops, and keep it in a prominent position ready for use. If any of the contents are used, replace them immediately.

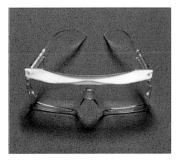

Eye protection Always protect your eyes with safety glasses or goggles when sanding, finishing or using power tools. When operating a machine that produces large quantities of chippings at high speed, wear a full-face visor.

Ear protection When using power tools or machinery, wear approved ear defenders (protectors) or earplugs to keep noise to an acceptable level. Some people think that it is safer to operate a machine by listening to its performance. They are wrong, and they risk permanent impairment of their hearing in the future.

Dust masks There are several types of mask to choose from, including the frame mask with replaceable pads and disposable masks that cover the whole of the mouth and nose. Choose the right product for the level of dust generated in the workshop. The dust produced by sanding machines is the most hazardous and needs a mask with a fine filter. Use sanders that are fitted with their own dust collection bag to cut down on the amount of dust produced. Clear, full-face safety masks are available now and are easy to put on and comfortable to wear, especially when using power tools.

When working with hazardous finishing materials, keep the workshop well ventilated and wear a respirator if necessary. Always be guided by the manufacturer's safety data, which by law must be supplied with any hazardous product. In general, if a product is so dangerous as to cause serious problems, you should consider an alternative.

Gloves and boots It is advisable to wear heavy-duty rigger's gloves when handling sawn timber (lumber) or large, heavy sheets of material. When you are using adhesives or finishing materials that are harmful to the skin, wear rubber or latex gloves. It is best to wear sensible and sturdy boots to keep toes protected in case you drop any wood.

Above Wear gloves when handling large pieces of wood.

Dust extraction

By far the best way of reducing the risk of inhaling sawdust is to install a dust extraction system. Compact units designed for the small workshop are available from all good tool suppliers. Many portable power tools are supplied with adaptors for direct connection to an extraction unit.

PLANS AND DRAWINGS

Drawing plans before starting a job is an important part of the design process. They will help you to visualize how the different components of your woodworking project fit together and how the two dimensions on the paper are translated into the three dimensions of a solid object. They also take the guesswork out of calculating the quantity of materials required, keeping costs down. No special skills are required, merely the same methodical approach that is part of any woodworking operation. Even a quick sketch on the back of an envelope can be enough to clarify an idea or reveal any discrepancies of scale or measurement before proceeding.

Views

These are usually the most helpful drawings when designing a project. The plan view shows the object viewed from above, and the elevation as viewed from one side. A section view shows a slice through the object. For a complex design with many components you may need more than one section to develop the idea.

There is no need to spend a long time on a complicated piece of artwork – a good drawing shows just the right amount of detail, clearly set out, and no more. Include the scale you have used to avoid errors and get a feel for the proportions of the design.

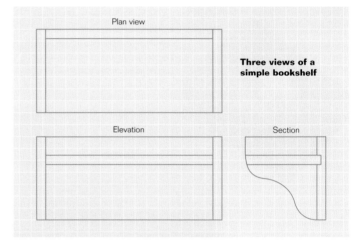

Plan view

Three views of a simple bookshelf

Elevation

Section

Left All of these items will prove invaluable for drawing plans for your projects: graph paper – useful for scale drawings and templates; plain paper or a sketch pad; a clipboard or drawing board; masking tape; a pair of compasses (compass); dividers or callipers – for the accurate transfer and duplication of measurements; drawing pens, pencils and a carpenter's pencil; eraser and pencil sharpener; a set square and protractor; templates for circular cutouts or other necessary shapes; rules (imperial or metric scales); scale rule and a pocket calculator for converting measurements and making calculations.

Scale drawings

Scale drawings are the best way to design a job accurately. They will allow you to get a feel for the proportions of the finished article. A scale rule converts dimensions on to the paper automatically; otherwise an ordinary rule can be used for simple scales such as 1:10 (when working in metric units) or 1:12 (imperial units – 1in equals 12in). You can also use graph paper, in either metric or imperial scales, to establish a grid on to which quite complex shapes may be plotted. Choose any scale that allows the overall dimensions of the object to fit neatly on the page.

Scaling-up

When dealing with complex curved profiles, it is useful to be able to scale-up a detail to produce a working template. Make a tracing of the small-scale drawing and lay it over a sheet of graph paper. Then transfer each section to a similar grid on a larger scale to reproduce the full-size pattern. The more intricate the design, the finer the grid should be to capture every detail.

Isometrics

This simply means "of equal measurement". An isometric drawing does not give a true idea of shape or perspective, but to the draughtsman or designer it is invaluable, allowing true measurements to be scaled from a drawing in all three dimensions. Simply divide a circle into three equal segments of 120 degrees to establish an axis for each side of a three dimensional object. When drawn to this format, the exact measurements in any direction can be reproduced faithfully on the page to establish how a construction will fit together.

Cutting lists and plans

From an accurate scale drawing, it is easy to work out a detailed cutting (cut) list for all the materials needed for a project. This helps when selecting the wood, making sure that you do not run short. When making an item where the grain of the timber is to be displayed at its best, it is important to purchase one batch of material so that all the components are of a matching colour and figure.

Label each part to identify it on the cutting list, and mark each piece of wood as it is finished to avoid confusion. Record any alterations you make on the cutting list and file it away safely as you might want to repeat the project in the future or use it as the basis for a similar job.

Cutting plans are slightly different: if you need to cut large sheets of plywood or MDF (medium-density fiberboard) into a set of different sized pieces, it is worth taking a few minutes to sketch out the most efficient layout to avoid waste.

All components of a similar width, for example, can be cut from one strip, then cross cut to length one at a time. Try combining different sizes to make up the full width or length of a sheet so offcuts (scraps) are kept to bare minimum.

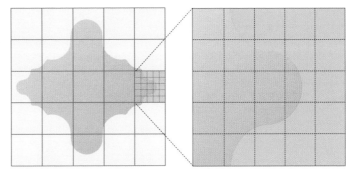

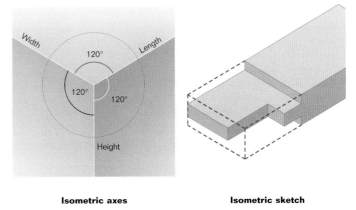

Isometric axes   **Isometric sketch**

DESIGN

Wood has so many variable qualities and such wide potential as a construction material that it is difficult to make any hard and fast design rules. Every piece of work is unique, and a common creed among woodworkers is to allow the wood to "speak for itself" and the natural qualities of each piece to suggest the best way of using it.

Grain direction

The pleasure of woodworking lies in working with it and not against it to express organic forms. Designing around the material in this way is an intriguing process of developing ideas in new and unexpected directions. As you will generally not be making free-form sculpture, to produce a well-constructed design requires the careful selection of material, tools and techniques to achieve the best results. Over the years, certain species of wood have become associated with specific types of furniture for the qualities they possess.

When working a piece of wood with hand tools, you will discover that it will behave better when cut or shaped in a particular direction, and can be most "unfriendly" if you try to force it in another. Thus, you should have no qualms about altering a design to reflect this changing quality as you work; this is one reason why no two pieces of work will be the same.

Right Directional table by Christopher Rose, made from maple with a veneered top and detachable solid leg frames.
Below Boxwood stringing provides a hardwearing edge to this steamed pear desk by Nicholas Pryke.

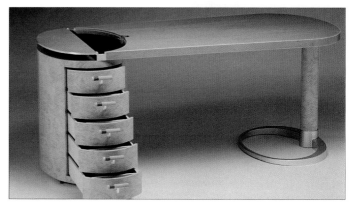

Design properties of wood

Beech was used for making chairs because of its good bending properties. The resistance to splitting of *elm*, with its knotty grain, makes it ideal for chair seats and table tops. *Ash* possesses a natural flexibility and springiness, and traditionally was used for carriage making. The high density of *maple* makes it ideal for hardwearing applications, notably chopping boards and butcher's blocks. *Oak* is uniquely impervious to water, but can be softened with steam and bent into shape. It was widely used for boatbuilding.

Above An elegant bureau designed by Tony McMullen, using a mixture of solid wood and veneers in contrasting colours.

Above Mapa stacking dining chair by the vk&c partnership. The design benefits from the contrast between native cherry and sycamore.

Ergonomics

Whatever the appearance of a piece of furniture, certain principles should be carefully observed to ensure that it performs its function correctly. A chair that is impossible to sit on comfortably could be said to have failed as a chair, no matter how striking, inventive or original the design.

A desk or workstation at the wrong height may encourage an unhealthy posture and you could easily do yourself harm without realizing it. By maintaining certain basic dimensional relationships when making furniture, you can still develop original designs while making sure that form and function work together to make a well-balanced product.

Therefore, good woodworking design is achieved by combining well-established principles with a feel for the potential of the material. The colour and figure of different types of wood are so variable that there is no limit to the effects that can be achieved. Even so-called defects in the grain can be displayed to advantage by emphasizing the natural qualities of the wood.

Choosing the finish can make a difference to the design – a high gloss will scatter light and add depth and colour, but also it can seem cold or formal in the wrong context. A simple wax finish generally adds warmth and lustre, which grows deeper with every new coat. Although the natural colour of wood is highly regarded, the creative use of stains or coloured polish can produce unusual and quite striking results.

Good contrasts can be obtained by working with light and dark woods. For example, a light wood interior will "expand" the space inside a cabinet and dark wooden legs on a light coloured table top will give it a more solid appearance.

Chair to table height

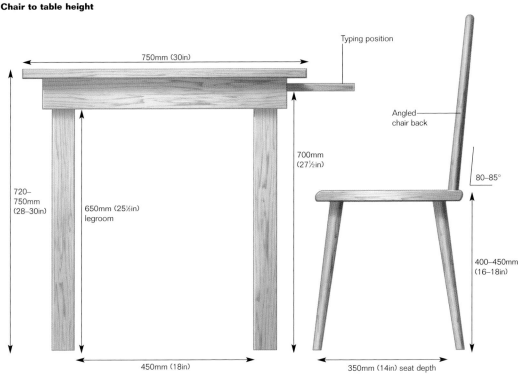

750mm (30in)

Typing position

Angled chair back

700mm (27½in)

720–750mm (28–30in)

650mm (25½in) legroom

80–85°

400–450mm (16–18in)

450mm (18in)

350mm (14in) seat depth

CONSTRUCTION TIPS

No matter how creative your design, it is sensible to observe sound
construction principles to make your work safe to use and give it a long life.
Some of these are common sense; others have been developed from years of
experience. Depart from traditional techniques by all means, but not without
considering their purpose.

Strengthening a shelf

The shape and size of a storage cupboard or bookshelf
should not encourage overloading. Strengthen shelves by
adding a length of rebated (rabbeted) moulding along the
front edge.

Fittings for safety

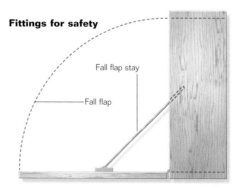

Fall flap stay

Fall flap

Choose the correct fittings so that moving parts do not
open too far and strain the hinges or cause injury. A fall
flap stay allows the flap of a bureau, or the lid of a box, to
fold out and come to rest in the right position.

Stiffening corners

Using knock-down fittings

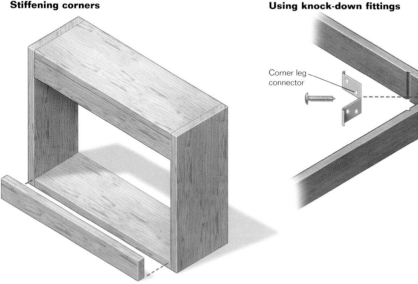

Corner leg
connector

Stiffening members can be added, concealed if necessary,
to hold a wooden frame square and prevent the joints from
working loose. In a wall cupboard, even two relatively thin
strips across the back will stiffen the structure without the
need for a solid back panel.

Steel angle plates or brackets, or knock-down fittings, can
be used to strengthen joints, as well as allowing a piece
to be taken apart if required. These ingenious corner
brackets are used to fix the detachable legs and connect
the side rails at the same time.

Movement

Even well-seasoned wood is prone to movement under different conditions of humidity and temperature. Understanding the behaviour of wood helps in developing construction methods to allow for its natural tendency to move. Even though modern adhesives are much more permanent than those used previously, they will not prevent wood from swelling or splitting.

A moisture-resistant finish coat may help to stabilize a piece, but as soon as the film is penetrated, it can lift or craze. In earlier times, woodworkers understood this and designed furniture to allow for natural movement.

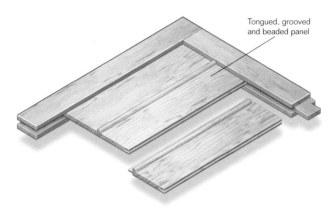

Tongued, grooved and beaded panel

It is better not to fix panelling into its surrounding frame, but allow it to move naturally within a groove. The beaded edge on a tongued-and-grooved moulding is not merely decorative – it creates a shadow line to distract the eye from the gap caused by natural shrinkage.

Gluing boards

When several boards are glued together on edge, the direction of the growth rings should be alternated to counteract the "cupping" tendency of the wood. Quarter-sawn boards, with the rings running at right angles to the surface, are much more stable in this respect.

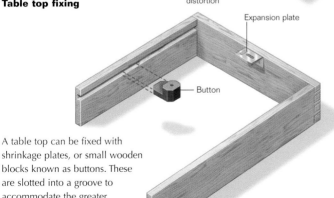

Growth rings in same direction – will lead to cupping.

Alternate growth rings on plain-sewn boards minimize distortion

Quarter-sawn boards

Table top fixing

Expansion plate

Button

A table top can be fixed with shrinkage plates, or small wooden blocks known as buttons. These are slotted into a groove to accommodate the greater movement of the wide boards relative to the narrow members of the supporting frame.

Finishing

Safety principles should also be observed when selecting the finish for your work. Never use oil-based paints or varnishes on toys or children's furniture – acrylic-based stains and coatings are non-toxic and safe. Oiled wood is heat-resistant, but modern finishing oils contain mineral extracts and should not be used on items that come into contact with food, such as bowls and countertops.

French polish provides a high-quality finish, but is not heat-resistant and will soften on contact with alcohol, so it is not always the ideal choice for a table top.

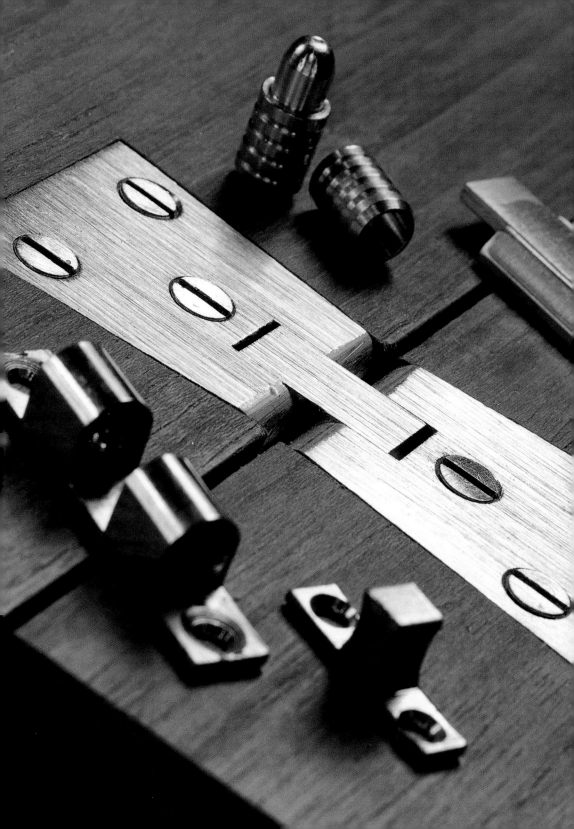

4

FIXINGS AND FITTINGS

Fixings and fittings, or hardware, play an important part in almost every wood project, and it is worth getting to grips with the different types to be able to choose the most suitable. There is a wide range of sizes and patterns, but each has been devised and developed over the years to meet a specific need. Nails and screws, whether designed for mechanical strength or more decorative qualities, can make all the difference to a job when used correctly.

In the same way, the choice of hardware fittings is so vast that you are certain to find the right item to complete a project. Some have a purely functional purpose, while others are more decorative. A pair of well-designed brass hinges, for example, has both qualities and can really add the finishing touch to a well-made piece of work.

SCREWS AND NAILS

Given the many types of nail, pin and screw that are manufactured, you can be sure that there will be one to suit any application. Inevitably, over time, you will build up a huge collection of fixings, and it is always worth the effort to keep them sorted into different sizes and types ready for use. Nothing is more frustrating than to reach the assembly stage of a piece of work and find you cannot complete it for the lack of the right size of screw and nail. It is very easy to ruin the work by making do with something fairly close, but if it is a little too long or too wide, it can easily split the wood. Use small jars or tins to store different types, sorting them by size and length, and labelling them so that they are easily identified.

Screws

These provide a more positive fixing than nails and generally are more useful for strong construction work. The size of the screw is determined by the size of the shank or the diameter of the gauge, and is denoted numerically. A No. 4 gauge is slightly smaller than 3mm (⅛in) in diameter and about the smallest size in common use; a No. 12 is 6mm (¼in) in diameter and used for heavy-duty constructional work. The gauge of the screw does not change with the length of the screw.

In general, the smaller the gauge, the shorter the range of lengths that will be available. For general cabinet work, a No. 8 screw is a convenient size, and is available in lengths from 19–75mm (¾–3in).

Regardless of size, all screws should be long enough to pass through the piece to be secured and penetrate approximately three-quarters of the depth of the second component. If there are lots of screwholes in a piece, wrap a piece of tape around the bit to mark the depth on the bit.

Wood screw The standard traditional wood screw, with a single slotted head and tapered shank. It requires a clearance hole of the correct size, counter-sunk to accommodate the head. It is the cheapest type of general-purpose screw and it is made in mild steel with a "self colour" finish. This means that the steel is untreated and will corrode easily in damp conditions.

Roundhead screws These are intended to be seen; the flat underside of the head provides extra grip.

Raised and countersunk wood screw This has a shallow domed head, which projects slightly above the surface and looks quite decorative.

Pozidriv head This is a more modern and very popular form of wood screw with a cross-head for extra grip. It is countersunk with a cross-head slot and zinc plated for rust-resistance. The shank is parallel, rather than tapered, making it suitable for driving into manufactured boards, using a suitably sized pilot hole, without splitting. Made of hardened steel, it is suitable for use with a powered screwdriver.

Black japanned roundhead screws are commonly used with black iron fittings for decorative purposes.

Brass screws These are less strong than steel screws of the same gauge, but have the great advantage that they will not rust or bind in the wood. Brass countersunk wood screws are perfectly acceptable in cabinet-making. They look neat when they are sunk flush with the surface. In hardwood, first drive in a steel screw of the same size as the brass screw, and then drive in the brass one.

Nails and pins
By far the most common type is the standard wire nail, which is available from 19–150mm (¾–6in) in length. These are fine for structural work, but are best used where they will be concealed, as the heads are difficult to sink down below the surface of the wood without causing it to split.

Brass panel pins will not rust or cause stains and can be left with their heads showing if desired.

Carpet tacks have wide, flat heads and are made of hardened steel.

Upholstery pins provide a decorative means of securing upholstery work and have wide, flat-bottomed heads so that they grip the fabric.

Surface screws Modern furniture is frequently assembled using these, with the heads being concealed by plastic caps. These allow the unit to be taken apart if required. Each small plastic cap clips on to a washer under the screwhead. Different colours are available to suit the material's finish.

Mirror screw and cups This has a chrome-plated cap that screws over the head after fixing it. Domed (top) and flat versions are available as above.

Lost head nails solve this problem. As their name implies, they can be set just flush with the surface and filled in if necessary. They are ideal for nailing battens (cleats) down and some larger components.

Oval nails have an oval section throughout their length, making them less likely to split the wood.

Annular, or ring, nails have small rings or grooves formed in the shank in order to to grip the wood. They are ideal for permanent attachments, as they are difficult to remove.

Panel pins (brads) come into their own for fixing small sizes of wood and delicate mouldings.

When working with small sections of timber, or particularly brittle components, it is worth drilling small pilot holes for fixings to prevent the wood from splitting. Use a cross pein or pin hammer for delicate work, and leave the head of each nail protruding just above the surface.

To punch, or "set", the nail head below the surface of the wood, use a nail set, which has a small-cupped end to fit over the head and punch a neat hole in the wood. Nail sets are available in a range of sizes to suit different nails. The resulting hole can be filled with a coloured stopping for an undetectable fixing.

Brass cup and washer This is a more decorative version of the screw cap. It is designed for use with a brass countersunk screw and is ideal for fixing removable panels, such as bath panels. Screw cups and washers spread the pressure of the screw.

Recessed cup washer Available for recessing into the wood. Drill a counterbore of the correct size to sink the cup flush with the surface.

Nail set
(punch)

Security screws have shaped heads, allowing them to be inserted with a flat-bladed screwdriver, but making removal impossible. The slot in the screw head is shaped so that the screwdriver will only grip when turned clockwise.

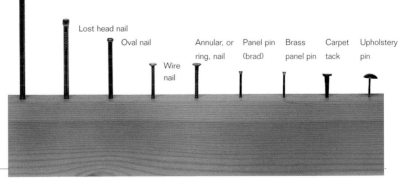

Wire nail

Lost head nail

Oval nail

Wire nail

Varieties of nails and pins

Annular, or ring, nail

Panel pin (brad)

Brass panel pin

Carpet tack

Upholstery pin

ASSEMBLY FITTINGS AND HINGES

The introduction of modern flat-pack furniture has generated a large range of custom-made assembly fittings, sometimes called knock-down or K-D fittings, which enable the home user to assemble and dismantle them without special tools. They are equally useful for making your own furniture, as they provide very rigid joints. All that is required is some care in drilling the correct locating holes. K-D fittings are obtainable from many good hardware stores, do-it-yourself stores and mail-order suppliers.

Brass guide dowel Used in conjunction with a cross-dowel to ensure perfect alignment as the joint is pulled up tight, preventing it from twisting. Guide dowels are equally useful for lining up the leaves of a table or an inserted panel.

Panel connector A device for connecting two panels side by side, as in a row of fitted base units. Also known as a *barrel nut* or *sleeve nut*. The bolt screws into the sleeved connector, clamping the units together and providing lateral location.

Expansion, or shrinkage, plate This angled bracket is ideal for attaching a table top or countertop made of solid boards. The slotted screw holes in the upper flange allow the top to expand or shrink slightly without becoming loose. It is also useful for attaching any kind of panel or fascia, and allows for accurate alignment.

Corner bracket Ideal for attaching a work surface or table top, it holds the corners of the framework square at the same time.

Cam fitting This ingenious cam fitting allows two panels to be joined at a right angle. A quarter turn of the integral screw tightens it against a cam, drawing the two components together. They can be disconnected easily when required.

Worktop connector Sometimes called a handrail connector. It uses a positive bolt action to draw two components tightly together.

Corner bracket This is designed for attaching table legs and strengthening the corner joints at the same time. The two lugs on the bracket locate into slots in the rails of the table and lock them together as the central bolt is tightened into the leg.

Countertop connector When attaching countertops made of chipboard and other man-made boards, expansion plates are not required as the materials are stable. These connector blocks are fitted into holes drilled inside the top edge of a cabinet and have holes for the screws. The holes are angled to allow easy access for a screwdriver.

Confirmat screw Designed for fixing into the edge of chipboard without splitting the material. A pilot hole of the exact size removes the chipboard core, and the parallel thread grips the chipboard fibres without expanding the board.

Cross-dowel connectors The small steel dowel, threaded to receive the bolt, is inserted into a hole drilled in the face of a panel. The bolt that connects the second component, passes through a hole drilled in the edge of the first panel that intercepts the dowel hole. The recessed bolt provides a strong, square connection.

T-nut This is tapped into the reverse side of a panel. A T-nut acts as a captive nut when access is restricted.

Hinges

Any device that includes a pivot action can be called a hinge, and there are many different variations. Some are designed to be concealed within the framework of a cabinet, or the carcass, while others are intended as decorative features in their own right.

It is important to choose hinges of the correct size and robustness when hanging a door so that it is well supported when it swings open. If a hinge or hinge pin is strained in any way, the door will not fit in the frame and may become detached, causing injury.

Fitting hinges

Attaching small hinges to cabinet doors requires patience. The style of door will determine the type of hinge required.

Doors which overlap the front of the cabinet can be fitted with butt hinges screwed to the front of the frame, or concealed hinges which are invisible when the door is closed.

Flush doors, which fit inside the cabinet frame, are normally fitted with butt hinges. They need to be recessed into the wood. Mark around the leaf of the hinge with a craft knife or sharp pencil, and form a recess with a chisel.

Flush hinges have very thin leaves, which avoid the need to cut a recess. They are small enough to fit into the small clearance gap surrounding the door.

Concealed hinge Originally designed for use in self-assembly base units, this hinge is concealed from view when the door is closed. It clips on to the base plate, allowing the door to be removed easily, and is adjustable in all three directions. A mounting hole is required, using a boring bit to suit the hinge boss.

Cylinder hinge Even more discreet, the barrel of the cylinder hinge is concealed in the edges of the door and frame, and is almost invisible when the door is opened. This is only suitable for light-duty use.

Counter hinges These are decorative brass hinges, suitable for bar flaps, counter tops and table leaves. Double hinge pins allow the hinge to fold back on itself without binding.

Lay-on hinge This is also a concealed hinge, but it requires no mounting holes. It is laid on the surface of the door and frame, and simply screwed in place. The linked pivot arms allow 180 degree opening and are spring-loaded for a positive closing action.

Pivot hinge A very discreet and neat hinge, suitable for small cabinet doors. One half screws directly into the frame; the matching half (not shown) screws into the edge of the door and slips over the brass pin of the former, allowing the door to be lifted on and off.

Lift-off hinge A decorative hinge in polished brass with finials at the ends, which can be separated, allowing the door to be lifted on and off at will.

Flush hinges The slimline design of these hinges allows them to be fitted without the need for chiselled recesses. One leaf folds inside the other to provide a very neat connection.

Butt hinges The classic hinge style that is machined from solid brass for a smooth action. It requires a recess chiselled in both door and frame. Butt hinges are available in sizes from as small as 12mm (½in), for use in a jewellery box for example, up to 100mm (4in) for hanging full-size doors.

Piano hinge A continuous brass-strip hinge, sold in lengths up to 1.8m (6ft) and having all kinds of use. It is ideal for fitting a lid to a box or, indeed, a lid to a piano.

STAYS, CATCHES AND DOOR FITTINGS

You should consider buying these fittings in advance. They are an important part of making and designing furniture and especially in the case of door and drawer handles, they will add the finishing touches to your design. There are many specialist outlets that sell all manner of stays, catches and door fittings and most can be ordered by mail order. The style and size of fittings should be chosen with some care to suit the overall design.

Shelf support

A small torpedo-shaped shelf support that fits into a 5mm (³⁄₁₆in) hole in the side of a cabinet, making a very unobtrusive fitting.

Stays and catches

Features such as nylon bearings and spring-loaded magnets make all kinds of ingenious fitting possible, expanding the range of hardware available to the cabinet-maker. For example, they can be used to design a cabinet door that springs open with a slight touch, requiring no handles at all. If you intend using any of these devices, it is advisable to obtain a sample first and study its operation before building the project. Although any hardware may be the last item to be installed, it must be included in your plans at the design stage.

Drawer runners Epoxy-coated drawer runners with nylon bearings make sticking drawers things of the past. In left- and right-handed pairs, these runners are available in various lengths to suit different sizes of drawer, but are a consistent 12.5mm (½in) wide when assembled. Therefore, a drawer box should be made exactly 25mm (1in) smaller than the internal size of the cabinet or cupboard.

Flap stay A reasonably heavy-duty, long-throw, solid brass flap stay, suitable for vertical and horizontal flaps, with self-lubricating nylon glide bearing. Reversible for fitting to the left- or right-hand end of a unit.

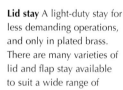

 Glass shelf support A small shelf support made of transparent plastic so that it is hardly visible. Incorporates a safety catch to prevent the shelf from being knocked accidentally out of place.

Lid stay A light-duty stay for less demanding operations, and only in plated brass. There are many varieties of lid and flap stay available to suit a wide range of applications.

Brass shelf support

Small brass clips that fit into a slotted bookcase strip, allowing shelves to be positioned at will.

Magnetic touch latch

This latch is spring-loaded so that a light touch on the closed door will release it and throw it open. To close the door, gently push it until the keeper plate and latch connect, and it clicks shut.

Bed fitting Used for connecting two panels at a right angle, such as the end and side panels of a small bed or cot. Screw one half to each panel, slot together and they interlock with a tapering fit. However, they can be detached easily when required.

Keeper plate
Used with a furniture bolt.

Miniature magnetic catch A very discreet catch, suitable for small cabinet doors. The barrel containing the magnet is recessed into the door frame, while the tiny striking plate is simply tapped into the door like a drawing pin (thumb tack).

Keeper plate
Used with an auto latch.

Furniture

bolt Unlike a barrel bolt, a furniture bolt has a flat profile and is much less obtrusive. It is spring-loaded to prevent it from rattling.

Door fittings

Whether the style of your project is traditional or ultra-modern, there is sure to be a range of door hardware to suit. Cabinet doors can be fitted with a variety of handles and knobs. Often, changing the handles can improve the appearance of a cabinet considerably.

For a set of doors or drawers, you can fit knobs or drop handles ranging from a reproduction style in Florentine bronze to slimline chrome or satin aluminium. Natural wood, ready for staining and polishing, or ceramic knobs to match a painted finish are other options. The size of fittings should be chosen with care to suit the overall proportions of the design.

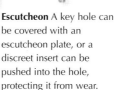

Door handles D-shaped handles in oak and pine, can be unfinished for staining or polishing to match the finish of the unit. A recessed oak handle, for flat mounting to a door or drawer front, provides a finger pull with no holes required.

Escutcheon A key hole can be covered with an escutcheon plate, or a discreet insert can be pushed into the hole, protecting it from wear.

Fall-flap lock This type of lock is designed for the fall flap of a bureau or cocktail cabinet and has a special security feature: the key can only be removed when the flap is locked shut.

Auto door latch A spring-loaded door latch that allows a cabinet door to be closed or sprung open by gentle pressure, so you do not need a handle.

Wooden door knobs Turned knobs in oak, beech and pine, a few examples of the different sizes and styles available. Although these are sanded ready for finishing, they can also be obtained ready-lacquered.

Cabinet locks A rim lock fits on the inside of a cabinet door or flap, mounted on the surface. A mortise lock is neater and more secure, and is inserted into a mortise cut in the edge of the door.

Reproduction handles A wide range of pull handles is made for reproduction furniture, offering different decorative styles with interchangeable base plates. These items are made with a copper, brass, bronze or pewter finish.

Magnetic door catch A simple device, with a small keeper plate that is screwed to the inside of a door. The magnet in the body of the catch keeps the door closed.

Ceramic knobs White, cream and decorated ceramic knobs are made in a range of sizes and look good on painted furniture.

Satin aluminium knob Metallic knobs give a contemporary look. They may be made in aluminium, steel or brass, with a highly polished, brushed, chromed, satin or even gold-plated finish.

Shell handle Typical of Shaker-style furniture, this nickel-plated handle is suitable as a drawer pull.

5

BASIC
TECHNIQUES

Study the finest example of cabinet-making, and no matter how complex it may seem, you can be sure of one thing: when it was made, the same skills were used as in the simplest of projects. Selecting wood and cutting it to size, shaping the individual components, assembling and gluing them together, then sanding and preparing for a final finish – all woodworking, at all levels, depends on these elementary principles. To develop your ability from novice to expert requires time, patience and application: persevere until experience begins to make the difference.

There are no easy short-cuts, but in the following pages you will find plenty of advice that will help you achieve your goals. An understanding of how hand and power tools work, and how wood behaves, will provide a good grounding for improving your skills and expertise.

MEASURING AND MARKING

There is a saying often repeated in woodworking: "Measure twice and cut once." It may seem obvious advice, but when woodworkers repeat it, you can be sure that they speak from experience – there is not a woodworker in the world who does not occasionally forget this basic rule. By adopting a simple discipline for measuring and marking out, you can reduce the risk of making mistakes in your work. Before even laying hands on your tools, check and double check. The simplest of errors can produce the most costly results.

Measuring tapes

A retractable measuring tape is a basic essential. Choose one with a lockable blade and clear markings – the quality can vary considerably. A double scale showing both imperial and metric measurements can be useful, allowing quick conversion across the scales.

Inspect the hooked end of the tape measure regularly for wear – this is a common cause of inaccuracy, so try not to let the tape spring back into its casing out of control, which could damage the end. The retracting spring in the centre of the tape will lose its effectiveness if fully extended, so if you find this occurring regularly, you should consider buying a longer rule. A 3m (10ft) or 5m (16ft) rule should be adequate for most workshop tasks.

It is a good idea to lubricate and clean the blade from time to time by applying a drop of oil with a soft cloth as the blade is retracted.

Marking rod

Marking rods

Shoulder line

Steel rules

A fixed steel rule with a permanently engraved scale will be better than a retractable tape where accuracy is required, such as when setting out joints and fine detail. A combination square is even more useful – it combines a steel rule with a sliding stock that acts as a try square and adjustable gauge all in one. If there are curves, you will achieve greater accuracy with a flexible steel rule.

Marking rods

When marking out a number of identical components, use a marking rod to reduce measuring errors. This is a straight length of square batten with suitable reference points marked on it. It is a simple matter to set out all the details of complex joinery on this master pattern without discrepancy. Keep it safe as a permanent record of each job you do – you never know when it might be useful again.

Above Use a combination square as a try square or as a normal rule.

Marking divisions

To divide the width of a board in half, or into any number of equal strips, you can save calculation and the risk of error with this quick method. Lay a steel rule at a 45 degree angle across the work with an even number of divisions from edge to edge. Simply use the scale to mark off the intervals you need; repeat at the other end of the board, and join the marks with a straightedge or chalk line.

Face and edge marks

Wood is an organic material and by its nature will be subject to variations in size, even after it has been cut from the tree. Woodworkers deal with this by always using one edge as a basis for all their measurements and setting out. Establish a procedure for marking up your work and follow it every time until it becomes second nature.

Select every component individually, bearing in mind its position in the construction. Grain pattern and direction, possible shrinkage, how much it will be seen, how it will be finished, and the strength and design of any joints required are all factors that should influence your decision in selecting the "face side" of any piece of wood. This attention to detail is the secret of quality woodwork. Square up the face of the wood with a try plane or jack plane. The surface must not only be straight, but free of any "wind" or twist between opposite corners.

1 On a wide piece of wood, use a pair of winding rods – place a straightedge at one end of the board and sight across it to another at the far end.

2 Use a try square or a combination square to check that one long edge is square to the face. Place the stock of the square against the face edge, with the blade on the face side.

When using a try square to check if the edge is square, sight along the surface toward a light source and slide the square from one end of the wood to the other – any small gaps will be visible. Adjust with the plane if necessary and mark the wood as shown where the two faces meet. Take all your measurements from the face edge/face side and you will eliminate any discrepancies in width or depth that might affect the overall dimensions of the finished piece.

Face and edge marks

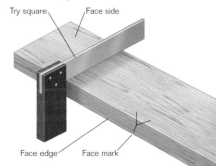

Try square   Face side

Face edge   Face mark

Marking and mortise gauges

A marking gauge has a single point and adjustable stock, and is used for scribing a line at a fixed distance from an edge; a mortise gauge (*left*) has two adjustable points, allowing parallel lines to be scribed.

To set up the mortise gauge, adjust the points and slide the stock to approximately the correct position, then turn the locking screw of the stock until it just "nips" on to the beam. Gently tap one end of the beam against the bench to make fine adjustments before finally tightening the screw. When gauging lines on timber (lumber), always run the stock of the gauge along the face side and edge. Set the points to the width of the chisel you intend to use to cut the mortise, not from a rule.

Scribing

When setting out lines for cutting or making joints, score across the grain of the timber with a bradawl or awl or sharp knife. This prevents the wood fibres from tearing out along the grain, and provides an accurate guide when paring down to the line with a chisel or plane for a final fit.

USING HAND SAWS

Cutting the material to size is the first stage of any project, and without doubt the art of sawing straight and true is the first vital skill to acquire. You should persevere with the correct technique until it becomes instinctive. Understanding how a saw works, and how the wood behaves as it is cut, is the key. If the teeth lose their cutting edge, or the set of the teeth becomes uneven through constant use, you will find it impossible to saw straight.

Sawing technique

Hand saws come in many types and sizes. An all-purpose panel saw and a good-quality tenon saw are the two basics to get you started. As your technique improves, and you explore the different demands of woodworking and the different properties of hardwoods, softwoods and sheet materials, you will soon find your collection of saws expanding. Nevertheless, the essential technique remains the same.

First of all, clamp the wood firmly to the bench. Forgetting this simple step is the most common cause of accidents – sawing accurately requires both hands for good balance, even though a hand saw looks like a one-handed tool.

Position yourself squarely over the piece, with your line of sight directly above the cutting line. Always make sure the saw cuts just to the waste side of the line to allow for the width of the cut, or kerf.

Start the cut slowly and form a groove. Some saws have a group of finer teeth at the tip of the blade for this very purpose. Hold the blade at a steep angle, sighting down and over the edge of the work to keep the cut absolutely square and vertical. This first step guides the saw for the rest of the cutting action.

Gradually decrease the angle of the cut and lengthen the strokes of the saw blade. Allow the blade to do the

work – do not force it through the wood. You will learn what it means to hear a good sharp hand saw "singing" as it cuts rhythmically. Use all your arm to generate the sawing action, keeping the upper arm, elbow and wrist in line; use your forefinger to direct and steady the saw. When cutting large boards, arrange a support to take the weight of the scrap, but make sure it does not force the work upwards and cause the saw blade to bind in the cut.

1 Start the cut very slowly with the tip of the saw blade, drawing it back and forth to form a groove, and guiding it with your thumb.

2 As you near the end of the cut, support the waste with your other hand and use shorter, gentler strokes to sever the last few fibres.

Ripsaw	Crosscut saw	Fleam cut saw
Use this for cutting along the grain of wood with a ripping action. The teeth are coarse set with a deep gullet to clear the waste quickly and prevent the saw from binding, particularly in resinous softwoods. The size and spacing of the teeth are specified as Teeth per Inch (TPI) – very coarse ripsaws can have as few as four or five TPI.	A crosscut saw is designed for cutting across the grain of timber. Each tooth is sharpened at an angle to the grain to prevent it from tearing. The teeth are smaller and finer than those of a ripsaw, up to 12–13 TPI.	Many modern saws are made with dual-purpose teeth for general use. The teeth are specially hardened and are ideal for cutting sheet materials, but they cannot be resharpened.

90°   TPI   Gullet   Set   65°   45°

Tenon saws

Sometimes called backsaws, tenon saws produce a finer cut for joinery work. A stiff spine along the top of the blade keeps it straight and adds weight to the saw. This weight will cause it to find its own way through the work as you guide it.

When cutting end grain, turn it around for the second cut so that the waste is always on the same side of the saw blade.

1 Make a small nick in the wood at an angle to start off the saw cut. Sight down the line to establish a good square cut. Concentrate on the direction of the saw.

2 Slowly increase the length of your stroke and lower the saw with each cut until it is completely horizontal to the wood. Do not grip the saw too tightly.

3 To make cuts in the end grain, clamp the work or piece of wood upright in a vice and saw down to the shoulder line, stopping exactly at the line.

Mitre saws

For cutting very fine mouldings and angles, this relatively new type of saw will soon repay its modest investment, especially if you intend to do a lot of framing work. The wide tensioned blade with specially hardened teeth slides within its own carriage, which can be set to any angle between 45 and 90 degrees.

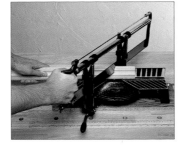

1 Hold or cramp the wood firmly against the backstop and work the blade back and forth with a smooth cutting action. Very little downward force is required, as the saw operates under its own weight and has its own guide mechanism. Always cut on the waste side of the marked line for perfect results.

Sharpening saws

A good-quality hand saw will last for years if looked after well; indeed, many woodworkers will say that a saw improves with age. If it needs sharpening, check the set of the teeth first. Each tooth on a saw is a miniature cutting blade that slices through the wood and clears a path for the next one. The teeth are "set" (angled) alternately to each side to prevent the saw blade from binding in the work.

When using a saw file, work systematically along the saw, sharpening each alternate tooth, then work from the other side to complete the process.

 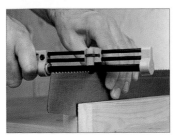

1 To reset a saw, clamp the blade between two strips of wood to protect and support it. Adjust the gauge of the saw setting tool to suit the number of teeth per inch, and work down the blade, applying the correct amount of set to each alternate tooth in turn.

2 A saw file is a triangular file with a sliding carriage that fits over the top of the blade. Set the carriage to suit the cutting angle of the teeth, settle the file in the gullet, and slowly draw it back and forth a few times until you see bright steel on the face of the tooth.

USING POWER SAWS

Portable power saws come into their own when cutting large quantities of wood, especially sheet materials, but they may not be as accurate as hand tools for fine work. Most woodworkers will employ a combination of both to suit each job. As always, follow the manufacturer's guidance for their safe use, and always fit sharp blades. It is false economy, and very dangerous, to work with a cutting tool unless it is set up properly and working efficiently.

Circular saws

Choose a model with the motor power and type of blade to suit the work. For cutting most sheet materials up to 19mm (¾in) thick, a 1,000W motor and tungsten-carbide-tipped blade, with a diameter of 165–180mm (6½–7in), will be adequate. Heavier work, especially in hardwood,

requires a more powerful motor and a greater depth of cut. You will soon burn out the motor if you overload it. Make sure that the spring-loaded safety guard is in working order, and regularly clear it of sawdust as you work. Make a habit of checking the power cord after every use, and attend to any signs of wear immediately.

With practice, you will be able to cut straight lines freehand, but using a guide is safer and more accurate. An adjustable fence is often supplied, but this will be useful for cutting strips only up to about 150mm (6in) wide. For larger sizes, pin a straight-edged batten to the wood as a guide for the saw's sole plate.

Cutting straight stock from a board

1 Make sure the power saw is disconnected from the power supply, then measure the distance from the edge of the base plate to the blade. To be absolutely accurate when cutting, you should allow for the extra thickness of the tungsten-carbide tips on the blade.

2 Mark the distance away from the cutting line and draw a parallel line along the work. Pin or clamp a straight-edge along this line, then run the sole plate of the saw along it. In some cases, the body of the saw will overhang the base plate, so choose a batten thickness that will not obstruct the saw.

3 Fit the parallel fence to the base plate and saw back in the other direction to reduce the board to the correct width. Make sure it is clamped firmly to the bench. A circular saw will make light work of cutting wood, but be sure not to overload it, and always have the guards in place.

Making a circular saw jig

If you want to cut large quantities of sheet material, make up a simple sawing jig for quickly setting out square cuts.

Cut two strips of 12mm (½in) plywood as shown and assemble them to form a table on which the circular saw's base plate can travel. Set the upper strip back from the cutting edge by the exact width of the base plate to the left of the saw blade. Fix a cross-batten square across the bottom of the jig. Now place the jig on the panel of sheet material, line it up with the cutting line and run the saw along the line.

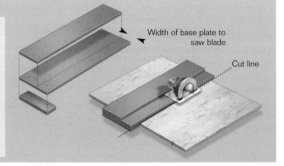

Width of base plate to saw blade

Cut line

Jigsaws

A jigsaw (saber saw) is one of the most versatile cutting tools you can have in the workshop, being suitable for both straight and curved cuts.

It has a small, reciprocating and narrow blade. It is hand held and easy to use without much setting up. As it is so portable, take particular care to keep the power cord out of the way when working.

If possible, buy a model with a pendulum blade action – this clears the sawdust better and makes a straighter cut in wood. Electronic speed control allows you to slow the cutting action for very delicate work. The variety of jigsaw blades available makes this tool useful for cutting many sheet materials into smaller pieces, including thin sheet metal.

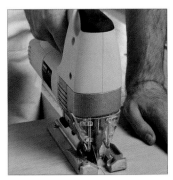  

1 Because the jigsaw (saber saw) blade cuts on the upward stroke, there is a greater risk of splintering the wood, particularly when cutting across the grain. When working with veneered panels, score along the cut line with a knife and cut just outside the line, then pare down to the cut line with a plane.

2 An alternative is to fit a small, transparent shoe that clips around the blade and presses down on to the surface directly in front of it to keep breakout to a minimum.

3 A useful accessory with some machines is a plastic cover that fits over the sole plate to protect delicate surfaces. If you find that the sole plate is bruising the wood surface too easily, you are probably forcing the saw too much – use a slower speed or fit a new, sharp blade.

Crosscut saws

Powered crosscut saws, also called mitre saws or "snip-off" saws, make accurate crosscutting of timber (lumber) a simple matter. The best models extend to a capacity of 250mm (10in), allowing extra wide boards to be cut.

Note that the blades are not interchangeable with other circular saws – the plunging action of the saw requires a different tooth profile. It is best to check what type of blades you'll need by reading the manufacturer's instructions.

1 The saw body can be adjusted to any angle, and a compound mitre saw, as shown, will cut two angles simultaneously. It is ideal for framing work and cutting mouldings and coving sections.

2 To save time when making a number of identical components for a piece of work, establish the correct size for the first one. Then clamp a small spacing block to the table to save marking up the rest.

USING CHISELS

Always aim to remove as much excess wood as possible from the cut before using your chisel. For example, remove the wood with a saw before cleaning up with a chisel or, when cutting a mortise, drill out as much of the waste as possible and use the chisel to clean and square-up the sides.

Chisels

There are two principal types of chisel used for general woodworking and cabinet-making: firmer and bevelled, or bevel-edged. A firmer chisel, with a stout blade and heavy-duty handle designed to accept blows from a mallet, is used for making mortises by chopping down across the tougher end grain of wood. Bevelled chisels may be more familiar, and they have many more uses. The bevelled tip of the blade is weaker and will not stand up to continuous heavy use, but it will suffice for most medium-duty work. This type of chisel comes into its own when used by hand alone for removing small amounts of wood with a gentle paring action.

1 Scribe the width of the mortise with a mortise gauge and cut across the grain at each end to prevent breakout. Use the firmer chisel, almost vertical with the bevel down, to make a series of deep cuts. Start at the middle and work toward one end, then reverse the chisel for the other end. Clear out any waste as you work – large, wedge-shaped chunks of wood can be chopped out quite easily.

2 When you have reached sufficient depth, place the chisel at the very end of the mortise with the bevel facing inward. Strike sharply with the mallet to plunge the blade vertically down and form a good square corner. Push the chisel blade slowly forward to disengage it and square up the sides at the same time.

Care of chisels

Chisels should always be kept sharp – they can slip away from the work and cause a lot of damage as soon as they lose their edge. Make a habit of sharpening them at the end of every work session (in the same manner as plane blades), and store them safely, either in a box or in a wall-mounted rack that protects the tips. A well-maintained set of chisels should last a lifetime.

3 To clean up the shoulder of a joint, hold the chisel vertical and steady the blade with your other hand. Lean over it and slice down for a clean cut.

Practical tip

Do not leave chisels lying on a bench where the blades can come into contact with metal objects. Fit them with plastic blade guards or keep them in a chisel roll.

4 In the absence of a shoulder plane, a bevelled chisel can be used to pare across the grain of a tenon joint. Use the widest chisel available, and hold it perfectly flat so that it slides evenly over the surface of the wood, removing the minimum amount with each stroke. A paring chisel has an even longer blade and is ideal for this kind of finishing work, but it should never be struck with a mallet.

USING PLANES

A woodworker will build a collection of planes over time, each having a different use. Planes should have a good-quality "iron" (blade), made of tool steel with a bevelled edge for removing fine shavings of wood. Good-quality planes are sufficiently weighty to avoid "chatter". The size and shape of the sole, or base, and the angle and adjustment of the iron will determine a plane's best function.

Block plane

Use the block plane for all kinds of fine finishing. Its blade is set at a shallow angle, allowing the removal of very fine shavings; the bevel on the blade faces upward, rather than down to the wood surface as in most other planes. It is very controllable, being designed for one-handed use.

A sharp and finely set block plane will remove the end grain quite easily. Make up a simple shooting board, as shown, to square the ends of components before jointing. It hooks over the edge of the bench and provides a firm support for the work, while holding the plane body square. Turn the board over for use as a straightforward bench hook.

Jack plane

This is used mainly for dressing large areas of sawn or uneven wood. The sole, at 300–380mm (12–15in) long, acts to even out high spots and ridges as you work. Use with a slicing action, angled slightly across the grain, to make a level surface, then make even strokes along the grain to finish off. The try plane, or jointer plane, is longer – up to 610mm (24in) – and is used to true-up (square) the long straight edges of boards before joining.

Rebate plane

The rebate, or filister, plane has a cutting blade that extends to the full width of the sole, making square-edged rebates (rabbets) simple to achieve. Adjust the side fence and depth stop to suit the size of rebate, then start the cut at the end of the timber (lumber) farthest from you. As the cutter forms the rebate, gradually increase the length of stroke, using your left hand to support the plane and hold it firmly in position.

Moulding plane

More often found in antique shops these days, old moulding planes, in good condition, can still be useful. The plane iron is held in a hardwood body by a wooden wedge and tapped into place. As with a rebate plane, start shaping the moulding at the farthest end of the piece and work with increasingly longer strokes as the profile is formed.

Smoothing plane

Ranging in length from 225 to 265mm (9 to 10½in), the smoothing plane is an all-purpose plane for most general carpentry and joinery work. It is an excellent plane to start your collection with.

Shoulder plane

This miniature rebate plane is good for fine joinery work, as it cuts at a shallow angle, both across the grain and on end grain. The mouth is adjustable to allow the removal of small slivers of wood when paring down for a final fit.

USING POWER PLANERS AND ROUTERS

Power planers are ideal machines for removing large amounts of waste quickly, but they can also be used with some accuracy for fine finishing. Different models on offer vary in size and capacity – look for a minimum depth of cut of 3mm (⅛in) and a dust extraction facility or dust bag to collect the copious shavings produced. Tungsten-carbide-tipped (TCT) disposable blades are best when working with manufactured boards.

Electric planers

These can be very aggressive when removing stock, so hold the tool with both hands and keep it moving so that it does not cut for too long in one spot. As with the hand tool, an electric planer can also be used across the grain of wide boards for quick results, provided final finishing is with the grain. Although the electric planer is very fast, the hand-held version rarely gives the quality of finish that can be achieved with a well-set and sharpened bench plane. Check for sharpness and adjustment each time an electric planer is used – and make sure the wood to be planed is held firmly in a vice or clamped down.

1 The depth of cut is controlled by the rotary knob at the front, which doubles as a handle. Push down firmly and evenly on the machine to remove a constant thickness of stock in one pass. The side fence keeps the sole plate square to the edge.

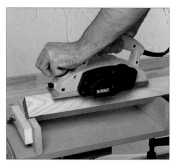

2 Most planers have a V-groove machined in the bottom of the sole plate to permit chamfering. Locate the groove on the square edge of the work to position the cutters at 45 degrees to each adjoining face. The work is in a jig to hold it in position.

Sharpening plane irons

Remove the lever cap from the plane by raising the lever at the top, then take out the blade assembly. Slacken the screw on the cap iron and swivel the plane iron until it can be lifted over the screw head. Do not allow the sharp end of the iron to contact the cap iron body. Apply a coat of thin oil to the oilstone and rest the bevel of the iron on the stone. Rock it up and down until you feel that the bevel is perfectly flat on the stone. Hold the iron at this angle, then slowly slide it backward and forward. Use the forefingers of your other hand to apply pressure evenly over the width of the iron, and move your arms from the elbows, not the wrists.

Check the bevel by turning it face upward – any slight unevenness will indicate that you need to adjust your grip. Increase pressure with even strokes until the whole face of the bevelled edge has been finely ground and you can feel a small burr running evenly along the back edge of the iron. Turn the iron over and press it flat on to the stone. Remove the burr with a few short strokes.

Keep the iron flat – any slight rounding over on the back face will ruin the cutting edge. Wipe off any excess oil and refit the cap iron. Clean any debris from inside the body of the plane before reassembly, and apply a drop of oil to the moving parts of the adjustment mechanism.

3 Some models allow you to form rebates (rabbets) up to 25mm (1in) deep, using the side fence to control the rebate width. The design of the planer body dictates the maximum rebate capacity, so always check this when buying new equipment to ensure that the tool meets your needs.

Routers

A router is one of the most versatile power tools available to the home woodworker. It uses high-speed rotary cutters, in a variety of profiles, to remove controlled amounts of material with great accuracy. However, certain safety rules should always be observed when operating a router. The router cutter should be presented to the work in the correct direction, so that the cutting edge bites into the wood. If you get this wrong, the cutter will spin out of control and ruin the work. Take the trouble to double check this every time you use the tool by observing the "clockwise" rule: looking down at the router, the cutter will always turn clockwise into the work. Always clamp the work firmly to prevent accidents, and keep the power cord well out of the way by draping it over your shoulder.

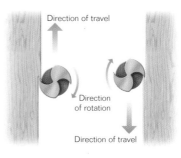

Direction of travel

Direction of rotation

Direction of travel

1 Always clamp the work to the bench. Never use the tool single-handed. Grasp it firmly with both hands and push slowly but surely through the wood, letting it cut at its own rate.

2 When using the side fence, a vernier scale allows fine adjustment of the cutter position. It is a good idea to keep plenty of offcuts (scraps) to hand for trial runs to ensure that the router is operating correctly.

3 Do not remove too much waste in one pass – use the adjustable depth stop to lower the cutter into the work in two or three steps. Remove 6–8mm (¼–⁵⁄₁₆in) at a time and you will produce a smoother cut.

Template follower

A template follower allows the repeated production of identical components by following a master pattern. It is particularly useful for creating curved shapes. Disconnect the power cord when making adjustments. Make sure it is completely seated in its recess.

1 Fit the follower attachment to the base of the router using the screws supplied.

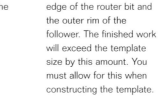

2 Measure the distance between the cutting edge of the router bit and the outer rim of the follower. The finished work will exceed the template size by this amount. You must allow for this when constructing the template.

3 A trammel point fitted to the side bars will simplify forming circular shapes to a fixed radius.

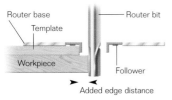

Router base
Template
Router bit
Workpiece
Follower
Added edge distance

USING POWER DRILLS

Without doubt, a power drill will be one of the most useful tools in your workshop. It is worth investing in a reasonably powerful model, not so much for heavy-duty use, but to guarantee that the motor will last a long time without working at the limit of its capacity.

Drill accessories

If your workshop does not have the space to install a free-standing bench (pillar) drill, a vertical drill stand accessory for your standard power drill is well worth considering.

Many drill bits and accessories depend on precise and controlled operation for accuracy and safety.

Hole-saws

These make short work of cutting large-diameter holes, but they do have to be mounted in a vertical drill stand. Sizes range from 12mm (½in) up to 100mm (4in). Set the drill to a very low speed when drilling large-diameter holes, and clamp down the work securely.

Spade bits

Also called a flat bit, these are useful for drilling large holes. Before you start drilling, the point of the bit needs to be engaged with the timber (lumber).

1 The traditional spade bit is much safer and more accurate when used in a drill stand. For a neat hole, set the depth stop so that initially the bit sinks just far enough into the wood for the pointed end to pierce the far side and mark the centre of the hole.

2 Turn the work over and use the small hole to centre the spade bit, then complete the hole. In this manner, you will avoid any breakout in the wood.

Power drill key features:

● Minimum chuck capacity of 10mm (⅜in); ideally 13mm (½in).
● Detachable side handle for extra grip.
● Keyless chuck, allowing the quick change of drill bits with a simple twisting action.
● Variable speed and reversible action for maximum flexibility.
● Lock-on button for continuous running.
● Automatic clutch or torque control, with variable settings, allowing use as a screwdriver.

Hinge borers

Many furniture fittings are designed to fit in standard hole sizes – for example, concealed cabinet hinges. The two standard sizes are 25mm (1in) and 35mm (1⅜in), and it is worth acquiring the purpose-made hinge boring bits that produce a neat, flat-bottomed blind hole to suit them.

Sanding accessories

The rotary power of a drill makes it ideal for many sanding and shaping tasks, without using a special tool. Drum sanders use a small sanding belt fitted on a rubber or foam cylinder in various sizes up to 150mm (6in) in diameter. For smoothing curves or cleaning up the edges of a piece of work these small accessories come easily to hand without the cost of a special tool for the same purpose. If using the drill freehand, always fit the side handle to steady the machine, and work against the motion of the rotating drum or disc to give you greater control.

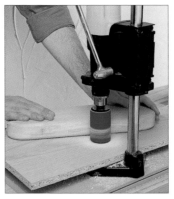

1 Fit a small sanding drum to the drill and pass the work over it, applying gentle pressure. Always wear a dust mask and eye protection when working in this way.

2 You can attach a sanding disc to the drill and use it freehand for shaping curved objects and removing large amounts of surface material extremely quickly.

Plug cutters

A very useful tool for cabinet-making is the plug cutter. It is fitted into a pillar drill and used to make small wooden pellets or plugs. These are then plugged into holes in the workpiece to conceal fixing screws. Plug cutters are matched to counterbore, or three-in-one, bits in a range of sizes to suit the size of screw, from No. 6 gauge upwards.

1 Use a counterbore or three-in-one drill bit to form the screw hole, sinking the counterbore to a depth of approximately 10mm (⅜in). The tip of the bit, which provides a pilot hole for the screw, is quite fragile, so it is good practice to use a drill stand for this to keep the drill absolutely vertical and avoid breakages.

2 Fit the plug cutter in a drill stand and make a series of small pellets in a matching material. Use stock of suitable thickness (19mm/¾in) and set the cutting depth to about 12mm (½in), leaving all the plugs in place until needed.

3 The easiest way to snap out each pellet is by using a small screwdriver blade or chisel. Apply a drop of wood glue and tap into the screw holes. Match the colour and grain direction of the wood as closely as possible.

4 When the glue is dry and clear, use a very sharp bevelled chisel to pare each pellet flush with the surface of the timber. This will leave it virtually undetectable when finished.

ASSEMBLY TECHNIQUES

When all the components of your project have been made, you can begin to assemble them. It is always good workshop practice to have a separate area for this operation, so that glued items can be left undisturbed to dry, preferably overnight. A solid bench is essential, and its surface should be perfectly flat. If the assembly bench is warped or uneven, this deformity will be transferred to the item you are making, no matter how accurate the woodwork.

Drilling

Plan your assembly carefully so that you have enough time to work in stages without rushing the job. A carpenter's brace is a very efficient tool and can sometimes be a quicker option than resorting to a power drill. Auger bits remove large amounts of waste much more accurately in a controlled fashion. Stand directly over the piece of work, using one hand to apply downward force and keep the bit vertical while turning the brace handle with the other hand. Drill pilot holes for any screws, especially in hardwood, countersinking them if required, and clear any debris before fixing the screw.

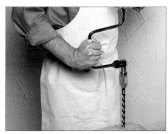

1 Choose a brace with a ratchet drive if possible, as this will allow you to make half a turn at a time and stand close to the bench.

2 Here a counterbore bit drills a pilot for the screw, a clearance hole for the screw shank, and a recess for the head, all in one operation.

3 Always choose a screwdriver bit to suit the screw heads. Do not allow the screwdriver to slip out of the head and ruin a piece of work.

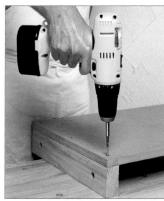

4 Some cordless drills can be used for inserting screws. You can also obtain purpose-designed electric screwdrivers. An adjustable torque setting ensures that you do not strip the head as the screw is tightened, while a magnetic bit holder saves time when working with steel screws.

Gluing

Before applying any glue to the assembly, always "dry fit" components together and prepare the work. Always seal glue containers after use to prevent the build-up of dried glue in the nozzle. Modern quick-setting PVA woodworking glue should be applied and clamped tight within ten minutes for the strongest bond. Be warned, however: on fine cabinet work intended for a clear finish, the dissolved glue should not be left to soak into the grain, as it may cause discolouration at the final stage. Sometimes it is advisable to leave the glue to set, then carefully cut away the excess with a sharp blade.

1 Apply PVA woodworking glue evenly to the entire joint surface, using a stiff brush to spread it out.

2 Wipe off any excess glue with a damp cloth as soon as a joint has been assembled and clamped.

Clamping

Apply pressure to a joint as soon as possible after gluing – make a habit of preparing everything you need in advance. Keep a box of small scraps of wood handy and use them to protect the surface of the work. It is a known fact that you can never have too many clamps, and you will soon start collecting a selection of different types and sizes to suit all kinds of assembly technique.

Adhesives

The traditional woodworker's adhesive was animal glue. While it has been superseded by more modern glues, it is still obtainable and is useful for restoration work and veneering. Small pearls of the material are melted to form a liquid and brushed on to the wood. Unfortunately, the glue is not heat-resistant and can deteriorate, becoming brittle with time.

For most tasks, the standard adhesive is a quick-setting, water-soluble PVA adhesive or wood glue. Generally creamy white in colour, it becomes transparent when dry, leaving an almost invisible glue line. It is non-toxic, non-flammable, safe to use and easy to remove before it dries with a damp cloth. Wood glue can also be yellow in colour. Rapid-drying and waterproof versions are available.

For heavy-duty applications, or exterior use, a more robust glue is recommended. Two-part adhesives are ideal, hardening by curing chemically. They cannot be dissolved or removed when dry. The glue is mixed by adding a liquid hardener to a powder; only mix a small quantity at a time – sufficient for the job in hand. Resorcinol glue is waterproof and heatproof. It is slightly toxic, so wear gloves to protect your hands when using. Another drawback is that it is a dark reddish brown, which makes it very visible on pale coloured wood.

1 G-clamps come in all sizes, ranging from 25mm (1in) up to 250mm (10in) or more. When buying G-clamps, beware of cheaper types made of low-quality castings – they may shatter as they are tightened. Look for high-grade malleable iron in the specification.

3 Use sash clamps in pairs to apply pressure evenly. They are ideal for assembling doors and panels that require a parallel clamping action to remain square. Think through the sequence for the clamping process and make sure you have enough clamps to hand.

2 Keep a few quick (spring) clamps handy for fast one-handed clamping. They are not suitable for high-pressure applications, but can be useful for fixing complex assemblies temporarily while making final adjustments. Do not be tempted to release clamps too quickly. Allow time for the glue to dry.

4 Check that a panel is square at the internal corners before applying glue. Accuracy in cutting the shoulders of joints is the key to a square assembly. If the shoulders are slightly out of square, the panel will become permanently deformed when pressure is applied.

Practical tip

A good tip for checking the squareness of a panel is to measure the diagonals. If one corner is true, and the diagonals are equal, the panel must be therefore a perfect square or rectangle. Measure both diagonals to make absolutely sure.

SANDING AND FINISHING

Before applying any finishing coat to your completed work, the wood should be sanded and prepared well. A coat of varnish or polish will show up any blemishes in the surface that were hardly detectable beforehand. Sometimes it is very tempting to rush this part of the process, but there is no substitute for careful and methodical preparation. A power sander will deal with most of the work, but you should always finish off by hand. This gives you the opportunity of checking every part of the assembly and correcting any small defects.

Using wire wool

Wire, or steel, wool produces an even finer finish than sandpaper. The tiny strands of spun steel fibre burnish the surface of the wood.

The most useful grades range from 0 (coarse) through 00 and 000 to 0000 (very fine). On oily wood, this can leave the surface so smooth that any further finishing is unnecessary. Form a pad from the wire wool when using it, and rub in the direction of the grain. Gently brush along the grain afterwards to remove any fine dust and debris.

1 Form a pad from a small amount of wire (steel) wool and work it along the grain, using smooth, even strokes.

Using sandpaper

Sandpaper grades are denoted in "grit size". This refers to the size of abrasive particles that are applied in an even coating to the backing paper. Begin with a fairly coarse grade, such as 60 or 80 grit, then use progressively finer grades until the surface is smooth and silky to the touch. Each grade removes the minute scratches left by the previous one. A good range of paper to stock would include 80, 120, 240 and 320 grit for the finest finish; 400 grit is so fine that it is normally used for cutting back the first coat of finish.

1 Use a cork or rubber block on flat surfaces to obtain the right amount of flexibility as you work. You can use a wooden block, but it could tear the sandpaper. Clear the dust away as you work to avoid clogging the paper, particularly on resinous and oily wood.

2 A surform tool is very useful for rounding off the edges of wood, and it is surprisingly accurate. The rows of miniature cutting edges on the blade pare away the surface of the wood with a continuous motion.

3 To finish off a rounded edge, wrap a small square of sandpaper around a section of moulded timber (lumber) of the correct profile (taking care not to tear the sandpaper). Work down through the different grades of sandpaper as normal.

Using a cabinet scraper

This is a flexible rectangle of high-quality tempered steel, which when used properly makes a versatile cutting tool capable of producing a highly polished finish. Use it before you use abrasive papers, such as garnet paper or silicon carbide, to remove small tears and blemishes.

When you use a cabinet scraper, always with two hands, you should vary the angle of the scraper to fine-tune its cutting action as you push it away from you with smooth strokes.

1 Hold the scraper as shown, flexing the blade between your fingers and thumbs until the cutting edge just begins to bite into the wood surface.

2 You can use other scraper profiles on moulded and curved surfaces, like the gooseneck scraper, which you can turn to suit any concave profile.

Sharpening a cabinet scraper

A cabinet scraper must be prepared before use and sharpened regularly to maintain its efficiency. The blade is made to scrape rather than cut. The cutting edge must be perfectly flat and square, so it should first be prepared with a file and then polished on an oilstone or grindstone. With the blade fastened in a vice, a hard steel shaft is run along the edge to raise a burr and produce the new cutting edge.

1 The cutting edge of the scraper must be perfectly flat and square before you begin. Clamp it upright in a vice and use a metal file to prepare the edge.

2 Place the edge of the scraper flat on an oilstone and work it back and forth to polish it.

3 Now raise a burr all along the edge by drawing a bar of hardened steel swiftly along and across the square edge. A proprietary burnisher should be used for this, but you can improvise with the shaft of a screwdriver or any similar tool steel. The burr acts as the cutting edge and should be renewed whenever the scraper becomes difficult to work.

Concave, gooseneck and flat cabinet scrapers

USING POWER SANDERS

Power sanders are most useful for the quick removal of waste stock before finishing by hand. A belt sander is worth considering if you have a lot of heavy-duty work, but does not produce an acceptable finish on its own. For general use, an orbital sander is by far the most versatile power tool to buy. When choosing a power sander, an important feature to look for is an efficient dust-collection facility. This not only reduces the amount of dust in the air, but also increases the working life of the machine and the sandpaper. Even with dust extraction, you should always use eye protection and a dust mask for your own health and safety.

Belt sanders

A belt sander must be used with great care as the rotating belt removes large amounts of waste and you can easily create deep marks in the work, thus spoiling the piece. Keep the base moving constantly and always flat on the surface without forcing the machine. Its own weight will provide sufficient sanding pressure.

Use a belt sander to deal with uneven ridges in a laminated surface and for scouring off old paint finishes, but never use it for fine sanding and finishing work.

Always use the dust bag supplied with the belt sander, but preferably fit an adaptor to accept a dust extractor. You should empty the bag regularly to prevent the motor from overheating. Always wear a dust mask to prevent inhalation of dust particles, particularly if removing old paint, stains or varnish.

Sanding belts

These sheets, like sandpaper, come in different grades, but the belts have a cloth backing for longer wear. They range from 40–60 grit (coarse grade) to 180 grit (extra fine). When fitting belts, look for the arrow printed inside, which indicates the direction of rotation.

1 Use the belt sander with a scouring action across the grain to level an uneven surface. The rotary action of the belt will tend to pull the work towards you, so clamp it firmly or use benchstops to prevent it from moving.

2 Using the same grade of belt, change direction to run the sander up and down the grain, removing the sanding marks running across the work. Change to a finer belt and repeat the process until the surface is flat.

Multi-function sanders

Relatively new is a family of sanders with differently shaped base plates and attachments for sanding difficult profiles. They come with self-adhesive sanding pads, specially shaped to fit the triangular base. While very useful for cutting into corners and mouldings, they are not really suitable for heavy-duty work.

Right and far right The pads of these sanders fit easily into the corners of drawers and doors.

Orbital sanders

As the name implies, an orbital sander moves the sanding pad in a circular motion for a much finer finish than a belt sander. It will still leave small circular marks on the work, however, which can only be removed by hand sanding with a sanding block. As the sandpaper collects more dust, the swirl marks tend to become more obvious, so change the paper regularly and use progressively finer grades, finishing up with 180 or 240 grit paper.

To prevent dust build-up, choose a model with a dust-collection bag that extracts dust from the surface of the wood through holes punched in the base as you work.

Orbital sanders are sold as half-sheet, third-sheet and quarter-sheet models. This allows you to cut a standard-sized sheet of sandpaper – 280 x 230mm (11 x 9in) – to fit the base without waste.

When buying sanding sheets, look for heavy-duty backing paper designed for use with power sanders. Aluminium oxide paper, sometimes called production paper, is by far the most durable and most efficient type.

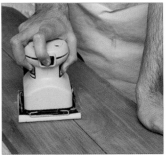

1 Ready-sized sheets of sandpaper are available to fit each particular model, but they are more expensive. However, they do have the advantage of being pre-punched to allow dust extraction from the base. Some models are supplied with a small template for punching your own holes.

2 A small palm sander is ideal for the final finishing grades of paper. Work all over the surface with a series of overlapping circular motions, before finishing off with long strokes parallel to the grain.

3 The orbital sander in use is a much less ferocious cutter than a belt sander, and easier to control. The base plates are often made of foam rubber, which makes them gentle in use and more forgiving to the surface being worked on.

Go with the grain

Always work "with the grain" when finishing wood – work along the wood fibres and in the direction in which they lie.

Study the edge of the timber (lumber) to obtain a clear picture before you begin. Sometimes the grain will change direction within the length of the same piece, so be prepared to change with it as you work.

On very coarse or uneven wood grain, there may be no easy solution – a block plane (right) set for a very fine cut can do the trick if used with a slicing action around difficult areas.

Alternatively, employ a cabinet scraper if you have one – it is well worth mastering the art of this simple tool.

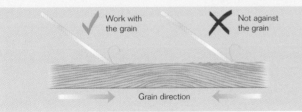

✓ Work with the grain

✗ Not against the grain

→ Grain direction ←

MAKING JOINTS

The basic techniques of woodworking are all that you need to begin to master the fine art of joinery. Patience, care and attention to detail provide the key to accurate joints; an understanding of how they work will allow you to choose the correct type for a given job. The techniques of joining wood have been developed over centuries, and there is satisfaction to be gained from employing these tried and tested methods. While it can be daunting to look at a long list of different joints with strange names, the following pages will demystify the whole subject. Ranging from the simplest of lap joints to more complex and decorative types, the joints shown cover most applications. As always, practice and good, sharp tools make perfect.

MAKING BASIC JOINTS

The techniques of joining wood have been developed over centuries, and there is satisfaction to be gained from employing these tried and tested methods. Patience, care and attention to detail provide the key to making accurate joints; an understanding of how they work will allow you to choose the correct type for a given job. The basic joints shown here are suitable for many projects.

Dowel joints

Beech dowels offer a quick and simple means of strengthening corner joints and aligning two components to prevent them from twisting. Three common sizes are available: 6mm (¼in), 8mm (⁵⁄₁₆in) and 10mm (³⁄₈in). Choose the diameter to suit the material; as a general rule, do not exceed half the thickness of the timber. There are several easy methods of locating them accurately.

Centre-point method

Small brass or steel centre-points that match the dowel diameter come in dowelling kits that are available from hardware stores and also include a drill bit and dowels.

Mitred joints

A frame with mitred corners can be reinforced with biscuits if the parts are thick enough to accommodate them. A versatile jointing machine can save time and improve accuracy in many applications.

Making a dowel joint

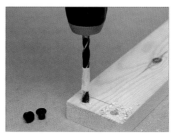

1 Use a dowel drill bit, also called a spur-point bit, to centre each hole. A strip of tape wrapped around the bit makes a depth gauge. Hold the drill truly vertical.

2 Insert the centre-points in the holes and push the adjacent component toward them, making sure that it is in its correct position. Use a square to check the edges are flush.

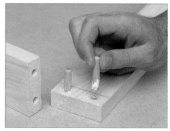

3 Clamp the second piece in a vice and drill to the correct depth for the dowel.

4 Apply glue to the dowels, insert in the holes and tap the joint together.

Making a mitred joint with biscuits

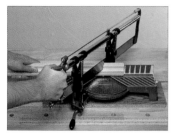

1 A mitre saw will cut through the timber easily and accurately.

2 Use a try or combination square to align the corners accurately when marking.

3 The oval shape of the biscuit automatically centres the mitred joint as it fits together.

Joining boards and knock-down fittings

Manufactured sheet materials are available in large sizes, but occasionally it is necessary to join them together neatly. Because they lend themselves to machine-made joints, there are several options to choose from. Knock-down (K-D) fittings are used extensively in the furniture industry for manufacturing self-assembly units. They are useful for furniture that needs to be reassembled easily.

Lap joint

A lap joint is easily made with a router machine and is useful when matching veneered boards to make decorative panels.

Loose-tongued joint

An even stronger bond can be achieved by using a "loose tongue", which acts as a key for the adhesive. This type of joint takes little time to fabricate.

Scarf joint

Two panels can be joined with a feather-edged scarf joint, which will provide a large surface area for the glue. When made correctly, this type of joint will allow the completed panel to be formed into a curve without the joint separating or kinking.

Practical tip

Use special construction screws when joining chipboard (particle board) panels. They have a coarse thread designed to grip the fibres in the panels without splitting them.

Making a lap joint

1 Use a router fitted with a fence to form the lap, cutting it to exactly half the thickness of the material.

2 Apply glue and clamp the boards together. When the veneers are well matched, the seam will be almost invisible to the eye.

Making a loose-tongued joint

1 Use 6mm (¼in) plywood for a loose tongue. The cross-ply structure is stronger than a long-grained section of hardwood. Apply glue and insert into a routed groove.

2 Firmly clamp the two panels flat to the bench before applying longitudinal pressure to the joint. This will keep it perfectly flat and produce a strong bond.

Making a scarf joint

1 This straightforward joint can be made easily with hand tools. Make up a simple wooden jig on the workbench to control the angle of the plane.

2 Before clamping the joint together, drive in a few panel pins (brads) to prevent the boards from sliding around. Remove them when the glue has dried.

LAP AND HALVING JOINTS

The simplest and most basic of joints is created where one piece of wood overlaps another. It is not the strongest method of joining two components, and may need reinforcing with extra fixings, but it is a straightforward technique. Where two pieces of the same thickness are to be connected, the strength of the joint can be greatly increased by forming a halving (half) joint.

Corner lap joint

A typical use would be to form the corners of a drawer or simple box, where the shoulder of the joint adds strength and helps to keep the construction square.

Right The finished corner lap joint.

1 Mark out the thickness and depth of the lap with a scribing knife and gauge, then cut along the shoulder line with a tenon saw, keeping to the waste side of the line.

2 Clamp the piece firmly to the bench in a vice or use a G-clamp. Remove the waste wood with a series of small cuts, using a chisel and carpenter's mallet.

3 Pare down the wood to the scribed line with the chisel to complete the joint. Check the fit of the joint and make any fine adjustments. Pin and glue the joint together.

Mitred halving joint

When glued and pinned from the underside, this more than doubles the strength of a simple mitred corner joint. Note that the end grain is revealed on one edge only.

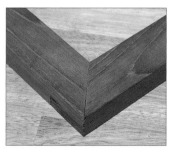

Above The finished mitred halving joint.

1 Mark out a half lap and the depth of the join on the top half of the joint using a try square and pencil, then remove exactly half the thickness of wood. Pare down to the shoulder with a very sharp bevelled chisel.

2 Mark out the mitre on the top face of the lap and remove the waste with a tenon saw. Lay the finished piece over the lower section and use it as a guide for scribing the other half of the joint.

3 Cut along the shoulder line and remove waste wood by tapping gently with a chisel. Pare away the seat of the joint to make a snug fit. Glue the joint together.

Cross-halved (half-lap) joint

This is the classic method of joining two intersecting pieces of equal thickness. Cut the shoulders accurately to form a very strong and square connection.

Above The completed cross-halved joint.

1 Mark the width of the bottom member on the underside of the top piece, then gauge the depth to half its thickness. Make a series of saw cuts across the waste area.

3 Pare down to the scribed lines using a bevel-edged chisel to ensure a flat and even seat for the joint. Hold the chisel blade perfectly horizontal and work toward the centre.

2 Remove the waste by chopping down sharply with a chisel to snap out small sections of waste at a time. This removes the risk of splitting the timber (lumber).

4 When the top half of the joint fits the bottom piece snugly, use it as a guide for scribing the exact width of the cut-out on the bottom half, then repeat steps 1–3.

Lapped dovetail joint

An elegant means of creating a very strong joint that prevents one component from pulling away from another. It is useful for connecting rails and cross-members.

Above The finished lapped dovetail joint.

1 Cut the top half of the lap first, as for a straightforward lap joint. Use a bevel gauge to mark the dovetail on the top face.

3 Lay the finished dovetail over the lower piece to mark out the socket, and cut away the waste. Pare down to the scribed lines carefully with a shoulder plane to make a tight fit. Glue the joint together.

2 Clamp the work in a vice and cut down to the shoulders with a fine tenon saw. Remove the waste and pare down to the lines with a chisel.

Housing and Bridle Joints

Another simple method of joining two pieces of wood where the end of one meets the side of the other is to cut a slot (housing) in the latter for the former. This provides positive location and strength.

Full housing joint

This is a simple means of joining two parts of a frame at right angles, for example where a cross-rail meets an upright. In this case, the full width of the rail is housed within the cut-out. You can also stop the housing short of the face side of the job.

Above The completed full housing joint.

1 The rail must be of a length that allows for the depth of the housing, and its end must be cut square. Use a vernier gauge to check the width of the rail accurately.

3 Use a sanding block, or an offcut (scrap) of wood wrapped with sandpaper (take care not to tear the paper), to trim the housing for a snug fit. Keep it absolutely flat to avoid rounding off the shoulders. You may have to plane the corresponding part of joint to make a good fit.

2 Use the other side of the vernier gauge to set the width of the housing. Scribe and cut the shoulders, then remove any waste to half the thickness of the rail.

Bare-faced housing joint

When creating a housing joint in a corner, as for a door or window frame, leave an extra amount on the end of the cross-member for maximum strength. The bare-faced tenon on the upright is formed by removing waste from one side only.

1 Cut the shoulder for the tenon on the outer face. This puts the bare face on the inside of the joint to give a fixed internal measurement. Pare the tenon and shoulder to the scribed lines.

2 Set the two pins of a mortise gauge to match the width of the tenon you have made, then adjust the stock so that the housing groove will be positioned correctly.

Bridle joint

A neat method of joining two components where they meet at a corner. This joint is versatile because it does not have to be a right angle and it is suitable for small sections. The tenon part of the joint is usually one-third of the thickness of the wood.

Above The completed corner bridle joint.

1 Use a mortise gauge to mark out the mortise, making it one-third of the thickness of the wood. Cut down to the required depth and chop out the waste with a chisel.

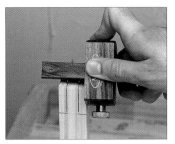

2 Without altering the mortise gauge setting, scribe the tenon to suit the mortise, making sure that you gauge from the face side of the wood. Shade the waste areas with a pencil.

3 Clamp the tenon member firmly. Cut the shoulders of the joint with a tenon saw and remove the waste. Leave the tenon oversize at this stage for final fitting.

4 Trial fit the joint by sliding both members together on a flat surface. This will indicate any high spots that need removing from the tenon for a flush fit.

3 Scribe the position of the housing with the mortise gauge, then mark the required depth for the tenon. Cut down to the lines with a tenon saw, and chisel out the waste.

Above The finished bare-faced housing joint.

MORTISE AND TENON JOINTS

These are some of the most useful joints you can master. They are the basis for most panelled doors, windows and joinery. The secret of success lies not so much in achieving a good fit for the tenon in the mortise, but rather in the accurate cutting of the shoulders of the tenon, which ensures a square and rigid construction when the joint is drawn up tight.

Basic mortise and tenon

The mortise and tenon joint has been adapted to meet a number of specific jointing needs, particularly to provide additional strength. The main types are shown here, and will prove useful as you develop your jointing skills.

Always cut the mortise first. Set the pins of a mortise gauge to suit a convenient size of chisel, about one-third the thickness of the wood.

1 Set the stock to centralize the mortise, and run the mortise gauge along the face side of the timber (lumber). Set the gauge aside without altering the setting of the pins – it will also be needed to mark out the thickness and the position of the tenon.

2 Drilling a row of holes between the gauged marks is a quick means of removing the majority of the waste. Use a spur-point drill bit (dowel drill bit) to ensure that the holes are kept in line. Make sure the holes are truly vertical – use a drill stand or pillar drill if possible.

3 Chop out most of the remaining waste from the mortise, then begin to pare down to the scribed lines with a broad chisel. Don't be hasty and try to remove too much at a time, otherwise you run the risk of splitting the wood along the grain.

4 Use a small chisel that matches the width of the mortise to chop out the ends. A firmer chisel can be used with a mallet to remove most of the waste. Finish off with a bevelled chisel, as shown, to get right into the corners for a perfectly square mortise.

5 Set out the tenon by marking the shoulder line with a carpenter's pencil on all sides. Use the mortise gauge to scribe the blade of the tenon, again working from the face side. Mark the waste to be removed with a saw and use a knife to scribe the cutting lines for the shoulders.

6 Cut across the grain at the shoulders with a fine-toothed tenon saw, keeping to the waste side of the scribed lines. Take care not to cut too deep, stopping just short of the scribed marks for the tenon blade. It is best to clamp the piece of work in a vice or with G-clamps for a positive hold.

7 Clamp the wood upright in a vice and remove the two outer sections, sometimes called tenon cheeks, again keeping to the waste side of the lines. Making sure that the wood is truly vertical will help you to produce straight cuts and taking time to cut accurately will save later adjustment.

8 Place the wood flat on the bench and pare down to the scribed marks. Use a paring chisel, pressing down on the blade with your forefinger to keep it absolutely horizontal. Try the tenon in the joint as you work, noting where it feels tight and paring gently until you achieve a perfect fit.

Wedged-through tenon

By far the strongest form of mortise and tenon joint, in which the tenon passes right through the matching component and is locked in place with small wedges.

This method is often used for doors and windows where the frame has to endure a high degree of stress and movement. Gluing the wedges in place ensures that the joint will never come apart, even if the wood shrinks slightly as it dries.

1 A very slight angle for the wedge is all that's needed to lock the joint. Mark out the waste areas beyond the ends of the mortise, and start the cuts with the tip of a small dovetail saw.

2 Use a chisel to complete the bevels. Note how the angle has been marked on the outside of the rail to act as a visual guide. Use the same angle when cutting wedges from small offcuts (scraps) of wood.

3 Apply glue to the joint and fit the pieces together. Slowly tap the wedges into place, alternating from one to the other to draw the joint up square. Leave to set before trimming off the excess.

Double tenon

Where you are joining a very wide component, such as the middle rail of a door, a continuous mortise would cause too much weakness in the receiving member. You can solve this problem by cutting two tenons side by side. The best door frames usually have mortise and tenon joints and they are frequently used in joinery and cabinet-making.

1 Form the double mortise in the usual way. If the tenons are 50mm (2in) wide, leave about the same distance between them. Pare the sides of each mortise.

2 It is more accurate to cut the tenon as a single piece, then remove the section in the middle. Pare down the shoulders. Clean up any waste with a chisel.

3 Fit the joint together. Both tenons should fit snugly into their mortises. Make sure there is a very small space for glue and then clamp when setting.

Fox tenon

This variation is similar to the wedged tenon, but is used where the tenon is "blind" and does not pass completely through the receiving member.

It is an elegant and secret joint that will remain locked together. Great accuracy is required, though, because you only get one chance to assemble it. The size of the small "fox" wedges is critical.

1 Form a stopped mortise and tenon joint, then cut two slots about halfway down the length of the tenon. Note their positions – the idea is to force the edges of the tenon sufficiently outward to grip the inside of the mortise.

2 Cut two small wedges to such a size that, when the joint is assembled, the bottom of the mortise will drive them home and lock the joint. Set them in the slots, apply glue and fit the pieces together. Clamp them together while the glue dries and sets.

DOVETAIL JOINTS

The dovetail joint is a fine example of the woodworker's art, combining a sound structural connection with a decorative appearance. You will come across many examples of furniture where dovetails have been used deliberately to display the cabinet-maker's pride in the work.

Making a basic dowel joint

Accuracy and forethought are called for in setting out the joint correctly. The orientation of the dovetail determines how the components will be assembled.

1 Begin by setting out the "tails" of the joint from which the dovetail joint gets its name. The end of the tail member must be perfectly square, so be sure to use a shooting board and block plane to square up the end grain.

2 With hardwood, an angle of about 7 degrees (or pitch of 1:8) will ensure maximum strength from the joint without weakening the pins. Note how the waste at each end of the joint is roughly half the size of the gaps between the tails.

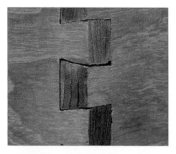

3 Always mark the waste areas between the tails as you work, because it's easy to become confused at this stage. Use a knife to scribe across the grain and mark the shoulder lines between the tails.

4 Clamp the work upright to make saw cuts for the tails, keeping to the waste side of the lines. Set the wood at an angle so that you hold the saw blade vertical for half the cuts, then reposition it to finish.

5 Use a coping saw to remove the waste from between the tails. Having the waste sections clearly marked out will prevent you from making any mistakes.

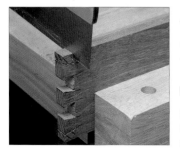

◄ 6 Turn the work horizontally to remove the last two portions of waste at the ends of the joint. Use a fine-toothed dovetail saw for this work.

► 7 Finally, use a bevelled chisel to pare down to the shoulder line and finish the tails. Work gradually towards the line, taking care to make the sides absolutely straight and square.

8 When marking out the pins, it helps to hold the work in a vice about 25mm (1in) proud. Highlight the end grain with a piece of chalk, especially on a dark hardwood such as the teak, used here.

9 Use the tails as a guide for marking out the positions of the pins. Place a block of scrap wood beneath the dovetail member so that it is square to and level with the pin member. Shade in the areas to be cut with a pencil.

10 Scribe the cut lines and shoulders for the pins with a knife, mark the waste sections, then remove them with a dovetail saw and chisel. Pare the pins to match the tails until the joint slides together smoothly.

Varieties of dovetail joint

Over the years, cabinet-makers have developed many varieties of dovetail joint to suit different applications. After you have mastered the basic principle, try some of the other types. The lapped dovetail conceals the end grain of the tails, which are fitted into sockets in the pin member. You might find this in use on the front panel of a drawer. A mitred dovetail is even more challenging – both sections of end grain are concealed by mitred housings. Modern machine-made joints use more permanent adhesives than were available previously, so some of the more artful dovetails have fallen out of use. A comb joint is simple to machine, depending entirely on glue to form the bond, and it can look attractive.

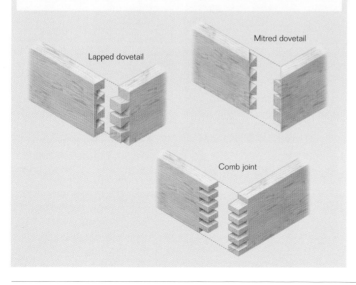

Lapped dovetail

Mitred dovetail

Comb joint

Above The completed dovetail joint. The dovetails take their name from their fan shape and the pins form the top and the bottom of the joint and sit in between the tails. Sometimes the pins are smaller in width than the dovetails.

To ensure a good fit, the pins must be scribed accurately and directly off the corresponding part of the dovetail.

ROUTERED JOINTS

A router is a powerful tool that comes into its own for making accurate joints, especially in large panels for carcass assembly. It is particularly useful for repetitive operations that demand a series of identical joints in several components. Accurate setting up and a methodical approach are essential for the best results. Always try out the router on a scrap of wood before starting on the work to ensure that the settings are correct.

Housing joints

Routered housing joints are a simple means of locating shelves and dividers in a carcass. The housing is a groove that is precisely cut with a router to accept another piece of timber (lumber) at right angles to it. The strength of the joint depends on a tight and secure fit. The router will cut the shoulders and the base of the housing at the same time.

A stopped housing joint conceals the front edge of the joint from view.

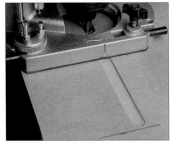

1 Mark the end of the groove at the front edge. Work toward this end if possible, stopping the router cutter just short of the pencil line.

2 To prevent any breakout, use a knife to scribe the square end of the joint.

◀ 3 Cut out the rounded portion of waste at the end of the groove with a bevelled chisel.

▶ 4 Apply some glue to the bottom of the groove and slot the panel into position.

Tongued-and-grooved housing

A router is useful for cutting continuous grooves accurately in long lengths of timber (lumber). This technique allows you to form the tongue to fit the groove exactly, whatever the thickness of timber.

Above The finished tongued-and-grooved housing joint.

1 Using the side fence of the router as a guide, rout a continuous groove in the first component.

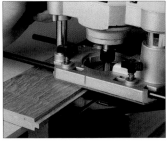

2 Now form the tongue, gradually increasing the depth of cut until it is a perfect fit. Alternatively, you can purchase a matching cutter that forms the tongue in one pass of the router, but it is a lot more expensive and less versatile.

Dovetailed housing

A dovetail profile cutter makes this self-locking joint easy to fabricate. There is no other practical way to form a long, dovetailed housing. To make a dovetail housing by hand would generally be too difficult and time-consuming.

The housing is of dovetail section. The corresponding part of the joint has a dovetail tongue. This type of joint has great structural strength. The dovetailer cannot be lowered into the work. The depth setting of the groove must be established before you begin working, and completed in one pass of the router.

1 Rout a square-section groove before using the dovetail cutter – this puts much less strain on the router and the cutter blades, as there is a lot of waste to remove.

2 Use a shoulder plane to trim the excess from the dovetail tongue to its finished size.

Right The finished dovetailed housing joint.

Scribed joints

Profile cutters in matching pairs allow you to form perfectly fitted scribed joints for making panelled doors and mouldings.

1 When using scribing cutters, the depth setting is critical for a good match, so make sure you have a good supply of extra material of the same thickness to allow a few trial runs.

2 Machine the male portion of the moulding before forming the female half of the scribed joint. Work slowly and steadily to produce a smooth ripple-free finish.

3 The two profiles should match each other exactly. Slide them together on a flat surface to check for perfect alignment.

DOWEL JOINTS

Beech dowels offer a quick and simple means of strengthening corner joints and aligning two components to prevent them from twisting. Three common sizes are available: 6mm (¼in), 8mm (⁵⁄₁₆in) and 10mm (⅜in). Choose the diameter to suit the material – as a general rule, do not exceed half the thickness of the timber. There are several easy methods of locating them accurately.

Centre-point method

Small brass or steel centre-points that match the dowel diameter come in dowelling kits that are available from hardware stores and also include a drill bit and dowels.

Above Dowels provide an invisible means of joining two sections of wood.

Practical tip

The best dowels are slightly fluted to allow the glue to spread through the joint.

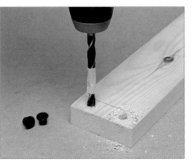

1 Use a dowel drill bit, also called a spur-point bit, to centre each hole accurately. A strip of tape wrapped around the bit makes a simple depth gauge. Hold the drill truly vertical – use a drill stand or pillar drill if you have a lot of holes to drill.

2 Insert the centre-points in the holes and simply push the adjacent component toward them, making sure that it is in its correct position. Use a square to check that the edges are flush.

◄ 3 Clamp the second piece in a vice and drill to the correct depth for the dowel.

▶ 4 Apply glue to the dowels, insert in the holes and tap the joint together.

Dowel drilling jig

Slightly more expensive than a centre-point kit, but well worth the investment if you are making a lot of joints, the dowel drilling jig comes in several forms. The type illustrated offers a choice of bushes to take three sizes of dowel drill.

1 Mark the components carefully to ensure the correct orientation in the drilling jig. Clamp the two components together with the jig, making sure that the outer faces are touching.

2 Tape the bit to allow for the depth of the drilling bush. Drill the end grain of the first part. Without altering the position of the jig, drill the matching hole(s) in the second part.

3 Apply glue to the dowel and the face of the joint, and simply push together.

BISCUIT JOINTS

"Biscuit" is the term for a flat wafer of compressed hardwood, usually beech, that acts in the same way as a dowel. However, it must be fitted into a slot cut with a biscuit jointer. Again, they are available in three common sizes: size 0 (16mm/⅝in), size 10 (20mm/¾in) and size 20 (25mm/1in). The biscuits are baked to a low moisture content so that when water-based glue is applied, they swell and make a tight joint – store them in a sealed container to keep them dry.

Edge joints

The beauty of biscuit jointing is that marking out is easy – simply place the two components together in their intended positions and make a series of pencil marks at suitable intervals.

1 To make a simple plinth, cut the components to size and align them for marking out, ensuring that all the edges are flush.

2 Clamp each side upright in a vice to cut the slot. The reference mark on the jointer automatically centres it on the pencil mark.

3 Cut a slot for the other half of the joint by clamping the piece to the bench. It must be held firmly as you plunge the cutting blade into the wood.

4 To cut slots for biscuits in a mitred corner joint, simply adjust the jointer's scale to 45 degrees and proceed as before. A spacing block is sometimes needed to position the carriage at the correct height.

5 Clear any sawdust from the slots before inserting the biscuits. Coat each with a small amount of glue and tap into place.

6 Apply glue to the faces of the joints and fit the parts together. Apply clamping pressure to pull everything tight – an easy, fast and accurate system.

Mitred joints

A simple frame with mitred corners can be reinforced with biscuits if the components are thick enough to accommodate them. The versatile jointing machine can save time and improve accuracy in a multitude of applications.

1 A mitre saw will cut the timber (lumber) easily and accurately.

2 Use a try square to align the corners accurately when marking.

3 The oval shape of the biscuit automatically centres the mitred joint as it fits together.

JOINING BOARDS AND KNOCK-DOWN FITTINGS

Manufactured sheet materials are available in large sizes, but occasionally it is necessary to join them together neatly. Because they lend themselves to machine-made joints, there are several options to choose from. Knock-down (K-D) fittings are used extensively in the furniture industry for manufacturing self-assembly units. They are useful for furniture that needs to be reassembled.

Lap joint

A lap joint is easily made with a router and is useful when matching veneered boards to make decorative panels.

1 Use a router fitted with a fence to form the lap, cutting it to exactly half the thickness of the material.

2 Apply glue and clamp the boards together. When the veneers are well matched, the seam will be almost invisible to the eye.

Loose-tongue joint

An even stronger bond can be achieved by using a "loose tongue", which acts as a key for the adhesive. This type of joint takes little time to fabricate.

1 Use 6mm (¼in) plywood for a loose tongue. The cross-ply structure is stronger in bending than a long-grained section of hardwood. Apply glue and insert into a routed groove.

2 Firmly clamp the two panels flat to the bench before applying longitudinal pressure to the joint. This will keep it perfectly flat and produce a strong bond.

Scarf joint

Two plywood panels can be joined with a feather-edged scarf joint, which will provide a large surface area for the glue. When made correctly, this type of joint will allow the completed panel to be formed into a curve without the joint separating or kinking.

1 This joint can be made easily with hand tools. Make up a simple jig on the workbench to control the angle of the plane.

2 Before clamping the joint together, drive in a few panel pins (brads) to prevent the boards from sliding around. Remove them when the glue has dried.

Cam fittings

A cam fitting forms a solid connection by a single turn of a screwdriver, which locks a lever arm into place on the mating part of the joint. Such joints allow you to prefabricate a set of components and insert the fittings in the knowledge that they will automatically line up when assembled.

1 Drill a hole in each component for the two halves of the fitting. The exact dimensions for their size and location will be supplied with the fittings. Insert them in the holes.

2 Simply locate the peg of one half of the fitting in the matching hole of the other and turn the cam to lock the joint together.

Construction screws

These special screws have an extremely coarse thread that is designed to grip the fibres in chipboard panels without splitting them – a common problem when using ordinary wood screws.

Jointing blocks

This is a modern substitute for the traditional glued wooden block, allowing panels to be dismantled easily. Simply screw the block to each panel.

1 A drilling jig will be supplied with the screws. Drill a clearance hole in the outer panel to suit the shank size of the screw.

2 Using the same jig, drill a pilot hole of smaller diameter into the end of the second panel. A depth stop on the drill bit will allow the depth of the hole to be controlled. Note how the jig locates the hole automatically. Assemble the panels by driving in the screws.

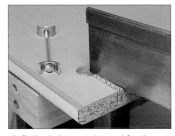

Panel connectors

When joining large sections of worktop, for example, a positive mechanical connection will hold them tightly together, but still allow the two parts to be dismantled if necessary.

1 Drill a hole in each panel for the connector boss, using a hinge boring bit. Mark out a slot for the bolt, as shown, and cut down with a tenon saw. Remove any waste with a chisel.

2 Align the panels, using dowels or biscuits if desired, and tighten the connecting bolt until the joint is rigid. to the required depth.

SCRIBING JOINTS

"Scribing" can be a confusing term. It is often used to describe the marking out of a piece of wood with a sharp knife, but it also specifically refers to the method of transferring the shape of one piece of wood on to another. The latter is a particularly useful technique when working with mouldings of complex profile.

Using a profile gauge

A profile gauge incorporates a large number of plastic "fingers" that are free to move independently in the body of the gauge. When pressed against a moulded surface, they duplicate its profile, allowing this to be transferred to another component.

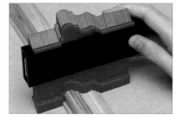

1 Place the moulding on a flat surface, hold the gauge level and press down slowly to achieve an accurate profile.

2 Square across the back of the second piece of moulding to provide a base line, then position the gauge and transfer the contours of the moulding with a pencil.

3 Mitre the end of the moulding back to the base line, which gives you a pattern to follow over the moulded surface. Follow this pattern with a coping saw, using the outline on the reverse side to keep the saw straight.

4 Clean up the cut with a gouge until the moulding is a perfect fit. Pare away small shavings at a time to prevent the end grain breaking away.

Scribing by hand

On less complex shapes, a simple method is to use a scribing block. Any suitable scrap of wood can be used as a spacer to follow the shape.

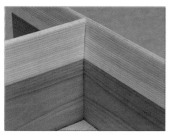

1 Grip a pencil against the scribing block and run it down the surface to transfer the outline on to the adjoining piece.

2 Cut down the line with a coping saw. The result is a neat fit between the two pieces.

Left The finished scribing joint.

USING MOULDINGS AND TRIMS

Small sections of decorative moulding can be used to form joints and to add solid wooden edges to manufactured boards and panels. Ready-made mouldings, in a number of different shapes and sizes, are commonly available, and you can usually match solid hardwood trim to the veneered boards used for shelves and carcass work.

Adding and gluing mouldings

1 Use a length of triangular moulding, sometimes called arris rail, to make a neat connection at an internal corner. This is more discreet than a square section of batten. Match the trim to the material you are working with.

2 Here, the arris moulding has been used to form the corner, leaving both edges of the panels exposed. Complete the joint with a section of scotia glued and pinned into the external corner.

3 If the moulding is thick enough, you can use biscuits to strengthen the joint and hold the moulding flush to one edge. This will provide extra stiffness to a shelf as well as concealing the exposed edge.

4 Finish off with small panel pins (brads), concealing their heads in the moulding detail. Set them in with a nail punch.

Adding pre-glued veneers

1 Pre-glued edging strip can be obtained in a variety of types to suit veneered boards. It is simply applied by pressing into position with a hot iron. Keep the iron moving to avoid local discolouration.

2 Leave the glue to harden (no more than half an hour is needed), then remove the excess veneer. Wrap some fairly coarse sandpaper around a block of wood and use it with a slow knifing action to cut away the veneer.

ADVANCED TECHNIQUES

One of the earliest woodworking principles for the novice to grasp is the importance of accuracy in fashioning the raw material, and an essential skill is the ability to produce flat surfaces, straight edges, accurate square corners and perfectly fitted joints. Nevertheless, as any experienced woodworker instinctively understands, wood is an organic material that is never naturally straight or uniform. To exploit the material's potential fully, the craftsperson will progress to exploring the manner in which wood behaves in other ways. From the earliest times, wood has been carved, sculpted, bent and shaped into curved forms. The right tools and techniques make it possible to create a seemingly endless variety of items, from simple wooden bowls to the most intricate of sculptural forms. The following pages show some of the many directions that can be followed to develop your skills as an expert practitioner in the craft of woodworking.

Forming Curves

One of the most attractive qualities of wood is its tactile nature, and many wooden items are made to be handled as well as enjoyed for their visual appeal. When working with wood, there is a natural tendency to soften the sharp edges of an object to break up its outline, making it more comfortable to use at the same time. Whether it is the bow front of a dressing table, the smooth curve around the back of an armchair or simply the rounded edge of a table, few woodworkers can resist the urge to include curved forms in their work. Moreover, there is no limit to the shapes that can be achieved.

Fret saws

Decorative work

Pierced panels with decorative fretwork make attractive features to include in many designs. A fretsaw or piercing saw can be used freehand to form the most intricate patterns. The very fine blade of a fretsaw is fed through a hole drilled in the centre of this veneered panel. Note that the teeth face toward the handle.

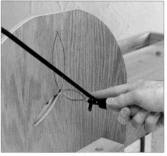

1 Squeeze the free end of the frame inward to attach the saw blade, then release it to tension the blade. The frame of the fretsaw can be up to 305mm (12in) wide, allowing a design to be located some distance from the edge.

2 Clamp the work vertically for the best results and keep the blade horizontal. The cutting action is applied on the pull stroke for greater control and accuracy, and the blade is so narrow that extremely tight curves can be formed.

Routers

A router is a powerful tool that needs to be kept under control, although it is possible to use it freehand for carving and lettering work if only small amounts of waste are removed. For making smooth curves, especially when you are producing a number of identical shapes from a template, it has no equal.

Alternatively, a trimming cutter could be used to make curves. This has a bearing on the end that matches the size of the cutting blade, allowing the shape and size of the template to be reproduced exactly.

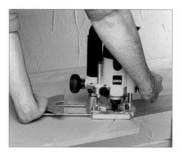

1 To make a circular template, fit a trammel arm to the router base. The trammel pin acts as a pivot point for the router. Slide the pin along the arm to the required radius, press it firmly into position, and move the router to describe an arc. Clamp the work firmly, place a piece of scrap wood beneath the router cutter, or work with the template overhanging the end of the workbench, moving it as required.

2 A template follower is a small circular disc that fits around the cutter and is screwed to the base of the router. A small lip around the edge of the follower slides smoothly on template to reproduce the latter's shape. Note that the finished size of the work is larger than the template. The diameter of the template must be set accordingly.

Jigsaws

Cutting curves is one of the primary uses of a jigsaw (saber saw). Ideally, use a saw with a variable speed and work slowly around the shape to be cut, steadying the base plate with your free hand. Always keep fingers clear of the path of the blade. You can obtain "scrolling" saw blades specifically designed for curved work and made to a narrow section to prevent the blade from binding in the cut as it changes direction.

1 In the absence of a scrolling blade, you can resort to this neat solution. Make a series of cuts in from the edge, stopping just short of the line of the curve. Guide the jigsaw just to the waste side of the cutting line, allowing the waste to fall away in small sections and leaving the back of the blade free to turn without binding or overheating.

Kerfing

Every saw blade leaves a narrow slot behind it as it cuts through the wood. This is called the "kerf" of the blade. Kerfing is the technique of using these small slots to allow a solid piece of wood to bend around a curve.

A series of parallel saw cuts is made on the back face of the wood, being carefully machined to a fixed depth to leave a thin layer of unbroken material at the front. The slots allow the entire piece, no matter how thick it is, to be pulled into shape and glued around a former. If the kerf is of the correct depth, the wood will then bend easily.

This technique was commonly used to make the curved "bullnose" of a stair riser, or the former for the bow front of a veneered cabinet.

1 This example of a kerfed panel was made from 19mm (¾in) plywood, using a circular saw set to a 16mm (⅝in) cutting depth, which left only one or two layers of plywood on the front face. To achieve a radius of 200mm (8in), make a trial cut that distance in from the end of the plywood strip. Adjust the depth of the saw blade if it feels too stiff. When the two edges of the kerf touch, measure how far the plywood has moved, as shown in step 1. This is the exact spacing required between the saw cuts.

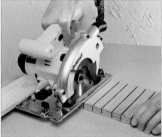

2 This operation will be easier with a circular saw table, but it is possible to achieve equally good results with a portable power saw on the workbench. Clamp a straightedge to the end of the panel to guide the baseplate of the saw, and make a series of cuts to cover the required length of the panel. Make sure the cuts are parallel and square to the edge of the work.

Circular saw

3 The closer the kerfs, the smoother the curve that can be achieved. The ideal is for the edges of the cuts to meet to produce the desired radius. They should be filled with glue to form a strong construction.

LAMINATING

This is the process of building up a composite form by gluing separate layers, or laminates, together. Because wood is so flexible, all manner of complex structures are made possible by this simple principle. Like a leaf spring, thin strips of wood can be bent around a curved former and glued together to produce a permanent curved shape. It is ideal for fabricating curved work or it can be used to glue blocks of timber on edge to create solid forms. A single large piece of wood, no matter how well seasoned, will be prone to splitting or deformation as it continues to dry out. The problem can be eliminated by laminating small pieces together.

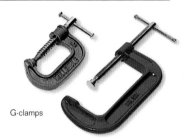
G-clamps

Laminated corners

A good way to add strength to a shelf or worktop is to trim the front edge with a batten (cleat), fixed on edge to prevent it from sagging. If the shelf is curved at the ends, the laminating technique allows the edge to be trimmed with a continuous length of wood, even though normally the batten may be too thick to bend in one piece.

1 With a circular saw or bandsaw, make a series of longitudinal cuts in the end of the batten, approximately 3mm (⅛in) wide. Then cut a matching number of thin strips from the same material, making them fractionally thinner than the width of the saw cuts to allow for the adhesive. Apply wood glue to both sides of each strip and insert them between the leaves of the batten.

2 With the straight section of the batten fixed to the front of the shelf, apply a layer of glue to the end and gradually and carefully bend it around the curve, using small G-clamps to prevent the assembly from springing back out of shape. Note how the batten has been cut over-length to provide added leverage while you are bending.

3 Continue the bending process around the end of the shelf. A tip is to cut some small wedges and tap them into place between the frames of the G-clamps and the batten, as shown, to force the laminates into good contact with the curved edge of the shelf. Note how the thin strips have been cut slightly wider than the batten to allow for any slight misalignment.

4 Leave the glued assembly to dry for as long as possible, preferably overnight. Plane the protruding strips flush with the top of the shelf, cut off the projecting end of the batten, sand smooth and round off the edges for a perfect curve. Using PVA wood glue, which is transparent when dry, will ensure that the laminates are almost undetectable.

Making formers

To make a free-form laminated object, first build a former to act as a jig. This example shows how the S-shaped legs of a small chair were made using 3mm (⅛in) strips of softwood. The result was legs that were strong enough to support the chair, but still flexible enough to allow some springiness in the construction.

An offcut (scrap) of kitchen countertop was used to make the baseboard for the former. The plastic facing made the glued assembly easy to remove. As an alternative, use a sheet of plywood coated with wax, or covered with a sheet of newspaper or kitchen film (plastic wrap).

1 Draw the shape on the baseboard and cut curved formers to match. Screw the formers to the baseboard and add a series of wooden blocks to receive the cramps. Carefully space the blocks evenly around the curves.

2 Apply glue to the laminates and insert them into the jig. They will tend to slide around and be difficult to handle, so use a small panel pin (brad) to keep them aligned until the first cramp is fitted.

3 Add further clamps, working from the centre toward the ends. The laminates must be of generous length, as the difference in radius between the inside and the outside of each curve requires the strips to move relative to each other as they bend.

4 To ensure no lateral twist in the final assembly, all the laminates must be in contact with the baseboard. Tap them down with a mallet and block of wood. Tighten each cramp in turn from the centre, to maintain a curve.

Joining blocks

By gluing together blocks of wood on edge, you can create solid shapes and patterns. Composite blanks for carving are built up in this way. You can make items, such as a butcher's chopping block, from small pieces of solid maple, which is a very hard species of timber (lumber), traditionally used for flooring and chopping blocks.

1 To make the joints as accurate as possible, each piece is fitted individually before laminating. Cut the first piece slightly oversize and use a small offcut (scrap) to mark its exact length. The blocks are simply butt-jointed, so accuracy is essential. Each piece should be a sliding fit in the jig.

2 Continue working around the jig in a clockwise direction, numbering each piece to avoid confusion later. Working from the outside toward the centre in this way ensures that no cumulative discrepancies occur in the overall size of the block and keeps it all square.

VENEERING

The art of veneering has a long history and demonstrates some of the finest qualities of decorative woodwork. By gluing a thin layer of high-quality wood to a substrate of cheaper, more workable material, the finest finish could be achieved at a lower cost. The same applies today, but often for different reasons, as exotic hardwoods are in short supply. Veneered panels of manufactured boards extend a limited resource and are in common use commercially. They have their uses for constructional work, but the home craftspeople can soon learn traditional veneering techniques, which will open up new avenues of creative woodworking.

Using veneers

Originally, veneers were cut with a saw, which must have been no easy task. Now they are produced by peeling or slicing the log into thin sheets, no more than 1mm (¹⁄₂₅in) thick.

Veneers are not only produced from exotic species, but also from any type of wood with an attractive figure or colour, and the best-quality logs are reserved for the process. Of notable value are burr veneers, which display intricate colours and distorted grain that is both visually stunning and difficult to work in solid form.

Veneers are supplied in sheets of varying size and sometimes in rolls. They should be flattened out as soon as possible and stored under a flat sheet of thick plywood in warm, dry conditions until needed. They are extremely delicate, so handle them with care. Keep your working area clean and free of dust.

The base on to which the veneer is glued must be dry, clean and perfectly smooth. Manufactured boards, such as MDF (medium-density fiberboard), make perfect substrates for veneers, as they are stable and uniform in structure. When applying veneer to solid wood or plywood, make sure the grain of the veneer runs at right angles to the grain direction of the board below, to counteract any tendency to move.

The veneering process

Veneers can be cut easily with a sharp knife or craft knife, but a veneer saw, with no set on its very fine teeth, is worth having. It is designed for use against a straightedge and is less likely than a normal saw to follow the grain or split the veneer. Veneers can be matched and butt-jointed undetectably if cut with perfectly square edges. Small strips for inlays can be produced with a strip cutter, which has two sharp blades mounted in a wooden stock.

Gluing

The traditional glue for veneering was animal glue, which is still obtainable and preferred by many woodworkers. It is sold as small pearls, and should be mixed and heated with water to dissolve it for use. Always warm the glue in a double boiler to prevent it from overheating. Spread the glue on the substrate while it is still warm. It will soon start to cool and become tacky. Lay the veneer over the glue, cover with a sheet of clean paper and run over it with a smoothing iron, set to a very low temperature. As the glue softens, it is absorbed into the fibres of the wood. Use a veneer hammer to

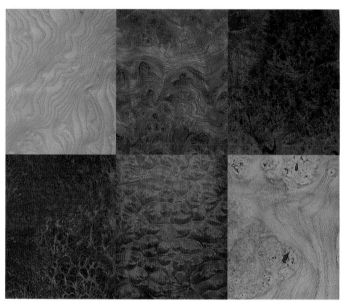

Left From left to right, the decorative burr patterns of ash, elm, walnut, (top row) vavona, myrtle and oak (bottom row).

press the veneer down and seal the glue as it dries once more. A veneer hammer should never be used as a regular hammer – it has a wooden head with an inserted strip of brass, which is used to press down on the veneer, using long firm strokes and working from the centre of the panel toward the edge. Iron out any uneven areas or bubbles, and if any air becomes trapped, forming a high spot, make a small slit in the veneer to release it. Use the warm iron to reheat any areas that show signs of lifting.

Local repairs to defects or damaged areas in a veneered surface can be made with a veneer punch. With a sharp blow from a mallet, this will punch through the veneer and create an irregular shape. Also, it produces a patch of identical size from a matching piece of veneer, allowing a repair that is almost undetectable.

The main drawback of using animal glue is that it is not heat-resistant and dries out, becoming brittle with age. A modern contact adhesive can be used, but this is unpleasant to work with and emits a flammable vapour as it dries. Employ a backing sheet of greaseproof paper between the glued substrate and the veneer, pulling it away and firming down the veneer in overlapping strips. Contact adhesive is more permanent than animal glue, but it makes repairs difficult and is almost impossible to remove.

Matching veneers

Veneers were often used on large panels to overcome the problem of using solid wood, which had a tendency to shrink or warp over time. They can be used to even greater effect when mixed in contrasting colours to make decorative patterns.

Veneers can be *bookmatched* or *quartered* by selecting leaves of similar grain, cut from the same log, and arranging them in a mirror-image

design. Hold the veneers firmly in place with veneer pins as you position them, and tape across the seams with veneer tape before gluing them down in the normal way. From this process, it is a small step to more complex designs, inlaying thin strips of veneer to create borders and crossbanding. These are produced commercially in a multitude of patterns, incorporating contrasting colours, shapes and grains for ornamentation of great complexity.

Right A beautiful veneer-fronted cabinet by furniture designer Tony McMullen. Tiny pieces of veneer were taped together to create a complex, geometric design (*below*).

Bookmatched

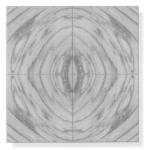

Quartered

TURNING

Woodturning adds a whole new dimension to the art and craft of woodworking. Shaping wood in the round as it spins on a lathe opens up many possibilities, ranging from straightforward spindles and table legs, through bowls and platters, to free sculptural forms. As an occupation for the home woodworker, turning has many attractions. A lathe and a bench will take up less space than a fully equipped workshop, and you can spend a lifetime exploring the potential of the craft.

Woodturning lathe

The lathe, uniquely among woodworking machines, requires that the cutting tool is offered up to the work, as opposed to the operator moving the wood on to a cutting blade. Therefore, a different approach is required, and a new discipline and technique for handling the tools must be learned. Although no more dangerous than any other woodworking operation, turning is a skill that must be gained under instruction. The first advice for any would-be turner is to attend a course in woodturning, to study the principles of safe working practice. One-day workshops and weekend training courses are commonplace, so it is not difficult to get started. Any adult education establishment, or even your local toolshop, is a sensible place to make enquiries. Attending a course also gives you a chance to try different lathes and tools before purchasing your own.

The lathe itself is a big investment and should be chosen carefully. As with most tools, the cheapest "beginner's" model may not necessarily be the best option. Even a novice will progress quite swiftly and soon find that a small, lightweight lathe has severe limitations. A robust machine at the lower end of the professional range will be a much wiser investment in the end.

Lathes are denoted according to the distance "between centres", which indicates the longest piece of work that the machine will accommodate. A variable-speed motor provides rotary power to the *headstock*, which turns the work. The *tailstock* supports the other end. Some turners concentrate on bowl making and hollow work, in which case a swivelling head is ideal, allowing large diameters to be worked. A *faceplate* to support the base of the bowl would also be needed. Alternatively, a self-centring chuck is a more versatile option. Whatever the style of turning envisaged, a robust machine with solid mountings and a sturdy tool rest is essential.

Turning tools

Although traditionally made of carbon steel, turning tools are increasingly being offered in high-speed steel (HSS). While this is more expensive, it keeps an edge for much longer and sharpens more easily.

Good-quality turning chisels are not cheap, and it is best to start off with a core of the essentials, adding to them as your technique develops. Chisels are classified according to the basic operations they perform.

Left Turning tools and the woodturning lathe.
Above A turned oak bowl by Anthony Bryant.

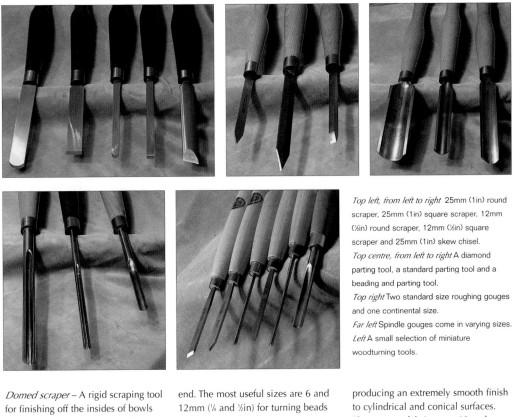

Top left, from left to right 25mm (1in) round scraper, 25mm (1in) square scraper, 12mm (½in) round scraper, 12mm (½in) square scraper and 25mm (1in) skew chisel.

Top centre, from left to right A diamond parting tool, a standard parting tool and a beading and parting tool.

Top right Two standard size roughing gouges and one continental size.

Far left Spindle gouges come in varying sizes.

Left A small selection of miniature woodturning tools.

Domed scraper – A rigid scraping tool for finishing off the insides of bowls and goblets with a curved profile and flat end. Sizes vary from 12 to 25mm (½ to 1in).

Parting tool – A diamond-shaped cutting tool designed for parting off, or removing, the workpiece when finished. It is also commonly used for notching and grooving operations.

Roughing gouge – This is a deep U-shaped gouge with a 45 degree outside bevel for the rapid removal of waste. Use it for turning square stock into round. Ideal size: 19mm (¾in).

Skew chisel – A very versatile tool with an angled, V-section blade that can be used for smoothing and shaping. The most useful sizes are 12 and 25mm (½ and 1in).

Spindle gouge – An all-purpose turning gouge with a shallower bevel than a roughing gouge and a rounded end. The most useful sizes are 6 and 12mm (¼ and ½in) for turning beads and other profiles.

Square-end chisel – This is ideal for producing an extremely smooth finish to cylindrical and conical surfaces. The most useful sizes are 19 and 25mm (¾ and 1in).

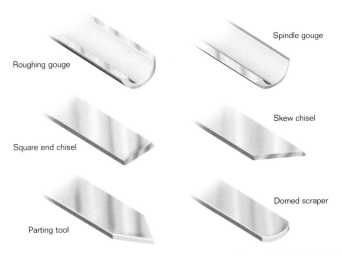

Roughing gouge

Square end chisel

Parting tool

Spindle gouge

Skew chisel

Domed scraper

TURNING TECHNIQUES

Acquiring confidence when working the lathe is the first step to developing further techniques for particular projects. Before committing yourself to an important piece of work you should prepare a selection of different sizes of wood, or blanks, and practice the basic skills of reducing square stock to a round section safely and accurately. Turning chisels are very sensitive tools when properly handled. The long handles become an extension of the arm and allow small amounts of presssure to be applied with great precision.

To start turning

Your lathe should be set at the right height to suit your working position, and so that the tool rest is level with your elbow. A well-balanced stance when working is essential – if you stand awkwardly the work soon becomes tiring and there is a great danger of digging the edge of the tool into the workpiece. To start turning, practice turning a square or octagonal length of stock to a round cylinder, which is the first step of most turning projects. Centre the work on the headstock, mount in the lathe, and slide the tailstock to meet it. Clamp it

tight and turn it by hand to make sure it revolves evenly, with no obstruction, before starting the lathe.

Take a roughing gouge and position it on the tool rest just away from the work so that it will only remove a small amount of wood. Move the gouge sideways along the rest as it cuts, and roll it slightly in the direction of movement to produce a slicing rather than deep cutting action. Only when you are confident that you have mastered this basic technique should

Below Note the angle of the gouge; this causes a slicing rather than a cutting action.

Above, from left to right Centre finder, bevel gauge and inside/outside calipers.

you progress to cutting, scraping and profiling. Always observe the safety points, be patient, and let your skill and feel for the work develop at its own pace.

Wood for turning

Almost any type of wood can be turned successfully, but the properties of certain species make them favourites. Close, even-grained timber of medium hardness produces the best results. With more expertise, sharp chisels and the correct lathe speed, harder woods with more interesting grain effects can be tackled. The ultimate challenge is highly figured burr wood, which is always sought after for its wild colour and grain effects, making every piece made from it unique.

Wood species
with good turning properties

Basswood (lime)
Beech
Sycamore
Walnut
Maple
Yew
Ash
Cherry

Safety points

Even though a lathe has no sharp blades or cutters, like other machinery, it is still a machine that requires great respect. When in motion, the workpiece can catch the end of the working tool and cause serious injury.

- Work carefully and with concentration, keeping your eyes on the work at all times.
- Make sure that safety guards are fitted and that the workpiece is free to turn without obstruction.
- Always use the tool rest to support the tools.
- Offer the cutting tool slowly to the work, moving with the direction of rotation, and working "downhill" on curved and angled surfaces to prevent the tip from digging in.
- Maintain a tidy working area and do not allow debris to collect around you.
- Wear safety goggles or glasses and a dust mask when dealing with fine work.
- Avoid wearing loose clothing, and remove any jewellery.
- Always switch off the lathe to make adjustments and when leaving it, even momentarily.
- Allow the workpiece to stop rotating on its own, without touching it.

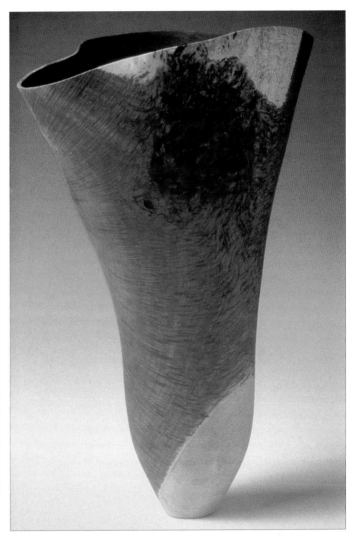

Above right and below left A beautifully fluid turned oak vase and a bowl turned from burr oak, by Anthony Bryant.

Below right A set of dishes, turned by Ian Durrant. Their solid, burnished form shows a quite different approach to turning.

CARVING

This skilled craft could be considered the most unrestrictive form of creative woodworking. Unlike most disciplines, in which a careful process of assembling separate components to complete a structure is routine, carving involves removing surplus material to reveal the hidden form concealed in a piece of wood. Perhaps the most successful carving is one that achieves a perfect balance between the sculptor's imposed ideas and the innate qualities of the material.

Types of carving

There is no limit to the scale and variety of what may be achieved by carving in wood; imagination is the only limiting factor. There are different approaches to the process, of course, and completely different styles.

Relief carving is a specialist form of carving whereby the background of a wooden panel is carved away, leaving a two-dimensional form in relief. Delicate floral carvings, in lime or basswood, have a long heritage, reaching their peak in the 17th century with the work of craftsmen such as Grinling Gibbons, the master of fine detail.

At the other end of the scale are pieces of a sculptural nature, carved from laminated composite forms to produce works of breathtaking realism. More abstract work simply lets the material speak for itself, with a little help from an expert hand.

Wood for carving

As with turning, the best species of wood for carving are close-grained and stable, but because the carver works at his or her own speed, and can choose how to approach every cut, it is true to say that any type of wood will be a candidate for the next subject. Even the most tortuous piece of wild or knotty grain will yield to the correct sharp tool, when approached with care from the right direction.

If possible, choose really well-seasoned wood to avoid the disappointment of cracks appearing as it dries. Work with intricate detail is particularly vulnerable in this respect. It is worth experimenting with polyethylene glycol (PEG), a waxy solution that penetrates the structure of the wood, replacing the water in the cells and stabilizing it. A good craft supplier or toolshop will stock PEG and may also be a good source

of small samples of unusual types of wood for carving, cut into small sections called *blanks*. These should have been sealed with a wax coating to keep them stable.

Wood species with good carving properties

Alder

Basswood (lime)

Jelutong

Mahogany

Ramin

Oak

Walnut

Yellow poplar

Below left Part of a highly-worked carved frieze by Kenneth Wilson.

Below This hand-carved frame by Ashley Sands incorporates Grinling Gibbons style foliage, grapes and acanthus leaves.

Carving tools

Tools for carving can range from the humble pocket knife to specially fashioned chisels and gouges with weird and wonderful names, such as *macaroni* and *fluteroni*, *dog-legs* and *fishtails*. The gouge is the basic carver's tool, its outside bevel allowing the wood to be chipped away piece by piece.

A spoon gouge has a cranked, spoon-shaped shaft to deal with deeply recessed work. For roughing out the work, use a *carver's mallet*, made of shock-resistant beech. It has a round head that allows the chisel to approach the work from any angle. The normal range of standard woodworking chisels and shaping tools will come in very useful for the more heavy work before addressing the fine detail.

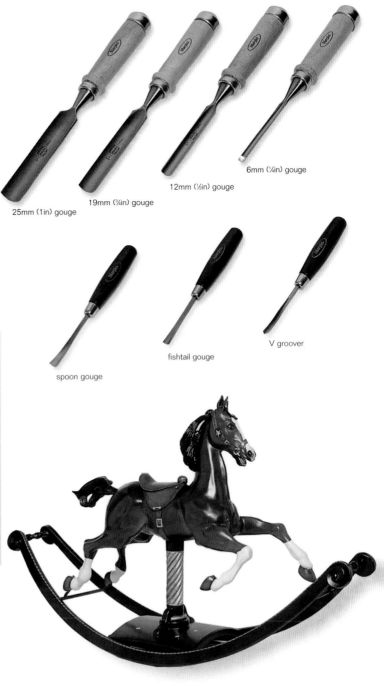

25mm (1in) gouge

19mm (¾in) gouge

12mm (½in) gouge

6mm (¼in) gouge

spoon gouge

fishtail gouge

V groover

Using gouges

Gouges are commonly used as carving tools, but occasionally they also come in useful when working with curved profiles. Use in the same manner as a straight chisel, with the bevel resting on the surface of the wood to control the depth of cut. Work slowly away from you, using light taps from a small mallet.

Right The rocking horse, carved by Bob Cleveland, was made in several stages using pieces of Jelutong laminated together. The fine detail and hand-painted finish make it almost too good to use.

CARVING TECHNIQUES

Carving work requires the ability to visualize a three-dimensional form on the flat surface of the wood, which takes some practice. It helps to break the subject down into a pattern of overlapping or interlocking planes, dealing with one at a time. On a square piece of stock, draw the shape on all four sides, and work on opposing faces in turn. The cylindrical form of this barley sugar carving presents more of a challenge. The secret lies in the marking out.

Marking out

1 It is important to use straight, square stock for good results. Begin by setting out the square capitals or blocks at the top and bottom of the column.

2 Use a fine tenon or dovetail saw to make cuts in at the corners, top and bottom, down to the circumference of the cylinder.

3 Pare away the corners with a spoon gouge until the ends of the column are perfectly round.

4 A spokeshave is the ideal tool for removing large quantities of waste around the centre of the column. Work from the middle of the piece towards each end, as the grain direction allows.

5 Keep turning the workpiece and removing shavings to make a perfect cylinder. With the blade of the spokeshave set for a fine cut, it is possible to work against the grain without encountering many problems.

6 Use masking tape to create a regular spiral around the column. Here, each strip of tape describes half a turn around the column, terminating on the opposite face at the other end. Draw along the margins of each strip with a soft pencil.

Roughing out

1 Always mark the area of each twist clearly to establish a reference. In the waste areas in between, work around the column with a bevelled chisel and mallet, cutting across the grain to form a deep channel.

2 Working from the top of each strand toward the waste area, gradually chisel away the margins to define the rounded profile. Direct the cuts down and across the grain. Change direction as required to avoid lifting the fibres of the wood.

3 Once the channels have been defined, it is quite simple to shape each twist, using a spoon gouge along the grain. Complete the roughing out process around the whole piece, leaving it 3mm (⅛in) oversize, before carving the final detail.

Carving a double twist

This column of four strands was carved out of ash, which is quite hard and positive to work with. Mark out as for the single twist, but give each strand a full turn around the column.

1 After roughing out each strand as shown above, use the gouge to pare away the waste in small flakes. Work patiently. Grip the tool between clenched fingers for greater control.

2 Use a small gouge or V-groove chisel to clear out the waste at the bottom of each strand, working carefully along the grain.

3 Finish off the column with a piece of coarse sandpaper wrapped around a small strip of wood to remove the marks of the carving tools. Fold the sandpaper into a V-shape to reach the smallest crevices.

Above The finished double twist spiral.

WOOD FINISHING

Applying a perfect finish to your work may seem to be the last stage in the construction process, but the secret of success is to consider it from the very beginning. From the moment you conceive an idea and determine its design, the finish will influence all your subsequent decisions. Some species of wood are better suited to certain types of finishing materials; conditions of use will dictate the degree of durability and water resistance required.

The orientation of each component and its grain pattern, the types of joint and glue, the tools and techniques used, even the order of work and assembly, will be affected by the demands of the finishing process. Keeping this in mind will help to focus your work, and will require great discipline and forethought. The visual appeal of the material is one of the attractions of woodworking, and the art of finishing is to display that to the best advantage.

FINISHING EQUIPMENT

There is a wide choice of finishes for your work, from materials that have been tried and tested over hundreds of years to modern products formulated to meet the demands of the furniture industry. Compared to the cost of timber, finishing materials are not that expensive, which allows you to experiment with every project to perfect your techniques and discover the features of each method. For a small outlay, you can assemble the basic equipment to get started, then add to this as you progress.

Preparation

The key to a good result, as always, lies in careful preparation. When a glossy finish is applied to a surface, small scratches or blemishes will be revealed that previously were barely visible to the naked eye. There is no substitute for a methodical approach, working through progressively finer grades of abrasive paper until you cannot feel any improvement.

A word of warning, though – your fingers can transmit greasy deposits and damp patches to the surface, so keep your hands clean and handle fine items with great care. Pick them up by the edges, or wear disposable gloves. Stack the finished components on clean softwood battens (cleats).

Carry out preparation work well away from the finishing area, and be prepared to move the work back and forth several times as you apply and rub down successive coats. Assemble a good supply of clean rags, wire (steel) wool, abrasive paper and scraping tools. Even used sheets of abrasive paper come in useful, as they lose some of their cutting ability and produce a progressively finer finish.

Dealing with blemishes

If you find a small blemish in your work at a late stage, all is not lost. There are various filling and stopping compounds, some of which are better than others. Soft interior stopping is fine for tiny cracks, and comes in a range of pre-mixed colours to suit different wood species. You can blend these together or add a drop of wood stain to match the wood's colour and tone, but check first that the stain you

Above, clockwise from top left Wire (steel) wool, filler, spatula, soft cloth, sanding block, abrasive papers and cabinet scrapers.

use is compatible with the final finish. Larger holes may need filling with a hard-setting exterior-grade filler. Leave this just proud of the surface, as it tends to shrink as it cures, then sand it flush. Shrinkage is a disadvantage of many fillers, which can shrink further and even fall out of the wood.

Workshop conditions

A suitable area in which to work is a priority. Sanding activities create dusty conditions, and dust is the enemy of a fine finish. It is best to work in a separate room, well away from the woodworking area. If you do not have this luxury, seal off an area of the main workshop with plastic sheeting or a partition. Organize your work so that you carry out finishing on a separate day, and keep away while each coat is drying.

Most finishing materials depend on the evaporation of solvents as they cure, so the area should be well ventilated, but you should prevent draughts and maintain a controlled temperature to ensure ideal drying conditions. Install good lighting, and position the finishing bench in the centre of the room so that you can move around your work without moving it. Drying racks fixed to the wall will be good for stacking small components.

Health and safety

Many substances that are used for finishing are flammable or contain ingredients that are hazardous. Keep them in a lockable area, out of the reach of children and preferably out of doors. Always keep containers sealed, and observe the manufacturers' instructions for the safe use of the materials. Do not pour used solvents or thinners into a domestic drainage system – take them to a safe disposal site at your local recycling centre. Old paintbrushes, rags and polishing cloths can also be hazardous – do not leave them lying around or mix them with other waste.

Brushes

You get what you pay for when buying brushes. Keep a stock of cheap disposable brushes for building up coats of primer and sealer – sometimes the price of thinners for cleaning a brush outweighs the cost of a new one. However, for finish coats, invest in good-quality brushes and keep them separate for different applications to avoid contamination. Clean them every time you use them, wash out in warm soapy water, and store them dry and in a dust-free container. A quality brush improves with age as the bristles become "worked in".

Right (Top row) 75mm (3in) disposable brush; 100mm (4in) lacquering brush; 50mm (2in), 38mm (1½in) and 12mm (½in) full-bodied paintbrushes. *(Bottom row)* Polishing mops and a variety of artist's brushes.

Shellac stopping

More traditional forms of filler, ideal for restoration work, can be obtained from specialist suppliers. Shellac stopping comes in stick form and a useful colour range. It sets quite hard and bonds well to the wood with minimal shrinkage.

1 During restoration of this table top, the removal of an old coat of varnish revealed a large knot. This was not unattractive, but needed to be treated and sealed before the application of a new finish. A cabinet scraper was used first to cut back the fibrous material around the knot.

2 The very centre of the knot had dried out and formed a small hole. The tip of the shellac stick was melted with an old soldering iron, and the small drops were allowed to fill the hole and soak into the wood surrounding the knot.

3 When the filler had hardened, the excess was scraped away with a sharp chisel until it was flush with the surface. More stopping was applied as necessary; several layers would be required for a deep blemish.

4 Wax filler was then rubbed over the areas of rough grain surrounding the knot. This sealed the entire surface and it should prevent further shrinkage of the wood.

5 The table top was smoothed with extra-fine sandpaper (320 grit) on a cork sanding block, using small circular motions at first, followed by working along the grain direction.

6 The entire surface was wiped down with a soft damp cloth, using long strokes parallel to the grain. This removed all final traces of dust and served to raise the grain slightly by adding moisture. When dry, it was rubbed down again with 400 grit paper before finishing.

STAINING

Stained and polished wood will be familiar to anyone who has seen antique furniture, such as "Jacobean" oak or mahogany from the 19th century. The use of wood stain is less fashionable today, the accent being on letting the natural colour of the material speak for itself. However, the purpose of staining is not always to make the wood appear darker. Creative use of a wood stain can enhance a grain pattern that otherwise would appear bland. With care, you can use very dilute stains to match different components in a construction, or to achieve attractive contrasts of tone. Even quite strong colours can be used to striking effect for a contemporary look on wooden toys and furniture.

Types of stain

Ready-mixed wood stains are readily available from all good hardware stores and paint suppliers, but care is necessary to ensure that the type of stain is compatible with the finish. All three common types have their advantages and disadvantages.

The colour of wood stain is often labelled according to wood species: pine, mahogany or oak, for example. This can be very misleading, as the result depends on the base colour of the wood to which it is applied. Always test the stain you want to use on an offcut (scrap) of the same piece of wood first and let it dry thoroughly. Apply a coat of the chosen finish over the stain to make sure that there is no reaction between solvents.

Bleaching

Bleaching is a technique that can be used to revive an old piece of wood or correct a patchy appearance. It can even out defects in the wood's appearance before more stain is applied. Always be careful when handling chemicals – wear heavy-duty rubber gloves, overalls and eye protection. Most wood bleach is applied as a two-part treatment. The base coat is washed into the grain, then the activator is added to set up the chemical reaction. Small bubbles appear on the surface and a noticeable colour change should be visible after 15–20 minutes. Rinse with plenty of water, or the required neutralizer, then sand down when dry. Some species of

wood, particularly oily varieties such as teak and rosewood, are not easy to bleach; mahogany, beech and light oak produce better results. Always test bleach on an offcut or concealed area of the workpiece before committing yourself.

Fuming

Fuming is another application of chemistry to the art of finishing. Wood with a high acid content, oak in particular, will react with ammonia gas and turn a deep rich brown. Not being a surface stain, the colour is fixed in the material. The process is particularly useful for treating an entire piece of furniture that has many detailed parts, which would make applying stain difficult. Ordinary household bleach contains ammonia, although more consistent results can

Above Different types and colours of stain, here being tested on strips of pine.

be obtained from a stronger solution. You can build a simple fuming chamber by constructing a light framework that is large enough to contain the object, then covering it with thin plywood or hardboard. Seal all the joints with plastic tape, then place the item inside with a wide, shallow container of ammonia solution. Handle the container with great care, making sure you do not splash the liquid on to any exposed skin. Wear gloves, goggles and protective clothing, and work in a well-ventilated area, preferably outdoors in a sheltered spot. Seal the chamber and leave for at least 24 hours. The amount of darkening depends on the exposure time allowed.

Applying wood stain

Wear a pair of disposable latex gloves to protect your hands, particularly when working with a solvent-based stain. This also prevents the workpiece from being marked by the oils in your hands when you move it. Shake the container well, and if you have mixed up your own blend, make sure that you have prepared enough to complete the job.

1 Use a small brush to test the colour or to apply small patches of stain to even out any pale areas of the wood. Dilute the stain when treating the end grain of timber, which is more absorbent and will take too much stain, leading to a darker finish.

2 With a soft cloth or ready-made staining pad, apply the stain with quick circular motions, keeping the pad fully charged. For an even coat, the wood should absorb as much stain as possible while it is still wet.

3 Before the stain has completely dried, rub the pad along the surface with long strokes up and down the grain to remove any excess colour.

Touching up

You can use a small watercolour brush to match the grain pattern of highly figured wood. Here, a small piece of veneer has lifted after the staining process.

1 Add a drop of stain to a small amount of stopping that matches the lighter background. Apply this to the damaged area with a spatula or modelling knife.

2 Rub down the repair very gently and dab with a light stain to blend it in. When dry, mix up a darker stain and copy the grain pattern with a fine-tipped brush.

3 The completed repair becomes almost undetectable when the finish coat is applied.

Wood stains

Water-based stains

Pros: Low in cost, safe to use and contain no harmful solvents. They are non-toxic and taint-free, and suitable for wooden toys, food utensils, storage units or items where safety is paramount.

Cons: These can produce uneven or patchy results, are slow drying and have poor penetration on oily and resinous woods. Not always colour-fast and can fade in strong sunlight. They will raise the grain of some woods, especially softwoods.

Solvent-based stains

Pros: These are quick drying; they use methylated spirit as a solvent. They will not raise the grain and can be inter-mixed successfully, or mixed with shellac sealer or polish to add body to further coats. Light-fast stains have a long life.

Cons: These require fast work to prevent blotchy results and variations in finish due to overlapping. They are not compatible with cellulose lacquers.

Oil-based stains

Pros: These come in a range of pre-mixed strong colours and are easy to apply evenly. Only one coat is required: further applications of stain tend to lift the first coat.

Cons: These are difficult to dilute or mix to create your own colours. They are not compatible with white spirit-based finish coats or wax polish. They give mixed results on close-grained wood.

VARNISH, PAINT AND LACQUER

For a hard wearing and waterproof finish, a coat of clear varnish takes some beating. Traditional, oil-based varnish is not ideal for finishing wood, as the resins in the varnish give an orange cast to the film and can obscure the natural colours of the wood.

Of the more modern varnishes, polyurethane is easier to apply and produces a clearer result. It requires white spirit (paint thinner) as a solvent and is safe to use with the normal precautions. Acrylic varnish is water-based, less toxic and quick drying, but it is less hard wearing in the long run.

Lacquers tend to be much thinner and require a build-up of several coats to be effective. The best results are obtained by spray application, which is not always a practical proposition for the home woodworker. Cellulose solvents for lacquer are quite unpleasant and flammable at lower temperatures.

Preparation

Varnish needs a good key to the wood surface to prevent blistering and peeling. On oily wood, apply a coat of shellac sanding sealer beforehand, as this will improve adhesion. Alternatively, apply a priming coat of varnish diluted with 50 per cent white spirit (paint thinner), allowing it to soak well into the grain of the wood. Leave to dry for 24 hours before rubbing down lightly with fine sandpaper.

Paint

While the benefits of a natural wood finish are undeniable, good paintwork also has its place. The brushing technique is much the same as for clear varnish and demands the same care in preparation. On very resinous and coarse-grained wood, apply a priming coat of shellac sanding sealer before painting to prevent patchy drying and cracking of the paint film. Continue with primer and several undercoats until the surface is smooth before applying the topcoat. Although paint is opaque, it will not necessarily mask unsightly blemishes.

Painted furniture and other woodwork is a subject in its own right, offering a wide choice of paint effects to explore. You can experiment with acrylic paints and glazes, which bond well to wood and can be used to good effect as tinted backgrounds with all manner of decorative touches.

Always seal the wood with a topcoat of clear lacquer to protect the finished paintwork.

Common finishing faults and their causes

Patchy areas in the finish coat
Uneven sanding of the surface during preparation
Oil or grease contamination

Ridges or ripples
Varnish drying too quickly as you join up the brush strokes – work on a smaller area at a time; check that the room temperature is not too high

"Orange peel" effect – small pinholes in a rough surface
Varnish applied too thickly in each coat
Uneven drying

"Bloom" – milky-white colour in the film
Presence of moisture on the surface or in the brush
Damp atmosphere or cold draughts

Crazing – small surface cracks developing in the glaze
Applying coats too rapidly without leaving time to dry
Using incorrect solvents that react with a stain or sealing coat

Top right The carcass of this display case was made from medium-density fibreboard, which was painted after assembly.
Left This table was finished with several coats of clear lacquer, rubbing down carefully between each coat for a mirror finish.

Varnishing technique

Use a good-quality brush with a full head of bristles, making sure that it is clean. Small flecks of dust or dried varnish in the brush will tend to loosen as you work and ruin the job. Pour a quantity of varnish, sufficient for one coat, into a small container and reseal the tin at once to prevent a skin from forming. Dip the brush no more than halfway into the varnish and avoid overloading it. Drips and runs are the most common causes of a poor finish.

1 If treating a complex piece of work, such as this panelled door, always begin with the fine detail. Use a small brush to work along the edges of mouldings and panelling, brushing out any build-up in the corners.

2 Change to a larger brush for the wider areas of panelling, using long strokes. Hold the brush at an angle to the surface and work quickly, but carefully. Pay attention to the V-grooves, which can trap small runs of varnish.

3 Support the work on small clean battens (cleats) to lift it clear of the finishing table. This allows treatment of the outer edges. Try not to overload the brush here – too much varnish will creep down and collect on the underside.

4 Move to the main members of the panel, treating the cross-rails first. Brush along the grain.

5 Finish off by brushing up and down the vertical stiles of the door, picking up the brush strokes at the ends of the rails and brushing out well along the grain. When dry, turn the door over and coat the other side in the same way before rubbing down.

6 Use 000 grade fine wire (steel) wool to remove any nibs of varnish on mouldings and edges. Brush the debris well clear to remove small fragments of wire wool, which easily become trapped in the corners.

7 Rub down all the flat surfaces with 320 grit silicon carbide paper until the first coat of varnish is silky smooth. For a quality finish, repeat the entire operation four or five times, building up a really flat and well-keyed surface.

8 Apply the final coat with a fine-haired polishing mop. If the surface is really smooth, this requires no effort and can be carried out very quickly, avoiding any streaks and ridges, for a mirror finish.

FINISHING WITH WAX AND OIL

Wax has been used as a treatment for finishing wood for centuries, and it is still very much in favour. Whereas a coat of varnish has to bond to the wood and provide a separate protective layer, wax sinks into the surface and produces a deep, lustrous finish that improves with age. Less skill is required for its application, and it is easy to refresh and renew. Oil is even more straightforward to use, and some modern formulations have the advantage of being slightly more durable and heat-resistant. No special equipment is needed to apply wax or oil, other than a soft cloth and fine wire (steel) wool.

Types of wax

Pure beeswax is a natural product that provides a wonderful finish for fine furniture. However, it is less durable than other types and can soften in warm temperatures.

The most common wax for wood is carnauba wax. It is much harder than pure beeswax – a mixture of the two can be successful. It is more resistant to wear, but more difficult to apply.

Beware of using silicone-based "wax polish" as a natural wood treatment. It is quick to apply and produces a glossy finish, but when this wears off, the result is patchy and dull. It attracts a build-up of dust and dirt, and is difficult to refresh. Silicone is not compatible with any other type of finish and is impossible to remove.

Furniture wax can be obtained ready coloured to suit different wood

types. It will not act as a stain on its own, but over time will build up a deep lustrous colour within the wood surface. It can be applied safely over a spirit wood stain, but can cause problems with oil-based stain. On soft wood with open grain, it helps to seal

the wood beforehand. When you are working on very dense, close-grained wood, warm the wax beforehand over a low heat, such as above a radiator. Finish off by rubbing along the grain and leave it for an hour or two to settle.

Left, clockwise from top left There are many different types and colours of wax for polishing woodwork and furniture: liming wax, carnauba wax, teak oil, soft cloth, wax filler sticks, beeswax, solid beeswax.

1 Apply a thin coat of sanding sealer or clear shellac. This provides a stable base for the wax, but does not prevent it from sinking deep into the grain. When dry, rub down very lightly with worn pieces of fine sandpaper and brush off.

2 Apply the wax with a ball of fine wire (steel) wool. The wax lubricates the cutting action and prevents too much abrasion, while being forced deep into the wood fibres. Use a strong circular motion to work the wax well in. The harder you work, the more friction is created, which softens the wax further.

3 Form a polishing pad from a soft duster and buff the wax vigorously. Add two or three more thin coats as the wax settles, then continue to build up the finish. To refresh a polished wax finish, first wash with warm soapy water to remove any debris. If the finish is really soiled, clean it with fine wire wool moistened with white spirit (paint thinner). Add another coat of wax.

Liming wax

A limed finish can be very attractive, particularly on oak and other wood with a strong grain figure. The white liming paste penetrates the grain and provides pleasing highlights. Over time, the lime continues to react with the acid content of the wood to produce a deep lustre.

Above A coat of liming wax accentuates the grain of the wood beautifully.

1 Apply a coat of sanding sealer. When it is dry, work the liming wax into the grain with fine wire (steel) wool. Use a circular motion, as you would for normal wax, but do not finish off along the grain. This would tend to lift the wax from the grain.

2 Wipe the excess wax away with firm strokes directly across the grain. Use a soft mutton cloth with a coarse weave for the best result. Leave to dry for about four hours, then buff with a soft cloth. Seal with clear lacquer, or add more clear wax for a silky finish.

Oil treatment

Oil is a natural waterproofer and, as such, is the perfect finish for outdoor furniture, especially on oily woods such as teak. It will outlast any varnish treatment, without the risk of water penetrating the film and causing it to lift, which is a common problem with exterior varnish. The correct oil will dry to form a protective film, but can be cut back and enriched by adding another coat at any time.

Linseed oil is not an ideal choice, as it remains soft and attracts the build-up of dust. Boiled linseed oil will form a protective crust, but is not heat-resistant and can become tacky in warm weather. Teak oil and Danish oil contain mineral extracts that help to preserve wood. They are more durable and are the best choice. One word of caution: oil is sometimes used to finish wooden culinary utensils and salad bowls. Clearly, metallic-based oils are not suitable for such items, so use thin vegetable oil instead.

1 Application of an oil finish could not be easier. Remove all traces of dust from the surface and work in the oil with fine wire (steel) wool. Allow it to soak in and, if uneven patches are visible, keep applying more until the wood achieves a uniform colour.

2 Finish off with long strokes up and down the grain, using a very soft cloth to work in the oil well. Leave it to dry overnight.

French Polishing

French polish is a general term that applies to many different products and techniques. However, all share the same basic raw material: shellac dissolved in methylated spirits (rubbing alcohol).

Shellac

This is derived from a sticky resin produced by small insects in the Indian subcontinent. Successive layers of shellac will bond together to form a deep protective coating that is not too brittle with a translucent quality and rich colour. The colour will vary with the method of preparation.

Common types of shellac

Button polish: more orange or golden in colour; the purest form of shellac.
French polish: a light to medium brown tone suitable for most finishes.
Garnet polish: a much darker richer brown for dark wood.
Shellac sealer: a useful product for building up or sealing the substrate before applying polish, or for use as a binder for stains and fillers.
White or pale polish: bleached shellac ideal for pale wood.

There is a great deal of mystique attached to French polishing, and certainly the best practitioners of the

art deserve the utmost admiration. The deep, rich quality of a well-polished piece of furniture is unmistakable, and difficult to reproduce by other means. "Instant" French polish treatments, which promise similar results in one coat, are not worth using. There is no substitute for good old-fashioned hard

Above, clockwise from top left Clear sealer, button, French and garnet polish, polishing mop, artist's brushes, cotton wadding, cloth.

work to achieve a fine finish. Try the technique on a spare piece of wood to get the hang of it – you will soon learn the basic principles.

Filling the grain

As you might expect, careful preparation is essential. For a mirror-smooth finish, most polishers like to fill the grain first to create a truly flat surface for the polishing process. On coarse-grained wood, this is essential, as the shellac sinks into the open pores and sometimes shrinks. Ready-mixed filling paste is sold as grain filler, and is not to be confused with wood filler or stopping. If the wood is to be stained, do this before the filling process, and stain the paste to match the final colour.

1 Press the paste into the surface with a broad-bladed filling knife. Work across the grain to prevent the filler from being pulled out.

2 Leave the filler for 24 hours to dry thoroughly, then rub down with 400 grit silicon carbide paper to remove excess paste from the surface.

3 Finish by wiping across, then along the grain with mutton cloth, moistened with a drop of methylated spirit to collect all traces of dust.

Applying the polish

French polish depends on friction to build up the coats of shellac, so it is applied with a polishing pad, or "rubber", rather than a brush. Plain unmedicated cotton wool (cotton balls), or upholsterers' wadding (batting), and clean, lint-free cotton cloth are all you need to make one.

There is no fixed size for a rubber pad – to some extent, it depends on the size of the work to be polished, and on the size of your hand. The base of the rubber pad must be completely smooth and free of creases and wrinkles. Make sure you always work on a dust-free surface.

1 Place a square of wadding in the centre of a square of cloth that is twice the size. Fold the front edge of the cloth over the wadding.

2 Fold the two front corners over to hold the wadding in place and form a point. Make sure the base of the rubber is free of dust.

3 Twist the "tail" of the rubber pad around the back of the wadding to form a pear-shaped pad that is comfortable to hold.

4 Charge the rubber pad with polish by unfolding it and pouring a small quantity into the centre. The idea is to use the wadding as a reservoir to feed the face of the rubber with polish as you work. Never apply polish directly to the face of the rubber pad.

5 Apply a base coat of the polish, working swiftly up and down the grain and squeezing out more polish as you proceed. Keep the rubber pad moving at all times, using long overlapping strokes to spread the polish around and fill the grain.

6 Leave the polish to dry for half an hour and begin the "body up" process. Add more layers of polish, using figure-of-eight motions to cover the surface. When the rubber begins to stick or drag, leave the polish overnight to dry. Store the rubber in an airtight jar.

7 The base coat will sink into the grain as it dries. Rub down with fine abrasive paper to remove any nibs from the surface, and brush away all fine particles. Do this away from the finishing area, which must be completely dust free from now on.

8 Build up further coats, working for half an hour at a time and allowing four or five hours between sessions for the polish to harden. As more is applied, you will find that the rubber pad begins to "pull" the surface as it softens the layer beneath. Lubricate by applying a dab of raw linseed oil to the face of the rubber.

9 You will soon see a high gloss forming as the polish is built up. Dull areas indicate too much oil. If this happens, leave to dry, then work over the surface again with a clean rubber pad charged with fresh polish. Use longer strokes, applying more pressure to harden the polish. This is called "stiffing up".

10 The final task is "spiriting off". This removes all traces of oil, a fresh rubber pad being charged with finishing spirit, or diluted polish, and applied with a light touch. Use long strokes, gliding the rubber on at one end and off at the other to avoid dragging. Leave the finish to harden for 48 hours before handling.

9

CARPENTRY PROJECTS

The previous chapters of this book provide an introduction to the raw material and the essential tools and techniques of woodworking. However, that information will go to waste if you do not put it into practice. All of the following projects were produced specifically for this book, in order to give you a flying start in the principles of design and construction. Whatever your level of expertise, there is sure to be something here to catch the eye and engage the imagination, which is all you need to get started. You can follow the plans and instructions in detail or simply use them as an aid in designing your own version to a different size or style. The nature of woodworking is that it is a continual journey of discovery and experience, and no two creations are ever the same. With each successful project, your confidence will grow, your technical skills will increase and, no doubt, you will obtain more satisfaction from the results.

WINE RACK

Materials

- 760 x 600mm (30 x 24in) of 12mm (½in) birch plywood

THIS SIMPLE PROJECT WILL PROVIDE practice in handling a few basic tools and learning one of the most important skills in woodwork – cutting straight and accurately to form simple halving (half) joints. It is made from birch-faced plywood, which can be attractive in its own right, and is finished with clear lacquer to seal it.

Construction

There are six components to this project, and only two different panel sizes. The only critical dimension is the width of each compartment, which must suit your chosen wine bottle – 90mm (3½in) is a typical size.

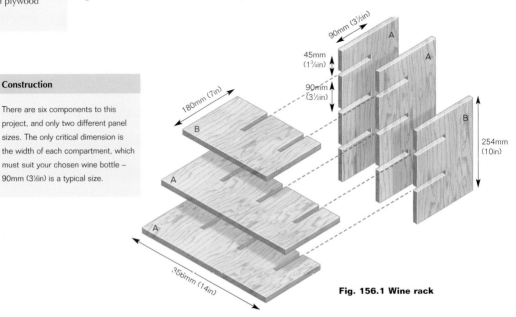

Fig. 156.1 Wine rack

1 Cut the panels to size (see diagram above) with a panel (crosscut) saw or jigsaw (saber saw), making sure that all are square. When cutting across the end grain of plywood, you will obtain a much neater finish by scoring along the cut line with a knife to prevent the saw from splintering the outer layer of ply.

2 Firmly clamp each panel upright in a vice and trim down to the scored lines with a smoothing plane to produce neat, square edges all round. Finish off with medium sandpaper wrapped around a sanding block, using long, smooth strokes to keep the edges straight and square.

3 Set out the lines for each slot as shown, using the dimensions given in the diagram. Draw along each side of a small offcut (scrap) of plywood to establish the correct slot width without measuring each time. Use the first panel as a template for marking out the others.

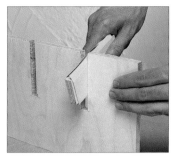

4 Clamp each panel vertically and cut downward carefully, keeping to the waste side of each line. A sharp panel saw will be more controllable than a power saw for making accurate cuts of this kind.

5 Use a mallet and a 12mm (½in) chisel to tap down at the ends of the slots. Each slot should extend to half the width of the panel so that the two halves of the joint slide together and leave the edges of the panels flush.

6 Wrap a strip of medium-grade sandpaper around a suitable offcut of wood and clean up the slots where necessary. The width of each slot must provide a good sliding fit for the 12mm (½in) plywood.

7 You will find it much easier to apply a finish to the components before assembling them. Clean up the panels with medium and fine sandpaper, then brush on a thin coat of varnish or clear sealer.

8 Slot the components together to join the rack. A dab of PVA wood glue may be needed on the inside of each joint, but if you have finished the slots well, it should not be necessary.

CD RACK

THE IDEA FOR THIS COMPACT DISC storage system came about because a piece of cherry wood, with distinctive figure in the grain, and a short offcut (scrap) of waney-edged yew with an interesting shape was leftover in the workshop. You can use any type of wood, of course, possibly something left over from another job. With a little imagination, you can turn short lengths of wood into all manner of items.

Materials

- 760mm (30in) of 125 x 25mm (5 x 1in) hardwood for the rack
- 760mm (30in) of 25 x 12mm (1 x ½in) hardwood for the sides
- 280mm (11in) of 150 x 19mm (6 x ¾in) hardwood for the base
- PVA wood glue
- Brass panel pins (brads)

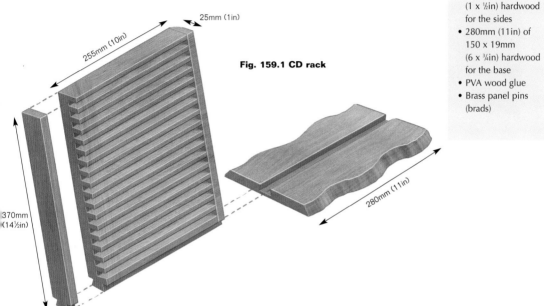

Fig. 159.1 CD rack

Construction

The design is simplicity itself – it uses the cantilever principle to support the weight of the CDs. A width of 255mm (10in) will allow two columns to be stacked side by side. The rack can be any height you like, provided the base is wide enough to make it stable. As a guide, ensure that the top of the rack, inclined at 10 degrees, is vertically above the back edge of the base. The diagram shows how to set out the ingenious dovetailed housing joint that holds the unit together.

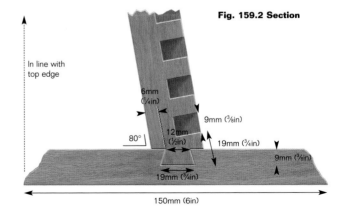

Fig. 159.2 Section

1 Cut the 125 x 25mm (5 x 1in) hardwood into two pieces 370mm (14½in) long for the main portion of the rack. Plane the edges square, glue and clamp them together. Simple butt joints are sufficient. To make sure that the board remains absolutely flat, clamp a stout batten over the top of the assembly before finally tightening the sash clamps.

2 Use a 9mm (⅜in) diameter router bit (to match the thickness of a CD cover) to rout a slot 19mm (¾in) up from the bottom edge, using the router fence as a guide. Then make a routing jig to do the rest by screwing a small strip of 9mm (⅜in) wide hardwood to the router base, exactly 9mm (⅜in) from the cutter's edge.

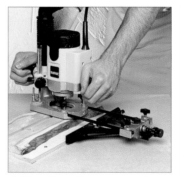

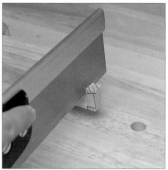

3 It is a simple matter to run the hardwood strip along each slot to position the next groove correctly. Continue in this way to the end of the board. Make sure the work is firmly clamped to the bench when doing this, or use a bench stop.

4 Use a dovetail cutter to rout the housing groove in the base. To deal with a waney edge, pin a straight-edged piece of plywood to the underside and run the router fence along it. Screw it down to the work surface so that it cannot move.

5 Cut the tails on the two side pieces with a fine dovetail saw. Use a bevel gauge to set the shoulders at an angle of 10 degrees, as shown in figure 159.2. Then make a small template to mark the shape of the tails to suit the profile of the dovetail groove.

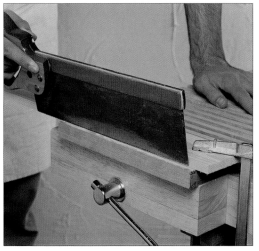

6 Use the same template to mark out the bottom edge of the main upright. Scribe the shoulders along its length with a marking gauge, and clamp a straightedge along the shoulder line to guide the tenon saw. Keep the saw blade perfectly level to ensure the shoulders are straight and parallel.

7 To form the tail on the upright, plane the required angle on a scrap piece of wood to make an accurate guide for a small shoulder plane. Use a paring chisel to remove the waste from the corners. The angles are different on each face because of the sloping profile, and should match those on the two side pieces.

8 Plane the bottom edge of the tail to the required angle to complete the joint, paring it down until the tail has a good sliding fit in the housing. Before fitting the side pieces, you should clean up each groove with a small sanding block.

9 Pin and glue the side pieces to the upright, using small brass panel pins (brads). Align the dovetails accurately and position the pins to avoid the slots. Apply glue to the dovetailed housing in the base and slide the rack into place. When the glue is dry, apply the desired finish.

Magazine Rack

This folding rack takes little time to construct and uses a few basic techniques. There are no joints to make, and no expensive tools are required; all you need are the basics of accurate marking out, cutting and fitting together. The materials are easy to obtain and are ready to use without further preparation. The interlocking design allows the rack to be opened up or folded flat and stowed away, with no need for clips or catches.

Materials

- 4.2m (14ft) of 75 x 12mm (3 x ½in) planed softwood for the slats
- 2.7m (9ft) of 50 x 25mm (2 x 1in) planed softwood for the legs
- 6mm (¼in) MDF (medium-density fiberboard) for the template
- 16 25mm (1in) brass wood screws
- 2 50mm (2in) brass wood screws
- Panel pin (brad)
- 2 65mm (2½in) coachbolts (carriage bolts), nuts and washers
- Thin cord

Fig. 163.1 Magazine rack

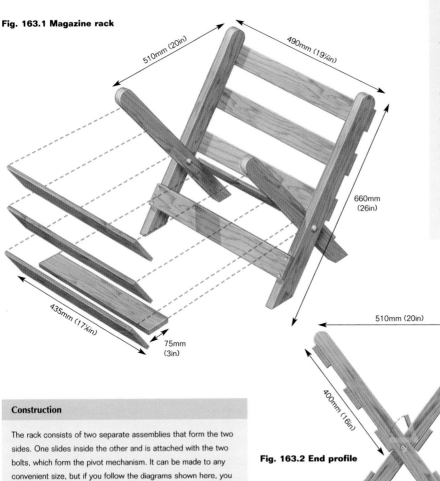

510mm (20in)

490mm (19¼in)

660mm (26in)

435mm (17⅛in)

75mm (3in)

Construction

The rack consists of two separate assemblies that form the two sides. One slides inside the other and is attached with the two bolts, which form the pivot mechanism. It can be made to any convenient size, but if you follow the diagrams shown here, you will not have to calculate the dimensions and angles required for the legs. Draw it out full size on a sheet of plywood or MDF to create a template for marking out.

Fig. 163.2 End profile

510mm (20in)

400mm (16in)

520mm (20½in)

190mm (7½in)

52.5°

345mm (13½in)

1 Cut the legs and the slats to their overall length. The slats for the inner frame are 55mm (2⅛in) shorter than those used for the outer frame, allowing them to easily slide within the latter. Cut a rounded profile at the top of each leg if desired, using the first as a pattern for the others so that they will be uniform.

2 Lay each pair of legs in turn over the template you have drawn out on a sheet of MDF (medium-density fiberboard) and mark the positions of the slats and pivot point. Support the upper leg with a small offcut (scrap) of wood to keep it level. Drill a small pilot hole through the pivot point of each leg at this stage.

3 Assemble the inner frame. Insert one screw at each end of the top slat, then use a try square to adjust the assembly before you proceed. It is essential that the frames are absolutely square. Make sure the ends of the slats do not protrude over the sides of the frame.

4 Add the third slat, then turn the frame over to attach the bottom slat. The final assembly will be easier if you omit the second slat at this stage; it can be added when the rack is bolted together. Three slats are sufficient at this stage to keep the assembly square.

5 Use the inner frame as a building jig for the outer frame. Position the components carefully, making sure that the pivot holes are in line. Insert a small panel pin (brad) to keep the legs aligned in the correct position as you work. Note how the angled ends of the legs face in opposite directions.

6 Use two small offcuts of 12mm (½in) wood at each side to support the outer legs at the correct level. Screw the top and third slats in place, checking they are square as before. All four legs should be parallel to allow the assembly to move freely.

7 Turn the assembly over to fit the bottom slat. At this stage, the two frames should enclose each other, but they can still be slid apart if required. Now is a good time to clean up any rough edges with medium-grade sandpaper before proceeding. You could also apply a coat of clear sealer or varnish.

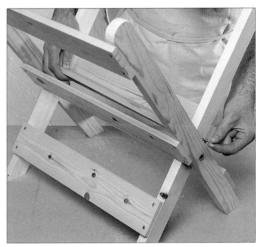

8 Drill through the legs for the coachbolts (carriage bolts), using the pilot holes to guide the drill bit. Fit a coachbolt to each side, inserting a large washer between the moving parts to reduce the amount of friction. Fit the nuts on the inside but do not over-tighten them or you will distort the framework. Note how the bottom slat on the outer frame will act as a stop to hold the rack in the open position.

9 Insert the bottom piece, which acts as a floor for the rack. Cut it to fit between the legs of the inner frame and attach with two long brass screws. It should pivot easily, allowing the rack to be folded flat for storage. Put in the remaining two slats. Add a couple of lengths of thin cord between the bottom slats as a final touch to secure the legs in their open position.

BOOKSHELF

MANUFACTURED BOARDS WITH VENEERED FACES, sometimes called decorative boards, can make quick work of any project. However, the exposed edges of veneered plywood and MDF (medium-density fiberboard), are vulnerable to damage and not at all attractive. To overcome this drawback, you can buy ready-made solid wood trim to match most common types of veneer, or you can make your own if you have the right tools. This bookshelf was made from boards veneered with American white oak, edged with darker oak trim to provide a contrast.

Materials

- 760 x 610mm (30 x 24in) of 12mm (½in) veneered plywood or MDF (medium-density fiberboard)
- 2.7m (9ft) of 19mm (¾in) angled moulding for edge trim
- PVA wood glue
- Panel pins (brads)

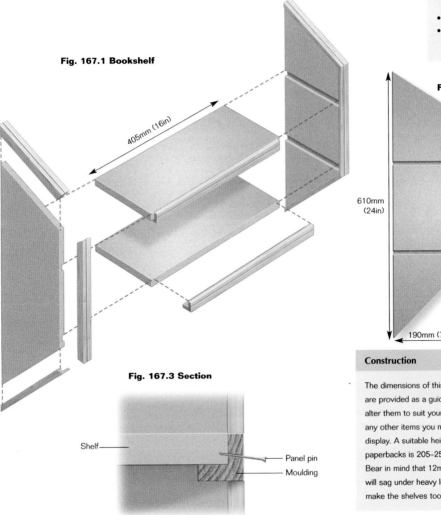

Fig. 167.1 Bookshelf

405mm (16in)

Fig. 167.2 Side

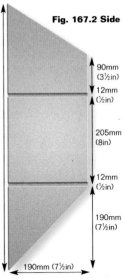

610mm (24in)

90mm (3½in)
12mm (½in)

205mm (8in)

12mm (½in)

190mm (7½in)

190mm (7½in)

Fig. 167.3 Section

Shelf

Panel pin

Moulding

Construction

The dimensions of this small shelf unit are provided as a guide only. You can alter them to suit your own books or any other items you may wish to display. A suitable height for most paperbacks is 205–255mm (8–10in). Bear in mind that 12mm (½in) boards will sag under heavy loads if you make the shelves too wide.

1 Set out the profile on one end of the unit, cut it out and use it as a pattern for the other end to ensure that they are a perfect match. Scribe the angled cuts across the grain with a sharp knife to avoid tearing the grain of the thin veneers. Cut just outside the line with a jigsaw (saber saw), if you have one, or sharp panel (crosscut) saw.

2 Clamp the angled ends in a vice so that they are horizontal, then plane them down to the scribed lines with a block plane. Work with the grain angled away from you to avoid damaging the veneer. The block plane, with a finely set, sharp blade, is the ideal tool for working this material.

3 Form the housings for the shelves with a router, running it along a straightedge pinned to the inner face. A good way to ensure accuracy is to clamp the two ends together tightly and cut the grooves in one operation. Pin a strip of scrap wood to the board edge to prevent breakout at the end of the groove.

4 The boards can vary in thickness depending on the type of veneer. It is not always possible to match the size of board exactly to the diameter of the router cutter. If necessary, plane small rebates (rabbets) on the underside of each shelf until it fits the grooves perfectly. This also improves the strength of the glued joint.

5 Apply glue to the housings and slot the unit together. It is good practice to use the glue sparingly. Any excess will have to be removed completely to prevent discoloration of the veneer at the finishing stage. Wipe off with a slightly damp cloth, and avoid rubbing glue into the grain.

6 Sash clamps are ideal for holding the assembly steady while pinning the shelves in place. Small panel pins (brads) are sufficient for a small unit such as this. Check that all corners are square and leave to set overnight. Note the small scraps of wood used to protect the veneer.

7 Cut two lengths of angled moulding to trim the front edges of the shelves. The moulding shown has a small shadow line, or "quirk", running along its length. This is designed to help conceal the heads of the panel pins when punched down with a nail set (see figure 167.3).

8 The same moulding is used to trim the end panels. Mitre the ends at the corners with a small tenon saw or adjustable mitre saw. To determine the correct angle for the mitred corners, place a short section of moulding in position and use it to mark pencil lines on the end panel, parallel to the front edges. Draw a line from the corner to the point of intersection to bisect the angle exactly. Then use this as a guide for setting an adjustable bevel gauge.

9 Apply PVA wood glue to the front edges of the end panels and pin the mouldings in place. Notice how the minimum of glue has been used. This is to prevent any excess from being squeezed on to the veneer surface when the pins are punched in with the nail set (punch). When the glue has dried, apply coloured stopping to each pinhole with a small spatula or modelling tool before sanding smooth all over, ready for finishing.

Bar Stool

THREE DISCS OF WOOD and three lengths of round-section dowel are all it takes to make this kitchen or bar stool. The simplicity of construction is reflected in the uncluttered design, reminiscent of Shaker style. Southern yellow pine, which has a distinctive grain figure and a deep colour to the annual rings, has been used here. It has the advantage of being commonly available in wider boards, allowing each round section to be made in one piece.

Materials

- 1m (39in) of 305 x 25mm (12 x 1in) softwood for the seat and stretcher
- 2.45m (8ft) of 32mm (1¼in) diameter softwood dowel
- 6mm (¼in) plywood or MDF (medium-density fiberboard) for template
- PVA wood glue
- 3 6mm (¼in) beech dowels
- Panel pins (brads)

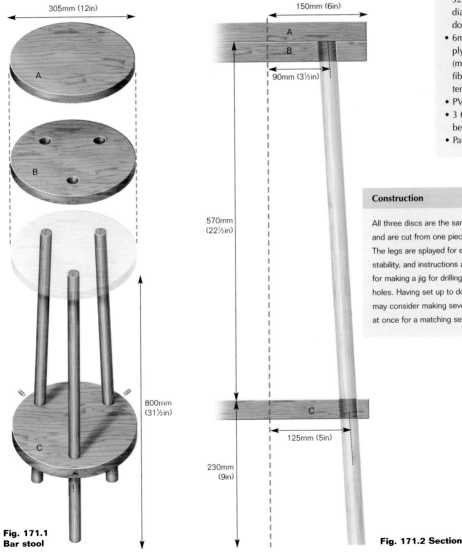

305mm (12in)

A

B

C

800mm (31½in)

Fig. 171.1
Bar stool

150mm (6in)

A

B

90mm (3½in)

570mm (22½in)

C

125mm (5in)

230mm (9in)

Fig. 171.2 Section

Construction

All three discs are the same diameter and are cut from one piece of board. The legs are splayed for extra stability, and instructions are given for making a jig for drilling the angled holes. Having set up to do this, you may consider making several stools at once for a matching set.

Fig. 172.1 Making a drilling jig

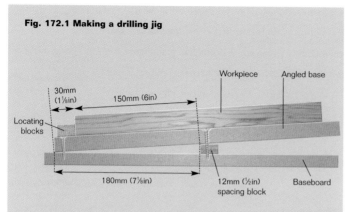

Workpiece   Angled base

30mm (1⅛in)   150mm (6in)

Locating blocks

180mm (7⅛in)   12mm (½in) spacing block   Baseboard

To drill the angled holes in the discs, make a drilling jig. First, cut a base board to fit under the drill stand, then screw a second board to it at an angle. You don't need to calculate the angle; simply screw a 12mm (½in) thick spacing block exactly 180mm (7⅛in) in from the front edge of the angled base. Provided you line up the centre of each disc with the centre of the jig, the holes will be set at the correct angle. Pin a couple of locating blocks to the angled base to position the disc accurately.

1 Make a 305mm (12in) diameter template from 6mm (¼in) MDF (medium-density fiberboard) and draw three radial lines at 120 degree intervals to divide it into equal segments. With a pair of compasses, mark the centres of the leg positions for the top and bottom discs, and drill a small pilot hole at each point. See figure 171.2 for the dimensions required.

2 Cut three discs from the board with a jigsaw (saber saw), making them oversize by about 6mm (¼in). Mark the discs A, B and C, as in the diagram. Pin the template to each piece in turn and use a template cutter fitted to the router to trim the edges to the finished size. Before removing the template from B and C, use a punch to mark the centres of the holes for the legs.

3 Fit a hole saw of the correct diameter in the drill stand and slide the drilling jig into place. Insert disc C in the jig and adjust it until the drill bit is centred exactly over one of the hole positions. Clamp the jig so that it cannot move and drill the hole. Repeat for the other two holes.

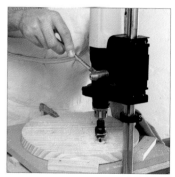

4 Drill holes in disc B in the same way – you will have to move the jig further toward the drill stand to allow for the holes being nearer the centre of the disc, but the angle remains the same.

5 Cut the legs to length and make a small wedge-shaped slot, 19mm (¾in) deep, in the top of each. Note the pencil line that identifies the outside of each leg to orient it correctly. This ensures that the angles at the bottom of the legs sit flat on the floor and keep the stool level.

6 Place disc B upside down on the workbench. Insert the legs into disc C and slide it to its position 230mm (9in) from the ends. Before gluing, locate the tops of the legs into disc B to hold them at the correct angle. Apply glue to the holes in disc C and tap it into place, making sure that it is level. Drill a 6mm (¼in) hole into each leg and glue in a small beech dowel to secure the disc.

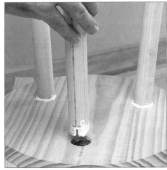

7 Leave the lower part of the assembly for the glue to dry before proceeding. When it is quite firm, carefully pull the legs away from the top disc one at a time, apply glue and tap them back into place. Keep the pencil line on each facing outward to prevent the legs from twisting out of position.

8 Turn the stool over and insert three small wedges, made from offcuts (scraps) of softwood, into the tops of the legs to lock them in place, as shown. Apply a generous amount of glue and tap the wedges firmly home. Allow the glue to dry, then plane flush with a block plane, set for a fine cut.

9 Finally, glue disc A to the top of the stool to complete the job. Two or three panel pins (brads) will prevent it from sliding around as the clamps are tightened. Note how the pattern of the growth rings has been reversed. This not only creates an attractive visual effect, but also serves to stabilize the two pieces by balancing any tendency to shrink or expand.

OCCASIONAL TABLE

No matter how fashions change, a low, neat table always makes a useful addition to the living space, and this one is a classic of its kind. With its well-proportioned, delicate frame supporting the bold, oval top, it combines clean, contemporary looks with all the best in traditional woodworking. White ash was used to make this example, and it was clear finished to bring out the honey colour of the wood.

Fig. 175.1 Occasional table

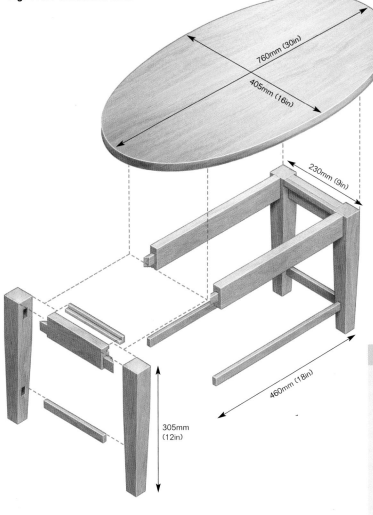

760mm (30in)

405mm (16in)

230mm (9in)

460mm (18in)

305mm (12in)

Materials

- 1.6m (63in) of 205 x 25mm (8 x 1in) hardwood for the top
- 1.25m (48in) of 38 x 38mm (1½ x 1½in) hardwood for the legs
- 1.4m (55in) of 50 x 19mm (2 x ¾in) hardwood for the top rails
- 1.4m (55in) of 25 x 12mm (1 x ½in) hardwood for the lower rails
- 6mm (¼in) MDF (medium-density fiberboard) for the template
- PVA wood glue
- Biscuits for jointing
- 38mm (1½in) brass wood screws
- Panel pins (brads)

Construction

The frame for this table provides a good exercise in classic carpentry, with fine detail to the tenon joints and a slight taper to the legs to add visual balance. The shape of the top was chosen, in part, to make the best of the attractive figure of the wood grain. Setting out the oval is simple with a neat geometrical device – a loop of string and two panel pins.

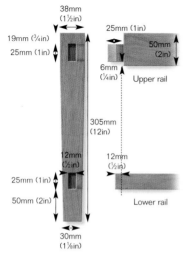

Fig. 176.1 Leg detail

38mm (1½in)
25mm (1in)
19mm (¾in)
25mm (1in)
50mm (2in)
6mm (¼in)
Upper rail
305mm (12in)
12mm (½in)
12mm (½in)
25mm (1in)
50mm (2in)
Lower rail
30mm (1⅛in)

1 The size of the top determines the proportions of the frame below, so start by setting out an oval shape to suit your pieces of wood. Cut a template panel so that it is slightly larger than the overall size of the top, and insert two panel pins (brads) on the centre line as shown. A loop of string placed over the pins will allow a pencil to describe a perfect ellipse. Practice with the length of string until you achieve a profile that looks right.

2 Cut two top boards to a suitable length, plane their edges square and insert biscuits in the edges prior to gluing them together. Position the biscuits in such a way that they will not be exposed when cutting the top to its final shape. Clamp the boards with sash clamps and leave to set while you make the frame.

3 Set out the mortises for the legs by following the dimensions in the diagram. The taper begins 50mm (2in) below the top of the leg so that the shoulders of the upper rails can be cut square. Note that the mortise for each lower rail is more of a socket, being the full size of the rail itself; no shoulders are required.

4 Pare the tenons on the upper rails with a wide bevelled chisel or shoulder plane. Accuracy is vital for this assembly to ensure that all mating parts make good contact for the adhesive. Even the small shoulders at the sides of the tenons play a part in keeping the frame square and rigid.

5 The tenons intersect inside the mortise at the top of each leg. Cut a mitre on the end of each tenon and check each corner in turn so that there is a snug fit. Mark up the rails and legs in their respective positions before moving on to fashion the tapers on the legs.

6 Scribe guidelines around the foot of each leg with a marking gauge. Use a straightedge to form the outline of the taper on two opposing faces and plane carefully down to the lines. Work from the top of each leg, with the grain, down toward the tapered ends.

7 On the faces you have just planed, mark the same taper profile for the remaining two sides and repeat the operation. Note the wedge in the vice that clamps the tapered leg in position. The tapered ends should be 30mm (1⅛in) square when you have finished.

8 The two short rails are grooved to receive the rebated (rabbeted) blocks that connect the frame to the top. Use a plough (bullnose) plane to form the 9 x 9mm (⅜ x ⅜in) housing, then fashion two fixing blocks from an offcut (scrap) of 19 x 19mm (¾ x ¾in) hardwood.

9 Assemble the frame, upside down, on a flat surface to ensure that it is square and level. Glue, clamp and leave to dry while you work on the table top. Cut out the oval shape of the template with a jigsaw (saber saw) and smooth the edges. Pin it to the underside of the top, and use a router with a template follower to transfer the shape.

10 Plane the table top flat, sand it smooth and, if desired, rout a profile around the edge. Drill and countersink the small fixing blocks for 38mm (1½in) brass wood screws and fix the frame to the top. There is no need to use glue – this type of attachment method allows the solid top to shrink or expand slightly without disturbing the frame assembly.

Storage Chest

This is a classic storage chest with traditional lines, which can be used as a linen chest in the bedroom, or perhaps as a window seat or toy chest. The clean design, with discreet brass fittings, makes it equally suitable for contemporary and period-style interiors. The chest was made from reclaimed pine floorboards, which have a deep orange colour that is rare in new-grown softwoods. A clear wax finish brings out the full character of the grain.

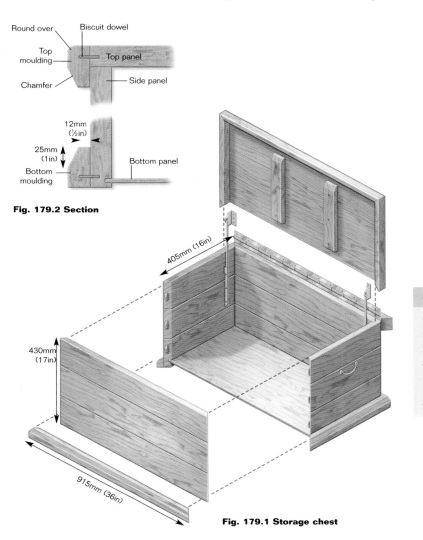

Fig. 179.2 Section

Round over
Biscuit dowel
Top moulding
Top panel
Chamfer
Side panel
12mm (½in)
25mm (1in)
Bottom moulding
Bottom panel

405mm (16in)
430mm (17in)
915mm (36in)

Fig. 179.1 Storage chest

Materials

- 11m (36ft) of 150 x 25mm (6 x 1in) softwood
- 6.7m (22ft) of 50 x 25mm (2 x 1in) softwood
- 915 x 380mm (36 x 15in) of 6mm (¼in) MDF (medium-density fiberboard)
- 915mm (36in) brass piano hinge
- PVA wood glue
- Biscuits for jointing
- 25mm (1in) panel pins (brads)
- 38mm (1½in) countersunk wood screws
- 2 brass lid stays
- 2 brass drop handles

Construction

This design relies on the gluing together of pine boards to make wide panels, the edges being butt jointed and reinforced with biscuits to align them. You will find a mitre saw invaluable for cutting all the joints for the sides and ends.

1 Cut all the boards roughly to length and plane the long edges square for butt joints. Align the boards with a try square and straightedge to set out mitre cuts at each end. Make pencil marks at about 300mm (11¾in) intervals for the biscuits.

2 You may find that the mitre saw is not quite accurate enough to produce a perfect joint every time. Make a mitred shooting board, as shown, so that you can square the ends of each piece with a block plane, set for a fine cut.

3 Rout a 6mm (¼in) groove in the bottom board of each panel to receive the base panel. The easiest way to clean up the groove is with a sheet of medium-grade sandpaper wrapped around a thin strip of plywood.

4 Insert biscuits and glue up each panel in turn. The biscuits will help keep the faces of the boards flush and level, as well as adding strength to the edge joint. Make sure the mitred ends are aligned perfectly, tidying them up with a block plane if necessary.

5 Use a biscuit jointer, set at 45 degrees, to cut slots in the mitred faces at the corners. Insert the biscuits and glue the box together with PVA wood glue. Slide the bottom panel into place before putting on the last side of the box. Clamp and leave to dry.

6 Cut the material roughly to length for the top and bottom mouldings, then plane a chamfer on one face of each piece. Figure 179.2 shows the dimensions used for this chest, but you can vary them to suit your taste. Check the angle with a bevel gauge.

◀ 7 Mitre the ends of the bottom mouldings so that they fit the external dimensions of the base. Use more biscuits to hold them flush with the bottom edges. Lock each joint with 25mm (1in) panel pins (brads).

▶ 8 Glue and clamp three boards for the lid. To make it stay flat, alternate the orientation of each board's growth rings. Clamp from above and below to equalize the pressure on the joints.

9 Apply a rounded edge to the top mouldings, then mitre the corners and fit to the front and sides of the lid. Omit the back edge at this stage.

10 Sand down the top of the lid and smooth the edges. The back edge is visible, showing how the ends of the mouldings are mitred.

11 Before fitting the lid, make up two battens to fit on the underside. These stiffen the top, keep it flat, and allow the chest to be used as a seat.

12 Chamfer the edges of each batten with a plane, and make matching cuts at the ends, using a dovetail or tenon saw. Glue and screw the battens to the inside of the lid. Note that they should be located at least 32mm (1¼in) in from the back edge.

13 The final length of top moulding is fitted to the chest, not to the lid. Use a rebate (rabbet) plane to cut a shallow rebate for the brass piano hinge. It must be deep enough to accommodate the thickness of both leaves of the hinge – no more than 1.5mm (⅟₁₆in).

14 Mitre the ends of the moulding to fit the back of the lid, and screw it to the chest so that it projects above the top edge to match the thickness of the lid. Double check that the hinge rebate lies parallel to the edge.

◀ 15 Screw the piano hinge along the back edge of the lid, using small countersunk screws, then put the lid in place, slotting the lower hinge leaf into the rebate. Attach it with a couple of screws at each end first, then check for smooth opening and closing before adding the rest.

▶ 16 Attach the brass stays. Adjust the sliding arm of each stay so that the lid is held in a position just beyond the vertical to prevent straining the hinge. Finally, attach the drop handles to each end of the chest.

THREE-LEGGED CHAIR

THIS THREE-LEGGED CHAIR is made in a traditional Windsor fashion, the seat acting as a mounting structure for the two front legs, which are wedged and glued. The back leg is attached by a tenon so it can extend above the seat to form the back. This form of chair was common in the medieval period, although all the elements would have been turned and the seat would have been a triangle.

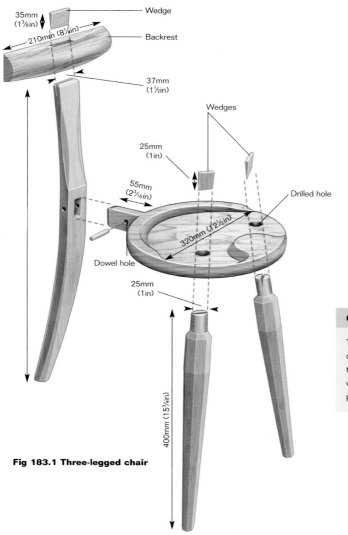

Fig 183.1 Three-legged chair

Materials

- 700mm (27½in) of 100 x 40mm (4 x 1½in) beech for the back leg
- 850mm (33½in) of 40 x 40mm (1½ x 1½in) beech for the front legs
- 210mm (8¼in) of 40 x 40mm (1½ x 1½in) beech for the back rest
- 2 330mm (13in) lengths of 135 x 40mm (5¼ x 1½in) beech for the seat
- 390mm (15¼in) of 60 x 40mm (2¼ x 1½in) beech for the seat
- Plywood for the template
- PVA wood glue
- Biscuits for jointing
- Small dowel

Construction

This chair relies on one of the most common joints, the mortise and tenon. Two of the joints are round and wedged but work on the same principle as the rectangular variety.

1 The seat is formed from three pieces of wood. Plane a face side and edge on each of these boards, prior to cutting them to length. Square edges are essential for jointing the boards if the seat is to be flat.

2 Cut the prepared boards to size and form a tenon on the end of the centre section, which will fit into the mortise in the back leg. The central square strip in the seat makes cutting this joint easier.

3 Join the boards together with PVA wood glue and biscuits, using sash clamps to hold them while the glue sets. Leave to set overnight as the joint is stronger if fully cured before removing the clamps.

4 Make a plywood template to match the profile of the back leg, then mark and cut out the leg from a planed piece of wood.

5 Cut out the seat shape with a jig saw and drill the angled holes for the front legs. Either make a drilling jig, or cut the angle on a scrap piece of wood and stand this next to each hole position so that the drill can be held at the same angle, as shown here.

6 Plane the front leg blank into a hexagonal section before cutting it in half to form the two legs. Allow enough timber for the saw cuts.

7 Plane a taper on each front leg, as shown in the diagram, working from opposing sides to form a square at the base.

8 Use a V-block to hold the leg firmly in place while you remove the corners to complete the tapered hexagonal section.

9 Make an angled cut with a tenon saw in the top of the leg to match the angle of the hole drilled in the seat. Using a chisel, form a 25mm (1in) round peg to fit the hole. Cut the mortise in the back leg to fit the seat tenon.

10 Use a spokeshave to form the chamfers on the back leg. Shape the leg in the same way as the front legs to create a tapering hexagonal section, taking care to leave the cheeks of the mortise square.

11 Having already cut the mortise in the backrest for the back leg, plane the backrest to shape, rounding off the front face. Create a taper on the back of the rest, as shown, using a block plane.

12 Using a shallow gouge, start carving out a concave shape in the seat blank.

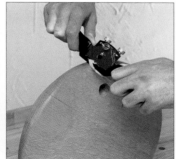

13 Continue in this way until you are satisfied with the shape; be careful not to remove too much material around the points where the legs join. Round the edge of the seat with a spokeshave.

15 Make a saw cut into the peg at the top of each front leg, apply glue and insert the peg into its hole in the seat. Secure the leg by driving a small wooden wedge into the cut in the peg. Secure the backrest to the top of the back leg in the same way. Remove any excess material when the glue has dried.

14 Drill a small dowel hole through the back leg mortise, insert the seat tenon and mark the position of the hole on it. Remove the tenon and drill the hole slightly off-centre, toward the seat. Attach the leg using a small dowel. When the dowel is driven home, it will pull the joint together.

DISPLAY CASE

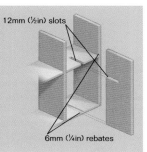

A COLLECTION OF INTERESTING OR PRECIOUS ARTEFACTS can be seen to best advantage if displayed in a purpose-made cabinet. Whatever you may want to show off, you can keep everything safe behind the sleek glass doors of this custom-built case. It is a simple pine box with a separate insert of pigeon-hole compartments, which can be removed for easy cleaning.

Materials

- 3.8m (12ft 6in) of 205 x 25mm (8 x 1in) softwood
- 1m (39in) of 38 x 38mm (1½ x 1½in) softwood for the corner blocks
- 1,050 x 775mm (41 x 30½in) of 6mm (¼in) MDF (medium-density fiberboard) for the back panel
- 1.65 x 1.25m (65 x 48in) of 12mm (½in) MDF for the inserts
- Glass doors cut to size
- Glass door hinges and magnetic catches
- PVA wood glue
- Biscuits for jointing
- 50mm (2in) countersunk wood screws
- Panel pins (brads)

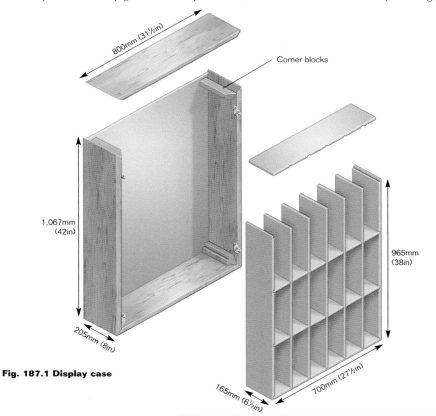

Corner blocks

800mm (31½in)

1,067mm (42in)

205mm (8in)

965mm (38in)

165mm (6½in)

700mm (27½in)

Fig. 187.1 Display case

Construction

This cabinet can be made to any size. This one was based around 18 compartments, each measuring 300 x 100mm (11¾ x 4in). Make a scale drawing of the ideal arrangement of compartments and calculate the external size of the box from this. This design features a 25mm (1in) gap between the insert and the outer box.

Fig. 187.2 Making the insert

The shelf insert is made from MDF and then painted to provide a contrast with the natural wood finish of the cabinet. The sides, top and bottom of the insert are rebated (rabbeted) 6mm (¼in) deep to receive the inner dividers, which are slotted to interlock and simplify assembly. The top and bottom are also rebated into the sides, making all the horizontal components the same length.

12mm (½in) slots

6mm (¼in) rebates

Fig. 188.1 Ordering the doors

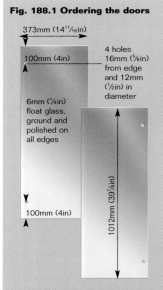

373mm (14¹¹/₁₆in)

100mm (4in)

4 holes 16mm (⅝in) from edge and 12mm (½in) in diameter

6mm (¼in) float glass, ground and polished on all edges

100mm (4in)

1012mm (39⅞in)

Measure the internal dimensions of the box and calculate the size of glass required for the doors. Subtract 1.5mm (¹/₁₆in) all round for clearance and a similar amount where the doors meet in the centre. The hinges used required small holes to be drilled in the glass – definitely a job for a specialist. Take a sketch to your glazier when you order the doors.

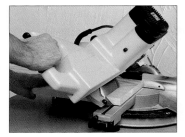

1 Cut the four sides to length, using a power crosscut saw to form the mitres in the softwood. This particular saw has sliding bars on the body that enables it to be extended in order to cut wide boards.

3 The corner joints are aligned using biscuits. This biscuit jointer has an adjustable front fence that makes it very easy to set the required angle, a feature to look for when buying.

2 A mitred shooting board is used to tidy up the face of each joint to ensure perfectly square corners. The end of the shooting board must be planed to a 45 degree angle to guide the sole plate of the block plane.

4 Use a router or rebate (rabbet) plane to cut a 6mm (¼in) deep by 12mm (½in) wide rebate along the back edges of the box to receive the recessed back panel.

5 Depending on the type of hinge being used, you may need to chisel a small recess for each hinge mounting plate. Glass door hinges are specialized items, so be sure to obtain them before you start the job.

6 Prepare four corner blocks from a length of 38 x 38mm (1½ x 1½in) batten. Cut a 12 x 12mm (½ x ½in) rebate along one edge and cut four pieces with angled ends. The overall length of each block is 150mm (6in).

7 Apply glue to the mitred ends of the boards, insert the biscuits and clamp the box together, face down on the bench. Use small offcuts (scraps) of rebated corner block to protect the corners under the clamp heads.

8 Check that the box is square, then lay the MDF (medium-density fiberboard) back panel into its rebate. Attach it in place with panel pins (brads). The panel will help keep the box square when you turn it over.

9 Install the corner blocks to ensure the box is square – vital for a good fit for the glass doors. The bevel at the front of each block guides the insert into position, making the block less apparent when the cabinet is complete.

10 To make the insert, cut the MDF into strips, 165mm (6½in) wide, then cut them to their respective lengths. Mark out all the rebates and slots on all parts, clamping them in pairs so that they match perfectly.

11 Set the depth stop of the router to cut 6mm (¼in) deep rebates and grooves in the outer panels. Use a fence when making the edge cuts. Clamp a straightedge to the work when forming the remaining housing joints.

12 Create the slots in the dividers by routing halfway across the width of the piece. You should square the end of each slot with a 12mm (½in) bevelled chisel.

13 Assemble the box using glue and panel pins. Slide each divider into place – the construction will become quite rigid as each bit is added. Check that all is square, wipe off any excess glue with a damp cloth and leave to dry.

14 Before attaching the insert, add the hinges to match the hole positions in the glass doors. This type of hinge is best for glass doors and provides a positive fixing through glass.

15 The chrome-plated clips on the doors act as striker plates for the magnetic touch latch. This device springs the door open with a light touch, so no handles are needed.

16 Offer the insert into position to ensure that it is a good sliding fit before painting. Tap it all the way in. Remove and apply the finish of your choice before fitting the doors.

BEDSIDE CABINET

This small cabinet is made of American white oak veneer with a liming wax finish to produce a smart, contemporary look. Solid wood trim and edging are easily applied to match the oak-veneered door and panels. The distinctive grain pattern of the oak is enhanced by the pale colour, while the lustrous wax finish suits the soft, comfortable feel of the bedroom.

Materials

- 1.5 x 1m (60 x 39in) of 12mm (½in) veneered MDF (medium-density fiberboard)
- 305 x 305mm (12 x 12in) of 6mm (¼in) MDF for the template
- 1.5m (60in) of 19 x 19mm (¾ x ¾in) hardwood moulding for the top
- 4m (13ft) of 12 x 6mm (½ x ¼in) hardwood edge trim
- Pre-glued veneer edging strip
- 2 brass hinges
- Ball catch
- Door handle
- 4 brass shelf supports
- PVA wood glue
- 19mm (¾in) panel pins (brads)
- 12mm (½in) countersunk brass wood screws

Construction

The distinctive profile of the cabinet sides incorporates a simple curve that forms the legs at the bottom and a matching handle detail at the top. Pre-glued strips of veneer simplify the process of applying edging to the shape. The top of the cabinet is finished with an angled moulding, which forms a shallow recess on the top to prevent stray items from rolling off. With a router and a few basic hand tools, this project can be constructed with ease.

Fig. 191.2 Profile

70mm (2¾in) 70mm (2¾in)

100mm (4in)

Shelf position

150mm (6in)

610mm (24in)

305mm (12in)

12mm (½in) rebates (rabbets)

50mm (2in)

Radius 180mm (7in)

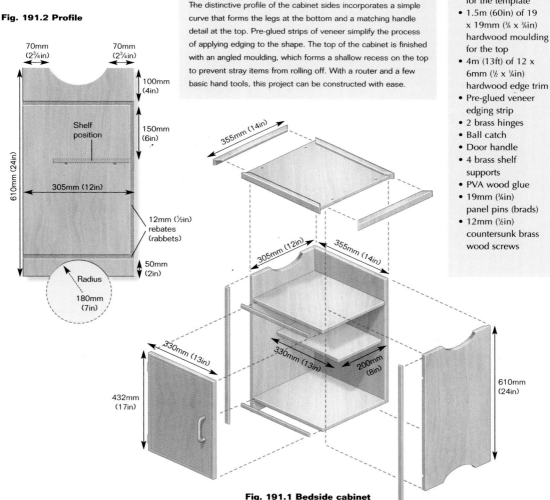

355mm (14in)

305mm (12in) 355mm (14in)

330mm (13in)

330mm (13in) 200mm (8in)

432mm (17in)

610mm (24in)

Fig. 191.1 Bedside cabinet

1 Cut the two side panels to their overall size, using a router with a 12mm (½in) cutter to rebate (rabbet) them for the shelves and back panel. Set out the rebates according to the dimensions given in figure 191.2. Cut out the back panel and rebate at top and bottom for the horizontal panels.

2 Make a template using 6mm (¼in) MDF to the radius shown. Line up the centre line of the template with the centre of the panel and transfer the shape to each end. Remove any waste with a jigsaw (saber saw), set to a slow speed to avoid forcing the blade through the work.

3 Smooth down the curves with a pad of sandpaper, taking care not to round over the edges of the cutout. The edging strip requires a perfectly flat surface when it is applied. Use a rotary sanding drum if you have one.

4 Using the tip of a warm iron, press the pre-glued strip into place so that it follows the curve. Keep the iron moving at all times to avoid overheating the delicate material. Leave for at least 15 minutes for the glue to set.

5 Trim off the excess veneer with a long, flat blade, pressed flat on the surface of the panel. This helps to prevent splinters from being picked up by the blade. Use a slow knifing action in long strokes to remove the small slivers of veneer.

6 Drill four small holes, 6mm (¼in) deep, for the support pegs of the removable shelf before assembling the cabinet. Note the masking tape on the drill bit, which acts as a depth gauge. Then sand down all the internal surfaces.

◀ 7 Assemble the cabinet face down on a flat worksurface. Apply glue to the rebates and slot in the horizontal panels. Push the back panel firmly into position to square the assembly.

▶ 8 Use 19mm (¾in) panel pins (brads) to attach the joints. Check the cabinet is square and that all front edges are flush. Wipe off excess glue with a damp cloth and allow to dry.

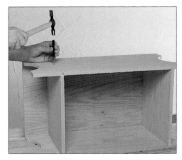

9 Cut short lengths of 6mm (¼in) hardwood edge trim to fit the front edges of the horizontal panels. Glue and pin them in place, taking care not to position the pins too close to the ends to prevent the material from splitting. A small pilot hole may be required for the pins.

10 Mitre four pieces of moulding to edge the top panel. Fit the front and back sections of moulding to the panel, gluing and pinning them as for the front trim. Centre the top on the cabinet and attach, using four narrow-gauge screws; they will be hidden by the remaining lengths of moulding.

11 Glue and pin the two side mouldings in position. Punch down all the heads, apply stopping to the pin holes and sand down ready for finishing. Take care when sanding veneered edges. Use a hand sanding block rather than a power sander.

12 Measure up and cut the door to size from a matching panel of veneered board, making it just over 6mm (¼in) smaller all round to allow for the edge trim. Mitre the ends of the trim pieces and glue them in place, then sand to a fine finish.

13 Flush hinges of the type shown require no recesses for the leaves. The barrel of the hinge pin lodges against the front edge of the side panel and automatically aligns the door. Fit with 12mm (½in) countersunk brass screws.

14 Screw the wooden handle of your choice to the door before fitting the catch. This allows you to control the closing action more easily and avoid straining the hinges. Now fit the brass ball catch just behind the handle.

► 15 A quick and easy way to align the tip of the ball catch is to apply a dab of ink to the base, and close the door on to it to make a small mark.

► 16 Make the removable shelf. Finish the front edge with a length of edging strip. Insert the shelf supports and offer the shelf into position. Coat the cabinet inside with clear lacquer.

Computer Cabinet

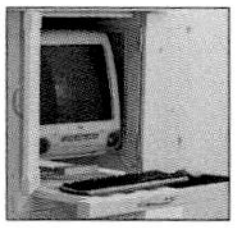

This cabinet is designed to hold the basic requirements for home computing – monitor, hard drive and printer. The plans can be adjusted as required to fit the size of your personal computer equipment. Readily available materials have been used throughout.

Fig. 195.1 Detail of pull-out shelf

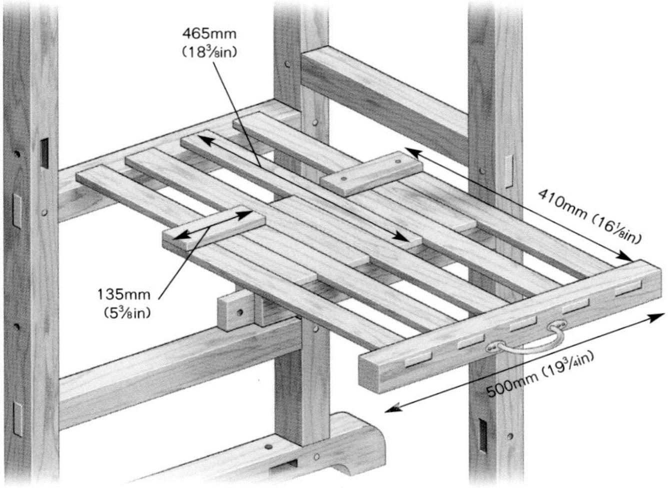

Construction

The cupboard is built using mortise and tenon joints throughout, secured with square pegs that pull the joints together with the aid of offset holes drilled in each mortise and tenon. These are achieved by drilling the mortise first, fitting the tenon and marking the position of the hole, then removing the tenon and drilling the hole slightly closer to its shoulder.

Materials

Unless specified otherwise, all wood is planed softwood

- 2 700mm (27½in) lengths of 70 x 45mm (2¾ x 1¾in) for the foot rails
- 4 1.06m (41¾in) lengths of 45 x 45mm (1¾ x 1¾in) for the uprights
- 8 510mm (20in) lengths of 45 x 45mm (1¾ x 1¾in) for the cross-rails A
- 3 510mm (20in) lengths of 45 x 20mm (1¾ x ¾in) for the cross-rails B
- 5 350mm (13¾in) lengths of 45 x 20mm (1¾ x ¾in) for the drawer rails C
- 4 465mm (18⅜in) lengths of 45 x 20mm (1¾ x ¾in) for the drawer members
- 2 510mm (20in) lengths of 45 x 20mm (1¾ x ¾in) for the shelf supports
- 510mm (20in) of 45 x 45mm (1¾ x 1¾in) for the drawer front
- 8 410mm (16⅛in) lengths of 19 x 19mm (¾ x ¾in) for side board supports
- 4 380mm (15in) lengths of 19 x 19mm (¾ x ¾in) for side board supports
- 2 135mm (5⅜in) lengths of 19 x 19mm (¾ x ¾in) for drawer connectors
- 225mm (8⅞in) of 19 x 19mm (¾ x ¾in) for drawer connector
- 4 410mm (16⅛in) lengths of 45 x 19mm (1¾ x ¾in) for shelf ends
- 4 205mm (8in) lengths of 45 x 19mm (1¾ x ¾in) for door ends
- 2 600mm (23½in) lengths of 90 x 19mm (3½ x ¾in) for top ends
- 3.2m (10ft 6in) of 10 x 10mm (⅜ x ⅜in) for pegs
- 22m (72ft) of 90 x 15mm (3½ x ⅝in) tongued-and-grooved cladding boards for cladding sides, top, doors and shelves
- PVA wood glue
- Galvanized fittings
- Castors
- 16 40mm (1½in) screws
- Panel pins (brads)

Fig. 196.1 Computer cabinet

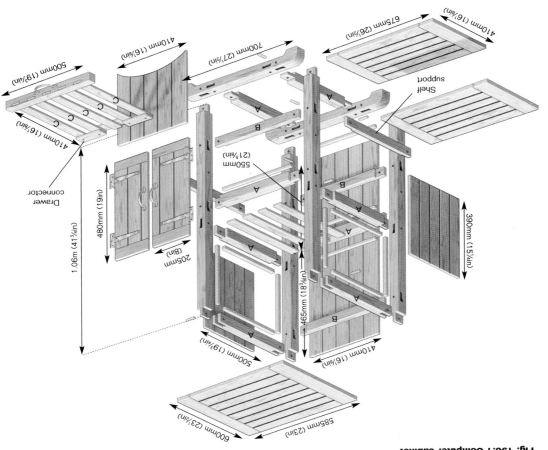

▶ **1** Cut the softwood sections to length as required for the frame, and mark out all mortise and tenon joints.

▶ **2** Start by cutting the profile of the bottom rails with a jigsaw (saber saw) and planing chamfers on all edges to finish off. Cut all the mortise and tenon joints.

500mm (19¾in)

410mm (16⅛in)

700mm (27½in)

675mm (26½in)

410mm (16⅛in)

Shelf support

410mm (16⅛in)

Drawer connector

480mm (19in)

550mm (21⅝in)

390mm (15¼in)

1.06m (41¾in)

205mm (8in)

465mm (18⅜in)

500mm (19¾in)

410mm (16⅛in)

600mm (23½in)

585mm (23in)

3 Assemble the base frame, pulling the joints together by driving square pegs into round holes drilled through the cheeks and blades of the mortise and tenon joints. Clean off any excess glue.

4 Drill peg holes in the uprights, making sure you keep the drill at 90 degrees to the workpiece and have a piece of waste wood underneath to drill into.

5 Assemble the front and rear frames of the cabinet by gluing and pegging the joints. Wipe away excess glue with a damp cloth before it dries. Check the frames for squareness by measuring the diagonals.

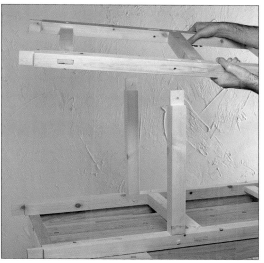

6 Fit the side rails to the rear frame. Make sure you label the rails to get them in the correct order, as three of the rails are slimmer so that they allow the cladding to sit on top of them.

7 Join the front to the back. Lay the assembled frame with side rails on a bench and then joint the assembled front to the back. Check the frame for squareness by standing it on a flat surface and check the angles with a try square.

8 Attach the base frame and then attach it to the main frame. Add the top rails. It may be easier to work on the floor to join all the components together. Glue and nail to the cross rails.

9 Where the sides and back are to be panelled with tongued-and-grooved cladding boards, you need to attach battens to which they can be nailed. These battens must be set back by the board thickness from the face side.

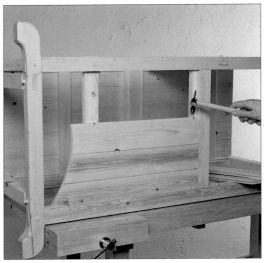

10 Pin and glue tongued-and-grooved cladding boards on to the back, driving the pins through the tongues of the boards and setting them with a nail set (punch). You will have to cut the outside boards down to fit.

11 Cut the cladding boards to size and attach them to the sides and front. Note at the front, the ends of the boards are cut to produce a curved edge to the panel to allow toe space.

12 Start to assemble the pull-out shelf, gluing and pegging the joints in the same way as before. Trim the pegs flush with the surface of the wood with a tenon saw. Finish off with a chisel.

13 Assemble the three central slats of the drawer, as shown, using the other slats as spacers so that the shelf will slide. Make sure that the fit is not too tight or it will be difficult to slide the shelf into position.

14 Turn the drawer over and join the two outer slats together. It is constructed in this manner so that the slats are not pinched and will not bind. Finish by attaching the "loose" slats to the cabinet with screws. Make sure that they are fitted parallel so they will not bind when the shelf is pulled out.

15 Cut shoulders on the ends of the tongued-and-grooved cladding boards that will form the top, shelves and doors. These shoulders will locate in a groove cut in each end piece, which helps to keep the boards flat. Use sash clamps when gluing these to the boards. Mark out the position of the hinges and handles on the finished doors.

16 Fit the top by gluing and pegging. Assemble the doors and attach the hinges and handles. Fit the shelf so that it will take the monitor using three pieces of tongue-and-groove. Complete the cabinet by adding castors and other fittings as required. The finish used on this cabinet was linseed oil mixed with white colouring.

BUTCHER'S BLOCK

NO WELL-EQUIPPED KITCHEN would be complete without a good, solid butcher's block to provide a self-contained workstation for chopping and preparing ingredients. Here, laminating is used to make the chopping block from solid, hardwearing maple. This project incorporates the worktop into a sturdy freestanding table unit. It includes an optional drawer for your chopping and cutting utensils.

Construction

The table legs are made from large-section timber (lumber), and the rails are equally sturdy, being tenoned into the legs to provide a strong support for the chopping surface. This assembly has a painted finish and a coat of hardwearing clear lacquer for hygiene and durability. The knots were treated with a shellac sealer so that they would cause no problems in the finished table.

Materials

- 3.6m (12ft) of 75 x 75mm (3 x 3in) softwood for the legs
- 3.7m (12ft 2in) of 75 x 38mm (3 x 1½in) softwood for the rails
- 2m (6ft 6in) of 75 x 12mm (3 x ½in) tongued-and-grooved cladding boards for the shelf
- 1.6m (63in) of 19 x 19mm (¾ x ¾in) softwood for the shelf battens
- 2.4m (8ft) of 25 x 12mm (1 x ½in) softwood for the drawer runners
- 400mm (15¾in) of 125 x 19mm (5 x ¾in) softwood for the drawer front
- 400 x 400mm (15¾ x 15¾in) of 12mm (½in) plywood for the drawer sides
- 400 x 400mm (15¾ x 15¾in) of 6mm (½in) plywood for the drawer bottom
- 7.3m (24ft) of 50 x 35mm (2 x 1⅜in) hardwood for the top
- PVA wood glue
- 38mm (1½in) lost-head nails
- 6mm (¼in) dowels
- 38mm (1½in) countersunk wood screws
- 25mm (1in) round-head wood screws
- 4 metal corner brackets
- Draw handle

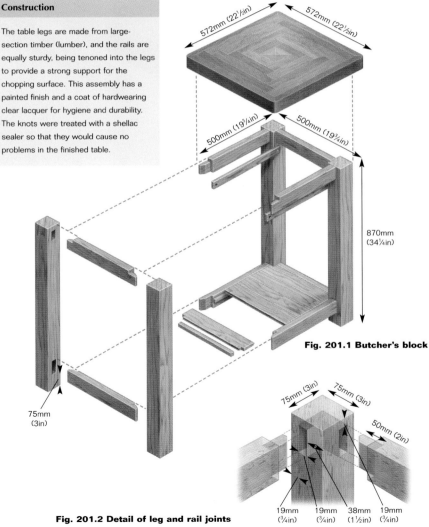

Fig. 201.1 Butcher's block

572mm (22½in) 572mm (22½in) 500mm (19¾in) 500mm (19¾in) 870mm (34¼in) 75mm (3in)

Fig. 201.2 Detail of leg and rail joints

75mm (3in) 75mm (3in) 50mm (2in) 19mm (¾in) 19mm (¾in) 38mm (1½in) 19mm (¾in)

Construction

The drawer is simply butt jointed together with dowels to strengthen the corners. Apply glue to the dowels and insert them into the drawer sides. Slide the bottom panel into place and tap the assembly together. Clamp the corners and leave to dry, after which the front panel can be glued and screwed to the carcass.

Fig. 202.1 Drawer

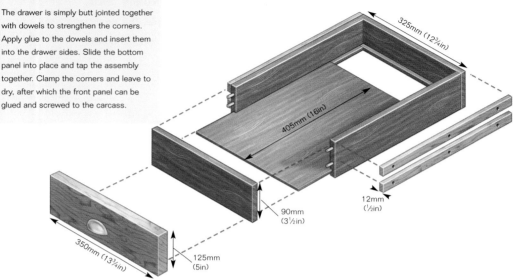

325mm (12¾in)

405mm (16in)

12mm (½in)

90mm (3½in)

350mm (13¾in)

125mm (5in)

1 To make the body of the block, cut the legs to length and make sure that their ends are absolutely square for a stable structure. Set out the mortises for the rails according to the dimensions in the accompanying diagram. Clamp the legs together in pairs to allow accurate marking out. Note that the mortises for the top rails are set back from the top edges, or "relished" (revealed), by 19mm (¾in).

2 Cut the mortises, cleaning out the corners with a bevelled chisel. The tenons of each adjacent pair of rails meet in the centre of the leg, at the bottom of the blind mortises, so make sure that they are deep enough and that all the waste is removed.

3 The tenons are "bare-faced" in that the shoulder is formed on only one side of the tenon. This has the effect of moving the inner face of the rail inward while centralizing the mortise in the leg for maximum strength.

4 Mitre the ends of the tenons where they will intersect, paring them down until they both fit together perfectly inside each corner joint. This allows longer tenons and provides a stronger glue bond. The lower rails are treated in the same way, but as they are located 75mm (3in) from the ends of the legs, no "relish" is required.

5 Begin assembling the components by gluing and clamping the legs and rails together in pairs. Set up two sash clamps on the workbench to tighten the joints of each sub-assembly. Note the small offcuts (scraps) of wood that protect the soft timber from bruising under the clamp heads.

6 Complete the construction with the legs inverted on a flat surface to keep the unit square. Slide the two leg assemblies on to the remaining rails, remembering to glue the mating surfaces of the mitred tenons where they meet inside each leg.

7 Apply sash cramps and lock the tenons in place with 38mm (1½in) lost-head nails at the inner corners of the legs. Punch the nail heads just below the surface. Check that the assembly is square, wipe off excess glue and allow to dry overnight.

8 Cut four shelf support battens from 19 x 19mm (¾ x ¾in) softwood and screw them to the lower rails as shown. Set them down from the top of the rails by the thickness of the shelf and clamp in place while attaching.

9 Cut the shelf material to size from 75 x 12mm (3 x ½in) tongued-and-grooved cladding boards. You will need to plane down the end boards to achieve the correct width for the shelf. Making it in boards allows you to fit each side in turn and cut notches to clear the legs.

10 Assemble the shelf. The boards can be sprung into place by fitting the last tongue into its groove and pushing firmly downward. The result is a perfectly fitting, strong assembly with no gaps.

11 If you want to make the optional drawer, refer to the diagram for details of its construction. Cut four lengths of 12mm (½in) plywood, 90mm (3½in) wide, for the drawer ends and sides. Then use a router with a 6mm (¼in) bit to groove them for the bottom panel. Fit centre-points to mark the ends for the dowel joints.

12 Screw the bearers for the drawer runners to the legs, using a small spacing block to position them. For 25 x 12mm (1 x ½in) runners, you should leave a gap of about 30mm (1⅛in). Drill the correct size clearance holes for the screws, countersinking the heads, to prevent the ends of the runners from splitting.

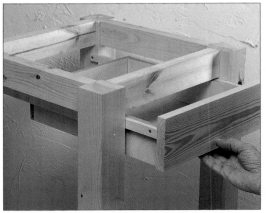

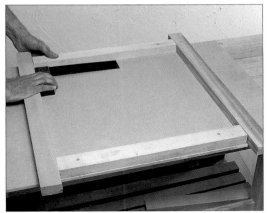

13 Finish assembling the draw, then fit the top runners to it, flush with the top edges of the drawer tray, and offer it up to the block to check for smooth operation. Then add the lower runners – these should be 25mm (1in) apart. The assembly is now ready for sanding and painting with the finish of your choice. Finally attach a handle to the drawer front.

14 The top of the block is made by laminating small components of maple together to make a herringbone pattern. All the components were prepared from quarter-sawn stock, the growth rings running vertically to the face of the block. To maintain the geometry of the design, the external size is determined by the building jig, made from straight lengths of maple screwed to a baseboard. Make sure the corners are perfectly square.

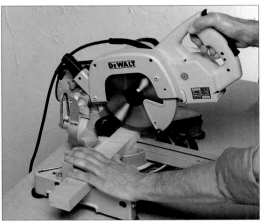

15 To make the joints as accurate as possible, each piece is fitted individually before laminating. Cut the first piece slightly oversize and use a small offcut (scrap) to mark its exact length. The blocks are simply butt-jointed, so accuracy is essential. Each piece should be a sliding fit in the jig.

16 A powered crosscut saw, is a quick means of cutting accurate square ends on each component. This machine can remove the smallest sliver of wood, so cut outside the line initially and slide the work fractionally toward the blade to make a second, or even third, cut at the exact length.

17 Continue working around the jig in a clockwise direction, numbering each piece to avoid confusion later when you start to laminate the blocks into position. Working from the outside toward the centre in this way ensures that no cumulative discrepancies occur in the overall size of the block and keeps it all square.

18 The centre of the block is formed by four triangular pieces. Mark the mitres with a mitre square and a sharp scribing knife for accuracy. The final central piece should be a really tight fit to lock everything together.

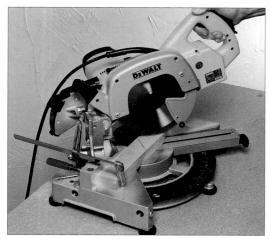

19 Making a mitre cut on a small length of wood will be safer if it is clamped to the saw table. Make the first cut, swing the saw body through 90 degrees, slide the wood along to align it, clamp it in position and make the second cut.

20 With all the components now fitted and numbered, start laminating, again from the outside toward the centre. Apply a thin film of glue to each piece and assemble the block, making sure that each piece is put into its correct place.

21 Tap the final piece of timber into position and wipe the excess glue from the surface with a damp cloth. If any hairline gaps remain, work some more glue into them and then give the piece a final wipe.

22 Tap the individual blocks firmly on to the baseboard and clamp a stout, straight-edged batten over the assembly to keep it flat as it dries. It is important to make sure the workbench underneath the board is also completely flat.

23 After at least 12 hours, remove the board from the jig and sand it down. Maple is so hard that a belt sander will probably be needed to create a flush surface, followed by a small orbital sander for a fine, smooth finish.

24 Place the top of the laminated block face-down on the workbench, align and position the leg assembly and attach the top with the corner brackets and round-head wood screws to create a sturdy fixing.

BOOKCASE

THIS BOOKCASE HAS A TOUCH OF THE CLASSICAL. With its solid proportions, clean-cut mouldings and fluted columns, this bookcase will make a stylish addition to any part of the home. The basic carcass is a straightforward box made of veneered MDF (medium-density fiberboard), with solid wood trim providing the extra detail. The example shown here was made from American cherry wood, left in its natural colour for the interior, but stained and polished on the outside to bring out the deep, rich figure of the grain.

Construction

The versatility of a router comes into its own for mounting the bookcase strip and fashioning the columns and mouldings, as well as making quick work of the carcass. The three types of router cutter illustrated below were used for this example, but you can vary the style of decorative detail.

Fig. 209.2 Router cutters

Core-box cutter

35° Chamfer

Stepped cutter

Materials

- 2.45 x 1m (8 x 3ft) of 12mm (½in) veneered MDF (medium-density fiberboard) for the carcass
- 1250 x 250mm (48 x 10in) of 25mm (1in) veneered MDF for the shelves
- 2.1m (7ft) of 100 x 25mm (4 x 1in) hardwood for the plinth
- 2.1m (7ft) of 50 x 19mm (2 x ¾in) hardwood for the bottom mouldings
- 2.1m (7ft) of 25 x 25mm (1 x 1in) hardwood for the top mouldings
- 1.8m (6ft) of 75 x 25mm (3 x 1in) hardwood for the columns
- 1.8m (6ft) of 19 x 19mm (¾ x ¾in) hardwood for the battens
- 1.2m (4ft) of 25 x 10mm (1 x ⅜in) hardwood for the shelf trim
- 2.45m (8ft) of brass bookcase strip and shelf clips
- Small countersunk brass screws
- Biscuits for jointing
- PVA wood glue

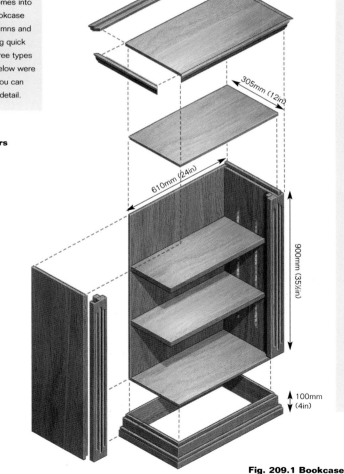

305mm (12in)

610mm (24in)

900mm (35½in)

100mm (4in)

Fig. 209.1 Bookcase

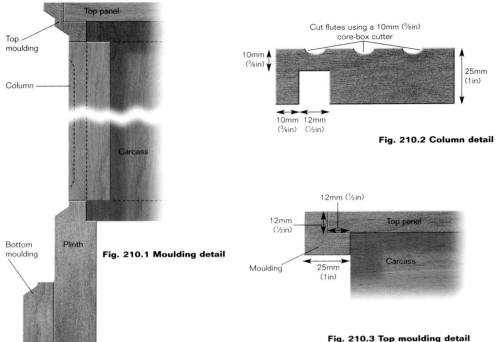

Fig. 210.1 Moulding detail

Fig. 210.2 Column detail

Cut flutes using a 10mm (³⁄₈in)
core-box cutter

10mm
(³⁄₈in)

25mm
(1in)

10mm   12mm
(³⁄₈in)   (¹⁄₂in)

Top panel

Top
moulding

Column

Carcass

Bottom
moulding

Plinth

Fig. 210.3 Top moulding detail

12mm (¹⁄₂in)

12mm
(¹⁄₂in)

Top panel

Moulding

25mm
(1in)

Carcass

1 The carcass for the bookcase is easily made. Cut the main components to size from the sheet of veneered MDF (medium-density fiberboard), and form edge rebates (rabbets) in the two sides to receive the ends and back panel. Clean them up with a sanding block, taking care not to damage the delicate veneer facing.

2 Before assembling the box, the recessed bookcase strips should be fitted to the sides. Cut the brass strip into four lengths, making sure that the slots for the shelf clips will align correctly. If the strips are not identical, the shelves will not sit level. The best course is to cut one strip to size and use it as a pattern for the others.

3 Mark out the positions of the strips on each side with a carpenter's pencil, using a try square to locate them. For maximum stability, each strip should be set back from the edge of the shelf by approximately 38mm (1½in).The strips do not need to continue to the full height of the bookcase, unless you want a very shallow top shelf.

4 Rout the grooves for the inset strips, squaring the ends with a bevelled chisel. Two grooves are required for each strip – one should be equal in width to the strip itself, and another slightly deeper and wide enough to provide clearance for the hooks of the shelf clips. You can do this with two separate cutters, or invest in a special stepped cutter (shown in figure 209.2), which completes the operation in one pass.

5 It is a good idea to sand down the inner surfaces of all the panels at this stage, so that they are ready for finishing. Then fit the brass strips, using small countersunk brass screws. Make sure the slots are correctly aligned, and that the top end of each strip is fitted toward the top of the bookcase.

6 Glue and screw the carcass together, checking that it is square. Make sure that the screwheads are countersunk well below the surface. The design of the unit ensures that the screws along the edges will be concealed by the top and bottom mouldings. Leave to dry.

7 Cut four lengths of 100 x 25mm (4 x 1in) hardwood for the plinth and form a 12mm (½in) wide by 6mm (¼in) deep rebate (rabbet) along one edge of each to receive the bottom of the bookcase carcass. Mitre the ends and insert biscuits to reinforce and aid the alignment of the joints.

8 Glue the plinth together, strengthening the corners by adding small glued blocks. Wipe away any excess glue. Note that the internal dimensions of the rebate around the inner edge of the plinth should match the external size of the cabinet, which simply slots into position.

9 Fit the plinth over the bottom of the cabinet and secure it with small wooden blocks and screws. There is no need to glue them, as the plinth will be removed later to add the decorative moulding before sanding and finishing. It needs to be fitted at this stage to assist in aligning the fluted columns.

10 Make the columns according to the dimensions given in the diagram. Cut a 12mm (½in) housing in the back to locate each column on the front edges of the carcass, and use a core-box cutter to add the fluting to the front face (see figure 209.2). Use a small cylinder of sandpaper to remove any marks left by the cutter in the rounded flutes.

11 Screw a 19mm (¾in) batten flush with the inner edge of the housing of each column to provide a secure attachment to the carcass without any visible fixings.

12 Apply glue to the front edges of the bookcase and tap the columns into place. They should fit exactly between the top and bottom of the carcass, stiffening the sides and giving a solid, well-proportioned appearance to the whole assembly.

13 Cut the panel for the top of the bookcase and glue on the edge profile. The latter is made from 25 x 25mm (1 x 1in) stock, rebated to suit the panel, as in figure 210.3. Mitre the ends and clamp around the edges, making sure that it is perfectly flush with the surface of the panel for a smooth finish.

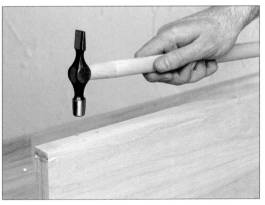

14 Check that the top panel is a good fit over the carcass – note how it locates over the top edges of the box, concealing the screws along the sides. Now you can add the moulding detail around the edges. Profile the top moulding using a 35 degree chamfer cutter (see figure 213.2). Sand, stain and polish the top and mouldings before finally attaching it to the carcass with screws from the inside. Use the same chamfer cutter to profile the plinth and bottom moulding.

15 Make two shelves for the unit, using 25mm (1in) board for extra strength. They should be slightly shorter than the internal width of the cabinet by about 1.5mm (¹⁄₁₆in), which will allow enough clearance for them to be tilted sideways for fitting. Glue and pin small strips of hardwood along the front edges to finish them off neatly.

16 Insert the shelf clips into the recessed brass strips and fit the shelves.

Practical tip

To avoid having to buy a small quantity of 25mm (1in) veneered board, you can use offcuts (scraps) from the sheet of 12mm (½in) material and laminate them together.

CORNER CABINET

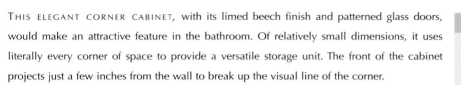

This elegant corner cabinet, with its limed beech finish and patterned glass doors, would make an attractive feature in the bathroom. Of relatively small dimensions, it uses literally every corner of space to provide a versatile storage unit. The front of the cabinet projects just a few inches from the wall to break up the visual line of the corner.

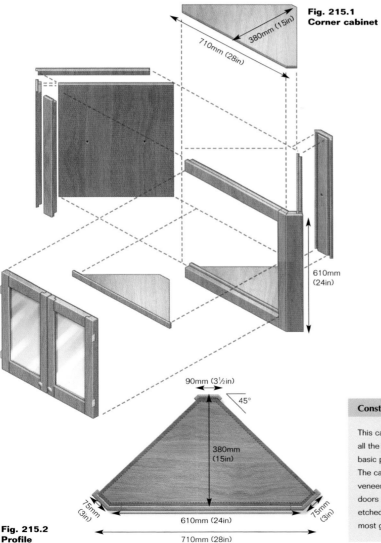

**Fig. 215.1
Corner cabinet**

380mm (15in)
710mm (28in)
610mm (24in)

90mm (3½in)
45°
380mm (15in)
75mm (3in)
75mm (3in)
610mm (24in)
710mm (28in)

**Fig. 215.2
Profile**

Materials

All materials are hardwood, unless specified otherwise:
- 1.25m (48in) of 75 x 25mm (3 x 1in)
- 3.3m (10ft 10in) of 38 x 25mm (1½ x 1in)
- 2.45m (8ft) of 50 x 25mm (2 x 1in)
- 1.25m (48in) of 50 x 10mm (2 x ⅜in)
- 610mm (24in) of 90 x 25mm (3½ x 1in)
- 3m (10ft) of 12 x 12mm (½ x ½in) glazing bead
- 1.25 x 1.25m (48 x 48in) of 12mm (½in) veneered MDF (medium-density fiberboard)
- Biscuits for jointing
- PVA wood glue
- 25mm (1in) and 38mm (1½in) wood screws
- 25mm (1in) panel pins (brads)
- Patterned glass for glazed doors
- Shelf supports
- 4 brass hinges
- 2 magnetic catches
- 2 door knobs

Construction

This cabinet is not as complex as it may appear – all the upright components are fitted around the basic profile, which determines the final shape. The carcass is made from 12mm (½in) ash-veneered MDF and solid beech was used for the doors and main frame members. Engraved or etched glass for the doors can be obtained from most glaziers, who will cut it to size.

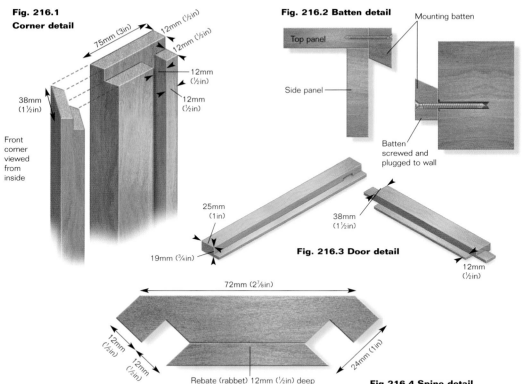

Fig. 216.1 Corner detail

75mm (3in)

12mm (½in)

12mm (½in)

12mm (½in)

12mm (½in)

38mm (1½in)

Front corner viewed from inside

Fig. 216.2 Batten detail

Mounting batten

Top panel

Side panel

Batten screwed and plugged to wall

25mm (1in)

19mm (¾in)

38mm (1½in)

Fig. 216.3 Door detail

12mm (½in)

72mm (2⅞in)

12mm (½in)

12mm (½in)

24mm (1in)

Rebate (rabbet) 12mm (½in) deep

Fig 216.4 Spine detail

1 Make a template for the basic profile, using the pattern shown in figure 215.2. The top and bottom panels, which determine the shape, are 12mm (½in) smaller all round than the external dimensions of the cabinet. Pin the template to the veneered board and cut out both panels with a jigsaw (saber saw), making them slightly oversize.

2 Use a router fitted with a template cutter to finish the shape of the top and bottom panels. For the best visual effect, the grain direction of the veneer should run from side to side across the cabinet. The small pin-holes can be filled later with light-coloured wood stopping (wood filler).

3 Cut all the vertical members to the same overall length, and plane the edges of the front pieces of wood to an angle of 67.5 degrees from the outside face. When joined, these form the required internal angle of 135 degrees at the front corners.

4 All the vertical members need rebates (rabbets) at the ends for the top and bottom panels. In addition, rout 12mm (½in) housing grooves in the outer corner pieces to receive the side panels. Figure 216.1 provides a clear view of the corner detail.

5 Join the angled faces of the corner members together with biscuits. Set the angled fence of the biscuit jointer to 67.5 degrees. The biscuits not only strengthen the glued joints, but also serve to align the front edges and prevent the components from sliding apart when clamped together during the gluing process.

6 Use the bottom panel of the cabinet as a template for assembling the corner joint. Apply glue, insert the biscuits and slide the two parts together. Note how the housing groove for the side panel is aligned with the outside edge.

7 Cut the cross rails to fit between the corner uprights, rebate them to fit over the top and bottom panels and glue in place. Each is locked in position with a strip of 10mm (⅜in) hardwood that also acts as a stop for the doors. It keeps the front of the cabinet square, too.

8 Insert a side panel into the groove in one corner post, and align the top and bottom panels with a couple of 25mm (1in) panel pins (brads). If you keep the edges flush, the cabinet will automatically conform to the desired shape as it is assembled.

9 The rear spine member locks the side panels together and stiffens the whole structure. Cut its housing grooves according to the dimensions given in figure 216.4. Rebate (rabbet) the top and bottom, and slot into position. Add the second side by sliding it into place in its housing grooves in the front and back members.

10 With the second side panel in place, apply tension to the whole assembly with a pair of web clamps. These will tighten all the joints and pull the cabinet into shape. Insert more panel pins to hold the top and bottom panels in position. Check that the front is square and leave the clamps in tension as the glue dries.

11 Add short battens to the top and bottom edges of the side panels. Notch the ends of the battens to clear the corner posts, as shown, and, if wished, plane bevels on the upper pair to make a neat system for mounting the cabinet. Figure 216.2 shows how the cabinet can be simply lifted into place and hooked on to a matching pair of battens screwed to the wall.

12 Use what remains of the veneered material to make a triangular shelf for the cabinet. Set it back by 50mm (2in) from the front frame, which will allow it to be tilted and offered into position. Glue and pin a strip of wood along the front of the shelf to trim the edge.

13 To make the doors, use 38mm (1½in) stock for the stiles, and 50mm (2in) for the horizontal rails. Set out and cut the 25 x 10mm (1 x ⅜in) mortises as shown, then form 19mm (¾in) deep by 12mm (½in) wide rebates in the rear faces for the glass and beads.

14 Cut the matching tenons and rebate the rails in the same way. Note that the 25mm (1in) tenons have unequal stepped shoulders to accommodate the rebates in the stiles. Pare down to fit with a bevelled chisel. See figure 216.3.

15 Glue and assemble the two doors, clamping them together flat on the bench. The joints are so small that no wedges should be required to secure the tenons if they are a good fit. When the glue has dried, remove the projecting horns with a small tenon saw.

16 Measure the size of glass required for the doors and order the two panes from your local supplier. If using decorative etched glass, be sure to mention that they must be a matched pair with symmetrical patterns. Cut the glazing bead into lengths to hold the glass in place, but hang and fit the doors before inserting the glass.

17 Mount the brass hinges on the doors, in line with the inner edges of the rails. The offset pins make it easy to locate the hinges accurately.

Practical tip

White liming wax accentuates the delicate flecked figure of the beech wood, preserves its pale colour and protects it from the humid conditions of a bathroom.

18 These miniature magnetic catches are very discreet and ideal for lightweight doors of this type. Each magnetic barrel is simply inserted into a hole drilled in the bottom rail of the frame. The small striking plate is tapped into position in the end of the door stile.

19 Finally, add two matching knobs to the doors. Sand down and apply a coat of sealer, then liming wax or your chosen finish, before fitting the glass into the doors. Cut small glazing beads and fit using small panel pins, taking care to protect the glass as you do so.

DINING TABLE

A COMPACT DINING TABLE OF striking appearance, this unique design is a composition of great subtlety and balance. The top displays the rustic quality of elm, with its swirling grain pattern and tight knot clusters. The supporting framework is made of straight-grained teak. Clear carnauba wax is the only finish required to bring out the character of the wood.

Materials

- 4.6m (15ft) of 230 x 25mm (9 x 1in) hardwood for the top
- 3m (10ft) of 75 x 75mm (3 x 3in) hardwood for the legs
- 2.1m (7ft) of 75 x 25mm (3 x 1in) hardwood for the rails
- 4m (13ft) of 50 x 25mm (2 x 1in) hardwood for the top frame
- PVA wood glue

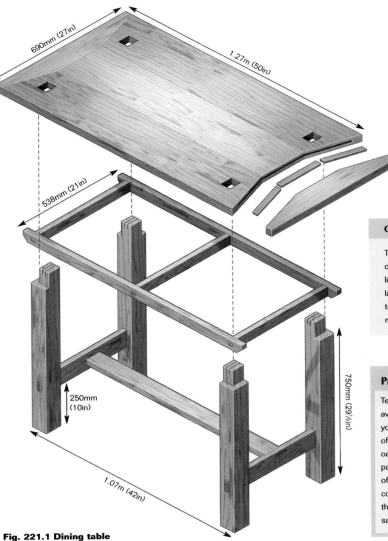

690mm (27in)

1.27m (50in)

538mm (21in)

250mm (10in)

750mm (29½in)

1.07m (42in)

Fig. 221.1 Dining table

Construction

The pieces for the table top are cut from two elm boards, one of lighter tone than the other, neatly laminated together. The legs are tenoned through the table top to make a bold geometrical pattern.

Practical tip

Teak may not always be readily available, nor affordable, in which case you could substitute a different type of wood of contrasting colour – dark oak, for example, makes a natural partner for elm. The attractiveness of the design is derived from the combination of the two species. Even the wedges for the tenons use the same contrast to highlight the effect.

Fig. 222.1 Top detail

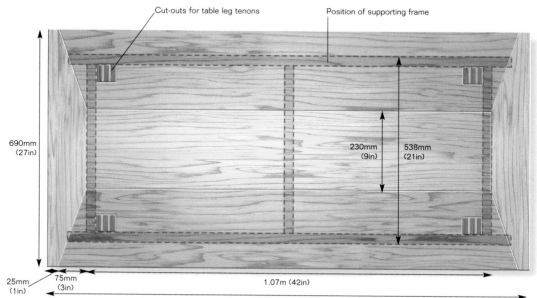

Cut-outs for table leg tenons

Position of supporting frame

690mm
(27in)

230mm
(9in)

538mm
(21in)

25mm
(1in)

75mm
(3in)

1.07m (42in)

1.27m (50in)

1 The "fishtail" design of the table top is not only attractive, but also serves to lock the ends of the boards together and keep the top flat. The five components are edge-jointed, using loose tongues made of 6mm (¼in) hardwood offcuts (scraps). Cut the three main boards to the sizes shown in figure 222.1 above.

2 It is best to laminate the top in two separate stages. First glue and clamp the three long boards together, making sure that the angled ends are aligned correctly. Use two straight-edged battens (cleats) to clamp the assembly flat on the bench while the glue dries.

3 Make an angled template as an aid to shaping the end sections. Pare down the edges if necessary to accommodate any discrepancy in the assembly. Position the template so that the most suitable and attractive portions of wood will be used to complete the table top. Mark out the end pieces and cut them to size.

4 Plane the edges of the end pieces so that they are absolutely square, and pare them down carefully to fit the table top. When they fit perfectly, rout the 6mm (¼in) grooves for the loose tongues. Stop the grooves short of the ends by 25mm (1in).

5 Apply glue, insert the hardwood tongues in the grooves and clamp the ends in place. Note how the grooves stop short of the ends to avoid weakening the corners. Set the top aside for the glue to dry while you work on the table frame and legs. Use weights or clamps to keep it as flat as possible.

6 Make the legs in pairs to suit each end of the table. Clamp each pair together, as shown, and set out the mortises for the lower rails. The mortises are sized at 68 x 19mm (2¾ x ¾in). This is slightly smaller than the rails, leaving a 3mm (⅛in) shoulder around each tenon.

7 At the outer face of each table leg, angle the sides of the mortise to receive the locking wedges. As the wedges have a decorative aspect, they can be generous in size, adding 6mm (¼in) to each end of the mortise.

8 Pare the tenons down to a good fit and dry assemble the legs, making sure that the shoulders sit squarely. Then set out the mortises for the horizontal stretcher bar in the centres of the rails.

9 The mortises for the stretcher are the same size as those for the rails, allowing a similar amount for the wedges. Good accurate joints are required for this assembly to ensure a rigid base for the table.

10 Assemble the stretcher to the rails and set aside. Then make the supporting frame for the top. Mark up all the components carefully to avoid confusion at the construction stage – each leg must be fitted individually to the table top.

11 The supporting frame is mortised and tenoned together, having three cross rails to span the laminated top and hold it flat, so make absolutely sure that the frame is not twisted. No wedges are used for these smaller tenons – they are simply glued and clamped together.

12 The longitudinal bearers of the frame extend beyond the outer cross rails, to provide full support for the table ends. Cut small bevels on the ends of each bearer to remove the bottom corners. Then glue and clamp the frame together, making sure that it is square.

13 The tenon at the top of each leg measures 50 x 50mm (2 x 2in) in section, being bare-faced on the inner edge. The shoulders locate under the supporting frame members. Add the thickness of the table top to the depth of the frame members to establish the length of the tenons.

14 Centralize the assembled supporting frame on the underside of the table top. Attach it in position with a couple of screws at each corner, then place each leg in turn in its corner of the frame as shown. Mark the positions of the mortises on the top, then remove the frame, marking it first so that you can replace it in the same position.

15 Use a try square to transfer the mortise positions to the upper face of the top and scribe around the edges of the cut-outs. Use a spade bit or auger mounted in a drill to remove the bulk of the waste, then pare down the sides so that the tenons are a sliding fit.

16 Clamp each leg upright and cut two small slots in the top of the tenon for the wedges. The slots should be no more than 25mm (1in) deep – the thickness of the table top – in order to avoid weakening the tenons more than necessarily.

17 Fashion a wedge-shaped section of wood from an offcut (scrap) of the table top material, using a bandsaw or circular saw to achieve a sharp feather edge. Note the grain direction. Using a hand saw, cut the strip into eight 50mm (2in) wedges.

18 Make 12 smaller wedges to fit the cross rail and stretcher tenons in the same way. Glue each pair of legs and corresponding cross rail in turn, keeping them flat and free from any twisting. Clamp them so that the assembly is square, insert the small wedges and tap them in.

19 Stand the two ends upright on a flat surface. Slip the support frame over the tops of the legs to position them correctly, then insert the connecting stretcher between the rails. Place the table top over the tenons, square up the legs and tap in the wedges. Leave both sections to dry before proceeding to the next step. Leave the top in position to keep the assembly square while the glue dries, then remove it for the final attachment.

20 Apply glue to the tenons at the tops of the legs, replace the table top and hammer in the wedges, using a small block of wood to protect the ends and keep them straight. Note the direction of the slots in the tenons – this prevents the wedges from applying pressure to the longitudinal grain of the table top. When the glue is dry, cut the excess from the wedges and sand the tops of the legs flush with the surface.

SETTLE

"SETTLE" IS AN OLD NAME for a wooden seat with a high back and raised arm rests. This version reflects the early origins of the concept by using wedged-through tenons, one of the earliest carpentry techniques, dating from medieval times. It departs from tradition, however, in the gently curved profile of the ends, which give a more contemporary feel to the whole design. The example shown was made from wide boards of sweet chestnut, a much neglected wood often mistaken for oak, with its attractive grain figure and delicate pale brown colour.

Materials

- 3.3m (11ft) of 305 x 2 mm (12 x 1in) hardwood for the ends
- 3.3m (11ft) of 150 x 25mm (6 x 1in) hardwood for the seat
- 4.9m (16ft) of 125 x 25mm (5 x 1in) hardwood for the back and arm rests
- 1m (3ft) of 50 x 25mm (2 x 1 in) softwood batten for the seat braces
- 1,100 x 610mm (43 x 24in) of 6mm (¼in) plywood or MDF (medium-density fiberboard) for the template
- PVA wood glue
- 8mm (⅜in) wooden dowels

Practical tip

Position the seat slightly lower if you want to add an upholstered cushion, maintaining the overall height above the floor of 460mm (18in).

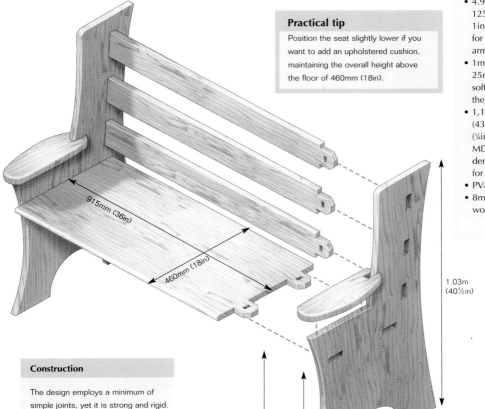

915mm (36in)

460mm (18in)

1.03m (40½in)

610mm (24in)

460mm (18in)

560mm (22in)

Construction

The design employs a minimum of simple joints, yet it is strong and rigid. The wedged-through tenons are not glued, and the whole assembly can be taken apart whenever required. The seat can be made to any width, but these dimensions are suitable for a two-seater.

Fig. 227.1 Settle

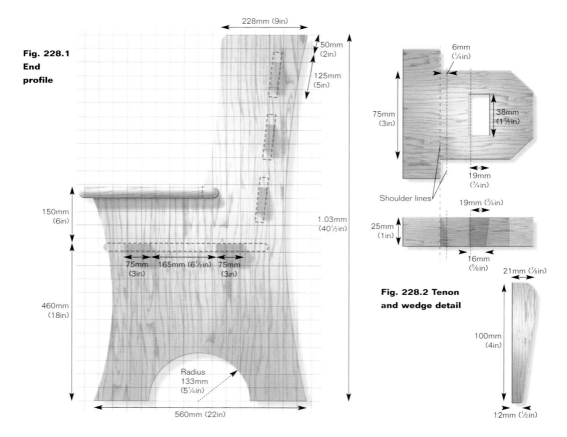

Fig. 228.1 End profile

228mm (9in)

50mm (2in)

125mm (5in)

1.03mm (40½in)

150mm (6in)

75mm 165mm (6½in) 75mm
(3in) (3in)

460mm (18in)

Radius 133mm (5¼in)

560mm (22in)

6mm (¼in)

75mm (3in)

38mm (1½in)

19mm (¾in)

Shoulder lines

25mm (1in)

19mm (¾in)

16mm (⅝in)

21mm (⅞in)

Fig. 228.2 Tenon and wedge detail

100mm (4in)

12mm (½in)

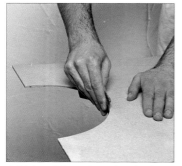

1 Make a full-sized template for the end profile from 6mm (¼in) plywood or MDF. Use the scale drawing provided (figure 228.1), plotting the outline on a scaled-up grid to transfer the shape accurately. Mark and cut out the mortise positions in the template at the same time.

2 Begin by edge jointing all the components for the seat and the ends. Rout grooves in the edges of the boards and clamp them together with loose tongues for extra strength. Note the straight batten clamped over the work to keep it flat as the sash clamps are tightened.

3 The arm rests are laminated from a double thickness of wood. Make a template of suitable shape, cutting a 50 x 25mm (2 x 1in) locating slot in it. Cut out and shape four pieces, using a router fitted with a follower cutter. Square off the ends of the locating slots.

4 Glue the arm rest pairs together and set aside for the glue to dry before shaping. Note the small block of wood inserted into the slot to keep the two pieces aligned. Remove the excess glue, sand smooth and round off the edges.

5 Cut the ends roughly to shape, slightly oversize, and pin the template to each in turn. Mark through the template to transfer the positions of the cut-outs for the tenons on to the workpiece so that both ends are identical.

6 Use a router fitted with a follower cutter to trim the ends to their final shape. The bearing on the end of the cutter follows the curved template beneath the work, which should be clamped firmly to the bench.

7 To make the cut-outs, drill a hole at each end of the slot and join them with a jigsaw (saber saw) to remove the waste. Cut just inside the line. Pin the template to the reverse of the work and then use the router to trim the slot to size, as in the previous step.

8 Square the ends of each slot with a bevelled chisel. A good tight fit to suit the thickness of the tenons will ensure a rigid construction when the latter are wedged in place. Ease the slots with a piece of sandpaper and a wooden block of the right size until a good sliding fit is achieved.

9 The seat is housed in a groove for maximum support. Clamp a straightedge to the inner face of each end to guide the router, aligning the groove exactly with the slots. A depth of 6mm (¼in) is sufficient for the housing. When the wedges on the seat are drawn up tight, the seat should fit securely in the housings.

10 Rout a similar 6mm (¼in) deep groove in the underside of each armrest to fit over the ends. Square off the end of the groove with a chisel to suit the exact length of the side location. Then radius the edges and sand smooth.

11 Drill two holes for 8mm (⁵⁄₁₆in) dowels in the edge of each end that supports the arm rest. Insert the dowel centre-points and slot the arm rest over the end piece, pressing down to mark the corresponding hole positions on the underside of the arm rest. Drill the holes.

12 Make a template for the tenons, using the diagram (figure 228.2) as a guide. Note the alternative shoulder lines that allow the same template to be used for both seat and back rails, the former being longer by 6mm (¼in). For the rails, the shoulders are flush to the inside face of the sides.

13 Cut the tenons on the ends of the back rails, and mark out the small slots for the wedges. Set the shoulder lines 915mm (36in) apart on each rail to the internal width of the seat. Trim the corners of the tenons, as shown, and sand them smooth.

14 Use the same template to mark out the tenons on the seat, but note how the shoulders are set forward by 6mm (¼in) to allow for the housing groove that receives the seat. Scribe along the shoulder lines and cut the ends carefully to shape with a jigsaw.

15 Drill out the slots for the wedges and remove the waste. Make each slot 16mm (⁵⁄₈in) wide, then use a chisel to form the small bevel shown in the diagram. Mark the bevel on the side of the tenon as a guide to keep the chisel at the correct angle.

16 Make ten wedges from offcuts (scraps) of wood, following the dimensions given. The angle of each wedge should fit the slot in its tenon exactly. Shape one wedge first, check for accuracy, then use it as a pattern for the others.

17 Before assembly, glue and screw two 50 x 25mm (2 x 1in) battens to the underside of the seat to stiffen it and help prevent any deformation of the edge-jointed sections. The battens are 25mm (1in) shorter than the width of the seat at each end.

18 Assemble the settle, easing each tenon into its slot and inserting the wedges temporarily to hold it together while you add the components. An assistant is useful at this stage to support the other end of the seat and rails.

19 Insert the rails with the slots facing forward, as shown, and tap all the wedges home. Because the slots are inset slightly from the outer faces of the seat ends, the wedging action will tighten the whole assembly until it is completely rigid.

20 Finally, attach the arm rests, locating them with the dowels and tapping them firmly into place. Use a block of scrap wood to protect the surface.

CONSERVATORY BENCH

THIS PROJECT WOULD LOOK PERFECTLY AT HOME in a conservatory or garden room. Its slatted construction allows plenty of light to pass through and around it, while keeping the weight down so that it is easily moved. For all that, it is remarkably strong, and being of generous length, it could even be used as a day bed if provided with a few loose cushions. It is made of iroko, a naturally hard and durable wood, so it would be equally suitable for use outdoors as a garden bench during the summer.

Materials

- 3.6m (12ft) of 50 x 50mm (2 x 2in) hardwood for the legs
- 10.7m (35ft) of 75 x 22mm (3 x ⅞in) hardwood for the rails
- 2.45m (8ft) of 65 x 19mm (2½ x ¾in) hardwood for the large slats
- 14.7m (48ft) of 19 x 19mm (¾ x ¾in) hardwood for the small slats
- 4m (13ft) of 38 x 25mm (1½ x 1in) hardwood for the seat battens
- 1.4m x 900mm (55 x 35in) of 12mm (½in) birch plywood for the seat
- 8 100mm (4in) bolts and cross-dowels
- PVA wood glue
- 8mm (⁵⁄₁₆in) wooden dowels
- 25mm (1in) and 38mm (1½in) wood screws

Fig. 233.1 Conservatory bench

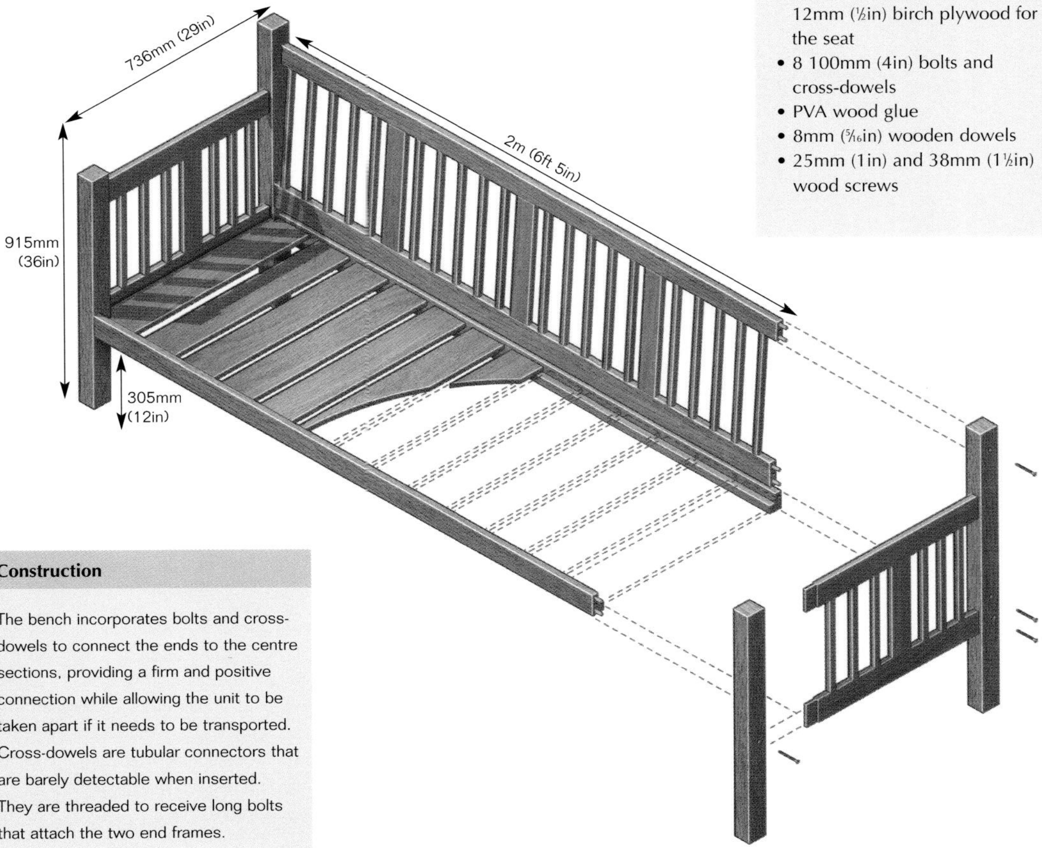

736mm (29in)

2m (6ft 5in)

915mm (36in)

305mm (12in)

Construction

The bench incorporates bolts and cross-dowels to connect the ends to the centre sections, providing a firm and positive connection while allowing the unit to be taken apart if it needs to be transported. Cross-dowels are tubular connectors that are barely detectable when inserted. They are threaded to receive long bolts that attach the two end frames.

Fig. 234.1 End profile

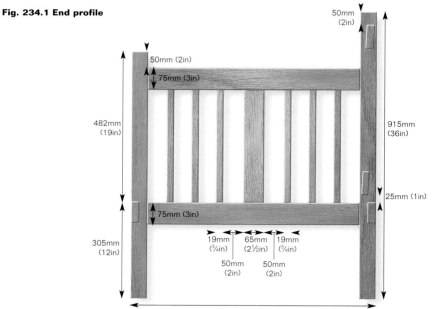

50mm (2in)

50mm (2in)

75mm (3in)

482mm (19in)

915mm (36in)

305mm (12in)

25mm (1in)

19mm (¾in)   65mm (2½in)   19mm (¾in)

50mm (2in)   50mm (2in)

736mm (29in)

1 Make the end frames first. Cut the legs to length, and scribe 12mm (½in) wide mortises with a mortise gauge as shown. Do this with the front and back legs clamped together, flush at the bottom. The diagram (figure 234.1) gives the dimensions required to set out the end frames.

2 Cut the mortises 32mm (1¼in) deep to leave enough room for the connecting bolts. Pare the ends and sides of each mortise true and square, making sure that the bottom is free of obstructions.

3 Set out the tenons on the cross rails, then clamp the rails together in pairs to mark out the mortises for the vertical slats. The wider, central slat is positioned first, then the smaller slats are placed at equal intervals along the rail.

4 Cut the tenons on the rails, and pare down with a shoulder plane for a good square fit in the mortises. Note that the shoulders only run along the wide faces of each rail. The mortise is the full height of the rail in this case.

5 Cut all the mortises in the rails. You can drill to a depth of 32mm (1¼in) and chisel them out, as shown, but there are a lot of them, so if you have a drill stand or, even better, a mortise attachment for a power drill, it's well worth setting up to do this.

6 Cut the tenons on all the slats and pare them to fit, clamping them together so that you can square up all the shoulders in one operation. This ensures that all will be drawn up tight when the frame is glued together.

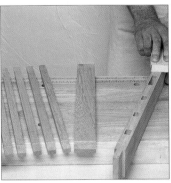

7 Before assembling the frame, sand all the surfaces that will be difficult to clean up later – it saves a lot of time and trouble.

8 Glue all the slats and fit them to the rails to make a sub-assembly that can be connected to the legs in one operation. It should not be necessary to wait for the glue to dry in this instance; the assembly should be rigid enough to proceed to the next step.

9 Clamp each frame together with a pair of sash clamps, keeping them flat on the bench to prevent any twisting. Wipe off any excess glue and continue with the slatted back section of the bench while the glue dries. Lay one frame on top of the other to make sure they are identical in size.

Practical tip

This project is made up in stages from several sub-assemblies. As each one is completed it can be easier to finish and apply a coat of sealer before constructing the finished bench.

10 Clamp the bottom rail in a vice and insert all the vertical slats. If you have worked accurately and methodically, all the narrow slats and all the wider slats should be interchangeable. Double check each one before applying glue, however, in case it should need easing slightly.

11 Attach the top rail, starting at one end of the assembly and then gradually working your way along. You will find it very useful to have an assistant support the free end. Tap the rail into place with a rubber mallet, locating all the slats before applying the cramps. Make sure the ends are aligned and the assembly is square, and leave to dry.

12 Mark the positions of the connecting bolts and dowels on the inner faces of the end frames. Note that the back is inclined outward at the top to provide a more comfortable seating position. The 50mm (2in) legs allow an angle of about 3 degrees within their width, which makes all the difference. Use a bevel gauge to set out the positions of the back rails.

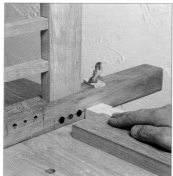

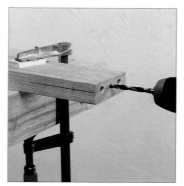

13 Each end of each rail is fitted with two 8mm (5⁄16in) diameter wooden dowels to locate it accurately and prevent it from twisting when the bolt is tightened. The central hole is drilled to suit the diameter of the bolt. Use centre-points to mark the hole positions on each rail – note the block of scrap wood clamped to the bench to hold the rail square.

14 Clamp the rails horizontally to drill the holes in the ends. The holes for the connecting bolts should be drilled to a full 75mm (3in) depth to allow plenty of clearance. Get someone to help you by standing to one side to check that your drill bit is truly horizontal.

15 Drill a hole for the cross-dowel, intersecting the bolt hole, and insert the cross-dowel from beneath the rail. Note the slot in the end of the dowel, which is used to align the hole to receive the bolt. When the slot is parallel to the sides of the rail, the bolt should enter the dowel easily.

16 Countersink the holes for the bolts in the outer faces of the legs so that the heads sit just below the surface. Align the wooden dowels, tap the end frames into place and tighten the bolts with the key provided. The result is a discreet and immensely strong connection.

17 Cut two battens to the full length of the front and back rails, and screw them in place to support the seat. The seat can be made of any suitable sheet material – in this case, 12mm (½in) plywood strips were used to provide a degree of flexibility.

18 The two endmost strips should be notched to fit around the legs. Note that the top edges of the plywood have been radiused with a rounding-over cutter to prevent splinters from catching on the upholstered seat cushions. Sand all the strips smooth before fixing.

19 Screw the plywood strips to the battens, using a block of wood to ensure regular spacing. Make sure that the screw heads are countersunk well to prevent them from snagging on the cushion material.

KITCHEN BASE UNIT

A FITTED KITCHEN DEPENDS ON a series of base units, built to standard sizes, to support a work counter and provide storage space. The easy option is to buy ready-made units in flat-pack form for self-assembly. Although economical, their main disadvantage is that the panels are made of chipboard or similar man-made materials, which are not durable. This project shows how to make your own units in solid timber (lumber), which will last longer and be more attractive. This example was made from good-quality pine, varnished to give a waterproof, easy-clean finish.

Materials

- 3.8m (12ft 6in) of 75 x 25mm (3 x 1in) softwood for the door and draw front
- 3m (10ft) of 90 x 10mm (3½ x ⅜in) tongued-and-grooved cladding boards for the door
- 2.1m (7ft) of 100 x 25mm (4 x 1in) softwood for the drawer
- 6mm (¼in) plywood for the drawer bottom
- 5.2m (17ft) of 75 x 25mm (3 x 1in) softwood for the sides
- 5.2m (17ft) of 90 x 10mm (3½ x ⅜in) tongued-and-grooved cladding boards for the side panels
- 2.2m (7ft 3in) of 100 x 25mm (4 x 1in) softwood for the plinth
- 1.25m (48in) of 50 x 25mm (2 x 1in) softwood for the rails
- 610mm (24in) of 50 x 19mm (2 x ¾in) softwood for the bottom panel trim
- 610 x 500mm (24 x 20in) of 19mm (¾in) MDF (medium-density fibreboard) for the bottom panel
- 760 x 610mm (30 x 24in) of 6mm (¼in) MDF for the back panel
- 8 bolts and cross-dowels
- 6mm (¼in) dowels
- 2 drawer runners
- 2 handles
- 2 concealed hinges
- PVA wood glue
- Panel pins (brads)
- Wooden or plastic joint blocks

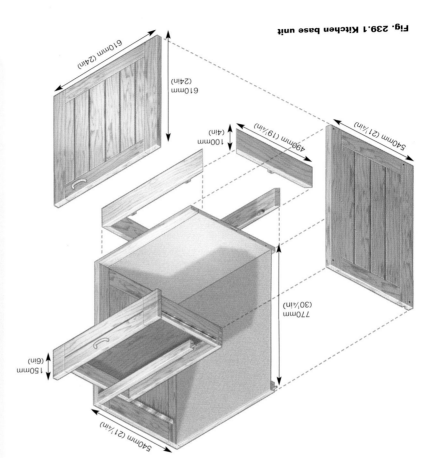

Fig. 239.1 Kitchen base unit

610mm (24in)

610mm (24in)

100mm (4in)

490mm (19¼in)

540mm (21¼in)

770mm (30¾in)

150mm (6in)

540mm (21¼in)

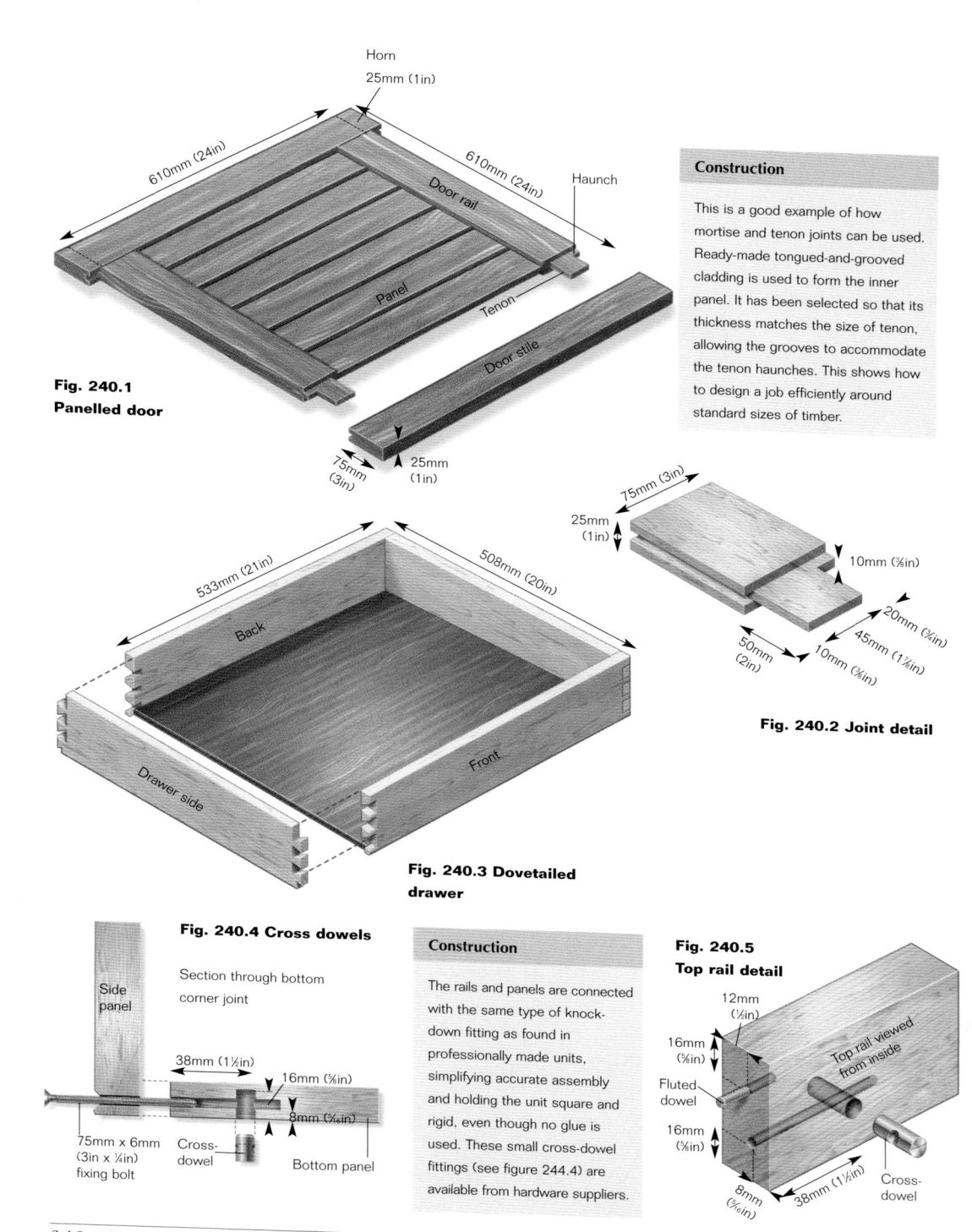

Horn
25mm (1in)

610mm (24in)

610mm (24in)

Haunch

Door rail

Tenon

Panel

Door stile

Fig. 240.1
Panelled door

75mm
(3in)

25mm
(1in)

Construction

This is a good example of how
mortise and tenon joints can be used.
Ready-made tongued-and-grooved
cladding is used to form the inner
panel. It has been selected so that its
thickness matches the size of tenon,
allowing the grooves to accommodate
the tenon haunches. This shows how
to design a job efficiently around
standard sizes of timber.

75mm (3in)

25mm
(1in)

10mm (⅜in)

533mm (21in)

508mm (20in)

20mm (¾in)

Back

50mm
(2in)

45mm (1¾in)

10mm (⅜in)

Fig. 240.2 Joint detail

Drawer side

Front

**Fig. 240.3 Dovetailed
drawer**

Fig. 240.4 Cross dowels

Section through bottom
corner joint

Side
panel

38mm (1½in)

16mm (⅝in)

8mm (⅜in)

75mm x 6mm
(3in x ¼in)
fixing bolt

Cross-
dowel

Bottom panel

Construction

The rails and panels are connected
with the same type of knock-
down fitting as found in
professionally made units,
simplifying accurate assembly
and holding the unit square and
rigid, even though no glue is
used. These small cross-dowel
fittings (see figure 244.4) are
available from hardware suppliers.

Fig. 240.5
Top rail detail

12mm
(½in)

16mm
(⅝in)

Top rail viewed
from inside

Fluted
dowel

16mm
(⅝in)

8mm
(⅜in)

38mm (1½in)

Cross-
dowel

Making the cabinet door

1 Set out the positions for the mortises on the door stiles, clamping them together for accuracy. Note how the stiles are left long at this stage. The extra 25mm (1in) at each end is called the horn.

2 Set the mortise gauge to the thickness of the panelling, which will also determine the size of the tenons. Scribe all along the inner face of each stile to mark out the groove and mortises in one operation.

3 Cut the mortises at each end of the stiles, but before cutting the tenons, use a plough (bullnose) plane to form the grooves 10mm (⅜in) deep. Check the panelling for a good fit before proceeding.

4 Cut the tenons on the rails, and form the haunches as shown. The depth of each haunch should match the depth of the grooves in the stiles – 10mm (⅜in) in this case.

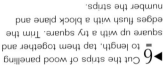

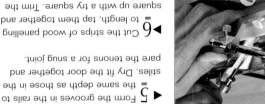

▶5 Form the grooves in the rails to the same depth as those in the stiles. Dry fit the door together and pare the tenons for a snug joint.

▶6 Cut the strips of wood panelling to length, tap them together and square up with a try square. Trim the edges flush with a block plane and number the strips.

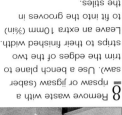

7 Trim the width of the panel to suit the door size. Measure out from the centre and mark the outer strips accordingly. This makes the layout of the panel symmetrical.

8 Remove waste with a ripsaw or jigsaw (saber saw). Use a bench plane to trim the edges of the two strips to their finished width. Leave an extra 10mm (⅜in) to fit into the grooves in the stiles.

9 Apply wood glue to the joints of one stile, insert both rails and carefully slide the panelling into place. The panelling itself is not glued, allowing each strip to expand or contract slightly without distorting the panel.

10 Gently tap the remaining stile into place and clamp the assembly on a flat surface. The horn at the end of the stile is clearly visible; it can be cut off when the glue is dry.

Making the drawer

1 When working in soft-wood, a shallower angle is required for the dovetails to ensure sufficient strength. An angle of about 10 degrees (pitch of 1:6) works well – draw up a simple scale on a piece of scrap wood to set the bevel gauge, and keep it safe for future use.

2 Mark the top face and edge of each drawer side and set out the tails. Note how the standard dovetail profile has to be altered to allow for a rebate (rabbet) for the bottom panel. Only the lower dovetail has a 12mm (½in) haunch that enters the rebate in the drawer front.

3 Cut out the tails and use a small bevelled chisel to pare down to the shoulder line. Mark the position of the bottom panel's rebate along the inner edge of each drawer side.

4 Apply chalk to the ends of the drawer back and front, align the sides and mark out the pins. The bottom pin must be cut short to accommodate the haunch on the dovetail. Here, the bottom rebate is being marked to suit.

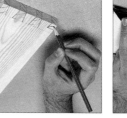

▶5 Cut out the pins, paring the bottom pin to suit the rebate depth.

▶6 Use a plough (bullnose) plane to rebate the inner edges of the drawer for the bottom panel.

7 Glue the joints and gently tap the drawer together. Use a rubber mallet to avoid bruising the wood.

8 Clamp the drawer together with a pair of sash clamps, using scraps of wood to protect the drawer sides. Wipe off excess glue and check for square with a try square.

9 When the glue is dry, fit the plywood bottom panel into the rebates and attach with panel pins (brads).

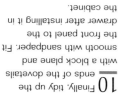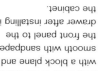

10 Finally, tidy up the ends of the dovetails with a block plane and smooth with sandpaper. Fit the front panel to the drawer after installing it in the cabinet.

Making the carcass

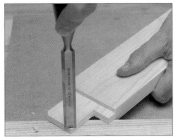

1 Make up the side panels in exactly the same way as instructed for the panelled cabinet door. Mark and cut out the mortises in the stiles as shown. The key to making the panels flat is to make sure that the cheeks of each mortise are cut accurately, providing parallel sides to receive the tenons.

2 The blind tenons do not pass completely through the rails. A useful tip when fitting a blind tenon is to nip off the corners to clear any obstructions at the very bottom of the mortise. Note the haunch on the tenon, which fits in the groove of the rail to help prevent twisting in the panel.

3 Use tongued-and-grooved cladding to form panel infills that match the door. This is particularly important for a freestanding unit where the sides will be visible. Cut the cladding to length and slot it together within the frame, as for the door. Glue and clamp the panels together in turn, making sure that they are kept flat and square.

4 Score across the ends of the stiles with a sharp knife and remove the horns with a tenon saw. Tidy up the end grain with a sharp block plane, and sand the panels before preparing them for assembly.

5 Use a router fitted with a 6mm (¼in) cutter to form a groove for the back in the inner face of each side panel. The groove should be set in from the back edge by exactly the thickness of the top rail, in this case 25mm (1in).

6 Cut the bottom panel to size, and rout a 6mm (¼in) groove in the back edge to match the side panels. Note how the depth of the panel is reduced by 50mm (2in) to allow the fitting of the front trim piece. Glue and clamp this in position so that it is flush with the surface of the panel, using biscuits to reinforce the joint.

Practical tip

A drawer box is a good project for practising dovetailing. The dovetail is a favourite joint for drawers, as it stands up well to the pulling action when the drawer is opened.

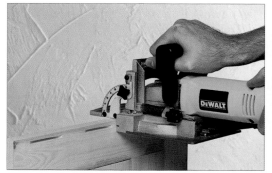

7 Biscuits are also used to set the side panels flush with the bottom of the unit. Cut three slots in the bottom rail of each side panel, keeping clear of the ends. Form corresponding slots in the edges of the bottom panel and insert the biscuits. No glue is needed.

8 Clamp the sides and bottom together so that the cross-dowels can be fitted at the corners. The cross-dowel is a neat device that allows small-section components to be bolted together to make a really strong assembly. Mark up each joint, using the dimensions given in the diagram (see figure 240.4), and drill a bolt hole through the side and into the rail.

9 Take the unit apart to fit the cross-dowels. Drill a blind hole of the correct diameter and depth to receive the metal cross-dowel. Note the tape wrapped around the drill bit to act as a depth gauge.

10 The top rails also need fitting with a 6mm (¼in) round wooden dowel to prevent them from twisting out of line when the bolts are tightened. Drill holes in the ends of the rails as shown in the diagram (see figure 240.5), use centre-points to mark the dowel positions on the side panels, and insert a dowel at each top corner.

11 Before finally assembling the unit, attach the fittings for the door. These adjustable base plates are required for the concealed hinges, allowing the door to be simply clipped into place. The exact fixing dimensions will be supplied with the hinges.

12 It is also easier to attach the drawer runners at this stage. They will be left and right handed, and must be fitted exactly square using a try square to the front edges so that the drawer runs level.

13 Connect the two sides to the bottom panel and the top rails, using the countersunk bolts and cross-dowels. The picture shows clearly how the connector operates – note how the slot in the top of the cross-dowel is used to align the threaded hole with the bolt.

14 Slide the back panel into its groove and attach it to the back rail with short panel pins. At this stage, the unit can be sanded and finished before attaching the plinth and adding the door and drawer.

15 Cut four lengths of timber to make a simple plinth, mitring the ends with a mitre saw. Fit a biscuit at each corner to aid alignment, then glue and clamp together, adding a couple of panel pins. Check that the assembly is square and leave to dry.

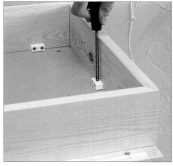

16 Note how the plinth runs the full width of the unit, but is slightly recessed at the front. Turn the cabinet upside down and attach the plinth to the bottom, using small wooden blocks or plastic joint blocks, as shown here.

17 Drill two holes in the door with a wood boring bit of a size to suit the concealed hinges. Position the holes following the instructions supplied with the hinges. Attach the hinges to the door, clip them into place on their backing plates and adjust until the door hangs squarely in its opening.

Practical tip

You can use MDF (medium-density fiberboard) for the internal panels of this unit provided you seal the edges for extra waterproofing. The sides, however, are solid wooden panels, properly jointed and finished for the extra quality that no man-made materials can match.

10

FRAMING PROJECTS

The ideal picture frame is one that effectively shows off what is contained within it, whether that is a photograph, a poster or print, a work of art, or the reflection in a mirror. It should not overpower the image, or clash with its style. Careful choice is one of the most important skills in framing, and knowing what will work best is something that often comes with practice. This chapter aims to show you how to take everything into account and frame your pictures successfully.

CUTTING AND JOINING A FRAME

Materials

- tape measure
- moulding
- mitre clamp or box
- saw
- pencil
- PVA (white) glue and brush
- frame clamp
- clean cotton rag
- V-nail joiner and V-nails or vice
- panel pins (brads) and tack hammer
- woodfiller
- cork sanding block
- medium- and fine-grade sandpaper

THERE ARE SEVERAL ways of cutting a length of moulding to make a basic frame, but the ends must always be cut at a precise angle. You can use either a mitre clamp or a wooden mitre box to guide the saw.

1 Measure the mounted artwork to give you the inside rebate measurement for the frame. Hold the length of moulding in a mitre clamp or box and cut the first end at a 45 degree angle. The edge of the moulding with the rebate should be the furthest from you.

2 Measure along the inside rebate of the moulding and mark the position for the next mitre cut on the face of the moulding.

3 Insert the moulding in the mitre clamp or box and saw at a 45 degree angle along the marked line.

4 Place the moulding in the mitre clamp or box. To make the next section of the frame, cut away the triangular "offcut" as in step 1 with the same 45 degree angle. Do this before you measure the second cut.

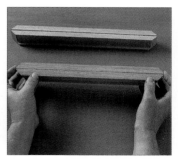

5 Measure and mark the second cut on the moulding. Repeat the steps until all four lengths are cut. Check that each pair – the two side lengths and the lengths for the top and bottom – is an exact match.

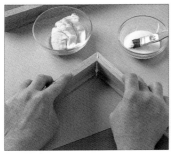

6 Using PVA (white) glue, secure two sections of the moulding together to make a right angle. Repeat with the other sections, then join them all together to make the frame.

7 Secure the frame clamp around the frame to hold the glued pieces together. Wipe away any excess glue with a damp cotton rag before it begins to set, otherwise it will form a waterproof barrier sealing the wood and any colourwash or woodstain you choose to use will not stain the wood around the joints.

8 Turn the frame right side down and insert V-nails into the corners of the back of the frame using a hand-held underpinner tool. Or, place the right-angled corners of the frame in a vice, and hammer panel pins (brads) into the corner edges of the moulding using a tack hammer. Once all four corners have been pinned, leave to dry.

9 Turn the frame right side up and fill the mitred corners with woodfiller. Wipe away any excess woodfiller with a damp rag. Allow to dry.

10 Use a cork block and medium-grade sandpaper to sand all over the frame and the rebate. Repeat with finer-grade sandpaper.

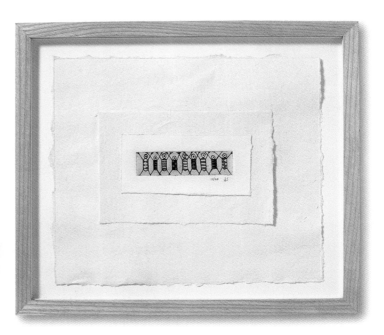

CREATING A REBATE

Builder's architrave, used for skirting (base) boards and door frames, can be used to make sturdy inexpensive frames. Architrave (trim) is flat on the reverse, so to enable it to hold a picture, glass and backing board you need to create a rebate (rabbet).

Using a router

A power router is quick to set up and the finished results are very professional. Edge-forming cutters have a rotating tip that runs along the edge of the wood. The rebate can be cut on lengths of moulding before making up the frame, or on the finished frame.

Materials

- power router
- rebate (rabbet) cutter with ball-bearing pilot tip
- spanner
- 2 G-clamps
- 2 lengths of architrave

1 Select a rebate cutter with a ball-bearing pilot tip. An edge-forming pilot tip allows the router to run along the edge of the architrave without a guide rail. Ensure the router is switched off, loosen the collet nut and fit the rebate cutter. Tighten the collet nut with a spanner (US wrench).

2 Clamp the length of architrave face down on a workbench. Clamp a second length in front of it on which to balance the router. Adjust the depth scale on the side of the router to the exact depth of the rebate required.

3 Balance the router on the two pieces of wood. Switch it on and use the plunge mechanism to drop the router on to the depth stop. Tighten the plunge-lock handle. Holding the router with both hands, advance the router into the architrave, using light pressure to move it along the length of the wood. Release the plunging mechanism when you reach the end and switch off.

Using fillets

Create a rebate (rabbet) by fitting lengths of wood, called fillets, on the reverse side of the frame. The depth of the wood should be the same as the required rebate – usually 1cm/½in. The width of the wood must be at least 5mm/¼in narrower than the architrave (trim), but if you do not want to see the fillet at the outer edge of the frame the width should be narrower still.

1 Measure the artwork to determine the inside measurement of the frame. Cut the first end of the architrave with a mitre saw set at 45 degrees. Measure the length required on the inside edge of the architrave. Turn the saw to the other side and line it up against the mark. Cut the second end. Cut two pieces of architrave for the sides and two for the top and bottom of the frame. Spread the cut ends with glue and assemble the frame.

Materials

- tape measure
- builder's architrave
- mitre box or clamp
- saw
- wood glue and brush
- frame clamp
- V-nails
- V-nail joiner
- mallet (optional)
- fillet of wood
- hammer
- panel pins (brads)

2 Fit a frame clamp on each corner and tighten the cord. Leave the glue to dry thoroughly.

3 Turn the frame over. Put a V-nail on the magnetic tip of the V-nail joiner with the sharp edge up. Check that the V-nail is correctly positioned across the joint and push down firmly. Repeat at each corner of the frame. You may need to use a mallet to drive the nails into harder woods.

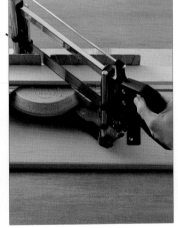

4 Cut the fillet at 45 degrees at one end. Add 1cm/½in to the inside length measurement of the frame, to allow for the rebate, and mark the fillet. Turn the saw to the other side. Line it up with the mark and cut the other end. Cut four pieces of fillet – one for each side of the frame.

5 Spread glue on the underside of the fillet pieces and arrange on the reverse side of the architrave frame. Butt the mitred corners together so that the rebate is the same depth all the way around. Hammer a panel pin (brad) through the fillet and into the architrave every 5cm/2in along each length and leave to dry.

DECORATIVE MOULDING FRAME

Materials

- tenon saw
- wood glue
- mitre block

Black Frame

- 1.6m/64in barley twist moulding
- 80cm/32in semicircular moulding
- 80cm/32in flat moulding
- black woodstain or ink
- paintbrush
- black shoe polish
- soft cloth
- shoe brush

Natural Frame

- 80cm/32in of 5mm/¼in square moulding
- 80cm/32in of 1.5 x 2cm/⅝in x ¾in flat moulding
- 2.4m/2⅝yd decorative moulding
- corner clamps
- clear polyurethane varnish and brush

COMBINE TWO OR THREE picture-framing mouldings to make your own made-to-measure frame. Two treatments are given to the mouldings chosen for this project: black stain, and a natural polyurethane varnish.

Black Frame

1 Using a tenon saw, cut 20cm/8in lengths from each piece of moulding. Using wood glue, join a barley twist and a semicircular moulding strip to each side of the flat moulding. (The semicircular moulding will form the rebate of the frame.) Allow the glue to dry completely.

2 Mitre the lengths of assembled moulding using a mitre block and tenon saw, and make up the frame (see Pressed Flowerhead Frame steps 1–4, p254). Mitre the remaining barley twist moulding and glue around the centre front of the frame. Allow to dry.

3 Stain the frame with black ink or woodstain applied with a paintbrush.

4 When the stain is dry, seal the wood and add a sheen with black shoe polish, applied with a soft cloth. Buff it up with a shoe brush.

Natural Frame

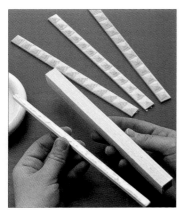

1 Using a tenon saw, cut four 20cm/8in lengths of square moulding. Cut four pieces of flat moulding to the same length. Glue a piece of square moulding to one edge of each piece of flat moulding.

2 Cut 12 pieces of decorative moulding, each 20cm/8in long. Glue two decorative mouldings to the front surface and one on the side. Leave the glue to dry thoroughly.

3 Mitre the ends of the assembled pieces, using a mitre block and tenon saw. Glue and clamp the corners accurately together.

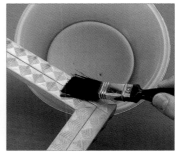

4 Apply one or more coats of clear polyurethane varnish to seal the wood and enhance the natural colours and grain of the wood.

PRESSED FLOWERHEAD FRAME

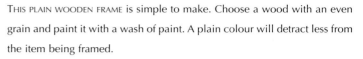

THIS PLAIN WOODEN FRAME is simple to make. Choose a wood with an even grain and paint it with a wash of paint. A plain colour will detract less from the item being framed.

Materials

- pencil
- ruler
- 80cm/32in length of softwood, 7.5cm/3in wide and 2cm/¾in thick
- mitre block
- saw
- wood glue
- staple gun
- white cardboard
- craft (utility) knife and cutting mat
- wine cork
- PVA (white) glue and brush
- small paintbrushes
- emulsion (latex) paint: white
- acrylic paint: pale green and dark blue
- artist's paintbrush
- pressed scabious flowerhead
- double-sided adhesive tape

1 Using a pencil and ruler, mark the softwood into four equal lengths of 20cm/8in, then mark a 45 degree angle at each end of each length.

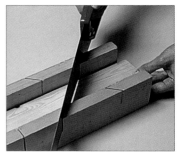

2 Place the wood in a mitre block and cut along the marked angles with a saw. These will form the mitres at the corners of the frame.

3 Glue the four pieces together with the wood glue to make a square frame. Leave to dry.

4 Reinforce the glued joins on the reverse side, using a staple gun.

◀ 5 Cut a piece of white cardboard the same size as the frame. Using a craft knife, and working on a cutting mat, cut a 1cm/⅜in slice of cork to support the flowerhead.

▶ 6 Glue the cork support to the centre of the cardboard. This will act as a backing board.

7 Apply two coats of white emulsion (latex) paint to the front of the frame and the backing board, allowing each to dry before applying the next.

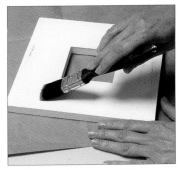

8 Take up a little green paint on a dry brush and lightly brush over the frame to leave a trace of paint on the surface.

9 Using an artist's paintbrush, colour the inside and outside edges of the frame with dark blue acrylic paint.

10 Glue the scabious flowerhead to the cork support in the centre of the backing board.

11 Centre the frame over the backing board and hold in place with strips of double-sided adhesive tape.

HALVING JOINT FRAME

Instead of making a mitre at each corner, this design for a sturdy frame employs halving joints, cut using a saw and chisel. Halving joints rely on glue for their strength but can be reinforced with dowels or screws.

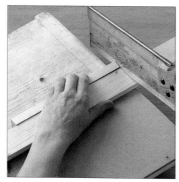

1 Measure the artwork horizontally and vertically to determine the aperture size of the frame. Add twice the width of the wood to each measurement to find the length and width of the frame. Cut two pieces of wood the length and two the width of the frame.

2 Use one of the cut pieces to mark the width of the wood at both ends of each piece. Use the square to mark the wood across the width and down the side. Mark the centre line on both sides at each end of the wood.

Materials

- tape measure
- pencil
- 12 x 50mm/½ x 2in wood
- tenon saw
- T-square
- bench hook
- clamp
- chisel and mallet
- wood glue and glue brush
- 5mm/¼in dowel
- drill and 5mm/¼in drill bit
- tack hammer
- medium- and fine-grade sandpaper

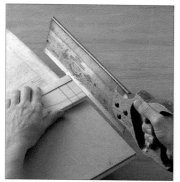

3 Fit the marked wood against a bench hook and saw along the line through to the halfway mark, bringing the saw to the horizontal to make a straight cut. Make two or three further saw cuts to make chiselling out the waste easier.

4 Secure the wood to the bench with a clamp. Using the chisel and a mallet cut away the waste wood above the line. Turn the wood round and chisel out from the other side.

5 Once most of the wood is removed, work with the chisel horizontally to remove the remaining raised portion in the middle. Cut all four frame pieces in the same way with the cut joints on the same side.

6 Turn the side sections over to the reverse side and assemble the frame. Glue the cut surfaces of the joints and clamp together. Check the corners are square and leave to dry.

7 For a stronger, more decorative dowelled joint, mark a diagonal line from the corner of the aperture to the outer corner of the frame. Measure along this line to mark the dowel positions. Cut eight pieces of dowel the same depth as the frame.

8 Clamp the frame to scrap wood and drill through at each mark. Drop a little glue into each hole. Tap the pieces of dowel into the holes and leave to dry. Sand the edges of the joints so that they are flush with the frame.

Materials

- wooden frame
- 4 decorative frame corners
- PVA (white) glue and brush
- acrylic paint
- paintbrush
- varnish or wax

Adding decorative corners

To give a plain frame a more individual appearance, add decorative corners and paint them to match the frame. Corners are available in a variety of styles and sizes and are sold by most art and picture framing suppliers.

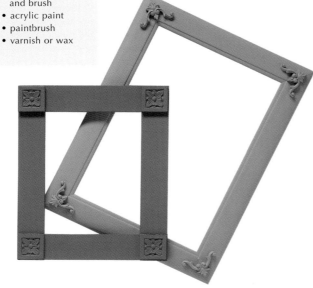

1 Apply glue to the reverse of each frame corner in turn, then position them at each corner of the frame. Leave to dry on a flat surface.

2 Cover the frame, including the corners, with two coats of acrylic paint and leave to dry. Varnish or wax the frame as required.

DEEP BOX FRAME

Materials

- 1.5m (5ft) of 50 x 25mm (2 x 1in) hardwood
- 355 x 280mm (14 x 11in) of 3mm (⅛in) hardboard for the backing
- PVA wood glue
- Panel pins (brads)
- Retaining clips
- Fixing attachment

VISIT ANY PICTURE FRAMING SHOP and you can take your pick from literally hundreds of different frames and mouldings. There is nothing to stop you making your own, however. Some pictures will look better if displayed in a deep box frame. This one was made from white oak with a clear lacquered finish.

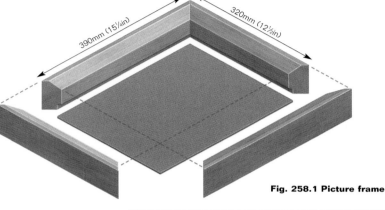

390mm (15¼in)

320mm (12½in)

Fig. 258.1 Picture frame

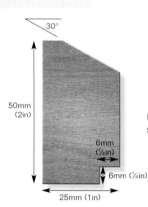

30°

50mm (2in)

6mm (¼in)

6mm (¼in)

25mm (1in)

Fig. 258.2 Section

Practical tip

To calculate the internal dimensions of the frame, the size of the picture should be measured off along the inner edge of the rebate (rabbet), then 6mm (¼in) subtracted from each end to determine the measurement along the inner face of the wood. Finally, add on a small margin for clearance.

Construction

This design has a chamfered profile to give the box frame added depth. You can improvise any variation to suit your own taste. A section of the profile used for this frame is shown in figure 258.2. The depth of the rebate is determined by the thickness of glass and backing board, plus the picture and its mount.

Cut the hardboard backing to size, then have a piece of glass cut to exactly the same size. Slip the glass into place. Fit small brass clips to act as retainers for the backing and check everything for a good fit before mounting the picture.

1 Cut the four frame members roughly to length before forming the rebate (rabbet). Leave them over-length at this stage. Use a plough (bullnose) or rebate plane to cut the rebate to a suitable depth in the bottom edge.

2 Turn the work over and plane a chamfer on the inner edge. Set a bevel gauge to 30 degrees, mark the angle at each end, and use a small block plane to trim accurately down to the line.

3 Check the angle of the chamfer with the bevel gauge as you work, particularly at the ends where the corners will meet.

4 Make a 45 degree mitre cut at one end of each frame member with a mitre saw. Calculate your internal measurements as instructed.

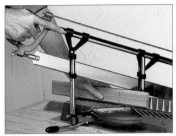

5 Mark this measurement on the inner face and square a line across the face. Align the mitre saw with this line and cut each piece to the right length.

6 Use mitre clamps to hold the assembly together while you check that the mitres are a good fit. Make any adjustments with a block plane, apply glue to each face and reassemble, tightening the clamps.

7 Fasten each corner with a couple of panel pins (brads) to lock them together. In a very hard wood such as oak, it is advisable to drill short pilot holes to avoid splitting the delicate mitre joints.

8 Before the glue has set, fit a web clamp around the frame. This helps keep the assembly square. Tighten the ratchet clamp with a spanner (US wrench), check the frame with a try square and leave for the glue to dry.

9 When the glue has set, clean up the edges of the frame and sand smooth all round by hand. Apply the finish and fittings of your choice.

MIRROR FRAME

It is remarkable how a plain mirror can be enhanced by adding a narrow bevel around the edge of the glass. This bevel-edged frame, which is built to generous proportions out of thick material, creates an even more striking effect. It was made from solid ash, which has a strongly figured grain, and it is simply finished with a coat of clear pale polish.

Materials

- Sufficient 75 x 30mm (3 x 1⅛in) hardwood to surround the chosen mirror
- 4 25mm (1in) barrel nuts
- fixing attachment

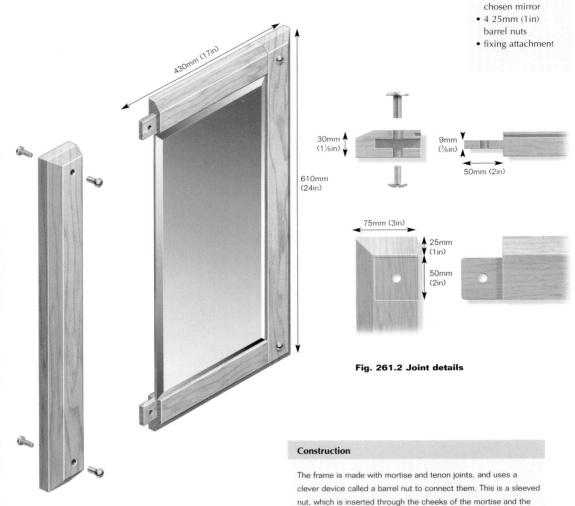

Fig. 261.2 Joint details

Fig. 261.1 Mirror frame

Construction

The frame is made with mortise and tenon joints, and uses a clever device called a barrel nut to connect them. This is a sleeved nut, which is inserted through the cheeks of the mortise and the blade of the tenon to lock them together. Should the worst happen and the mirror have to be replaced, simply remove the bolts, tap out the barrels and the frame will come apart easily.

1 Cut the frame members to length to suit the mirror. Set out the mortise and tenons according to the dimensions given in figure 261.2. Deduct 6mm (¼in) all round from the overall size of the mirror to determine the internal size of the frame. Chop out the mortise to a depth of 50mm (2in) and clean up the corners with a bevelled chisel.

2 Cut a 25mm (1in) haunch to each tenon with a tenon saw so that the blade is 50mm (2in) square. Pare down the tenon to be a loose sliding fit in the mortise – it should not be too tight. Nip the corners off the tenon to prevent it from fouling the bottom corners of the mortise.

3 Cut a slot on the internal edge of each component to receive the mirror. The exact dimension will depend on the thickness of the mirror glass and the size of the bevelled edge. This frame required a slot only 3mm (⅛in) wide and 6mm (¼in) deep, which was carefully cut on a circular saw bench.

4 Plane a 25mm (1in) bevel on the outer edge of each frame member. The ends of the upright members, often known as stiles, will also require matching bevels. It is better to leave these until the next step, after the joint is fitted together, in order to achieve a good match.

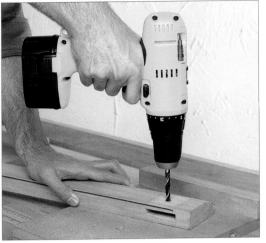

5 Before assembling the frame, drill an 8mm (⁵⁄₁₆in) diameter through-hole in the centre of each mortise. Clear the waste, insert the tenon and use the same drill bit to mark the centre of the hole on the blade. While the joint is still fitted together, mark the bevel required on the ends of the stiles. Finish the corner detail with a sharp block plane.

6 Take the frame apart again to drill matching holes in the tenons. For a really perfect fit, they should be offset slightly toward the shoulder. This will draw the joint up tight when the barrel nut is inserted. Use a bradawl to offset the centre point by 1.5mm (¹⁄₁₆in). Make sure the hole is drilled straight and square.

7 It is a good idea to assemble the frame first without the mirror so that you can check that everything fits perfectly. Tap two of the barrel nuts into place; you should find that the rails are drawn up tight on to their shoulders. Remove one side of the frame, slip the mirror into place and reassemble the frame.

8 Insert the male portion of the connector from the back of the frame into the threaded sleeve and tighten with a wide-bladed screwdriver. You now have a completely secure frame assembly that can be dismantled easily if you have to remove the mirror glass for any reason. Choose a suitable fixing attachment for the weight of the mirror frame.

CROSS-OVER FRAME

Materials

- tape measure
- length of square section wood, 15mm/⅝in wide
- pencil
- tenon saw
- bench hook or vice
- G-clamp
- chisel
- flat surform file
- coarse sandpaper
- fine sanding pad
- PVA (white) glue and brush
- board and weight
- rubber (latex) gloves
- soft clean cotton rags
- dark woodstain
- black patinating wax

THE TRADITIONAL CROSS-OVER FRAME, often known as a school frame, is quite easy to make. The skill is in making each joint exactly the right size so that the sides of the frame fit securely together.

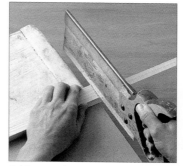

1 Measure the artwork and mount (mat) board horizontally and vertically to find the aperture size of the frame. Add 9cm/3½in to each measurement to determine the lengths of wood required for the frame. Cut two lengths and two widths.

2 Mark the wood 9cm/3½in from each end. Use a spare piece of the wood to mark the width of the joint and square the lines. Mark the halfway line on each side of the wood. Fit the wood in a bench hook or vice. Saw just inside each line down to the halfway mark. Turn the wood around and cut the other end in the same way. Cut all four pieces.

3 Clamp the wood to the bench and chisel out the waste wood a little at a time. On narrow wood strips use the chisel vertically with the flat surface towards the marked line. Push down firmly to remove the wood bit by bit.

4 To shape the edges of the frame, hold a flat surform file at an angle across the edge of the wood. File the wood between the chiselled-out sections until there is a 3–5mm/⅛–¼in flat surface that tapers off at each end.

5 Shape the ends of each piece using the surform. This time the shaped edge is tapered near the cut-out section and then comes right off the end rather than tapering again. Shape the ends of each piece.

6 Sand all the shaped edges with coarse sandpaper until they are smooth and rounded. Finish off with a fine sanding pad.

7 To assemble the frame, arrange the top and bottom sections of the frame the correct distance apart. Spread glue on all the sides of the cut-out sections of one of the side pieces and fit in place. Glue the other side in place. Place a board and weight on top of the frame until the glue dries.

8 Using a soft cloth, wipe the wood with a dark woodstain, making sure there is no bare wood showing in any inside corners around the cross-over joints. Leave to dry. To finish the frame, rub black patinating wax into the wood and buff up the surface with a clean cotton rag.

JIGSAW PUZZLE FRAME

Materials

- pencil
- cardboard
- craft (utility) knife
- cutting mat
- MDF (medium-density fiber-board), 9mm/⅜in thick
- marker pen
- 2 G-clamps
- protective face mask
- jigsaw (saber saw) with 2mm/¹⁄₁₆in blade suitable for MDF ruler
- offcut (scrap) of wood
- drill and 8mm/⅜in bit
- medium-grade sandpaper
- fine sanding pad
- router with rebate (rabbet)
- cutter
- clean cotton rag
- acrylic paint an paintbrush
- backing board
- panel pins (brads)
- tack hammer

ANY SHAPE OF FRAME can be cut from MDF using a carpenter's jigsaw. Draw your design and simply cut around it. You can cut the rebate (rabbet) into the aperture using a router.

1 Draw a jigsaw puzzle shape template on cardboard and cut it out using a craft knife and working on a cutting mat. Place the template on the MDF and draw around it using a marker pen. Clamp the MDF to the workbench so that the line you are going to cut first is clear of the bench. Wear a protective face mask when working with MDF to avoid inhaling dust particles.

2 Using a jigsaw, cut one side of the frame just outside the drawn line. Turn the template around to the next side. Continue turning and cutting until all four sides are cut.

3 In each corner of the aperture, draw an 8mm/⅜in square using a pencil and ruler and mark across each square on the diagonal to find its centre.

4 Place the frame on a piece of offcut (scrap) wood and clamp in position. Drill through the MDF into the offcut wood at each centre point. Secure the frame to the workbench so that the first side of the aperture is clear of the work surface. Cut along the line between the two holes. Turn the frame around and cut the other sides in turn.

5 Sand the frame edges. If you
are making frames to link
together, check the fit. Adjust as
necessary. Finish the frame with a
fine sanding pad.

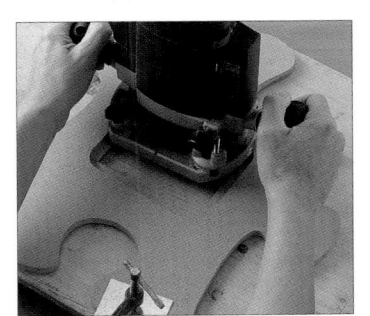

6 Fit a rebate cutter into the router.
Clamp the frame face down on the
workbench. Set the router depth.
Place the router in the aperture. Cut
out the rebate, then sand the frame.
Wipe the surface with a damp cloth.

7 Paint the frame as desired. Cut a
backing board to fit the aperture.
Insert the picture, then the backing,
and secure with panel pins (brads).

MULTI-WINDOW FRAME

SIMILAR IN EFFECT TO A MULTI-WINDOW MOUNT (mat), this frame is ideal for collections of objects – in this case, pressed leaves – and creates a dramatic three-dimensional effect. Finish the surface with Danish oil.

Materials

- tape measure
- T-square
- pencil
- 18mm/¾in birch plywood: 2 front verticals, 60 x 6cm/24 x 2⅜in; 4 front horizontals, 13 x 7cm/5 x 2¾in; back, 60 x 25cm/24 x 10in
- jigsaw (saber saw)
- tenon saw
- medium- and fine-grade sandpaper
- cork sanding block
- PVA (white) glue and glue brush
- self-adhesive sealing tape
- scissors
- soft cotton rags
- Danish wood oil
- dish
- rubber (latex) gloves
- sheer fabric
- metal ruler
- craft (utility) knife
- heavy weights or G-clamps
- tack hammer
- large-headed nails, 2.5cm/1in long
- epoxy resin glue and brush
- pressed leaves

1 With a tape measure, T-square and pencil, mark the lengths and widths of the plywood and saw the pieces to size. Butt the plywood pieces together to check that they fit. Cut the back of the frame and set aside. Sand down all the edges.

3 Once the glue has set, remove the tape. Use medium-grade sandpaper with a cork sanding block to sand the face and all edges of the frame. For a smooth finish, sand again with fine-grade sandpaper.

2 Apply PVA (white) glue to the ends of the horizontals and assemble the frame. Wrap self-adhesive sealing tape around the frame, both front and back. Wipe off the excess glue at once with a damp cloth and leave overnight to dry.

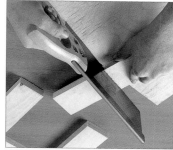

4 Place some Danish wood oil in a dish. Wearing rubber (latex) gloves, apply the oil all over the wood in a circular motion using a soft cloth. Work the oil into the wood. Buff up with a clean soft cloth.

9 Apply a coat of oil to the side edges of the backing board. Find the centre of each window and hammer in a large-headed nail, leaving approximately 1cm/⅜in showing. Mix a small amount of epoxy resin glue and apply this to the nail heads. Place a leaf on each nail and leave to set.

8 Place heavy weights or G-clamps on each corner and the middle section of the frame. Place a rag below the weights or clamps to prevent damage to the face of the frame. Wipe away excess glue with a damp cloth and leave to dry overnight.

7 Apply glue to the back of the frame front, then align the frame front and backing board and stick the two halves together.

6 Trim the excess fabric using a metal ruler and craft knife.

5 Apply a line of glue to the front of the backing board, approximately 3cm/1¼in in from the edge. Stick the fabric on to it. Leave to dry.

DRIFTWOOD FRAME

GOOD, CLEAN DRIFTWOOD can be hard to find even if you live near the sea, but you can make your own "driftwood" from old boards or packing crates. Break up the wood and distress the lengths with a chisel.

Materials

- packing crate or wooden board
- chisel
- hammer
- surform file
- coarse-grade sandpaper
- watercolour paints: green, crimson and blue
- paintbrushes
- epoxy resin glue
- coping saw
- hardboard
- chalkboard paint
- masking tape
- drill
- sisal string, 1m/1⅛yd
- scissors
- thick sisal rope, 1m/1⅛yd

1 Split the wood into narrower lengths using a chisel and a hammer.

2 Select four suitable lengths of similar width for the sides of the frame. Gouge chunks from the sides of the wood to make it look weatherbeaten.

3 Use a surform to file away the edges of the wood until they are smooth.

4 Sand the wood down with coarse-grade sandpaper to remove any splinters, and round off the edges.

5 Mix a thin colourwash using green, crimson and blue watercolour paints and brush it on to the wood. Allow the wood to dry.

6 Glue the frame together with epoxy resin glue and allow to dry. Cut a piece of hardboard to fit the back of the frame and paint the smooth side with chalkboard paint.

7 Tape the chalkboard to the back of the frame. Drill a hole in each corner through all the layers. Thread each end of a length of sisal string through the holes at the bottom of the frame, working from the back to the front. Knot the ends on the front of the frame. Trim any excess string.

8 Enlarge the two holes at the top of the frame and pass thick sisal rope through the holes as before, leaving enough excess rope to hang the frame. Tie a knot in each end on the front of the frame.

RECLAIMED TIMBER FRAME

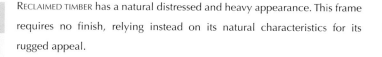

RECLAIMED TIMBER has a natural distressed and heavy appearance. This frame requires no finish, relying instead on its natural characteristics for its rugged appeal.

Materials

- reclaimed timber: 2 verticals, 62 x 10cm/25 x 4in, 2 horizontals, 18 x 10cm/7 x 4in
- tape measure
- pencil
- tenon saw
- sandpaper
- hardboard, 54 x 28cm/22 x 11in
- coping saw
- fabric glue and brush
- black felt
- decorative paper
- PVA (white) glue and brush
- chalk
- bradawl or awl
- 14 screws, 2.5cm/1in long
- screwdriver
- 4 reclaimed brackets
- 8 galvanized nails, 2.5cm/1in long
- hammer
- fillets, 5mm/¼in deep
- natural objects for framing

1 On the timber, measure and mark with a pencil the length and width of the frame verticals and horizontals. Use a tenon saw to cut the timber to the correct sizes. Lightly sand the sawn edges. Cut the hardboard backing board to size. Apply fabric glue to the back, then stick a piece of black felt on top. Glue decorative paper to the face of the backing board.

2 Mark out corner holes for the screws, using chalk. Turn the cut lengths of timber face down and butt them together at the corners. Place the felt-covered hardboard on the back of the timber. Make initial holes in the hardboard with a bradawl or awl, then screw into the back of the frame. The screws will hold the frame together.

3 Turn the frame the right way up and nail in the reclaimed brackets, using galvanized nails.

4 Cut small fillets to size, coat with PVA (white) glue, and use them to mount the framed objects to give a three-dimensional effect.

DISPLAY BOX FRAME

Materials

- length of batten, 30 x 5mm/1¼ x ¼in
- pencil
- metal ruler
- junior hacksaw
- wood glue
- panel pins (brads)
- hammer
- hardboard
- jigsaw (saber) or coping saw
- white acrylic primer
- paintbrush
- length of batten, 30 x 2mm/1¼ x ¹⁄₁₆in
- masking tape
- PVA (white) glue and brush
- tissue paper in assorted colours
- acrylic paint: yellow and blue
- artist's brushes
- small Indian shisha glass

A DEEP-SIDED, SECTIONED FRAME is the perfect way to display a collection of small objects such as ornaments, jewellery or badges. Custom-build the sections to suit the size of the objects in your collection.

1 Using the thicker battening, measure and cut four sides of the rectangular frame, then glue them together with wood glue and secure with panel pins (brads).

2 Cut a piece of hardboard to fit the frame and paint the smooth front side with acrylic primer. When dry, glue and pin it to the back of the frame.

3 Measure and draw out all the compartments. Cut the dividers from the length of thinner battening.

4 Assemble the compartments inside the box frame with wood glue, taping them in position with masking tape until the glue has set.

5 Coat the inside of each compartment with PVA (white) glue and cover with pieces of torn tissue paper. Work the tissue paper into the corners and keep applying the glue. Use light colours over strong colours to create depth.

6 Carefully retouch any areas of the compartments that need more colour, using yellow acrylic paint. Allow the paint to dry.

7 Use wood glue to attach lengths of the thinner battening to the outer edge of the frame, in effect creating a rebate (rabbet). Leave the glue to dry.

8 Cover the edge of the frame with a collage of blue tissue paper, using PVA glue.

9 Using an artist's brush, lightly brush over the tissue paper with blue acrylic paint. Leave to dry.

10 Glue small Indian shisha glass all around the frame. Arrange your collection in the compartments, securing the pieces with glue.

FRAME RESTORATION

BEAUTIFUL OLD FRAMES can often be found in junk shops, but are usually in need of some restoration. You can restore a frame to its former glory using cold-curing silicone rubber to make a mould for missing details.

Materials

- damaged gilded frame, cleaned
- cold-curing silicone base
- curing agent
- plastic container
- spoon
- small spatula
- bag of sand
- casting plaster
- small plastic pot
- craft (utility) knife
- 2-part epoxy resin glue
- 2-part epoxy putty
- artist's paintbrush
- emulsion (latex) paint: red
- picture framer's gilt wax

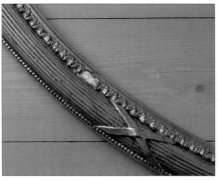

1 A small area on this frame is missing. Because it is intricately moulded it needs to be copied exactly in order to blend in with the rest of the frame.

2 Mix the cold-curing silicone and spread a thick coat on to an identical area that is clean and not damaged. Remove when dry.

3 Support the rubber mould on a bag loosely filled with sand. Mix a small amount of plaster in a plastic pot and pour the plaster into the mould. When it is full, shake it slightly to allow any air bubbles to rise. Leave to dry for 2 hours.

4 Remove the cast from the mould and use a craft (utility) knife to cut it to the right size to fit the missing area. Stick it to the frame with epoxy resin glue, then leave to dry for 24 hours. Fill any gaps between the cast and the frame with two-part epoxy putty, using a small spatula. Leave to dry for 2 hours.

5 Using an artist's paintbrush, paint the repaired area with red emulsion (latex) paint. Repeat if the plaster is not completely covered by the first coat. Leave to dry for 3 hours. Dip your finger in gilt wax and gently rub it over the red paint. Blend it in carefully at the edges of the repair to match the existing gilding.

11

HOME
MAINTENANCE
AND DIY

Where your home is concerned, prevention is often better, and certainly less expensive, than cure. A regular programme of inspection and maintenance will prevent small problems from becoming large and expensive ones. From time to time, however, repairs will be necessary, and their successful completion depends on having all the necessary tools and equipment to hand, and understanding how to use them.

FITTING LIGHTWEIGHT FIXTURES

Installing new fixtures and fittings is a basic do-it-yourself activity that covers a variety of tasks, such as hanging a picture, fitting drawer and door handles, putting up lightweight shelving, and fitting hooks, locks, clasps and catches on all manner of items. Many are very straightforward jobs, which involve simply screwing, pinning or sticking the fixture in place.

Supporting lightweight hooks and shelving

Fixtures of this kind include coat hooks, cup hooks and dozens of other quickly fitted aids and clips of all types. Threaded hooks and eyes need a pilot hole to be made with a bradawl (awl), after which they can be screwed in place with finger and thumb. Small shelves can be supported in a variety of ways, including using screw eyes, dowels and lengths of wood. All these methods are suitable for shelving that will carry little weight.

Fixing hanging rails to walls

When attaching a clothes or towel rail to a plaster or plasterboard (gypsum board) wall, it is best to fix a small wooden block to the wall at each end, using a single, central screw, then screw the rail brackets to the blocks. This avoids the need to drill closely-spaced holes in the wall for the fixing plates, which could cause the surface to crumble, or for the holes to merge into each other.

Below A variety of lightweight hooks.

Regency and Victorian style brass hooks

Brass cup hooks

Lightweight shelf bracket

Plastic self-adhesive dish towel hooks

Rubber dish towel hook

Lightweight shelf bracket

Tool hooks

Lightweight shelf bracket

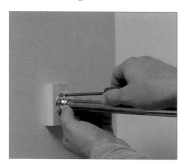

Above When fixing hanging rails, insert a wooden block between the fitting and the wall.

Hanging a cabinet

A good way to hang a small cabinet is with a wooden batten (furring strip) fixed to the wall with screws and plugs. The tapered top edge of the rail engages with a recess in the back of the cabinet, providing a safe mounting, yet allowing the cabinet to be lifted down when required. It is essential to ensure that the angles of both nails are the same for a good and secure fitting.

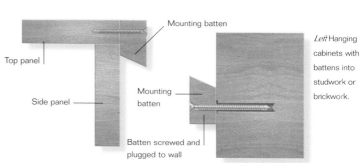

Top panel

Side panel

Mounting batten

Mounting batten

Batten screwed and plugged to wall

Left Hanging cabinets with battens into studwork or brickwork.

Hanging a picture

When hanging any artwork, it is important to consider the weight and size of the frame. Use picture wire or strong cord to hang any weight of frame. Light pictures can be hung with a single picture hook, which incorporates a hardened pin rather like a masonry nail and is driven directly into the wall.

Single or double D-rings are strong fixings for light to medium-weight frames, but you should use strap hangers for heavy or large frames. These are screwed on to the back section of the frame and wire or cord can be attached in the same way. However, if the frame is very heavy, it is recommended that you hang the picture from the loops of the strap hanger on to screws inserted directly into the wall.

Anti-theft devices (ATDs) and mirror plates work in much the same way as strap hangers. The straight section is screwed into the back of the frame, and the curved section is screwed to the wall.

Setting a striking plate (keeper) for a door catch

Fitting a striking plate incorporates the tasks likely to be encountered in the fixing of many small fittings: accurate positioning and marking, skill in cutting recesses to different depths, and the accurate fitting of countersunk

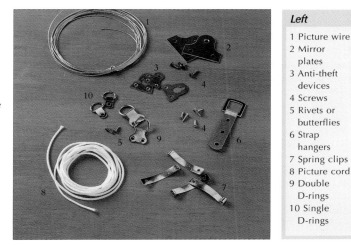

Left

1 Picture wire
2 Mirror plates
3 Anti-theft devices
4 Screws
5 Rivets or butterflies
6 Strap hangers
7 Spring clips
8 Picture cord
9 Double D-rings
10 Single D-rings

screws. You should offer the striking plate to the timber, making sure that it is in the correct position and square with both the lock and the door frame. Scribe around it, including the hole in the centre. Carefully chisel along the marked outline, starting with the cut across the grain at each end. Then chisel out the waste to the depth of the plate.

You will need to cut deeper with the chisel to create the mortise for the catch. Hold the plate in position and use a bradawl (awl) or gimlet to prick the positions of the screw holes. Drive in the screws, making sure that they fit flush into the countersunk holes in the plate.

Surface-mounted catches

The roller catch is often used on small cabinet doors, especially those in a kitchen. Offer up the striking plate first, marking the screw positions, drilling pilot holes and screwing the plate to the frame. Both striking plate and roller have elongated holes to allow for adjustment. The roller is fitted in the same way and adjusted accordingly.

The magnetic catch is also common. This is even simpler to fix, since it can be placed in a variety of positions on the door. Large doors may be fitted with two catches, one top and one bottom. Slotted mounting holes allow adjustment so that the catch works efficiently.

Above A striking plate set in an internal frame.

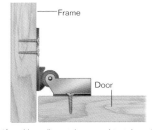

Above Use roller catches on cabinet doors for a smooth opening action.

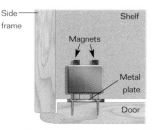

Above A magnetic catch is easy to fit but you may need to use more than one on large doors.

FITTING HEAVYWEIGHT FIXTURES

Heavyweight fixtures around the home tend to be of a permanent nature. Items such as sturdy shelving for books, and cabinets, wall-mounted televisions and cabinet speakers are very heavy, need a lot of support and tend to remain where they are installed originally. For this reason, heavy wall fixings are designed to be permanent.

Obtaining a good fixing

A frequently encountered problem with heavy fixtures is obtaining a good fixing in masonry. A traditional method, which is quite acceptable, is to drill and plug a wall with home-made tapered wooden plugs, driven in hard, and then screw into them.

There are some useful commercial products, too, such as the rawl bolt, which expands inside the hole as it is tightened and will provide a secure fixing for heavy shelving or wall units.

Post anchors are another option, although they are designed mainly for vertical posts outdoors. Some are adjustable to take either 75 or 100mm (3 or 4in) posts and can be used

horizontally to fix the frames for stud (dry) walling to concrete or stonework. Hanger screws are an easy method of fixing into woodwork to leave projecting studding, which can be used to secure heavy bookcases and room dividers, yet allow them to be removed simply by undoing the nuts.

Angle brackets

Many sizes of angle and straight steel bracket are available, and they have a variety of uses. Among them are fixing the top and bottom frames for wardrobes. They should be fitted inside the framing so that they cannot be seen. The top brackets should be screwed into the ceiling joists, which

you might have to locate by prodding with a sharp tool through the plaster, while the floor brackets should be screwed directly to the floorboards. Much the same applies to fitting the sliding rails for the doors.

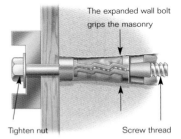

The expanded wall bolt grips the masonry

Tighten nut   Screw thread

Above How to fix a wall bolt.

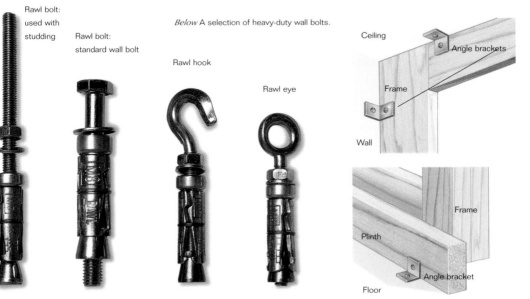

Rawl bolt: used with studding

Rawl bolt: standard wall bolt

Below A selection of heavy-duty wall bolts.

Rawl hook

Rawl eye

Ceiling

Angle brackets

Frame

Wall

Frame

Plinth

Angle bracket

Floor

Above Angle brackets positioned as above ensure stability and squareness.

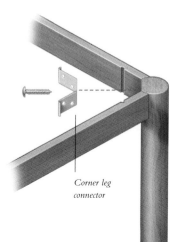

Above Steel angle plates or brackets, or knock-down fittings, can be used to strengthen joints, as well as allowing a piece of furniture to be taken apart if required. These ingenious corner brackets are used to fix the detachable legs and connect the side rails at the same time.

Corner leg connector

Heavy-duty brackets

There are many heavy-duty brackets to choose from, making all manner of joints possible. One of the most frequently used in the home is the joist hanger. This may be nailed or screwed to an existing timber beam to carry flooring joists, very heavy shelving or similar constructions. Some joist hangers are designed to lip into brickwork. Simple angled plates can be used for bracing the frames of stud walls. They may be nailed or screwed in place. You can also buy heavy-duty fixings for putting up bicycles, racks and ladders in garages. Most are simply bent angle irons with pre-drilled holes.

Fitting a television shelf

In a small room, a television is best mounted in a corner, otherwise it will have to be fixed high on the wall, which will make viewing difficult. When installing a television (or microwave) shelf, always follow the

Above A heavy steel bracket can be used for bracing a frame joint.

manufacturer's instructions, but generally you should offer the backplate to the wall at the desired height, making sure the television can swing around to the angle required, and mark its position. Drill holes for the bolts, screw them into place and add the movable shelf. Position the television and arrange the wiring so that it will not tangle.

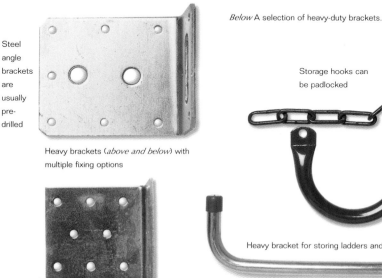

Steel angle brackets are usually pre-drilled

Heavy brackets (*above and below*) with multiple fixing options

Below A selection of heavy-duty brackets.

Storage hooks can be padlocked

Heavy bracket for storing ladders and bikes

FITTING SHELVES

Putting up shelves is a fundamental do-it-yourself task, and is probably one of the first jobs the newcomer will tackle. With a little thought, shelving can be made to be decorative as well as functional, and a variety of materials, including wood, metal and glass, can be used to good effect. All require firm wall fixings and always use a spirit level when fitting shelves.

Simple shelving

Ready-made shelving systems can be employed, both wall-mounted and freestanding. The basic methods of fitting shelving are the same, no matter what material is used. Essential requirements are establishing a truly level surface with a spirit level, obtaining firm fixings in the wall, and being able to fit accurately into an alcove.

Use your spirit level to ascertain the height and horizontal run of the shelf, then mark the positions for the brackets. Mark the positions of the screws through the holes in the brackets, drill with a masonry bit and insert wallplugs. Hold each bracket in place and start all the screws into the wallplugs before tightening them fully. This will ensure that they engage properly.

If fitting more than one shelf on an uninterrupted run of wall, mark them out at the same time, using a try or combination square. Cut them to size, then screw them to the shelf brackets.

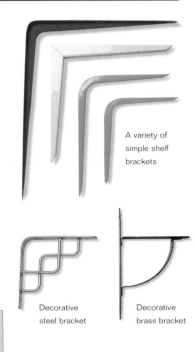

A variety of simple shelf brackets

Decorative steel bracket

Decorative brass bracket

Above A variety of very lightweight plastic shelf fittings

Fitting a simple shelf

1 Mark the position of the shelf with a level placed on top of a batten (furring strip).

2 Mark the position of the screws through the bracket holes.

3 Drill and insert your plugs. Start all the screws before tightening up.

4 Screw up the bracket into the shelf to make a secure fixing.

5 You can also attach the shelf to the brackets before mounting the brackets to the wall.

Fitting shelves in an alcove

1 Use two battens (furring strips) clamped together to measure in a confined space.

2 Transfer the measurement on to the wood to be used for the shelf and cut to length.

3 Align the position and fit the rear shelf using a spirit level and screw in position.

Alcoves

An easy way to measure the internal width of an alcove is by using two overlapping strips. Allow them to touch each end of the alcove and clamp them together on the overlap. Transfer this measurement to the shelving material and carefully cut it to length.

Establish the position for the back batten with a spirit level. Drill and plug the holes, then screw the batten in place. Using the back batten as a reference point, fit the side battens to the end walls of the alcove.

Drill screw clearance holes in the shelf, place the shelf on the battens and screw it down. When fitting shelves into an alcove, do not cut all the shelves to the same size. If the sides of the alcove are plasterwork, brick or stone, there will almost certainly be some discrepancies in the width from top to bottom, so measure for each shelf individually and cut them separately.

If there is an uneven gap along the back of a shelf, caused by an uneven wall surface, you can hide the gap by pinning quadrant moulding (a base shoe) along the back edge of the shelf.

4 Drill the holes in the side battens and screw into place using the back batten as a guide.

5 Pre-drill the screw holes in the shelf and screw on to the side battens from the top.

Planning shelves

Think of how to make best use of the new storage space. Make a rough sketch of the plans, in order to take into account which items are going to be stored, such as the height and width of books, or the clearance that ornaments and photographs require. Aim to keep everyday items within easy reach, which in practice is between about 750mm (2ft 6in) and 1.5m (5ft) above the floor. Position deep shelves near the bottom so that it is easy to see and reach the back. Allow 25–50mm (1–2in) of clearance on top of the height of the objects to be stored, so that they are easy to take down and put back.

Think about weight too. If the shelves are going to store heavy objects, the shelving material must be chosen with care, since thin shelves will sag if heavily loaded unless they are well supported. With 12mm (½in) chipboard (particle board) and ready-made veneered or melamine-faced shelves, space brackets at 450mm (18in) for heavy loads or 600mm (2ft) for light loads. With 19mm (¾in) chipboard or 12mm (½in) plywood, increase the spacing to 600mm (2ft) and 750mm (2ft 6in) respectively. For 19mm (¾in) plywood, blockboard, MDF (medium-density fiberboard) or natural wood, the bracket spacing can be 750mm (2ft 6in) for heavy loads, 900mm (3ft) for light ones.

FITTING SHELVING SYSTEMS

Storage can be provided in one of two ways. One is to buy or make pieces of freestanding furniture that match the required storage function. The other is to use raw materials such as wood and manufactured boards plus the appropriate hardware to create built-in storage space, arrays of shelving, closets in alcoves, wardrobes and so on.

Buying shelving systems

Shelving systems abound in do-it-yourself stores for those who prefer simply to fit rather than to make the shelving. There is a range of brackets on the market to cater for every need, and these clip into slotted uprights screwed to the wall. The bracket positions can be adjusted to vary the spacing between the shelves to accommodate your needs. Shelving systems are a versatile way of dealing with changing requirements, and they have the distinct advantage of being portable when you need to move them. They are capable of holding quite heavy weights, but remember that ultimately a shelf's capacity depends on the strength of the wall fixing that you have employed.

First measure the distance between the shelving uprights, bearing in mind the thickness and material to be used for the shelf. Books can be very heavy, so do not set the uprights too far apart, otherwise the shelf will sag in the middle. About a quarter of the length of the shelf can overhang each end. If necessary, cut the uprights to length. Drill and plug the wall so that you can attach one upright by its topmost hole. Do not tighten the screw fully at this stage. Simply allow the upright to hang freely.

Hold your spirit level against the side of the upright, and when you are satisfied that it is vertical, mark its position lightly on the wall with a pencil. Mark in the remaining screw positions, then drill and plug the rest of the screw holes.

Fitting a shelving system

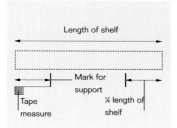

1 Measure the distance between the uprights. Do not set the brackets too far apart.

2 Fix the first screw loosely and let the upright hang.

3 Check the bracket is absolutely vertical with a spirit level.

4 A little packing card may be necessary if the wall is uneven.

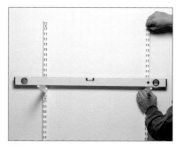

5 Mark the position for the second upright using the first as a guide.

6 The shelf brackets can be inserted at different heights and can be easily moved.

You may find that when you tighten the screws, the upright needs a little packing here and there to keep it vertical in the other plane. If these discrepancies are not too large, this adjustment can be done by varying the relative tightness of the screws, which will pull the upright into line. You can mark off the position for the second upright and any others, using a spirit level on top of a shelf with a couple of brackets slipped into position. Fitting the second upright entails the same procedure as before.

Freestanding shelving

These shelving units usually come packed flat for home assembly. They can be very useful and versatile pieces of furniture. They are available in a variety of materials, including pine, manufactured boards and metal. Knock-down joints are often used in their construction.

There is a possibility that boisterous children could pull freestanding shelving over, so it is worth attaching a unit to a wall, if only temporarily until the children are a little older. This can be done with a couple of brackets screwed and plugged to the wall, or with brackets to the floor.

Above A well-organized shelving arrangement for a wardrobe system.

Left Knock-down joints are used primarily in symmetrical structures to ensure squareness.

Practical tips

- If there is a gap along the back of a shelf, caused by an uneven wall, you can hide the gap by pinning quadrant moulding (a base shoe) along the back edge of the shelf.
- Select the screw sizes according to the load that a shelf will have to take.

Corner units

A popular form of shelving, corner units represent an efficient way of using what otherwise might be redundant space. They can be made from plywood with some form of lipping applied to the front edge to hide the laminations, or they can be quite ornate and made in an expensive hardwood. Cut the triangular shelves so that the angle at the apex, which fits into the corner, is slightly over 90 degrees. This will ensure that the front edges touch the wall where they will be seen. Mirror plates provide a neat, unobtrusive means of fixing corner units.

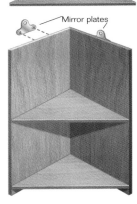

Mirror plates

Above Mirror plates hang the cabinet rather than pinning it to the wall.

HANGING DOORS

Installing a new door is not a difficult task, but the job does need patience, precision and organization to go smoothly. A methodical step-by-step approach will pay off. The following sequence relates to hanging a new door, and you may only need to trim some of the door. If you are fitting an old door or simply moving one, advice is given in an earlier section of the book.

Types of door

Many modern internal doors are hollow structures with "egg-box" centres and solid timber lippings around the edges. They offer little flexibility for trimming to fit frames that are out of square, which often occurs in an old building. For this reason, as well as for aesthetic appeal, use only solid doors in older houses.

Putting in a new door

Measure the frame accurately, top to bottom and side to side, then choose a door that will fit as closely as possible. Even so, it will probably need to be cut to fit.

Joggles, or horns, may project from the ends of the door to protect it in transit. Mark these off level with the top of the door, using a try square. Place the door on a flat surface and

carefully cut the joggles flush with the ends of the door, using a hand saw. Offer up the door to the frame, placing wedges underneath (chisels are handy) to raise it off the floor by about 12mm (½in) to allow for a carpet or other floorcovering.

Mark the door in pencil while it is wedged in place to allow for a 3mm (⅛in) clearance at the top and sides. Place the door back on the flat

Hanging a door

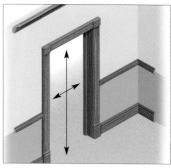

1 Measure the door frame to assess the size of the door you require.

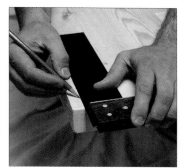

2 If there are joggles, square them off accurately using a try or combination square.

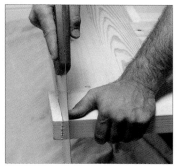

3 Remove the joggles with a hand saw making a clean, square cut.

7 Plane the edges, working in from both sides. Offer the door into the frame to check it fits.

8 Lay the hinge on the door and cut around it with a sharp knife.

9 Alternatively, scribe the outline of the hinge on to the door with a marking gauge.

surface and saw off the bulk of the waste, leaving the marked lines still visible. Plane down the sides of the door to the marked lines, working with the grain, then plane the top, working in from each side to avoid splintering the wood. Replace the door in the frame, wedging it once more to hold it. If you are satisfied with the fit, you can hang it.

Hold each hinge in position, about 150mm (6in) from the top and 225mm (9in) from the bottom of the door, with the knuckle projecting just beyond the face of the door; mark it with a knife. For a heavy door, a third hinge will be needed, positioned the third hinge centrally between the other two. Working around the marked outline, cut vertically down into the wood to the depth of the hinge flap with a chisel.

Make a series of cuts across the width of the recess, to the same depth, and remove the waste with a chisel. Place the hinge in the recess, drill small pilot holes for the screws, but fit only one screw at this stage. Repeat with the other hinge.

Open the hinges and offer the hinge side of the door to the frame, placing wedges under it to raise it to the correct height. Press the free flap of each hinge against the frame and mark around it in pencil. Cut the recesses. Drill pilot holes and hang the door, again fitting only one screw in each hinge flap. When you are satisfied with the fit and operation of the door, insert all the screws, making sure that the heads lie flat in the countersinks of the hinges, otherwise the door will not close properly.

Practical tip

When hanging a door, you'll need someone to help with positioning.

4 Offer the door into the frame. Use a wedge to square up if need be.

5 Mark the clearance on to the frame using a pencil and a 3mm (⅛in) washer as a guide.

6 Saw off the bulk of the waste using your knee as a support on the end of the door.

10 Chop out the waste with a chisel working along the scribed line.

11 Insert the hinge into the recess and screw up tightly.

12 Mark the other part of the hinge on the door frame with a pencil.

REPLACING CABINET DOORS AND DRAWERS

Old and tired-looking cabinets can often be revived by a coat of paint, the addition of stencilled patterns or the application of decorative laminates, however, sometimes the only way to revive them is to renew the doors and drawer fronts themselves. This is neither a complex nor very expensive job and it can be fun to do.

Replacing chipboard doors

This may also be necessary if the hinges have failed in chipboard (particle board) doors, which can occur with kitchen furniture after a number of years because of its heavy workload. If you replace old chipboard doors with new ones, they must be exactly the same size and be hung in the same way as the originals, since they cannot be trimmed to fit. Doors such as these are readily available, along with the chipboard hinges necessary to fit them. It is important to ensure that the hinge positions are perfectly accurate

and that their recesses are of the correct depth, so careful measuring and a reliable drill stand or pillar drill is essential.

Remove the old door from the hinge baseplates by slackening each retaining screw, not the adjuster, and sliding the door off. Then release the two retaining screws and remove each hinge from the door, leaving a circular hole.

Place the new door over the old one so that the top edges are aligned, then measure down to the centre of each hole. Next measure to the centre of each hole from the edge to locate

Above Revive tired-looking kitchen cabinets with a new coat of paint or new doors.

their positions exactly. Use a combination square as a gauge to take the centre position from the old door and transfer it to the new one. Mark the positions of the hinge holes on the new door with a centre punch. Bore the hinge recesses with a pillar drill or a drill mounted in a drill stand for accuracy. Be sure to set the stop to the correct depth.

Insert the hinges, making sure they are square to the edge of the door and screw them in place. Replace the door, using the adjustment screws to obtain a perfect fit with the face of the unit.

Replacing a door

1 Take off the old hinge simply by unscrewing it from the side.

2 Measure accurately from the edge of the old door to the hinge hole.

3 Transfer the mark to the new door to ensure a perfect position for the new hinge.

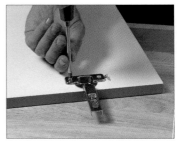

4 Drill out a new hole, preferably using a static drill stand for accuracy

5 Attach the new hinge in the same position on the new door as the old.

Replacing a drawer front

1 Remove the old drawer front by unscrewing it from behind.

2 Drill the new front using the existing holes as a guide.

3 Screw the new drawer front into position from behind.

Drawer fronts

The drawers of modern furniture are often made with false fronts that allow a basic carcass to be used in a number of different styles. To replace, open the drawer or, better still, remove it completely. From inside the drawer, slacken the screws holding the false front to the carcass and remove it. Place the old front over the new one, aligning it exactly, drill down through the screw holes and into the new front to make pilot holes for the screws. Take care not to drill right through the new face and spoil the finish. Use a depth stop to prevent this. Finally, screw the new front to the carcass from the inside.

Practical tip

When fitting screws in hardwood doors, always drill pilot holes for them, otherwise it may be impossible to drive them in completely. Brass or small gauge screws may even snap.

Fitting a louvre door

1 Fit a flush hinge to the door. Surface mounting makes this easy.

2 Screw a magnetic catch beneath the bottom shelf of the cabinet.

3 Screw a magnetic catchplate to the door, both the top and bottom.

4 Change the handle or knob to suit the style of your door.

Fitting solid wood doors

With solid-timber-framed cabinets, an attractive option is to fit louvred doors, which are made of solid timber and are available in a host of standard sizes.

Fitting louvre doors, or other solid wooden doors, to cabinets follows the basic procedures for hanging any door. First fit the hinges to the inside of the door, then open the hinges and fit them to the cabinet stile. Note that fitting a cabinet door with butt hinges is only recommended for solid timber framing.

Cabinet doors can be fitted with a variety of handles and knobs to suit the style of furniture. Often, changing the handles alone can improve the appearance of a cabinet considerably. A small brass handle, for example, makes a nice finish or use stainless steel for a modern look.

REPLACING WALL-MOUNTED BOARDS

Skirting (base) boards receive a lot of wear and tear from scuffing by feet and furniture, which is why they are there in the first place, of course. From time to time, the damage may be so great, such as after replacing flooring, including woodstrip or laminate flooring, that sections of skirting or even complete lengths of it need to be replaced.

Types of boards

Skirting boards may vary from simple rectangular sections of timber to quite ornate moulded profiles. Similarly, picture rails and dado rails, sometimes called chair rails because they protect the walls from damage by chair backs, may need to be renewed or repaired. In many ways these tasks are similar.

Dealing with corners

When fitting a moulded shape with concave curves into a corner, the correct way to achieve the joint is to scribe it. This is done by marking the profile of one board on to the back of the other with the aid of a small offcut

of the moulding. Then a coping saw is used to cut along the marked line, allowing the board to fit neatly over its neighbour. This technique avoids the mismatch of ends that can occur when some mouldings are mitred at 45 degrees, using a mitre box or mitre saw. However, to cut an external mitre for a wall return, use a mitre saw or mitre box in the normal way.

Skirting board

In a rectangular room, it is always best to fit the two long sections of skirting board first and then fit the shorter ones to them. It makes handling, lifting and fixing much easier. To fit the boards, first prise the

Replacing a section of skirting board

1 Prise away the old skirting board with a crowbar and a wedge.

2 Cut away the damaged section with a mitre box and a saw.

3 Mark each end of the new section of board and mitre the ends.

4 Hammer nails into the new section of board while holding a plank against the wood.

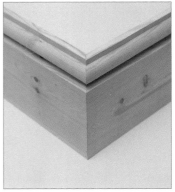

Above Internal and external mitres of a skirting board.

Putting up a new dado (chair) rail

1 Prise away the old rail from the wall using a crowbar.

2 Remove any residual nails in the wall or plaster with a pair of pincers.

3 Fill any cracks or holes in the plasterwork with filler.

old board partially away from the wall, using a crowbar, then insert wedges to hold it far enough away to allow you to get at it with a saw. Place a mitre block tight against the board and, with a tenon saw, nibble away at it at 45 degrees until the board is cut in half. Repeat the 45-degree cut at the other end of the section to be replaced and remove the length of old skirting. Then offer up the replacement section, mark each end with a pencil and mitre accordingly.

A good way to hold the new section in position is to lay a plank so that it butts up against the skirting and kneel on it while driving the nails home.

Replacing a picture or dado (chair) rail

Use a crowbar to prise the picture rail away from the wall, inserting a block of wood under its head to protect the plaster and to give extra leverage.

Remove any nails that remain in the wall with a pair of pincers, again using a block of wood to protect the wall. Make good the nail holes with filler, leaving it slightly proud at this stage. When the filler is completely dry, sand it down with sandpaper wrapped

4 Sand off the dry filler with sandpaper to get a smooth finish.

around a cork block or block of wood to give a perfectly flat, smooth surface. Fit the new picture rail, scribing or mitring the ends as necessary.

Fixing methods

Cut-nails, such as those used to fix skirting boards, have long been used to fix picture rails, Delft rails and the like, but you may find that they are not available in your local store. Any ordinary wire lost-head nail is a good alternative when fixing through plasterwork into stud (dry) walling, as long as you know where the studs are.

5 Fit the new rail to the wall, making sure it is properly level.

Cutting a scribed joint

Use a scrap of the board as a guide. Grip a pencil against the scrap of wood and run it down the surface of the back of the board to transfer the outline. Cut it out with a coping saw.

WORKING WITH MOULDINGS

A moulding is the term used to describe any section of wood that has been shaped, either by hand or by machinery, to alter the square profile of the original piece. This may range from rounding over the sharp edges of the finished work to adding more decorative detail. Alternatively, profiled cutters can be fitted in a router to make your own mouldings and create a range of decorative effects.

Cutting angles

In most applications, mouldings are not difficult to fit, but there is a small range of handy aids that make cutting accurate angles a simple process. The most basic of these is the mitre box or block. Essentially, this is a small jig with slots, in most cases cut to 45 and 90 degrees since these are by far the most commonly used angles for saw cuts. The slots hold the saw blade at the correct angle for making the required cut through the moulding. Normally a tenon or backsaw is used. More complex is the hand mitre saw,

Quadrant moulding (base shoe)

Ovolo

Scotia (cove)

Astragal moulding

Ogee moulding

Angled hockey stick moulding

Hockey stick moulding

Skirting torus moulding

Chamfer skirting base

Tongued-and-grooved moulding

Tongued, grooved and beaded moulding

Above Typical mouldings used on frames, architraves (trims) and skirting (base) boards.

Fitting a shelf moulding

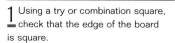

1 Using a try or combination square, check that the edge of the board is square.

2 Cut the mouldings at 45 degrees to go around the edges of the board.

3 Glue and fix the mouldings to the board with masking tape. Leave overnight to dry.

4 Clamp the board and carefully clean up any rough edges with a plane.

the blade of which can be set to any required angle, although usually stops are provided for the most commonly used ones: 90, 45 and 22.5 degrees. This tool can be used for cutting mouldings, lippings, architraves (trims), picture rails and skirting (base) boards. The most sophisticated aid is the powered mitre saw, which will do all that the hand mitre saw can do and cut compound mitres as well. These saws produce perfectly angled cuts and are often used by picture framers.

Fitting a moulding without nails

Small-section mouldings can often be fixed with glue rather than nails. First, establish that the edges of the panel to which the mouldings will be attached are true, using a try square. Cut the mouldings to length, mitring the ends at 45 degrees. Attach the mouldings to the edges of the panel using wood glue and hold them in place with masking tape. Alternatively, special

Fitting an architrave (trim) around an internal door

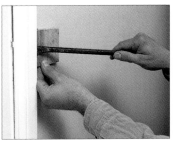

1 Remove the old architrave with a crowbar.

2 Scrape away any old filler or paint from the face of the frame.

3 Measure the internal door frame width and cut the top of the architrave. Mitre the ends.

4 Pin the new piece of architrave in place about 6mm (¼in) above the bottom of the top member.

5 Measure, cut and fit the side pieces of architrave and pin in position.

6 Any gaps between the mitres can be filled with wood filler and sanded down.

edging clamps are available that grip the panel and allow pressure to be applied to the moulding.

When the glue has dried, trim the moulding with a plane, or sand it, so that it is flush with the panel.

Fixing mouldings

Generally speaking, it is wise to drill pilot holes in hardwood mouldings before nailing, especially when fixing close to the ends, since small-section hardwoods, especially ramin, which is often used, will split readily.

Softwoods are far more forgiving, and it is unnecessary to drill a softwood architrave (trim) before nailing. Simply drive the nails in, punch the heads below the surface, and fill before finishing. Panel pins

(brads) or lost-head oval wire nails are the preferred fixings for architraves: they should be spaced at intervals of 230–300mm (9–12in).

Typical applications

Mouldings are ideal for improving the appearance of a fireplace surround, which is usually the focal point of a room. Metal brackets holding the mantel shelf can be hidden with cornice (cove) moulding, while half-round nosing applied to the front of the shelf will soften the overall effect.

Fitting internal architraves

The range of mouldings includes larger-section profiles such as architrave, which can be ornate. Fitting architrave is fairly

straightforward. Measure the internal width of the door frame and mark out the top piece of architrave so that its bottom edge is 12mm (½in) longer. Mitre the ends at 45 degrees, using a mitre box or mitre saw, so that the top edge is longer than the bottom.

Pin the top piece of architrave to the top of the frame so that it projects by an equal amount each side and is 6mm (¼in) up from the bottom edge of the top frame member. All architrave should be set about 6mm (¼in) back from the inside edge of the door frame.

Measure for each side piece separately, as they can vary quite considerably over the width of a door, especially in older houses. Cut each to length and pin in position.

FIXING CLADDING

Wooden cladding may be fixed to walls and ceilings for a variety of reasons. These include: cosmetic, to hide the existing finish; acoustic, to deaden sound; and thermal, to insulate against heat loss. Sometimes cladding has a structural quality, for example, when it is part of a stud (dry) wall, in which case all three qualities may be desirable.

Types of cladding

Cladding can take the form of manufactured boards such as chipboard (particle board), plywood and hardboard, often faced with either melamine in coloured patterns or imitation woodgrain, or wood veneers. It can also be solid timber (lumber) such as shiplap or tongued-and-grooved, V-jointed boards, which come in different profiles, widths and thicknesses.

Basic requirements

Cladding is only as good as the framework to which it is attached, so it is essential to ensure that any wall is solid and properly prepared with a framework of battens (furring strips), or that a sturdy stud frame is built before proceeding. The positioning of battens and studwork, both vertically and horizontally, is critical when using standard sheets of manufactured board. Each sheet should finish in the middle of a frame member to allow the adjoining sheet to butt against it for nailing. Allowing for likely cable positions, if any, is also advisable.

It is recommended that any wall cladding affixed to the inner surface of an exterior wall should be fitted with a barrier of building paper and insulation material, such as glass fibre, during construction.

Battening a wall

Drill pilot holes in the battens for the masonry nails, as this will prevent the wood from splitting, if it is a thin section. Hammer the masonry nail home at one end. Level the batten with a spirit level and drive home the nail at the other end. Finish by

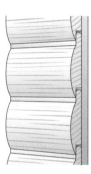

Above Cladding comes in a range of profiles and can be fixed to a framework of battens using nails, screws or adhesive.

driving in more nails along the length of the batten. If the wall is crumbly, you may prefer to attach the battens with screws and wall plugs. The security of the battening is essential for a good job.

Right Finish the sheet of manufactured board in the centre of the stud.

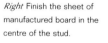

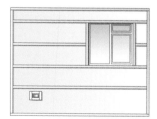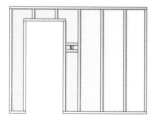

Above The framework of battens has to be tailored to suit the size and position of obstacles such as doors, windows and electrical fittings. Shown are positions for vertical cladding (*left*) with a likely cable point and batten positions and for horizontal cladding (*right*).

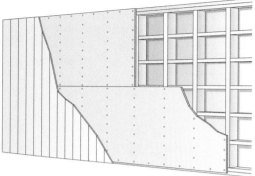

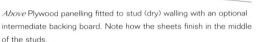

Above Plywood panelling fitted to stud (dry) walling with an optional intermediate backing board. Note how the sheets finish in the middle of the studs.

Above A section showing plywood cladding fixed to battens that have been attached to a masonry (plaster and brick) wall.

Fitting sheet panelling

Cladding can be fixed to the framework of battens (furring strips) using either nails or screws. If screws are used, especially brass ones, a feature can be made of them, so they should be equally spaced in a pattern formation.

Alternatively, a panel adhesive can be used for fixing cladding. Apply this to the battens and push the sheet firmly into place. If it fails to adhere immediately, tap nails part way through into the battens. The nails can be removed when the panels are secure.

To cut cladding, use either a hand saw or power saw. If using a hand saw, have the decorative face uppermost and cut on the downstroke to limit the chances of damaging it. With a power saw, turn the decorative face of the wood downward. Ensure that the cladding is resting on a firm, level surface. Before using the saw, score the cutting line carefully using a straightedge as a guide. If you need to leave a perfectly straight edge to a cut

sheet, where it is to be butted up against another board, then clamp a straightedge to the board as a guide for the saw.

After cutting, use a fine abrasive paper wrapped around a wood or cork block to smooth down the rough edges.

Foot fulcrum

Using two pieces of wood as a foot fulcrum, pivoting one on top of the other, simplifies holding a panel off the floor for fixing. Wedges can be used, but they are not as versatile.

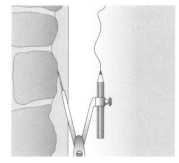

Above A pair of compasses is useful for scribing the edge of a panel where it butts against an uneven surface such as stonework.

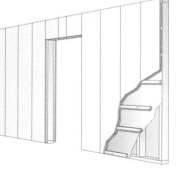

Above Work from each end of the surface to be covered, using cut panels in the middle to retain symmetry.

TONGUED AND GROOVED BOARDING

Fitting tongued-and-grooved boarding is more time-consuming than using sheet materials, but the supporting framework can be made simpler because the boards are relatively narrow and rigid. As with all cladding, it is essential to ensure that the battens (furring strips) are laid securely, and are reasonably spaced for adequate support.

Types of boarding

For vertical boarding, only horizontal battens (furring strips) are required; for horizontal boarding, vertical battens are needed. The spacing of the battens is not critical unless you intend having staggered joints in alternate rows of boarding, in which case you must make sure that a batten runs beneath each joint position to allow for fixing.

You can also fit boarding in diagonal patterns, which is not too difficult, but it pays to keep things simple by using only 45-degree angles. This can be done in several well-known configurations.

Tongued-and-grooved, V-jointed boards are usually referred to as TGV, and a common size is about 9 x 100mm (⅜ x 4in); allowing for the loss of the tongue in the fitting, each board covers an area about 90mm (3½in) wide. Various decorative profiles are available.

Shiplap is normally heavier. A typical size is 12 x 121mm (½ x 4¾in), the actual coverage being about 110mm (4⅜in). TGV is usually fixed by secret nailing. Panel pins (brads) are driven diagonally through the

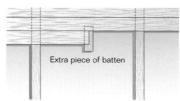

Above Add in an intermediate batten to pick up any short boards.

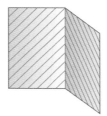

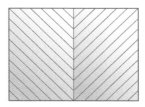

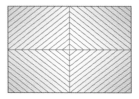

Left and above Three different options for diagonal cladding.

base of the tongue and into the framework. Decorative surface nailing can also be used.

Mouldings are commonly used to finish around the edges of cladding. For example, quadrant beading (a base shoe) can be pinned in internal corners, while simple square or hockey-stick beading will fit around an outside edge. Both TGV and

sheet materials can be used for cladding ceilings. Battens (furring strips) can be fixed directly to the joists above through the ceiling, or a suspended framework installed to support the cladding and lower the ceiling at the same time. This treatment can be attractive, help to conserve heat and add a feeling of cosiness to a room.

Practical tip

With a soft or crumbly plaster wall, it is often better to hack off the old plaster and attach battens (furring strips) straight on to the brickwork, rather than try to fix into it. On good flat plaster, battens can be fixed with adhesive.

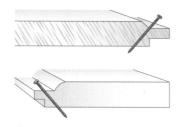

Above Secret nailing through the tongue of the board.

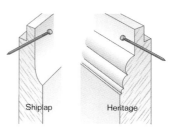

Above Nailing below the tongue can be done when the overlap of the next board is greater.

Shiplap   Heritage

Fitting the boarding

First, square off the end of the board to ensure that it is at 90 degrees, or 45 degrees if required. Mark off the length of board required with a craft (utility) knife or pencil and cut it to size with a tenon saw. Place the board in position on the battens, making sure that the tongue is left exposed for the next board to slot over, and in the case of TGV that the correct face side with the chamfer is showing. Secret nail the board with panel (brads) pins. Repeat this procedure with the remaining boards, tapping each firmly home with a mallet and an offcut (scrap) of the wood to prevent damage to the tongue before nailing. Leave the second to last board slipped over the previous tongue, but before nailing, use an offcut and pencil to scribe the cutting line on the final board if it needs trimming to fit. Cut and plane the board to width. You might need to fit the last two boards by springing them

Fitting cladding

into place, in which case, both will have to be nailed through the face, since the tongues will not be accessible. Punch the nail heads down and fill.

1 Tap fixing nails into each support strip at 300mm (12in) intervals. Check that it is level and drive in the nails.

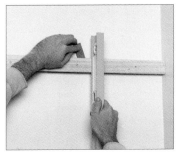

2 If the walls are out of true, insert slim packing pieces between the strips and the wall to keep the faces of the strips level.

3 Scribe the wall outline on to the face of the first board by holding its grooved edge to the wall and running a block and pencil down it.

4 Fix the boards by interlocking their tongued-and-grooved edges and driving nails through the exposed tongue of each board.

5 When fixing subsequent boards, close up the joints by tapping the board edge with a hammer. Protect the board edge.

6 Saw or plane the final board down to the required width and spring the last two boards into place. Secure the last board.

7 Neaten internal corners by pinning or gluing a length of scotia (cove) moulding into the angle. Use this at ceiling level too.

8 Butt-join the two boards that form an external corner, and conceal the joint with a length of birdsmouth (corner bead) moulding.

BOXING-IN PIPES

Some people regard visible pipes in the home as an eyesore, but with a little time and minimal woodworking skills they can be hidden successfully from view – and completely concealed if the boxing is decorated to match the room. Be sure to allow for the box work to be easily removed in situations where it may be necessary to gain access, such as around valves.

Accessibility

Bear in mind that stopcocks, drain taps, pumps, hand-operated valves and the like will need to be readily accessible and require some form of removable box system. For this reason, the boxing around them should be assembled with screws rather than nails. If a panel needs to be regularly or quickly removed, turn buttons or magnetic catches are a good idea.

Boxing basics

Steel anchor plates and screws can be used to secure the sides of boxing to walls, and these will be easy to remove when necessary. Battens (furring strips), either 50 x 25mm (2 x 1in) or 25 x 25mm (1 x 1in), can be used to fix boards at skirting (base) board level. Disguise the boxing by decorating it to match the rest of the room. If pipework is running along a panelled or boarded wall, construct

the boxing so that it follows the general theme, using similar materials and staining and varnishing the boxes accordingly.

Wall pipes

Measure the distance the pipes project from the wall, taking account of any joints and brackets. Cut the side panels from 25mm (1in) board slightly over this measurement and to their correct length. Fix small anchor

Boxing-in wall pipes

1 Measure how far the pipes protrude from the wall.

2 With a pencil, mark the positions for the side batten fixings.

3 Attach the side battens, screwing them firmly into position.

4 Cut the front panel of the box to size with a jigsaw. Use 6mm (¼in) MDF (medium density fiberboard).

5 Drill pilot holes and screw the front panel into position, using 19mm (¾in) No. 6 screws.

6 Trim the edges of the front panel with a block plane.

plates flush with the back edge of each panel and spaced at about 600mm (2ft) intervals.

In plywood, you may need to drill pilot holes. Hold the panels against the wall and mark the positions of the screw holes on the wall. Drill the holes and fix the panels to the wall with rawl plugs and screws.

Cut the front panel to size from 6mm (¼in) plywood. Drill evenly spaced screw holes in the front panel and fix it in position with 19mm (¾in) No. 6 screws. Use cup washers under the screw heads to protect the panel if it is likely to be removed often. Trim the edges flush with a block plane.

Floor pipes

Screw battens to the wall above the skirting (base) board and to the floor at the correct distance from the wall to clear the pipes. Screw a 25mm (1in) thick board to the floor batten so that it is level with the top of the wall batten, using 37mm (1½in) No. 8 screws. Fit a 6mm (¼in) plywood top panel to the wall batten and top edge of the front panel with 19mm (¾in) No. 6 screws. Trim the edge flush with a block plane.

When boxing-in pipes at floor level, you can use a section of skirting board for the front panel. This will help blend the boxing into the overall room scheme.

Waste pipes

Often, where a house has had an extension added, it is possible that the waste-water pipe from a first-floor bathroom will have to be run to the main waste-water drainpipe via a route that will take it across the ceiling line of the ground floor of the extension.

The main problem here is one of noise, as the sound of the waste water flowing away will be clearly audible. In a case like this, the best course of action is to muffle the noise by using 12mm (½in) thick plywood for the boxing, and encasing the pipe by using fibreglass insulation material within the box.

Boxing-in floor pipes

1 Attach wall and floor battens at the correct distance to clear pipes at 60cm (2ft) intervals.

2 Fix the front board to the floor batten, level with the top of the wall batten and screw up.

3 Add the top board and screw into position so that it can be easily removed.

4 You may find it better to use a piece of moulded skirting (trim) to match the room.

WOOD FINISHING

Although there are many techniques for finishing wood, a number of basic steps are common to all of them. Carry out preparation work well away from the finishing area, and be prepared to move the work back and forth several times as you apply and rub down successive coats. Remember that any finish on wood will enhance defects as well as good points, so preparation is important.

Preparation

Not often mentioned is the fact that wood must be dry, regardless of the treatment applied. Another requirement is that when several applications of a finish are called for, they must be rubbed down, or "flatted", between coats.

Many different types of wood will need filling. This can be as simple as rubbing in a grain filler, which will give a more even and less absorbent surface. It may involve using a wood filler, which can be bought to match the colour of the timber being used, to fill cracks, blemishes and knot holes. Soft interior stopping is fine for tiny cracks, and a two-part exterior-grade wood filler for making-good large holes.

The tools required for finishing are simple, and most of the work can be done entirely by hand. A few scrapers, some sandpaper in various grades, wire (steel) wool, soft cloth, a cork sanding block and some filler or stopping are the basic requirements.

Left (Clockwise, from top left) Wire (steel) wool, filler, spatula, soft cloth, sanding block, a selection of abrasive papers and cabinet scrapers.

Typical finishing processes

Apply any filler that is necessary to knot holes and blemishes in the wood, allow to dry and remove the excess gently with a chisel. With this done, the wood can be rubbed down with sandpaper wrapped around a cork block, working along the grain.

Wipe over the surface with a clean, damp rag to raise the grain very slightly, allow it to dry, then cut it back lightly with 400-grit sandpaper, again working along the grain. If you want to stain your timber (lumber), test the stain on a spare piece of the same wood to check the final colour and depth.

Remember that end grain will absorb a lot more of the stain and will be darker. Stain can be applied with a soft cloth or brush. Keep a wet edge all the time to avoid a patchy finish. Apply the stain in short circular motions.

Filling in wood

1 Apply filler to match the colour of the wood. Cut away any excess with a sharp chisel.

2 Sand down with sandpaper wrapped around a cork block, working along the grain.

3 To remove dust, wipe down with a soft cloth, using long strokes parallel to the grain.

Applying stains and varnish

1 Use a small brush to test the colour. Dilute the stain when treating end grain.

2 If satisfied with the colour, apply the stain with a soft cloth (cotton rag) in quick, circular motions.

1 For large panels, use a wide brush to apply varnish using long strokes.

2 Rub down the surface using 320-grit silicon-carbide paper, varnish and repeat.

Varnishes, such as polyurethane, or acrylics, which are quick drying, should be applied along the grain with a soft brush. Be sure to get into all corners and recesses but do not leave pools of liquid. Make sure there are no runs, allow to dry and flat down with 400-grit sandpaper or a fine grade of wire (steel) wool.

Wax and oil finishes

With the wood sanded down, apply a coat of sanding sealer, lightly rubbing it down when dry. This gives a good base for the oil or wax. Apply the wax or oil with a ball of fine wire (steel) wool, using a circular motion to work it well into the grain. Polish off with a soft cotton rag.

Types of stain

Take care when you are choosing wood stain to ensure that the type of stain is compatible with the finish. The colour is often labelled according to wood species, such as pine, mahogany or oak. This can be mis-leading, as the result depends on the base colour of the wood to which it is applied. Test the colour on a small piece of scrap (offcut) wood.

Practical tips

- Varnish is best applied in a cool environment: otherwise problems with a "ripple" finish can occur.
- To achieve a better finish with wax and oil, build up layers slowly.

Waxing wood

1 Apply a thin coat of clear shellac to provide a stable base for the wax. Leave to dry.

2 Apply the wax with a ball of fine wire (steel) wool in a strong circular motion.

3 Buff the wax vigorously with a polishing pad made from a soft duster. Add more coats.

REPAIRING AND REPLACING FLOORBOARDS

The majority of floors in older homes will have individual floorboards nailed to floor joists. In modern homes, sheets of flooring-grade chipboard (particle board) will be nailed or screwed to the joists. If a new floor covering is to be laid, it is essential that floors are in good condition. If floorboards are to be exposed, they need to be in even better condition, as any defects will be visible.

Lifting floorboards

To inspect the underfloor space or fit new floorboards, you will need to lift existing floorboards. You may find some that have been cut and lifted in the past to provide access to pipes or cables. These should be easy to lever up with the flat blade of a bolster (stonecutter's) chisel – do not use a screwdriver as you will damage the floorboard.

To lift boards that have not been cut, check first that they are not tongued-and-grooved – a tongue along one edge of each board fitting into a groove along the adjacent edge of its neighbour. If they are, use a floorboard saw or a circular saw with its cutting depth set to 20mm (¾in) to cut through the tongue.

Lever up the floorboard with your bolster chisel, and use a floorboard saw to make a right-angled cut across it. Make the cut exactly over a joist so that the two parts of the board will be supported when they are replaced.

Chipboard sheets are easy to unscrew, but you may need to cut through tongues in the same way as for traditional floorboards.

Repairing joists

Above Cut the new joist section to length and clamp it in place while you drill holes through it and through the old joist.

Joist problems

Most of the problems associated with floor joists are due to dampness, which may occur if airbricks (vents) have become blocked or if there are not enough airbricks to ensure adequate ventilation of the underfloor space.

Lift a few floorboards and inspect the joists with a torch and a mirror, prodding any suspect areas with a

Above Pass bolts through the holes and add a washer before securing the nuts with a spanner (US wrench).

bradawl or awl. If sections of joist are damaged, you should be able to cut and lift floorboards or chipboard sheets over the damage and bolt on a new section of joist of the same size, making sure that it is fixed to solid wood. Do not bother to remove the old joist unless it is actually rotten. If you do find signs of dry rot (typically white strands), all damaged

Removing a section of floorboard

1 If it is a tongued-and-grooved board, cut through the tongue with a circular saw.

2 Lift the end of the floorboard by levering with a bolster (stonecutter's) chisel.

3 Wedge the board up and cut, over a joist, with a floorboard saw.

Fitting floorboards

Above Plane down floorboards if they are too wide to fill the gap.

Above Use card or plywood packing pieces over the joists if the board is too shallow.

Above Use a chisel to cut a slot to fit over a joist if the board is too thick.

wood must be removed by a firm of professionals. If you find signs of woodworm attack, treat the affected areas with a recommended woodworm eradicator or call in a professional firm.

Loose floorboards

If floorboards are loose, the best answer is to replace the nails holding them down with screws. Do not put a screw in the middle of a board – there could be a pipe underneath. If nail heads are protruding, use a hammer and nail punch to set them below the surface of the floorboards. This is essential before attempting to use a sanding machine or laying carpet or sheet vinyl.

Damaged floorboards

If floorboards are split or broken, the damaged section, at least, will need to be replaced. The most likely problem is that old floorboards will have become "cupped", or turned up at the edges. You can overcome this by hiring a floor sanding machine.

You do not need to replace a whole floorboard if only part of it is damaged; simply lift the board and cut out the damaged section, making the cuts over the centres of joists.

If replacement floorboard is too wide, plane it down to fit the gap – do not fit a narrower replacement floorboard, as you will get draughts. If the board is slightly thicker, chisel slots out of it where it fits over the joists; if it is thinner, use packing

pieces of cardboard or plywood between the joists and the board.

Secure each floorboard with two floorboard nails at each joist, positioning them about 25mm (1in) from the edge of the board and exactly in the middle of the joist. It is a good idea to drill nail pilot holes in the board first.

> ### Practical tip
>
> When laying new floorboards or new floor coverings, make sure that you can still gain access to pipes and cables underneath.
> If necessary, cut a removable inspection hatch in both the floor and the floor covering.

Fixing floorboards

Above Drill pilot holes for floorboard nails to avoid splitting the wood.

Above Hammer down protruding nails to prevent them damaging the floor covering.

Above Secure loose floorboards by replacing the nails with screws.

CONCEALING THE CEILING-TO-WALL JOINT

Coving (crown molding), a quadrant-shaped moulding made from polystyrene, plaster or timber is fitted between the walls and ceiling of a room. It has two functions: to be decorative and to conceal the joint between the walls and ceiling. An ornate coving may be referred to as a cornice; old plaster cornices may be clogged with years of paint and need cleaning to reveal the detail.

Preparing for coving

Using a short length of coving as a guide, draw pencil lines all around the room, on the wall and ceiling, to indicate the position of the coving. Make sure the lines are straight and continuous. If you are fitting polystyrene or plaster coving, any wall and ceiling coverings must be stripped off between the pencil marks. Run a trimming knife along the lines, then lift the paper with a flat stripping knife, using water and wallpaper stripper if necessary.

Left Plaster coving is held in place with adhesive (plus nails if heavy) and painted.

Left Timber coving is nailed in place and usually varnished or stained (nail holes filled).

Left Paper-covered polystyrene coving is held in place with adhesive and it is usually painted.

Left Plain polystyrene coving is held in place with adhesive and usually left untreated.

If you are fitting plaster coving, score the surfaces of the walls and ceiling with the edge of a filling or putty knife, or trowel, to provide a key for the adhesive.

Dealing with corners

With polystyrene and plaster coving, you can often buy moulded internal and external corner pieces that fit over the coving at corners, saving you the trouble of having to make neat joints. With timber (lumber) coving, you may find pre-scribed ends to fit both internal and external corners.

If you have no ready-made corners, you will have to cut 45-degree mitres on the ends of lengths of coving where they meet at a corner. Special jigs or paper templates are often sold with polystyrene and plaster coving to help with this. The alternative is a deep mitre box. For plaster and wood, use a fine-toothed panel or tenon saw to cut the coving; with polystyrene, use a sharp trimming knife. Be prepared to make slight adjustments to the mitres if the room is not absolutely square.

Practical tip

When removing wire nails used to hold coving temporarily in place, employ pliers rather than pincers or a claw hammer, which could damage the mouldings.

Polystyrene coving

The corner pieces for polystyrene coving have square ends designed to be butted against the straight pieces. Start by fitting an internal corner, spreading the recommended adhesive and simply pushing the coving into place. Then fit the straight pieces, working toward the next corner, where you may have to cut a straight piece to fit.

If the walls are uneven, it is better to use ceramic tile adhesive rather than the coving adhesive, since it will provide a thicker adhesive bed.

Plaster coving

Special adhesive is available for fixing plaster coving, and it should be spread on the back edges of the mouldings. To hold the coving in place while the adhesive sets, drive wire nails into the wall and ceiling along the edges of the coving (not through the coving), after using a damp cloth to remove excess adhesive that is squeezed out along the joints. Once the adhesive has set, remove the pins and, if necessary, make good the corners and joints with plaster filler.

Left A template is used to guide a trimming knife to make mitres in polystyrene coving.

Putting up plaster coving

1 Use the coving and mark out two parallel guidelines on the wall and ceiling of the room.

2 Remove old coverings. Score the surface of painted or plaster walls to improve adhesion.

3 Cut the mitre for the corner, press the length into place and support with nails.

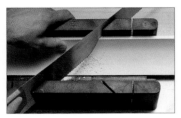

4 Cut a mitre using a mitre box and tenon or panel saw.

5 Butter the back edges of the plaster coving with good adhesive.

6 Fit the adjacent corner piece which has been carefully mitred for an external corner.

Timber coving

This could be put up with adhesive in the same way as plaster coving, but it is easier to use panel pins (brads), making sure they will protrude about 20mm (¾in) from the back of the moulding. Drive them home with a nail punch, then use matching wood filler applied with a putty knife to conceal the holes.

As an alternative to mitring internal corners, they can be scribed – that is, the end of one piece of moulding is cut to the profile of the adjacent piece. The first piece is cut square to butt tightly into the corner, and the second piece fits over it.

External corners will have to be mitred, and all corners must be made good with wood filler once the coving is in place.

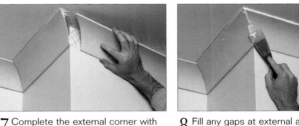

7 Complete the external corner with another length of coving, butting the ends together.

Fixing timber coving

8 Fill any gaps at external and internal angles with cellulose filler and sand down once dry.

1 Fix with a punch and panel pins (brads).

2 Fill the nail holes with matching wood filler.

REPAIRING WINDOWS

The most obvious signs that there is something wrong with a window are when it starts to rattle in the wind or to stick, making it difficult to open and close. Rattling is most likely to be caused by worn hinges or wear of the window itself; sticking by swelling of the wood, build-up of paint or movement of the frame joints. All these faults can be repaired.

Repairing hinges

Loose or worn hinges are often a cause of window problems. To start with, try tightening the screws or replacing them with slightly longer screws of the same gauge. If that does not work, replace the hinges with new ones of the same size and type plus new screws. Remember that steel hinges will rust quickly, so apply suitable primer immediately and then repaint to match the window when this has dried.

Check the opening and closing of the window. If the window is sticking on the far edge, it may be necessary to deepen the recess for one or both hinges; if it binds on the closing edge, one or both recesses will be too deep and may need to be packed out with cardboard. A rattling window can often be cured by fitting draught-excluder strip. Measure the gap, then buy a suitable draught excluder.

Above A loose window joint can be re-glued with fresh adhesive. Clamp it up while the adhesive dries.

Worn windows

Sash windows are particularly prone to wear. The best answer is to remove the windows and fit brush-pile draught excluder inside the sash channel. A new catch to hold the windows together may also be necessary. Fit a new inner staff bead around the window so that it fits more closely against the inner sash.

Warped windows

Timber, hinged windows can sometimes warp, so that they meet the frame only at the top or at the bottom. The best way to cure this is to fit some mortise window locks, which fit into holes cut in the actual window, with the bolts shooting into more holes in the frame. These allow the window to be held in the correct position (get someone to push from the outside while you lock it) so that the warp will self correct. You could position a tiny block of wood between the window and frame so that the warp is over-corrected – do not overdo this or you will break the glass.

> **Practical tip**
>
> When replacing painted steel hinges with brass versions, always use brass screws to match.

Dealing with binding windows

Above A binding window may be cured simply by tightening the hinge screws or replacing them with longer ones.

Above If a window is binding on the far side, it may be that the hinge recesses need to be deepened with a chisel.

Above A sticking window may be swollen or have too much paint on it. Plane down the leading edge of the window.

Reinforcing a window joint with dowels

1 To reinforce a glued window joint, drill holes across the joint.

2 Then, hammer in adhesive-covered dowels of the same size.

3 When the adhesive has dried, chisel or plane the dowels flush.

Sticking windows

Over time, a build-up of paint may cause windows to stick, especially when the weather is damp and the wood begins to swell. Use a plane to cut down the offending areas, which is much easier if you remove the window from its frame, then repaint before refitting the window.

Make sure that all bare wood is covered with paint, as this will prevent water from getting in, which causes the wood to swell. Also, check that the putty is in good condition and doing its job of keeping the water out and the glass in.

Loose window joints

If the paint on a timber window has been allowed to deteriorate, the joints may have dried out and shrunk, causing the window to sag and stick in the frame.

Remove the window and strip off the old paint. You will be able to see the gaps in a loose mortise-and-tenon joint, and it should be possible to work wood glue into these. Use sash clamps to keep the window square while the adhesive dries. There may be wedges in the mortise-and-tenon joint that you can replace with new glued-in wedges as with doors. If not,

you can drill holes across the joint and glue in lengths of dowel to reinforce it. Use a proper dowel drill – 6, 8 or 10mm ($\frac{1}{4}$, $\frac{5}{16}$ or $\frac{3}{8}$in) – and fit two dowels per joint. Chisel or plane the dowels flush once the adhesive has dried.

The alternative is to fit an L-shaped reinforcing bracket to each loose window corner. Make sure the window is perfectly square before you fit these and, for neatness, chisel out a recess in the face of the window so that the bracket is flush with the surface, or slightly below so that it can be covered with filler.

Reinforcing a window joint with a bracket

1 To fit an L-shaped corner reinforcing bracket, first chisel out a recess.

2 Screw the bracket in place so that it is below the surface.

3 Fill over the bracket and smooth down once the filler has dried.

Repairing Window Sills

A wooden sill is often the first part of a window to need repair, as the rain that falls on the window drips on to the sill and some of it may collect, resulting in flaking paint or crumbling, rotten wood. The treatment ranges from simple repainting to replacement. Since sills project from the wall, they are also prone to impact damage, which can affect concrete and stone sills.

Wet rot

This can be recognized by softening and darkening of the wood and often by severe splintering, the rotten wood falling out. Fortunately, it is fairly easy to repair; on the other hand, dry rot – recognizable by white strands on the surface and a musty smell – requires the services of a professional.

Provided the damage is not so severe that sill replacement is a better option, the first thing to do is remove all the rotten wood with a sharp chisel until you get back to sound, dry wood. Use a hot-air gun if necessary to dry out the wood.

Brush the wood with a wood hardener solution and leave this to dry. This prepares the wood for the application of exterior wood filler. Although this sets hard, it retains sufficient flexibility to be able to move with the wood as it expands and contracts with varying temperatures and humidity. The wood filler can be applied with a filling or putty knife and should be left to set. Substantial damage may need two or even three layers.

Once the filler has hardened, it can be sanded down and the whole area painted to match the surrounding wood – it is probably best to repaint the whole sill.

Some wet-rot repair systems include wood preservative sticks or tablets that you put in drilled holes in the wood surrounding the repair area to prevent future rot. The holes are concealed when the damaged area is filled.

A wet rot system cannot be used to make good dry rot, which can affect masonry as well as woodwork. In this situation, all damaged wood must be completely removed (along with any affected bricks and mortar) and the areas must be professionally sterilized before replacement materials are installed.

Repairing wet rot

1 Chisel out all the rotten wood, making sure only sound wood is left.

2 Brush the sound wood with hardener and leave to dry as recommended.

3 To fit wood preservative sticks, drill holes in the sound wood.

4 Push preservative sticks into the drilled holes and below the surface.

5 Fill the damaged area with exterior wood filler. Leave to dry before sanding.

Replacing a wooden sill

If only part of a sill needs replacing, you may be able to cut out the damaged section and fashion a replacement, screwing and gluing it in place. However, it is not always easy to achieve a perfect match.

Replacing the whole window sill may be easier than you think, and it can be done without removing the window frame.

First remove any opening windows and take out the glass from the fixed windows. Remove the window board, or inner sill, and saw down through the sill as close as possible to the jambs. Slide out the cut sill sections, then saw through the tenon joints between the jambs and the ends of the sill to remove them. Clean the brickwork below the sill and dry it if necessary.

Cut a new sill to the correct length and, if necessary, cut slots in the ends to fit under the jambs. Prime the sill and the ends of the jambs and leave to dry. Put the new sill in position on a mortar bed, driving in timber wedges to force it up against the bottom of the jambs before inserting countersunk screws at an angle through the jambs and into the sill. Fill the screw holes before painting.

Glue in wooden blocks to fill any gaps between the jambs and sill, and add more mortar under the window sill if necessary.

1 Cut out the old window sill close to the jambs after removing the inner window board.

2 Put in a new window sill, trimming it to fit underneath the jambs.

3 Secure the new window sill with screws angled down through the jambs.

Repairing a concrete or stone sill

A simple crack or small hole in a concrete or stone sill can be repaired in much the same way that you deal with a crack or hole in a wall or ceiling, using an appropriate exterior filler or ready-mixed mortar.

Damage to the edge is more difficult to repair, as it involves building timber shuttering to hold the new concrete while it sets.

Chisel away all loose concrete before fitting the shuttering, using temporary timber supports. Then fill the damaged area with fresh concrete – use dry readymix – using a trowel. Once the concrete has completely set, you can remove the shuttering. A similar arrangement is used to replace a whole concrete or stone sill, but in this case, it must take the form of a box with a length of rope pinned along the bottom to provide a former for the window sill's drip groove.

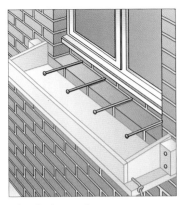

Above Fit shuttering for a new concrete window sill with a drip groove rope.

Above Fill the shuttering with concrete, making sure the surface is level.

REHANGING A DOOR

There may be occasions when the way in which a door opens is not the most convenient. Switching the hinges from one side to the other may provide a more attractive view of the room as the door is opened or allow better use of the wall space. Alternatively, making the door open outward may create more useful space. However, never have a door opening outwards on to a stairway.

Switching the hinged side

When switching the hinged edge of a door from one side to the other, you will need to cut a new mortise for the latch and drill new holes for the door handle spindles. The old latch mortise and spindle holes can be filled by gluing in small blocks of wood and lengths of dowel. Leave the blocks and dowels slightly proud of the surface, then plane and sand them flush when the glue has dried. If you reverse the door, you will be able to use the old latch and door handle spindle holes, but the latch itself will need to be turned around.

You will need to cut a new slot for the striker and striking plate (keeper) on the other side of the frame, and fill the old recess with a thin block of wood stuck in place. Again, make this oversize, planing and sanding it flush once the adhesive has dried.

You will also need to chisel out new recesses for the hinges in both the door and the frame; if the door is reversed, you may be able to use part of the old hinge recesses in the door and need only fill the unused portions. Fill the old hinge recesses with thin blocks of wood glued into place and sanded flush.

If the door has rising butts or other handed hinges, these will need to be replaced.

After re-hanging the door, the light switch may be in the wrong place if it is in the room the door opens into. There are two choices here: reposition it on the other side of the door (means running a new wire) or move it across the wall so that it is outside the room, but more or less in the same place (little or no new wire, but possible problems securing the switch mounting box).

Filling a recess

1 To fill an old hinge recess, cut a sliver of wood slightly over size.

2 Add adhesive and tap the wood sliver down into the recess.

3 When the adhesive has set, plane the surface flush and smooth.

In to out

When making a door open outward, you will be able to use the same latch and handle positions if the door is hung from the same side of the frame. You will have to reverse the latch, but will be able to make use of parts of the hinge recesses in the door. However, you will need to reposition the striking plate and make new hinge recesses in the frame, as described previously.

The one extra job will be to move the door stop, unless this is positioned centrally in the frame. Moving the door stop needs care to avoid splitting it – slide a chisel in behind the stop and lever it out. Remove the sides before the top, starting in the middle.

When repositioning the door stop, hang the door first, so that you can be sure that the stop fits snugly against the door all round. You can use the same nails to secure it, but reposition them and fill the old holes before repainting.

If you change the side of the frame from which the door is hung (as well as changing it from in to out), you can retain the existing door hinge, latch and door handle positions, although new recesses must still be cut in the frame for the hinges and striking plate, and the old ones filled.

Practical tip

To prevent the paint from chipping when you remove a doorstop, run a trimming knife blade along the joint between doorstop and frame to cut through the paint.

Changing door handles

1 Remove the existing door handle and latch from the door, along with the door spindle.

2 Fill the latch recess (not shown) and plug the handle spindle hole with dowel. Fill holes.

3 On the other side of the door, cut a recess for the latch and drill a hole for the spindle.

4 Fit the latch and the door spindle. Now fit the new door handle (here with a keyhole).

Repositioning the door stop

1 Slide a chisel under the door stop in order to lever it out.

2 Nail it to the door frame in its new position and fill in any nail holes.

Repairing Doors

Doors can develop all sorts of problems, from simple squeaks and rattles to suddenly refusing to open and shut properly. Fortunately, most of the problems are easy to solve, though for most door repairs you will need to remove the door from the frame. Some faults can be cured by fitting a draught excluder and others by fitting a weatherboard.

Squeaks

A door normally squeaks simply because the hinges need oiling. Often you can dribble sufficient oil on to the hinges with the door in place, but if they are caked in dirt and paint, it is best to remove the door and work the hinges back and forth with oil before replacing it.

A door may also squeak if the hinges are binding, usually because the recesses have been cut too deep into the door and/or frame. The solution is simple: unscrew each half of each hinge in turn, place a piece of cardboard behind the hinge and refit the screws. Experiment until the door hangs correctly – you may need more than one thickness of cardboard (or thin plywood).

A door can also bind because the screws are sticking out of the hinge. Normally these can simply be retightened; if they will not hold, fit longer ones of the same gauge, or a smaller size if the original screws had heads that were too large for the countersinks in the hinge.

Rattles

The simplest way to stop any door rattling is to fit a draught excluder. With an internal door, you could also try moving the door stop; with all types of door, you could try moving the latch striking plate, although this is not easy – drilling out and filling the old screw holes with glued-in dowels helps.

Binding

External doors often bind during cold, damp weather, becoming free again when the weather is dry and warm. This is a sign that the bottom of the door was not sealed when the door was painted, allowing moisture to get in and swell the door.

Binding doors can also be caused by a build-up of paint on the leading (non-hinge) edge. The cure is to remove the door and then to plane down the leading edge, repainting it once the door has been fitted. Add at least one coat of primer to the bottom of the door to prevent more moisture from getting in.

Practical tip

Door hinge screws are often caked with paint and can be very difficult to turn. Clean the paint out with a sharp screwdriver, held at an angle to the slot and tapped gently with a hammer. To release a stiff screw, place the screwdriver blade in the slot and strike the end of the handle smartly with a hammer, trying, in effect, to push the screw further in. If this does not work, try tightening the screw before unscrewing it.

If a door binds at the bottom, it may be because the hinges have worked loose. Try tightening the screws, fitting larger or longer screws if necessary. If this does not work and the door joints have not worked loose, you will have to remove the door and plane down the part that is rubbing. Use a block plane, working toward the centre of the door. Then repaint the bottom of the door. With an internal door, you may be able to remove sufficient material by laying a sheet of sandpaper on the floor (abrasive side up) and working the door back and forth across it. A door can bind seriously when you have fitted a new carpet or other floorcovering. In this case, remove the door and cut a strip off the bottom with a circular saw fitted with a rip guide. If there are several doors to shorten, consider hiring a door trimming saw, which can be used with the doors in place.

Adjusting hinges

1 Pack a hinge with cardboard to prevent a door binding.

2 Fit longer screws to a hinge if the old ones have lost their grip.

Door trimming techniques

Above Take the door off its hinges and plane the leading edge of a door if it is sticking.

Above Run the base of a door over sandpaper if it is binding.

Above Use a door trimming saw to adjust the height after fitting a new carpet.

Loose joints

Most doors will have a mortise-and-tenon joint at each corner where the side members, or stiles, meet the top and bottom rails. These can work loose with age.

You do not need to take the door apart: simply remove it, prise out any wedges, cut new wedges and glue them in place. For added security or if there are no wedges, drill 10mm (⅜in) holes through each stile and the tenon, and glue in 10mm (⅜in)

dowels, planing them flush once the adhesive has dried. When repairing a door in this way, use sash clamps first to square it up and then to hold it square while the glue dries.

Warped door

If a door has become warped, you can straighten it with pairs of clamps, stout lengths of wood and packing blocks. Mount the door between the timbers, say lengths of 50 x 100mm (2 x 4in), and position the packing

blocks to force the door in the opposite direction to the warp. Force it beyond straight by tightening up the clamps and leave for as long as you can. When the clamps are removed, the door should be straight.

Fitting a weatherboard

A weatherboard is a shaped piece of wood screwed to the bottom of a door to throw rainwater clear. For the best result, drill clearance holes for the screws, then counterbore them with a drill of the same size as the screw heads. That way, the screw heads will be below the surface and can be concealed by gluing in timber plugs.

Above Reinforce mortise-and-tenon joints with new tapering wedges.

Above Straighten a warped door with timbers, clamps and packing blocks.

Above Fit a weatherboard with screws tightened into pre-drilled holes.

FITTING DOORS

There is quite a lot to do when fitting a new or replacement door – even if it is the right size. You will need to fit the hinges to the door, together with some form of latch and may need to cut new recesses in the frame for the hinges and striking plate. If the door latch has a lock, you will need to drill and chisel out keyholes.

Size

Doors come in standard sizes, but you may need to trim the sides of a door with a plane or the ends with a saw before fitting it. There needs to be around 3mm (⅛in) clearance at the sides and top, and 5mm (³⁄₁₆in) at the bottom. Always take equal amounts off each side or end, and if planing the top and bottom, work from the edges toward the centre to prevent the wood splitting.

Fitting hinges

Hinges

A solid hardwood external door will need three substantial hinges: typically 100mm (4in), but most internal doors can be hung on two 75mm (3in) hinges. If you are using brass hinges, always use brass screws.

Choose the hinge positions, using an existing door as a guide – some hollow flush doors incorporate hinge blocks of solid wood – and mark lines across the edge of the door with the

aid of a try square. Then use either a hinge or a marking gauge set to the width of the hinge to mark out the recesses – each hinge should end up so that only the knuckle protrudes from the edge of the door. Also mark the thickness on the face of the door.

Cut out the recesses with a mallet and chisel, first cutting down along the lines with the chisel held vertically, then removing the wood with the chisel held at an angle, bevel down to prevent digging in. Take great care not to go beyond the marked recesses. When the hinges fit snugly, make pilot holes for the screws with a small drill or bradawl and screw the hinges in place.

Offer the door up to the frame, propping it on 5mm (³⁄₁₆in) blocks, and transfer the positions of the hinges on to the frame. Cut the recesses in the same way, check the fit, make pilot holes and, with the door propped on the blocks again, secure the hinges to the frame. Check that the door swings freely and closes properly without catching the frame. If necessary, remove the door and deepen the hinge recesses, or pack them out with cardboard.

1 Mark out the hinge using the hinge itself as a guide.

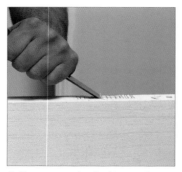

2 Cut a recess for the hinge with a chisel and wooden mallet.

3 Clean up the hinge recess, working from the side. Secure the hinge.

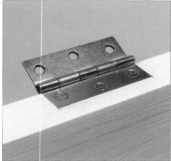

4 The hinge should sit snugly in its recess with the knuckle protruding.

Practical tip

As a guide for drilling holes to a specific depth, wrap insulating or masking tape around the drill shank at the depth required.

Fitting a mortise lock

1 Mark out the mortise lock using a mortise gauge.

2 After drilling out the main recess, remove the rest of the wood with a chisel.

3 Cut out a keyhole and spindle hole. Fit the lock and spindle and then the handle.

Latches and locks

Most doors are fitted with a mortise latch, ranging from a simple spring-operated affair to a sturdy high-security lock. The method of fitting is the same, except that with a lock you will need to make keyholes.

Check the instructions and mark out the position of the latch or lock and the handle spindle holes on the door – some hollow flush doors will have a solid block to take the latch/lock. To make the mortise, first drill as many large holes as you can within the outline, then use a chisel to remove the remaining wood. Put the latch/lock in place and mark around

the foreplate so that you can chisel out a housing for this – you may also need to deepen the main hole. Drill the handle spindle holes, checking the fit of the latch/lock and the positions of the handles.

Fit the latch/lock to the door and use it to transfer the position of the bolt to the door frame. Draw the outline of the striking plate, double checking its position in relation to the door stop – too close and the latch will not work, too far away and the door will rattle. Drill and chisel out recesses for the plate and screw it in place. Check the latch/lock operation; if necessary, reposition it.

Letter plate

This needs only a large rectangular hole and two smaller holes to fit it. Mark out the position of these on the door – in a solid central rail or bottom rail or, possibly, vertically on the closing stile. Drill the two small holes (for the letter plate securing bolts) and drill largish holes at each corner of the main outline to start the jigsaw (saber saw). Cut along the marked lines, working from the outside of the door, so that any splintering is covered by the letter plate. Do not force the saw or its blade will bend. Clean up the hole with a file and fit the letter plate.

Fitting a letter plate

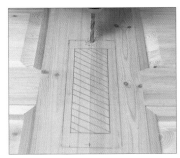

1 Work from the outside of the door. Mark out the letter plate and drill holes for the bolts.

2 Drill holes at the corners of the marked out letter plate and finish cutting with a jigsaw.

3 Fit the letter plate from the outside, securing the nuts inside.

REPAIRING STAIRS

The most common problem with stairs is that they creak. However, they may also suffer from physical damage and from missing parts, especially beneath the treads. The ease with which stairs may be repaired will depend partly on whether you have access to the underside. In some cases, plaster or boards may conceal it, which means working only from above.

How stairs are built

The flat parts of stairs that you walk on are called treads; the vertical sections connecting them are called risers. Treads and risers are joined to one another by various means: butt joints, housing joints or tongued-and-grooved joints. Both treads and risers are joined to the side timbers (strings) by butt joints if the strings are "open", that is shaped to follow the line of the treads and risers, or by housing joints if the strings are "closed", that is having parallel sides. The housing joints in closed strings are reinforced by long, thin glued-in wedges, while in both cases the joint between the front of each tread and the riser below is usually reinforced by small glued-in triangular blocks.

Blocks

Reinforcing blocks can work loose, and some may be missing altogether. If blocks are missing, you can make new ones by cutting diagonally down through a piece of 50mm (2in) square timber. When fitting new blocks, or refitting old ones, screw

Replacing blocks

1 Clean the old adhesive off loose reinforcing blocks and add fresh adhesive on the two meeting sides.

2 When putting the blocks back into place, screw them to both the tread and the riser to hold them securely.

them to both tread and riser as well as applying wood adhesive. With an existing loose block, it may be possible to prise open the joint to squeeze in some adhesive.

Wedges

Tapered wedges are used to hold the risers and treads firmly in closed strings, but with age, the wedges may become loose. It is best to remove all loose wedges so that you can clean

them and the grooves they fit in of all traces of old glue. If any wedges are missing, make replace-ments by cutting tapered strips from a piece of timber cut to length, using an old wedge as a guide.

Apply glue to the wedge and its groove, then hammer the vertical wedges home first, followed by the horizontal ones, which should make contact with the vertical wedges at the bottom.

Replacing wedges

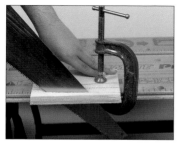

1 If any of the tapered wedges are missing, cut fresh ones from a block of wood.

2 Before applying each wedge, coat each side with adhesive. Remove excess afterwards.

3 Hammer the wedges into place; the horizontal ones under the vertical ones.

Securing treads

1 If you have access from underneath, drive screws up through the backs of treads into the bottom of the risers.

2 If access is denied, cut recesses towards the back of the tread and front of the riser and fit L-shaped brackets to secure the joint.

3 To secure the front of a loose tread, drill holes down exactly into the centre of the riser below and fit screws.

Securing treads

If the joint between the back of a tread and the riser above is loose, you can insert reinforcing screws from below, through the back of the tread into the bottom of the riser. Where access to the underside is impossible, reinforce this joint from above with a couple of L-shaped brackets recessed into the back of the tread and the front of the riser. Make the recesses slightly deeper than the thickness of the brackets and screw them in place.

If the joint between the front of a tread and the riser below is loose, and you cannot get below to reglue the blocks and/or wedges, you can reinforce the joint with screws. Drill pilot holes down through the tread into the riser, making sure they are centred in the riser, and enlarge the holes in the tread to clearance size before driving countersunk screws through the tread into the riser.

If possible, prise the joint apart with a bolster (stonecutter's) chisel, brush out any dirt and squeeze in some glue before screwing the joint together.

Repairing a damaged tread

It is very unlikely that an entire stair tread will need to be replaced. The more common fault is that part of the nosing, the front curved section, will have sustained damage.

Fortunately, this can be replaced relatively easily.

Mark out as much of the nosing as you need to remove, drill holes and cut it out using a circular saw, cleaning up the cut with a chisel. Saw the ends to an angle of 45 degrees. Shape a new piece of timber to fit exactly into the space, drilling pilot holes through it and into the existing tread for the securing screws. Enlarge the holes in the new section and countersink them before gluing and screwing it in place. Drive the screw heads below the surface and screw on a supporting batten (furring strip) while the adhesive dries. Fill the screw holes.

Repairing a damaged tread

1 Use a circular saw or jigsaw (saber saw) to cut out the damaged section, finishing off the ends of the cut with a sharp chisel.

2 Cut and plane the replacement wood to size and shape before screwing or gluing it in place with a supporting batten.

Practical tip

When replacing stair treads in an older house, you may well find that the replacement timber you buy will be too small because the original tread was an imperial size (in) and the replacement is metric (mm). If this is the case, buy a larger size and plane it down.

REPAIRING STAIR BALUSTRADES

"Balustrade" is the name given to the combination of balusters (banisters), posts and handrails that run up the side of a staircase. Over time, these components may become loose or damaged, but repairs are quite straightforward and may range from simply regluing a cracked baluster or repairing a short length of handrail, to replacing the entire assembly.

Baluster repairs

The most likely problem with a balustrade is a cracked or broken baluster. Often, it will be possible to prise a split apart with a wood chisel, squeeze in some adhesive and tape up the split, or clamp it with a small G-clamp, while the adhesive dries. Sometimes, a short dowel glued into a hole drilled across the split will help.

If the baluster is broken, it will be necessary to remove it and either fit a new one or glue together the original piece, which may be your only option if you cannot find a replacement of the same style. You

will need to work out how to remove the old baluster. Sometimes, this simply involves pulling out a couple of nails top and bottom. On other occasions, you may need to remove the nosing on the end of a tread, or prise out spacers fitted between the balusters under the handrail and in the base rail, or even cut through the baluster.

You can fashion replacement square balusters yourself and build up broken moulding on a damaged turned baluster with wood filler. If you need to replace a complete turned baluster, you may be able to buy a

new one of the same style, if the staircase is not too old, or a second-hand one from an architectural salvage yard, if it is. Failing that, you could approach a local woodturner to make a new one. Otherwise, the broken piece will have to be repaired.

Repairing a handrail

You can buy handrail moulding to repair a broken section, but you need a special type of bolt to hold the sections together. This passes through holes drilled into the ends of the new and old handrails, both cut square, and requires "pockets" to be cut out

Replacing a balustrade

1 If you have an old-fashioned balustrade like this, you may want to replace it completely.

2 Remove the old handrail and the wrought iron sections and prise up the base rail.

3 Cut through all newel posts with a panel saw, keeping the cut square to the post.

7 Hammer the newel post into place, using a piece of scrap wood to protect the top.

8 Cut the handrail to the correct length and angle before joining it to the newel post.

9 Fit a nut to the bracket bolt and tighten it with a socket spanner. Fit the cover plug.

to accommodate the nuts of the bolt. Two additional holes need to be drilled for dowels that prevent the handrail from turning around the bolt. To position these correctly, drill the holes in one part, using a dowelling bit, and fit centre-points into the holes so that their positions can be transferred to the other part.

Replacing a balustrade

You can buy kits for replacing a complete balustrade, using the bottom portions of the existing newel posts. The first step is to remove the existing balustrade – handrail, balusters and the bottom rail. Cut through the old newel posts with a panel saw close to the base, making sure the cuts are square. Then drill a large hole in each

stump of newel post to take the end of the new newel post and shape the stump to a gentle curve. The new newel post is glued into place with a dowel to tighten it. The new handrail must be cut to length with the correct angle at each end and secured with the brackets supplied.

The base rail must also be cut to the correct length and angles. Then each baluster can be cut to length, again with the ends at the correct angle, and slotted into the base rail and the underside of the handrail. The balusters are held in place with wooden spacers nailed to the base rail and the underside of the handrail. Special accessories are available to accommodate staircases that have 90-degree turns or half-landings.

Practical tips

● To reinforce a straight break in a baluster, first drill a 10mm (⅜in) hole in the centre of one of the sound sections. Then make a right-angled cut through the baluster, using the thinnest saw blade you can find, such as a junior hacksaw, to remove a portion of the drilled baluster. Glue this to the other broken piece and leave for the adhesive to set. Continue the hole through the glued joint into sound timber. Finally, glue the whole baluster together with a 10mm (⅜in) dowel bridging the original break and the new saw cut.

● When buying a handrail, look for the type that has a grooved underside to hold the balusters firmly and in a straight line.

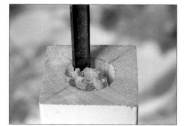

4 Mark out the hole for the new newel post, drill several holes and lever out the waste.

5 Use a plane (or a planer-file) to give the stump of the newel post a rounded top.

6 Using the dowel supplied, apply adhesive to the newel post and insert it into the hole.

10 Each baluster will have to be cut to the correct angle. Use a sliding bevel to mark it.

11 Spacers fitted to the handrail and to the bottom rail correctly space the balusters.

12 Enhance the final result by sanding and applying a stained varnish to the staircase.

WINDOW HARDWARE AND LOCKS

Over half of all home burglaries occur through a window and even the smallest one is vulnerable, so good locks are very important. The first line of defence is to fit key-operated locks to all ground floor windows, and those first floor windows that are easily accessible. It is also essential to provide secure ventilation around your home.

Basic hardware

The most common items of hardware fitted on hinged windows are a rotating cockspur handle that is used simply to fasten the window, and a casement stay which props it open in one of the several different positions. On sliding sash windows, the basic hardware is a catch that locks the two sashes together when they are closed.

Window locks

A wide range of locking devices for windows is available. Many are surface-mounted using screws and are quick and easy to fit, although for some types a drilled hole for a bolt or recess chiselled for a striking plate (keeper) may be required. Mortised locks and dual screws that fit into holes drilled in the window frame take longer to install, but they are very secure.

All window locks are supplied with fixing screws but these should often be discarded in favour of longer, more secure fixings. For extra security, it is also a good idea to fit two locks on casement windows more than 1m (3ft) high and all locking devices for sash windows are best used in pairs.

For ventilation, if the window has a stay pierced with holes, you can replace the plain peg with a casement stay lock. Attach the screw-on lock to the threaded peg with the key supplied. You can now secure the window in position.

If fitting lockable window catches and stays, do not leave keys in the locks where they might be seen by an intruder or in case they fall out as the window is opened and closed. Instead, hang them on a hook close to the window.

Fitting a window handle and stay

1 Choose the position of the cockspur handle on the casement and make pilot holes through it with a bradawl. Then screw the handle to the casement.

2 Fit the striking plate (keeper) to the frame so that it will engage with the cockspur. Drill out the frame to a depth of 20mm (¾in) through the slot in the plate.

3 Fit the casement stay by screwing its base-plate to the bottom rail of the casement about one-third along from the hinged edge.

4 Open the window to find the right position for the pins on the frame. Attach the pins, then fit the stay rest on the casement rail.

Practical tip

Ensure you have the right screws: a lock for wooden frames requires wood screws and metal windows require self-tapping screws.

Casement locks

Locks for wooden casement windows may be surface-mounted or set in the frame. In the former case, the lockplate is attached to the fixed frame and the body of the lock to the opening frame. With the window closed, mark the positions of the lock and plate on both frames, then screw them in place. For those with a locking bolt, you will have to cut a rebate (rabbet) or drill a hole to receive the bolt. Some surface-mounted locks are also suitable for metal casement windows. Check the instructions.

Locks that are set in the frame normally require holes to be drilled in both fixed and opening frames. Also, a hole must be drilled through the face of the frame for the key.

Sash locks

Some types of casement-window lock will also work with sash windows. Another option is key-operated dual screws, which bolt both sashes together. Use a flat bit the width of the lock barrel to drill through the inner meeting rail into the outer rail to the required depth, then tap the barrels into place with a hammer and piece of wood. Fit the longer barrel into the inner rail, the shorter into the outer rail, and screw the bolt into the barrel with the key.

Fire safety

Wherever possible, fit window locks that all use the same standard key so that any key can be used to open a window in the event of an emergency. Keep the key in an accessible position.

Fitting a casement lock

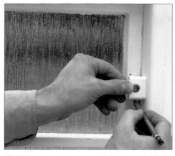

1 With the lock assembled, mark the position on the fixed and opening frames.

2 Separate the two parts of the lock and screw the body to the opening frame.

3 Fit the cover plate and insert the screws. You may want to use longer screws.

4 Some makes come with small covers to hide the screws. Tap these into place.

Fitting a sash window lock

1 Mark the drill bit with tape to the required depth and drill through the inner meeting rail of a sash window and into the outer rail.

2 Separate the two sections of the lock and tap the barrels of the dual screw into place in the meeting rails (mullions).

DOOR LOCKS

Doors, especially those at the rear of the house, often provide an easy entrance and exit point for intruders. Good locks properly fitted to a strong door and door frame are the basic requirements for ensuring that house doors are secure, while additional security devices may help you feel safer at home. The doors of garages and outbuildings are also at risk and need to be protected too.

Installing mortise locks

Align the mortise lock with the centre rail of the door and use the lock body as a template for marking the top and bottom of the mortise.

Draw a line down the middle of the door edge and, using a drill bit the width of the lock body, drill a series of overlapping holes along the centre-line to the depth of the lock. Chisel out the mortise so that the lock body fits snugly. Insert the lock, mark the outline of the faceplate with a marking gauge and chisel out a recess so that it fits flush with the door edge.

Mark the positions of the key and spindle holes, then drill them using a twist drill of the same diameter; enlarge the keyhole with a padsaw. Assemble and check the lock works. With the latch and bolt open, mark their positions on the door frame. Measure from the outside of the door to the centre of the bolt, mark that distance on the jamb and cut mortises in this position. Chisel a recess for the striking plate and check that the door closes properly before screwing it in place.

Practical tip

"Measure twice and cut once." Accuracy is vital when measuring out for door locks, so take your time with this part of the job and you will have fewer problems later.

Fitting a mortise lock

1 Mark out the dimensions of a mortise lock on the door edge.

2 Draw a vertical line in the exact centre of the door between the marked lines.

3 Drill a line of holes through the centreline to the depth of the lock body.

4 Insert the lock, then mark and chisel out the recess for the faceplate.

5 Using the lock as a guide, mark the position of the spindle and keyhole.

6 Drill, then use a padsaw to form the keyhole, then fit the covers.

7 Cut out mortises for the latch and the deadbolt on the door jamb.

8 Cut out a recess for the striking plate (keeper) so that it fits flush in the door jamb.

Fitting a rim lock to a door

Mark the position of the lock on the door, using any template provided, and bore a hole with a flat bit for the key cylinder. Push the cylinder into the hole, connect the backplate and secure it with screws. The cylinder connecting bar will protrude through the backplate. If necessary, cut it to length using a hacksaw.

Mark and chisel out the lock recess in the door edge, then fit the lock and screw it to the door, making sure that the cylinder connecting bar has engaged in the lock.

With the door closed, mark the position of the striking plate (keeper) on the jamb, then chisel out the recess so that the plate fits flush with the frame. Fix the striking plate with screws and check that the door closes properly.

Fitting rack bolts

Mark the position of the rack bolt in the centre of the door edge and on the inner face of the door, using a try or combination square to ensure that the two marks are level. Drill horizontally into the door edge to the depth of the body of the bolt.

Push the bolt into the hole, mark the outline of the faceplate, then withdraw the bolt and chisel out a recess for the plate. Hold the bolt level with the guideline on the inside of the door, and mark and drill a hole for the key.

Fit the bolt, following the manufacturer's instructions, check that it works properly and screw the keyhole plate to the door. Close the door and wind out the bolt so that it leaves a mark on the jamb. Drill a hole at this point and fit a recessed cover plate.

Fitting a rim lock

1 Mark the position of the cylinder on the door and drill its hole.

2 Insert the barrel of the cylinder into the drilled hole.

3 Fit the backplate to the door and secure it tightly with screws.

4 Mark the length of the connecting bar to be cut off if necessary.

5 Fit the lock case on to the connecting plate and screw up.

6 Mark the position of the striking plate. Chisel out the wood to fix to the frame.

Fitting a rack bolt

1 Use tape to mark out the drilling depth and keep the drill bit horizontal. Push in the bolt.

2 Mark the outline of the faceplate then withdraw the bolt to chisel out the recess.

PREPARING WOODWORK FOR PAINT

The secret of a good painted or varnished finish on wood is to spend time preparing the surface before you get down to the job itself. Wood must be sound and blemish-free, and any knots, common in softwoods such as pine, will need treating with a knotting solution (shellac) to prevent resin from seeping out and ruining the finish.

Pre-painted wood

If the existing paintwork is sound, there is no need to strip it back to bare wood. Simply wash the area carefully with a sugar soap (all-purpose cleaner) and water solution, lightly sand with sandpaper, then remove any traces of dust before painting. Where there are patches of bare wood, apply primer, then undercoat as normal. Finally, you should sand lightly before painting on the top coat.

However, if the paint or varnish is chipped or blistered, you will have to remove it. Use a scraper to get rid of loose fragments; a triangular scraper, known as a shavehook, is handy for getting into tight corners and mouldings.

For stripping large areas of wood, the choice is between a chemical stripper and a hot-air gun. If you opt for the former, you will need

to neutralize the surface, as recommended by the manufacturer, once the old paint has been removed. A hot-air gun will make light work of removing large areas of paint, but take care around windows, as the heat may damage the glass.

If you plan to paint over a faded woodstain, you will not be able to remove the old finish. In this case, simply sand the area, remove the surface dust, then apply one or two coats of an aluminium-based primer before over-painting.

If knots are showing through the painted woodwork, sand the paint film back to the bare wood and apply a knotting solution (shellac) to the knot, then prime and undercoat to bring the new paint film level with the surrounding paintwork. Sand between coats. Knots in bare wood should always be treated with a knotting solution.

Bare wood

- There is a three-step sequence to painting bare wood:
- First, coat with a primer and lightly sand when dry. Wipe the surface with a lint-free cloth and white spirit (paint thinner).
- Apply an undercoat as specified by the manufacturer of the top coat you'll be using, and sand again. Remove any traces of dust with a lint-free cloth moistened with white spirit.
- Paint on the top coat. Normally, this will be a gloss finish, as it is hardwearing and easy to maintain. When varnishing bare wood, sand away any rough edges, wipe off the dust, then apply the finish.

Using liquid stripper

1 Wearing gloves, brush the stripper on to the painted surface. Leave it until the paint starts to bubble, following the instructions.

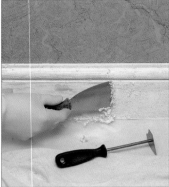

2 Scrape off the peeling layers of paint with a paint scraper. Use a shavehook for more intricate mouldings.

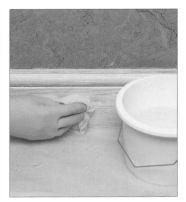

3 Wash the surface with water, white spirit (paint thinner) or neutralizer, as recommended by the manufacturer.

Using a heat gun

1 Move the heat gun over the surface so that the air stream heats and softens the paint evenly. Scrape off the paint as you work.

2 Be careful not to scorch the wood. Use a shavehook to scrape out the paint from intricate mouldings.

3 Rub off any remaining traces of paint with wire (steel) wool, soaked in white spirit (paint thinner). Work in the direction of the grain of the wood.

Filling defects in wood

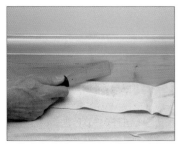

1 Fill splits and dents in wood using all-purpose filler on painted surfaces, and tinted wood filler on new or stripped wood.

2 Use the corner of a filling knife or a finger to work the filler into recesses. Smooth off the excess before it dries.

3 When the filler or wood stopper has hardened, use sandpaper wrapped around a block to sand the repair down flush.

Preparing painted woodwork

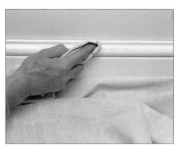

1 Use fine-grade sandpaper to remove "nibs" from the paint surface and to key the paint film ready for repainting.

2 Wash the surface thoroughly with a solution of detergent and rinse with clean water so that no residue is left.

3 Use a clean cloth moistened with white spirit (paint thinner) to remove dust from recessed mouldings and corners.

PAINTING WINDOWS, DOORS AND STAIRS

Windows and doors are key elements in the appearance of a house exterior. Flaking or badly executed paintwork will deter potential buyers and generally create a poor impression. Planning can be just as important as the mechanics of painting itself; discipline yourself to follow tried and tested painting techniques to ensure your home is presented to its best advantage.

The correct sequence

It is tempting simply to get on with a painting job to complete it quickly. However, there are logical sequences for painting windows and doors, which will streamline the process and give the best results. For instance, by following the illustrated guidelines for painting a panelled door, you will be joining a series of wet edges, allowing the paintwork to be blended completely before it dries. When using gloss paints, work with the grain and, since areas to be covered are typically small, aim to complete the job in one session.

Order of painting windows

When painting a casement window, keep the casements wide open as you work. Start with the glazing bars, followed by open casements, then paint the window frame last.

With sash windows, you will need to move the sections up and down to paint the various components. Paint the base of the top sash first, then finish the rest of this section. Next concentrate on the bottom sash, and finish off with the outer framework – take care not to splash paint on to the sash cords; it will be very difficult to remove.

Practical tip

Paint windows early in the day, so that they will be dry enough to secure firmly by night-time.

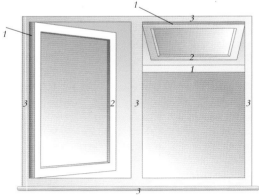

Left The correct order of painting a casement window. It is best to keep the casements wide open while you work (see below).

Preparing windows for painting

1 Unscrew all old or existing window fittings, prior to painting.

2 Screw a woodscrew into one of the holes to make a temporary handle.

3 Carefully scrape off any traces of old paint.

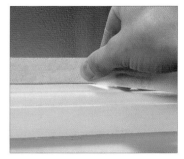

4 Apply masking tape, leaving a 1.5mm gap.

Above Always remove door furniture.

Above The correct order of painting a sash window.

Order of painting doors

The order for painting a door will depend on its construction. There is one set of rules for flush doors and another for panelled doors – see the numbered illustrations on the right. Complete a flush door in one session, starting at the top left-hand corner and finishing at the bottom right of the door.

Order of painting stairs

For each stage, start at the top and work downward. Begin with the banisters and bottom rail, followed by the newel posts, top rail and handrail (if painted). If you are laying a stair runner and want a painted border either side of it, paint the edges of the treads and risers next. Allow the painted areas to run 50mm (2in) underneath each side of where the carpet will lie so no bare areas will be visible. Continue with the skirting (base) board and finally the side of the stairs.

Above The order of painting a panel door.

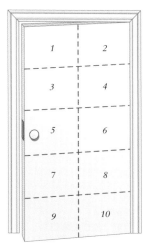

Above The order of painting a flush door.

Left The correct order of painting a staircase.

Practical tip

Try painting the treads and risers of stairs in shades that tone with the general decor, or use a co-ordinating stencilled effect on stair risers and walls.

PAINTING EXTERIOR WOODWORK

A wealth of products has been developed for painting exterior woodwork. Never try to economize by using interior gloss paints outside, they will not cope with temperature extremes and will soon flake and split. Do not be afraid to experiment with bright colours on woodwork, but choose a finish that complements, rather than contrasts with, other houses in the neighbourhood.

Fascias, soffits, bargeboards and weatherboards

Choose a dry, calm day to paint and avoid working in direct sunlight, as the glare will prevent you from obtaining good, even coverage. Furthermore, if you are using a water-based (latex) paint, it will dry too rapidly, leaving hard edges.

Start by priming any bare areas, then apply an undercoat and finally one or two coats of gloss. With a standard gloss paint, begin by applying the paint vertically, and then use sideways strokes to blend it well. Work in the direction of the grain, blending in the wet edges for a uniform finish. If you are using a one-coat paint, apply the finish quite thickly in close, parallel strips and do not over-brush. For weatherboarding (siding), paint the undersides first, then the faces, working horizontally.

Windows

Bare wood should be primed and undercoated, while old or defective paintwork will need sanding before over-painting. If existing paint is badly cracked or blistered, it should be stripped off completely and a new primer, undercoat and top coat applied. Exterior windows should be

Above Paint bargeboards early on in your work schedule. By starting from the top and working down you ensure that any dislodged dirt or paint droplets only fall on unpainted surfaces.

painted in sequence, broadly following the pattern for interior casement and sash window frames. However, when painting a sash window, start with the bottom sash, as opposed to the top in indoor work. Mask windows carefully before

starting work, or use a paint shield to protect the glass from splashes. Remember to let the paint extend a little way on to the glass to prevent rainwater from seeping into the frame.

Doors and fences

If you have an attractive hardwood door, think twice before covering it with several layers of paint. You may prefer to let the natural beauty of the wood show through by applying a stain or varnish.

Stains may be water-, oil- or spirit-based and are applied directly to the bare wood. Teak and Danish oils are also popular for hardwood doors. They give a waterproof, durable finish and enhance the natural look of the timber. Apply with a clean cloth or brush. The final coat can be applied with a scouring pad or 000-grade

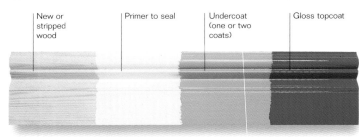

New or stripped wood	Primer to seal	Undercoat (one or two coats)	Gloss topcoat

Above The sequence for painting wood.

Painting a door

1 Remove old paintwork, then smooth the surface with a palm sander.

2 Apply a suitable primer and allow to dry completely before over-painting.

3 Apply one or two undercoats and lightly rub down with sandpaper between coats.

4 Apply topcoat to mouldings and panelled areas first, then move on to cross rails.

5 Finally, replace the door furniture. The finished door should last for years; simply give the paintwork an occasional wipe-down to keep it in good order.

wire (steel) wool. If you want a particularly hardwearing paint finish on an exterior door, consider a high-gloss enamel. With this type of product, you will obtain the best results by applying paint sparingly.

For fences and outbuildings, there is a wide selection of exterior wood stains and paints in all shades. Many are water-based and plant-friendly, while being tough enough to withstand the rigours of quite harsh

climates. Special paints and stains have also been developed for decking with a greater resistance to scuffing and cracking.

Painting a weatherboard (siding)

1 It is easy to miss sections of exterior weatherboarding, paint the undersides first.

2 Paint the facing boards next, and finish off with the end grains.

Above Fences and gates can be painted in all shades of bright colours.

PREPARING FLOORS

Do not ignore the decorative potential of the floors in your home. There is a wide range of attractive materials from vinyl and cork to ceramic and parquet tiles, but all need laying on a sound, stable surface. Cheapest of all are the floorboards beneath your feet, which, sanded and sealed, can be decorated to suit your colour scheme.

Basic requirements

The flooring is often the most expensive item in a room, so it must be laid and fitted correctly. All flooring requires a smooth, dry and level base, and a sub-floor will be needed over floorboards if sheet vinyl, parquet, or vinyl, cork, woodstrip, laminated or ceramic tiles are chosen.

Sheets of 3mm (⅛in) thick hardboard will be adequate for lightweight flooring such as cork and vinyl, but ceramic tiles will require a stronger base of plywood 6–12mm (¼–½in) thick. In bathrooms, it is worth paying the extra for marine ply, which offers greater resistance to damp.

Where flooring is to be laid directly on to floorboards, make sure that the surface is in good condition. Any protruding nails should be hammered in and loose floorboards secured with screws. A solid floor that is uneven or damaged should be repaired with a proprietary self-levelling compound.

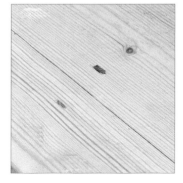

Above Punch any protruding floorboard nails below the surface of the wood to prevent them from damaging the new floorcovering.

Laying a hardboard sub-floor

1 To ensure a secure fixing for hardboard or plywood, use annular (spiral flooring) nails.

2 Condition the hardboard sheets by brushing or spraying with water before laying.

3 A piece of wood cut to size will allow you to space nails correctly and rapidly.

4 Use the offcut (scrap) from each row to start the next so that joins are staggered.

Laying a sub-floor

Before laying, condition the boards by spraying the textured side of each sheet with 450ml (¾pint) of water. Stack the sheets back-to-back flat, separated by strips of wood, on the floor of the room in which they are to be laid. Leave them for 48 hours.

Begin laying boards in the corner farthest from the door, fixing each sheet in place with 19mm (¾in) annular (spiral flooring) nails. Start to nail 12mm (½in) in from the skirting (base) board edge. To ensure the boards lay flat, work across the surface in a pyramid sequence, spacing the nails 150mm (6in) apart along the edges and 230mm (9in) apart in the middle.

Butt boards edge to edge to complete the first row, nailing the meeting edges first. Use the offcut from the first row to start the next row, and continue in this way, staggering the joins in each row.

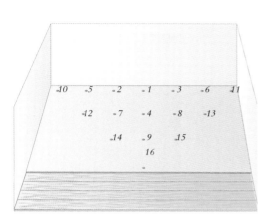

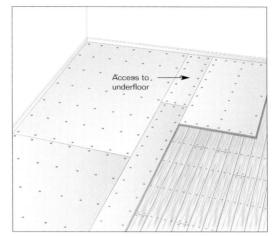

Above Nail across a hardboard sheet in a pyramid sequence to avoid creating bulges. Nails should be 150mm (6in) apart along the edges and 230mm (9in) apart in the middle.

Above If there are plumbing pipes or electric cables under the floor, lay narrow strips of board over pipe runs to ensure easy access for future maintenance.

Calculating quantities

Before buying new floorcovering, take note of any aspects that could make laying difficult.

Sheet materials (carpet and vinyl)

Measure the length and width of the room at its widest points, taking the tape right into alcoves and to the halfway point under doors.

Multiply these two figures together to obtain the floor area, which will give you an idea of the amount of flooring needed. Draw up a rough sketch of the room showing all the dimensions and take it to your flooring retailer, who will calculate the quantity required and advise on how to minimize wastage and plan any necessary seams.

Small-unit flooring (tiles, slabs and panels)

Measure the room and multiply the width by the length to obtain the floor area. If the room has a bay or recesses either side of a chimney breast (fireplace projection), measure and calculate these areas separately and add to the total.

Hard floor tiles and slabs may be sold by the square metre or square yard. Purchase the quantity required plus a ten per cent allowance for wastage and breakages when cutting. Soft floor tiles and parquet panels are sold in packs. To work out the number of packs required, divide the floor area by the area that one pack will cover, rounding up to the next whole pack.

Strip flooring (woodstrip and laminated boarding)

Measure the room and obtain the floor area as discussed above.

Strip flooring is sold in packs to cover a given area. To calculate the quantity of packs required, multiply the length of the room by the width to give the area of the room and divide by the area that is covered by one pack, rounding up to the next complete pack if necessary. Different makes of woodstrip vary slightly, so follow the manufacturer's guidelines when laying the floor.

Practical tips

- Boards can be nailed in place quickly if you cut a length of wood to the correct length as a guide for spacing the nails.
- Lay hardboard with the textured side up. This provides a good key for adhesive, while nail heads will be concealed.
- In an irregularly shaped room, set out the stringlines and adjust the starting point so that any obvious pattern is centred in the main part of the room.

SANDING AND FINISHING FLOORBOARDS

A natural wooden floor will allow you to appreciate the true beauty of the wood grain and can transform a room. A few simple checks will soon tell you if the floorboards beneath your feet are worth renovating. While the work itself is quite straightforward, do not underestimate the amount of time that may be needed to complete the job.

Assessing the floor

A mechanical sander will not only get rid of ingrained dirt, polish and stains, but also remove deep blemishes and ridges between boards. However, the result will only be as good as the base material. Thin and splintering floorboards are not worth the effort of renovating, while a floor that consists of many sizes and types of board will not look attractive unless painted or disguised with dark stain.

Gaps, however, are quite easy to remedy: small gaps can be filled with a neutral-coloured wood filler, while large gaps should be plugged with fillets of wood planed level with the surface. If the problem is extensive, it will be easier simply to lift and re-lay the whole floor. Protruding nail heads and heavy deposits of old polish will tear and clog abrasive paper, and must be dealt with first.

Tools and equipment

Stripping a wooden floor can be hard work, so make sure that you have the right tools – hire those tools you do not own. You will need a drum sander for stripping the main part of the floor, an edge sander to reach right up to the skirting (base) boards as well as different grades of abrasive paper, a shavehook (triangular scraper) and a hand sanding block for getting right into tight corners.

A nail punch, hammer and screwdriver will be needed to knock in protruding nail heads and screw down loose boards.

Right Sanding floors is a noisy, messy job. Protect your clothes and yourself with the right equipment.

Preparing the floor

1 Seal doors with masking tape to prevent dust from seeping into the rest of the house.

2 Screw down loose boards and punch down protruding nails.

Practical tips

- Using a sander creates dust, so wear a facemask and goggles.
- For safety, drape the electrical cable of a mechanical sander over your shoulder, and keep it behind you at all times. Use all power tools with a Residual Current Device.

3 Fill gaps between boards with a matching offcut (scrap) of wood or wood filler.

4 Remove traces of old polish with wire (steel) wool and white spirit (paint thinner).

Sanding

To remove the worst of the dirt, fit coarse sandpaper to the drum sander and work diagonally across the boards, overlapping each sanded strip by about 75mm (3in). If the boards are badly blemished or warped, vacuum to remove dust, then repeat this step, working diagonally in the opposite direction. Vacuum again, then fit medium-grade sandpaper to the machine and work up and down the boards along the grain, overlapping each strip as before.

Finally, repeat this step, after vacuuming, using fine sandpaper. Around the edges, use an edge sander along the grain, and finish corners with a shave hook and sanding block, or a disc sander.

If you are not careful, a floor sander can run away from you, and if used incorrectly it can spoil a floor. Therefore, it is important to know how to use it properly.

With a drum sander, tilt it back on its wheels, switch on and gently lower the belt on to the floor. Allow the machine to move forward slowly and do not try to hold it back or in one spot, or it will create grooves in the floor. Raise the machine back on to its wheels at the end of each pass, and do not be tempted to "spot sand" stubborn marks as you may end up with a deep groove.

Lay an edge sander on its side, switch on, lift it and lower it on to the floor. Keep the machine moving, otherwise it will create swirl marks.

Finishing and sealing

Once stripped and sanded, floorboards must be sealed with a flooring grade wax, oil, and polyurethane varnish or paint. Wax is the most traditional treatment, although it attracts dust and is not particularly durable, so it is best used in low-wear areas. Brush-on liquid floor wax is the easiest to use, but must be applied in several thin coats, otherwise it will stay soft and look dull.

Floor oils are very easy to apply and form a hardwearing, water-resistant finish, but will darken the surface colour of the wood slightly. Rub with wire wool before the final coat. Follow the manufacturer's instructions for the best finish.

Sanding a wooden floor

1 Sand diagonally across the boards, using coarse sandpaper.

2 Use a medium-grade sandpaper, working along the grain. Finish with fine-grade paper.

3 Use a belt sander to tackle edges. Use a disc sander or sanding block for the corners.

4 Remove all traces of dust with a brush and then a damp sponge or clean cotton rag.

5 Sand down any remaining rough spots by hand with a sanding block.

6 Build a new protective finish with several thin coats of varnish, applied along the grain.

PAINTING AND VARNISHING WOODEN FLOORS

A wooden floor makes an attractive feature in itself, but it can take on a whole new dimension when you experiment with colourful paints, stains, waxes and varnishes. Bare floorboards in pristine condition cry out for innovative treatment. If you prefer traditional treatments, look at oak, mahogany, or beech stains coupled with varnish or a clear wax finish.

Essential preparation

Prepare the surface by vacuuming up all traces of dust, then clean the boards with a lint-free cloth moistened with white spirit (paint thinner). If the boards are already painted or varnished, the floor will need sanding. A hardboard floor will look more attractive with a painted finish. Use a primer first, then apply two coats of paint. Allow each to dry thoroughly, sand lightly and finish off with two coats of varnish.

The most important rule when treating a floor is not to paint yourself into a corner. Start at the corner farthest from the door, then work back toward the doorway so that you can make a safe exit while the floor dries.

Limed boards

Liming is an easy technique and a good one for beginners to try. It can be used in conjunction with colour-washing – the colourwash goes on first, then the liming paste – to produce an effect known as pickling.

Strip back any worn or grimy floorboards and apply a coat of shellac to seal the wood. Allow the shellac to dry, then use a wire brush to expose the grains and provide a good surface for the liming paste.

For a very attractive finish, try using pastel shades such as pale green or blue for the background colour.

Wood dyes

For modern schemes, consider colourful wood dyes. These must be applied to a clean, sound, grease-free surface. If the preparation is not thorough, the result will be patchy and unattractive. Wood dyes penetrate

Liming a wooden floor

1 Stroke the floorboards with a wire brush, working gently in the direction of the grain.

2 Apply the liming paste with fine wire (steel) wool. Fill up the grain as you work.

3 Working on a small area at a time, rub the liming paste into the boards in a circular motion. Leave to dry thoroughly.

4 Remove the excess by rubbing in some clear paste wax with a soft cloth. Buff the surface with a soft cloth to give a dull sheen.

deep into timber (lumber), but they do not provide a protective surface and must be sealed after application.

It is advisable to test the dye on a similar piece of wood before you start work on the floor as the dye will give varying results on different woods and can change significantly as fresh coats are applied. Finish the test with a coat of varnish.

If you are happy with the finish, apply the dye with a 100mm (4in) brush in the direction of the grain,

working rapidly so that hard edges do not spoil the effect. Alternatively, you could use a soft cloth.

Practical tip

Use lacquer on your floor for a bright, durable finish. Keep it scrupulously clean, as every speck of dust will show up on the glossy wooden surface.

Wood stains

These do have a protective function and come in a wide choice of colours, in water- and solvent-based versions. The former dry more quickly, but this may not be an advantage when covering large areas, as patchy sections could develop. When staining a newly stripped floor, seal the surface with a thinned polyurethane varnish first.

Use a brush to apply up to three coats of stain, using the product sparingly and working with the grain. If, at some point in the future, you wish to over-paint a stained floor, you will need to strip the surface back to bare wood, then apply a primer and undercoat.

Floor paints

Specially formulated floor paints give a particularly durable finish, but in practice, many ordinary paints will suffice. The latter will need one or two coats of varnish to protect the surface. Although paint will conceal the natural grain of the wood, it can produce an attractive, hardwearing finish, which requires less preparation time as floors do not need to be stripped back to

Applying a wood wash or stain

1 Pour the pre-mixed wash or stain into a paint kettle. Brush the wash or stain evenly on the wood in the direction of the grain.

bare wood, although they must be clean and grease-free.

Varnishes

These are available in oil- and water-based versions, and in satin, gloss and matt (flat) finishes. Coloured varieties, a mixture of stain and varnish, give you the option of transforming pale floorboards into a rich spectrum of colours, ranging from light honey pine to deep mahogany.

2 While wet, wipe off any excess. This will even the effect and expose more of the grain. Leave to dry before varnishing, if required.

If you are applying a solvent-based product, ensure that the room is well ventilated. Stir the varnish well and use a wide brush to apply it. Apply a minimum of three coats. Rub the floor down with a fine sandpaper before applying the final coat of varnish. On the minus side, varnish will crack with time. Every two or three years, you will need to sand the floor back to bare wood and treat the boards again.

Applying satinwood paint

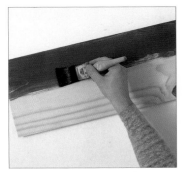

1 Dilute satinwood paint with 50 per cent white spirit (paint thinner). Brush on the mixture in the direction of the grain.

2 While wet, wipe down with a cloth to remove the excess and even the effect. Leave the surface to dry before varnishing.

Practical tips

- Colours that work well in wood washes and stains include yellow ochre, blue, Indian red, violet cream and pale green.
- If you use a solution of artist's oil paint and white spirit (paint thinner) to make up a thin wash, make sure you only use a small amount of oil paint, as the pigment produces intensely strong colours.

LAYING WOODSTRIP FLOORING

Woodstrip flooring is suitable for use in most rooms of your home and requires only basic carpentry skills to lay. The method used will vary according to the system you buy. Some strips need to be secret nailed to the floorboards, while others are designed to be a floating floor and may be glued, clipped or simply slotted together.

Expansion gaps

All woodstrip flooring requires an expansion gap around the edges of the room to allow the floor to expand and contract naturally. This can be achieved by removing and refitting the skirting (base) boards so that they cover the edge strips, or by filling the gap with cork strip or covering it with quadrant (base shoe) moulding, which are quicker and easier options. Floor laying kits that contain expansion-gap spacers are available. Laminated strip flooring can be laid in exactly the same manner as woodstrip flooring.

Fitting

Mark a guideline for the first run by snapping a chalked stringline 12mm (½in) away from, and parallel to, the longest or most convenient wall. Normally, woodstrip is laid lengthways in a room, or at right-angles to the floorboards.

Use a strip of wood or spacers to maintain the expansion gap and butt the grooved edge of the first strip tightly against it. Lay strips dry to complete the first run and, and if necessary, cut a length to fit, marking it with the aid of a try square.

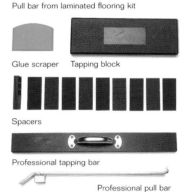

Pull bar from laminated flooring kit

Glue scraper   Tapping block

Spacers

Professional tapping bar

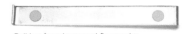

Professional pull bar

Laying a woodstrip floor

1 To allow for an expansion gap, butt the first length against 12mm (½in) spacers.

2 Drive pins at a 45-degree angle through the tongue into the floor.

3 If adhesive is recommended, apply glue to both the tongue and groove.

6 To ensure that the floor is strong and stable, stagger the joints.

7 Use an offcut to mark the architrave (trim) for cutting to the correct size.

8 Cut strips to size with a tenon saw and discard the tongue portions.

Once the first row has been aligned and is square with the wall, ease the boards apart and fix them in place according to the recommended method. For a glued floor, apply adhesive to both the tongue and groove of adjoining boards, wiping off any that oozes between the boards immediately. Boards held by clips should have them driven into adjacent lengths at 760mm (30in) intervals. If secret nailing is required, drive pins into the floor through the board tongues at a 45-degree angle, spacing them 200–250mm (8–10in) apart, up to 40mm (1½in) from each end.

To lay subsequent lengths, push the grooved edge of one strip on to the tongue of the strip laid previously, tapping it firmly with a hammer and protecting the edge from damage with an offcut (scrap). Lay the second and subsequent rows in this way, staggering the joints. An offcut longer than 300mm (12in) can be used to start the next row.

If a strip needs to be trimmed along its length to fit in the skirting, place it exactly over the last strip laid and put a spare board on top so that its tongue butts up to spacers against the skirting. Use the edge of the top board as a guide for marking the cutting line on the board below, and trim to size with a tenon saw. To ease the last strips into place, use a lever, or fitting tool if supplied, and pull them tightly against the previous row. If the flooring has been fixed by secret nailing, secure the last pieces by nailing through the face of the wood, punching the nails below the surface and disguising them with wood filler. Leave the floor to settle for 24 hours, after which the spacers can be removed and the expansion gap filled with cork strip or covered with quadrant moulding pinned to the skirting. If the flooring does not have a factory finish, it should be sealed as soon as possible with flooring grade wax, finishing oil or polyurethane varnish.

Cutting techniques

Cutting wooden flooring to fit neatly around a door frame can be difficult. Instead, use an offcut as a guide to mark a horizontal cutting line around the bottom of the architrave (trim) and frame. Saw through the architrave along the line and remove the narrow portion of wood. The wood strip should slip neatly underneath.

Sub-bases

Woodstrip flooring does not need a hardboard sub-floor, but it may require a paper underlay or polyethylene vapour barrier, so check the manufacturer's installation instructions. Floating floors and direct-fix systems can be installed over floorboards. A floating floor is the best option for a solid floor.

4 Tap each strip into place, using an offcut (scrap) to protect the edge from damage.

5 To mark a cutting line, align strips carefully and use a straightedge as a guide.

9 The last strip will need to be levered into place to create a tight fit.

10 Remove the spacers and fit cork strip into the expansion gap.

Practical tips

- Doors may need trimming to fit over the new floor, so remove them before you start.
- Use a detector to find the positions of pipes and cables.

LAYING WOOD MOSAIC FLOORING

Wood mosaic or finger parquet flooring is the least expensive type of decorative wooden flooring, and may be veneered or hardwearing solid wood. It is also easy to lay and economical to use, particularly in awkwardly shaped rooms. Some finger parquet is supplied pre-finished, while other types may require sanding as well as sealing after being laid.

Fitting

To mark a guideline for the first row, add 12mm (½in) to the width of one panel and snap a chalked line of string on the floor that distance from the wall farthest from the door. Butt a 12mm (½in) strip of wood or spacers against the skirting (base) board to maintain the expansion gap. Apply adhesive to the floor with a notched spreader, covering an area equal to two or three panels.

Lay the panels one row at a time, against each other. Do not push panels together, as this will force adhesive on to the surface of the wood. Wipe away excess adhesive immediately. Use a straightedge and spirit level to check that each row is straight and horizontal before going on to the next. Level uneven panels by tapping them down with a

softwood block and hammer.

Once all whole panels have been laid, cut others to fit around the edges of the room by using a spare panel to mark the cutting line. Butt the top panel up to the spacers against the skirting to allow for the expansion gap. When trimming panels to size, cut down through the decorative face with a tenon saw; apply adhesive to the back before fitting into place.

Attach quadrant (base shoe) moulding to the skirting with panel pins (brads) every 600mm (24in), or fill the expansion gap with cork strip. Punch pin heads below the surface

and disguise with wood filler.

Once the adhesive has set, the surface can be sanded if necessary. Use an electric orbital sander, paying particular attention to any uneven joints. Vacuum thoroughly and wipe with white spirit (paint thinner) to remove all dust. Then seal according to the manufacturer's instructions. Cutting techniques

To cut parquet or wood mosaic flooring to fit around a door frame, you can remove part of the architrave (trim) by using an offcut as a guide to saw horizontally through the frame as for woodstrip flooring and slip it

Practical tips

- To reduce the risk of warping, remove the wrapping and leave the panels in the room in which they are to be used for seven days prior to laying so that they will acclimatize to humidity levels.
- Set out panels dry first, adjusting the starting point if you will be left with awkward gaps to fill.
- The grain on parquet runs in different directions, making sanding difficult. To minimize scratching, lightly sand at a 45-degree angle to the grain.

Laying wood mosaic flooring

1 Snap a chalked line on to the floor as a guideline for the first row of panels.

2 Mark the expansion gap, and apply glue to the floor with a notched spreader.

6 Cut the wood mosaic panels face upward, using a tenon saw.

7 Wood mosaic can be cut to fit or slotted underneath a door frame.

underneath, or use a profile gauge to transfer the exact shape on to the panel and cut it out with a fine hacksaw.

To accommodate a pipe, measure and mark the position of the pipe on the panel, then drill a hole slightly larger in diameter than the pipe at that position. Remove a strip of wood between the drilled hole and the edge of the panel so that it can be glued in place, then fit the strip into the gap behind the pipe.

Sub-bases

Wood mosaic flooring must be laid on a clean, dry and level sub-floor. A self-levelling screed should be applied to uneven solid floors, while a hardboard sub-floor will be required over floorboards.

Above Use a profile gauge to transfer the shape of small obstacles to panels.

Cutting curves

Mark out a template on a piece of cardboard and transfer the shape to the wooden panel. Use a coping saw to cut along the guideline.

Above Drill a hole and cut out a strip to fit a panel around a pipe.

3 Butt panels against each other by aligning the meeting edges first.

4 Work in rows across the room, laying whole panels first.

5 Make sure that you allow for the expansion gap when cutting panels for edges.

8 Fix moulding to the skirting (base) board, not the floor. Punch the pins below the surface.

9 Remove all dust by wiping the floor with a cloth moistened with white spirit (paint thinner).

10 For unsealed floors, apply two or three coats of varnish or floor sealer.

FURNITURE
REPAIR AND
RESTORATION

M any of the techniques and methods used in the repair and restoration of furniture repair and restoration are shown in this section, from restoring damaged surfaces, to polishing and colouring, veneering, with step-by-step projects including chairs, tables, chests and desks.

RESTORING DAMAGED SURFACES

There are a great variety of surfaces associated with antique furniture and there are equally numerous ways in which they can be affected by excessive heat, water, moisture, grease, dirt or oxidation, to name a few. To remedy these problems each surface may need treating in a different way. Great care must be taken in the process, as a badly restored piece of furniture will not only look unsightly but be radically decreased in value.

The types of damage found on the surfaces of veneers, solid wood furniture, gilt, marble or leather fall mainly into two categories. That caused by accidental damage and that which has simply been a result of the passing of time and the action of normal wear and tear.

In some cases the damage can be corrected by little more than a light clean and a rewax, but occasionally the existing finish will have to be stripped and replaced. In the case of a gilt finish, for example, this will not be too much of a problem (the vast majority of gilded pieces have been regilded at some point). With polished surfaces, however, only the minimal amount of work should be undertaken and the work confined to the localized area of damage.

There is also the question of whether to restore a surface or leave it alone. When the damage has been caused recently, it is obvious that attention is needed. When the surface damage is old, the stain, dent or mark might have been covered with numerous generations of waxing so that it forms part of the "character" of the piece. The decision is whether to remove an unsightly mark or leave an otherwise excellent patinated surface well alone. The skilled restorer and polisher should be able to remove any localized damage successfully. The amateur

restorer should not attempt this type of work on good coloured and patinated pieces. Often collectors and furniture owners alike would rather leave a mark and retain the overall integrity of a piece.

Blisters

When the glue bonding a veneered surface to its core perishes due to heat or water damage, or simply because the glue has deteriorated through age, blisters will form. The solution is either to apply hot blocks or fresh adhesive.

Water marks

Caused by either the direct or indirect action of water on a polished surface, water marks are characterized by the appearance of white patches, known as blooming. This is usually treated with new applications of polish and wax, although occasionally the surface will need to be washed back and refinished.

Spirit and water stains

Should spilled water or spirit be left to penetrate through a polished surface into the wood beneath, the result will be a black or dark stain. This can sometimes be treated with mild bleach, which will improve if not always completely remove the mark. This is, however, a specialist procedure best left to the professionals.

Dents

If dents occur on legs they can be largely ignored; if they appear on a flat, top surface they need attention. If the dent is not too deep the most common method is to try and remove it with the action of steam, which raises the grain.

Burns

The most common type of burn damage is that caused by cigarettes. A considered view should be taken to restore or not, but a burn is easier to correct on a veneered surface than a solid one. However, it is a specialist job best left to the professionals.

Scratches

Scratches are one of the most common forms of damage found on antique furniture. Light scratches that only affect the polished surface can be waxed out, while deeper ones will need to be filled and coloured out with stain.

Sunlight

The action of direct sunlight will often have an adverse effect on a polished surfaces, causing the polish to dry out and the surface to change colour. If the overall change in colour is aesthetically pleasing, it can be left; if the damage is patchy then localized areas may need to be coloured to match the rest of the surface.

Above Burn damage

Above Scratch

Above Dent

Removing a blister

The figured walnut veneer on the top of this Regency chiffonier has blistered badly. The first solution to try is to apply a hot block in an attempt to soften the glue beneath the veneer so that it will re-adhere (see p.368). If that is not successful, the alternative is to introduce new adhesive through a cut in the veneer, but without marking the finish.

Materials

- sharp knife
- PVA (white) glue
- clean white paper
- wooden block
- G-clamp
- rubber
- polish
- wax
- clean cotton rag

1 Using a sharp knife, make small cuts in the blistered veneer to the core underneath. Follow the grain of the veneer to disguise the cuts.

2 Spread a little water on top of the cut blister; this will penetrate the incisions.

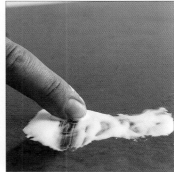

3 Spread some PVA (white) glue on top of the blister and work it in with a finger in a circular motion. The water under the veneer will draw the glue through the cuts and into the space between the veneer and core.

4 Wipe away the excess glue and place a sheet of clean white paper over the blister. Lay a hot block (heated on a hot plate or an iron, see p.368) on top and clamp it firmly in place. The paper will protect the block from the glue. Leave overnight so that the veneer can rebond with the core.

5 Remove the block and paper; carefully wash off any paper that has been stuck with excess expelled glue. If there are any minor heat marks from the hot block, charge a rubber with polish and apply a thin layer to the surface, before waxing to finish (see pp.356–7).

Above Once polished, no trace of the blister remains.

REMOVING A WATER MARK

The photograph below shows a common problem found on polished surfaces: a water mark caused by hot or wet items being placed directly on to a surface. In this instance, a wet vase has been placed on the table and has marked it. Fortunately, it has penetrated only the top layers of polish and not stained the actual wood. The solution is to remove the damaged polish and carefully build up the finish with fresh polish and wax so that it matches the surrounding finish. The top is quarter veneered, which means that the grain is split in four directions, so the wax must be applied in a circular motion.

Materials

- methylated spirits (methyl alcohol)
- clean cotton rags
- rubber
- polish
- wax

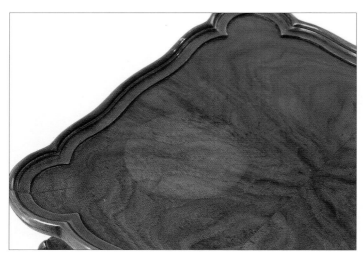

1 Gently wash just the affected area with a cotton rag dipped in methylated spirits (methyl alcohol). This will remove the perished polish.

2 Charge a rubber with polish (see p.356) and apply a light layer to the washed-off area to build up the surface. Then give the whole top a rubber of polish to produce a uniform appearance (see p.357).

Above The water mark has now been removed without touching or altering the table's colour or patination.

3 Allow the polish to harden, then treat the surface with a dark wax (see p.358), using circular movements.

RAISING A DENT

Dents and bruises are common problems with polished furniture, often caused by something being dropped on to the surface or the surface being damaged in transit. Most dents can be lifted with steam and then made invisible with polish, as shown here, but some dents are more difficult to remove. If they are not in a central position or on an otherwise unblemished surface, it is best simply to leave them alone and regard them as part of the history and character of the piece.

Materials

- clean cotton rags
- iron
- fine wire (steel) wool
- methylated spirits (methyl alcohol)
- fine-grade sandpaper
- fine brush
- spirit- (alcohol-) based stain
- rubber
- polish
- wax

1 Place a wet cotton rag over the dent and press the tip of a hot iron on top. This will generate steam, which will lift the bruised wood fibres. Take care to use only the tip of the iron in order to keep the steamed area as localized as possible.

2 The dent has been raised, but the steam has caused some localized damage. Use fine wire (steel) wool and methylated spirits (methyl alcohol) to wash off the areas of damaged polish.

3 The grain of the wood will have been raised by the heat. Using fine-grade sandpaper, lightly sand the repair until the wood is smooth.

4 Mix a spirit-based (alcohol-based) stain to match the colour of the table, then carefully apply this to the restored area, disguising the raised grain. Charge a rubber with polish and seal the area by rubbing in circular motions until it is covered (see p.356–7). Leave the polish to harden.

5 Wax the affected area using fine wire wool, then wax the rest of the surface with a soft cloth until the repaired area blends in.

Right When finished, all evidence of the dent should be removed and no trace of the restoration remain.

DISGUISING A SCRATCH

A deep single scratch is not uncommon on an otherwise unmarked surface, and the aim is to try to disguise the scratch as best as possible without disturbing the rest of the polished area. If the scratch runs parallel to the grain, the task will be that much easier. If, as in this case, it runs across the grain, it will be very difficult to disguise the damage completely, although filling wax, polish and stain can produce remarkable results.

Materials

- fine wire (steel) wool
- filling wax
- flat-bladed knife
- fine-grade sandpaper
- rubber
- polish
- spirit- (alcohol-) based stains
- fine brush
- clean cotton rag
- clear wax

Practical tip

Good craft stores should stock a range of coloured wax blocks for use in furniture restoration.

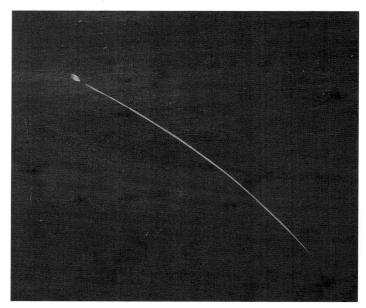

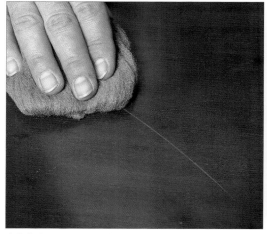

1 Rub the area around the scratch lightly with fine wire (steel) wool to remove the surface wax.

2 Choose a filling wax that is as close a match in colour to the table as possible. Fill the scratch with wax using a flat-bladed knife.

◀ 3 Allow the wax to harden, then gently scrape away the excess wax with a flat-bladed knife. Take great care not to mark the surface of the wood with the blade.

▶ 4 Remove the last traces of the surface filling wax with fine-grade sandpaper. Take care to avoid marking the existing polish.

5 Charge a rubber with polish and apply a layer over the scratched area to seal in the wax and blend the repair into its surroundings (see pp.356–7).

6 Mix a spirit-based (alcohol-based) stain to a colour slightly darker than the polished wax, and apply it to the scratch with a fine brush. When the stain is dry, seal the surface with another rubber of polish.

7 Now mix a spirit-based stain to match the original surface, and apply it to the scratch with a fine brush to blend the repair into the surrounding area. Leave to dry, then seal with a rubber of polish.

8 Once the polish has dried, apply a wax coat to the whole table top. Allow the wax to dry, then buff it to a shine (see p.357).

Right Although the scratch has not disappeared completely, it has been disguised and looks a lot less unsightly. Most importantly, the surrounding polished area has not been altered by the repair.

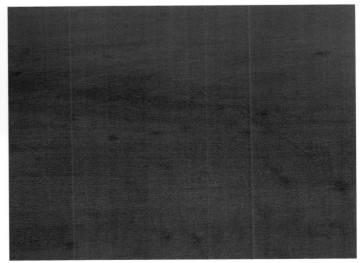

CLEANING AND REVIVING

By its very nature and with the period of time that passes, surfaces become oxidized or coated with dust, waxes and natural greases that combine to form a surface coating. While this is desirable with wood, other materials such as metal, marble and leather may on occasion need to be cleaned or the surface revived. Different materials will require different methods, but the one common theme is to clean a little at a time to enable the desired effect to be reached and not overdone. If you are over-zealous when cleaning, the result may look rather artificial.

There are a number of steps that can be taken to help keep the need to revive or clean a surface down to a minimum. The one measure that will apply to most materials is to wax on a fairly regular basis. The wax will nourish and feed both timber and leather.

Marble, it must be remembered, is porous and to help prevent stains on the tops of tables, for example, light waxing with clear wax should be regularly applied. As well as protecting the surface, the wax will help it to develop a lustre. Regular dusting will also help to avoid the build-up of a

surface coating. Dusting should be done with a dry cloth (cotton rag) – home recipes, such as the application of a harsh vinegar and water solution, should never be used. The following techniques will help to clean and revive the surfaces listed.

Cleaning marble

Over a period of years, there can be a build-up of dirt, grease and grime on marble tops. In fact, marble, like wood, often develops a warm surface patination over the years. While this can sometimes add to the colour and character, there comes a point when it will need to be cleaned. This piece of marble from an antique table is in good condition; it simply requires cleaning and sealing.

Materials

- soda crystals
- clean cotton rag
- clear wax

1 Dissolve approximately a handful of soda crystals in 4.5 litres (1 gallon) of warm water in a bowl. Use this solution to give the top a light clean, using a cloth (cotton rag) to lift off the surface dirt. Take care not to remove too much, as the natural character of the marble is part of its charm.

Practical tip

Marble can sometimes have an unseen fault line in it, which can crack under its own weight. When carrying a piece of marble, therefore, turn it on its side to minimize any possible risk of breakage. Remember that marble is very heavy, so enlist a helper if you have to move a large piece.

2 Using a clear wax, apply a thin coat with a cloth, rubbing with a circular motion, and allow it to harden.

3 When the wax has hardened, buff it to a soft sheen. Repeat the process until a warm patination returns to the marble.

Cleaning metal

Some metal fittings, usually brass, are gilded, while others have a lacquer coating to stop them oxidizing and the brass tarnishing. The cleaning of brass is very much a personal affair: some people may be happy to leave brass fittings completely tarnished, others may prefer to have just the highlights brightened, and others still may like to see the brass shining brightly like a soldier's buttons. If traces of the gilt or lacquer finish remain, surface grease and dirt should be removed without touching the finish underneath. In this example, two pieces of an early 19th-century cast brass moulding, known as a gallery, will be cleaned: one by a gentle method of washing with diluted soda crystals, the other using a stronger proprietary cleaning agent. The original finish on the gallery is fire-gilded.

Materials

- soda crystals
- soft toothbrush
- de-greasant agent
- protective gloves

Practical tip

When cleaning mounts, mouldings, galleries or handles, it is best to remove them from the piece of furniture, if possible, to prevent any damage to the polished surface. If this is done, make a note of their location to enable them to be refitted correctly.

1 The least severe method of cleaning is to use a solution of soda crystals and water. This will gently ease off the dirt and grease without removing the finish below. Dissolve a handful of soda crystals in 4.5 litres (1 gallon) of warm water in a bowl large enough to take the metal item.

2 With a soft toothbrush, gently scrub away the residue. As this is quite a mild form of cleaning, you can leave areas of dirt in the background to give the cleaned brass a softer look. If the host piece of furniture is of good colour and patination, this is often the best and most desirable finish.

3 If you want to remove all the dirt and grease and return the gilt as closely as possible to its original state, then a strong de-greasant is recommended. Leave the brass to soak in the cleaning agent for some minutes, then scrub it with a soft toothbrush. It is advisable to wear protective gloves to prevent your skin from being stained.

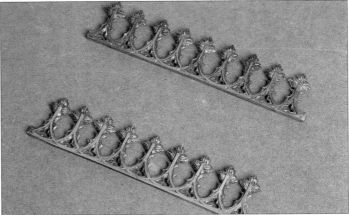

Above The top section of gallery has been cleaned with soda crystals, giving a softer, still slightly tarnished look, while the bottom length has been cleaned with a proprietary cleaning agent, producing a brighter, harder appearance.

REVIVING LEATHER

Leather was often used to cover writing surfaces as well as act as an upholstery material in antique furniture. Due to its nature, however, leather tends to become dry and brittle, and so usually has a shorter life than that of the piece of furniture it adorns. During the life of a piece of leather-topped furniture, therefore, the leather may have been replaced a number of times, and on occasion it may simply have been renewed because the owner wanted a colour change. Even so, a worn and textured leather surface can often enhance the character of a piece of furniture, and the surface can be revived. On this leather surface, you can see clearly where a blotter, which offered protection to the central area, has been laid. The outer, unprotected borders of the leather have become faded, worn and dry and so need to be revived.

Materials

- brush
- clear wax
- leather-reviving cream
- rubbers
- polish
- spirit- (alcohol-) based stain
- fine wire (steel) wool
- soft clean cotton rag

1 First, brush a coat of clear wax over the whole piece of leather. This will feed and nourish the leather and provide a protective coating. Coloured wax should not be used, as it could change the overall tone. In addition to the wax, a leather-reviving cream could be applied to the piece.

2 When the wax is dry, charge a rubber with polish and apply a thin layer to the surface (see pp.356–7). This will help to seal the grain, as well as giving a protective layer in readiness for the stain. If the grain is not stained first, certain areas will absorb more stain than others, giving a blotchy look.

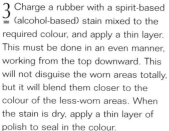

3 Charge a rubber with a spirit-based (alcohol-based) stain mixed to the required colour, and apply a thin layer. This must be done in an even manner, working from the top downward. This will not disguise the worn areas totally, but it will blend them closer to the colour of the less-worn areas. When the stain is dry, apply a thin layer of polish to seal in the colour.

4 When the polish is dry, cut it back with fine wire (steel) wool with wax on it. The wax ensures that the wool does not cut back the top too much. Finally, buff to a soft sheen with a soft cotton rag.

Right The leather is now revived and fed. All that is necessary in future is to wax it along with the rest of the piece.

REVIVING A POLISHED SURFACE

General wear and tear causes most items of furniture to become discoloured and marked over time. Water marks, light scratches and stains will penetrate only the first layers of polish, allowing surfaces with this type of damage to be revived rather than completely repolished (see pp.346 and 348–9). The process of revival requires care, patience and sensitivity, but with the right application the blemishes can be erased, and the original colour and sheen will be revealed.

This top from a Georgian chest of drawers has a variety of water marks, stains and scratches. Although they are numerous, it is immediately apparent that none of the blemishes penetrates beneath the top layers of the polish, so a systematic revival of the surface is all that is required. A variety of techniques are required for this, and, when used with care, these can produce quite dramatic results, as you will see on the following page. However, as mentioned previously, any restoration work should be carried out with great care, as the idea is to attend to existing damage and not cause further problems.

Materials

- flat-bladed knife
- fine wire (steel) wool
- linseed oil
- polish
- linen cloth
- wadding (batting)
- methylated spirits (methyl alcohol)
- fine brushes
- oxalic acid
- spirit- (alcohol-) based stain
- rubber
- coloured wax
- soft cotton rags

1 First remove any lumps and bumps, such as candle wax, by dragging a flat-bladed knife at a 45-degree angle across the surface. Be careful not to add any further scratches.

2 Rub the surface with fine wire (steel) wool, following the line of the grain. Failure to follow the grain could result in numerous tiny scratches, which will be difficult to remove at a later stage. Apply only very light pressure at this stage.

3 Apply linseed oil and polish to a piece of linen and rub gently in a circular motion. This will soften the top layers of polish, allowing the new colour and polish to bind to the existing surface.

4 Lightly moisten a piece of wadding (batting) with methylated spirits (methyl alcohol), and wipe it over the surface to remove any remaining traces of oil.

5 Paint over the dark inside and outside edges of the ring marks and stains using a fine brush and oxalic acid. Paint only the edges, which are always the darkest areas of ring marks and stains.

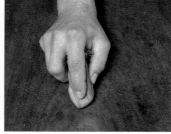

6 Mix a spirit-based (alcohol-based) stain to match the surface colour and apply it with a fine brush. Try to blend the blemishes with the surrounding area rather than masking the stain with solid colour. Then leave to dry.

7 Charge a rubber with polish and apply a layer of polish over the surface in even strokes (see pp.356–7). Allow to dry, then repeat until you have replaced the layers of polish removed by the linseed oil.

8 Cut back the surface by gently dusting with a piece of fine wire wool, following the grain. The idea is to even the surface and remove the glossy finish.

9 Select a wax to match the colour of the wood, and use a soft cotton rag to apply it, rubbing with a circular motion. Leave to harden for approximately an hour.

10 Buff the surface lightly with a soft cloth, following the grain. Work carefully, because the underlying polish will still be soft, and over-enthusiastic buffing will simply cause unsightly streaking.

Above The finished surface is now free from marks and blemishes, and the original grain, colour and patination have been revived.

POLISHING AND COLOURING

The term "polishing" is used to describe the overall method of filling the grain and enhancing the figure of any piece of wood using shellac polish. The vast majority of polishing work today is commonly known as French polishing, which involves the use of shellac polish combined with oil – often linseed oil – and applied to the wood with a linen rubber. Within the history of antique furniture, however, there are two very distinctive methods of finishing: varnishing using oil or spirit varnishes, and French polishing, which was introduced only in the 19th century. Both methods create distinctive appearances, and it is the effects of light, oxidation and time that make these polished and waxed surfaces so sought after by today's collectors.

The principles involved in polishing a new surface or repolishing an old surface remain the same: numerous thin layers are built up to form a combined surface. When completed, the polish should have a translucent quality that allows the colour and figure of the wood beneath to be seen. On occasion it may be necessary to tint the polish in order to adjust the final colour. This method of colouring is different from staining with spirit, water or oil, which is the process by which the actual wood tone is changed rather than colouring or tinting the polish. When removing polish from a piece of furniture, it must be done a layer at a time to minimize any damage to the colour and surface of the piece. When the damaged areas have been carefully lifted, further polish can again be applied, a layer at a time, until the required surface appearance is obtained. If too much polish is applied the surface will have a treacle-like appearance; if too little polish is used the grain in the wood will look open and "hungry", resulting in a blotchy effect once the surface has been waxed.

French polishing

Prior to the early 19th century the methods of finishing furniture were mainly the application of varnishes or oils such as linseed and various wax compounds. These were usually applied, often by brush or cloth (cotton rag), after the grain had been sealed with ground brick dust or pumice powder. They served to protect the wood and could be burnished to a soft lustre finish.

In 1820 a new practice, imported from France, came to favour. It was the use of shellac, which comes from the shells of the lac beetle. The shellac, which was dissolved in spirit, was applied layer by layer, giving a hard, glossy finish. Over the years, and with the application of wax, the hard, glossy surfaces mellow, and depending on the style and period of the piece, the surface finish can range from hard and glossy to a soft, almost matt appearance.

Materials

- wadding (batting)
- linen
- polish
- fine wire (steel) wool
- methylated
  spirits (methyl alcohol)
- soft cotton rag
- shellac
- linseed oil
- clear beeswax

Left This Regency table has become severely damaged on its polished surface and must be repolished.

Making and charging a rubber

A rubber is an essential tool for applying a French polish finish and is easy to make. All you need is some wadding (batting) or plain unmedicated cotton wool (balls) and a square of linen or similar lint-free cloth. The rubber acts in the same manner as a sponge, absorbing a quantity of the polish (known as charging), which is squeezed out on to the surface being polished when you apply pressure to it. A rubber can also be used to apply a stain to wood.

1 Lay a 15cm/6in long piece of wadding (batting) on the centre of a piece of linen the size of a large handkerchief.

2 Fold the ends of the linen inward and grasp them in the centre of your palm

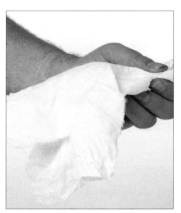

3 With all the outer edges gathered together, twist the ends of the linen to form a tail.

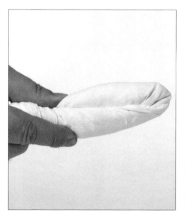

4 The rubber is complete when the tail is completely twisted. For a smaller, more intricate, polishing job, make a smaller rubber to suit.

5 To charge the rubber, open out the linen to expose the wadding, then pour a small amount of polish on to the wadding. With practice, you will be able to judge the correct quantity. Note that if the rubber is too dry it will not run smoothly over the surface; if it is too wet it will simply lay the polish on the surface.

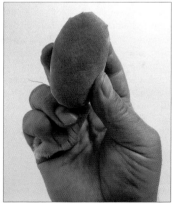

6 Refold the linen around the wadding. Squeeze the tail to apply pressure to the wadding, to force the polish through the linen. The more you tighten the tail, the more polish will emerge. After polishing, you can store the rubber for another day.

Applying the polish

If the damage to a surface is extensive, it will have to be stripped back with methylated spirits (methyl alcohol) before repolishing, as shown here. New wood is polished in much the same way, except that the grain is first filled with pumice and polish, then sanded flat with very fine or broken down sandpaper.

Once the rubber has been charged, the polish can be applied. This process takes time, and the finish must be left overnight for the polish to harden before it can be buffed to a high sheen or cut back to produce a matt finish.

Practical tip

When polishing with a rubber (step 3) the idea is to "body up" or fill the grain. This is done by first applying the polish in straight continuous strokes along the grain (below top). The polish is then applied in circular motions (below centre) and finally with wider figure of eight movements (below bottom).

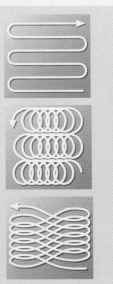

1 Remove the old polish and wax surface with fine wire (steel) wool and methylated spirits (methyl alcohol).

2 Once the old polish and wax have been removed, wash off the surface with a soft cotton rag and methylated spirits.

3 Polish the surface using a rubber and shellac (see Tip). Linseed oil can be dripped on to the surface to help lubricate the rubber. This technique, known as "bodying up", fills the grain. Leave for at least 24 hours to harden.

4 When the polish has hardened, cut it back lightly using fine wire wool and working in the direction of the grain. Use light strokes to remove any raised nibs of polish. This also produces a higher gloss finish.

5 Finally, apply a coat of wax. Use light strokes as the polished surface will still be delicate. Allow to stand for a week before use to allow the polish to fully harden.

Right When polished, the scratches become invisible and the table has an even, soft sheen that should last for years.

WAXING

All antique furniture will require waxing during its lifetime. Waxing feeds, protects and nourishes the wood. It is the combination of waxes with natural grease and oxidation that forms the surface patination that is so desirable. Over the generations, various types of wax have been used, with workshops producing their own secret recipes.

One of the most common misconceptions is that the more frequently a piece is waxed, the fuller the finish will be. Over-waxing will result in smeary surfaces, since wax softens wax. The only remedy for this is to remove all the wax and begin afresh. It is far better to wax at sensible intervals and apply only a very thin layer. Use only natural wax-based products.

Materials

- clear wax
- soft brush
- soft cotton rags
- brush

Waxing a flat surface

1 Apply a thin layer of wax using a soft cotton rag impregnated with the chosen wax. Never apply too thick a layer, as this will simply make the rubbing up more difficult and time consuming.

2 Even out the wax using a soft brush. Take care not to mark the surface and make sure you work along the direction of the grain. Use long, steady strokes, working from one side of the surface to the other.

3 Allow the wax to harden for a few minutes, then buff the surface vigorously with a soft cotton rag, working in the direction of the grain. Finally, use a clean cloth to give the surface a final burnish.

Waxing a carved surface

1 Due to the nature of the hollows and relief, it is better to apply a thin coat of wax with a soft brush, making sure that it is neither too hard nor too soft.

2 Allow the wax to harden for a few minutes, then gently burnish the carving with a soft brush. This will remove any surplus wax and even out what remains.

3 Finally, buff the highlights using a soft cotton rag. Mutton cloth, which is available from most trade suppliers, is ideal for this role.

STAINING

Paints and varnishes adhere to the surface of the wood, but stains penetrate it, changing its colour permanently. For this reason, stains are favoured by the restorer. They can enrich dull-looking wood or change the colour of new wood so that it blends in with the rest of the piece of furniture. This bureau has had a new piece of wood added to it that must be stained and polished so that it matches the rest of the piece.

Materials

- spirit- (alcohol-) based stain
- clean cotton rag
- wooden dowel
- fine brush
- rubbers
- polish
- methylated spirits (methyl alcohol)
- soft brush
- wax

Practical tip

Spirit-based (alcohol-based) stains, thinned with methylated spirits (methyl alcohol), are the best stains to use, because they dry very quickly. However, they are harder to obtain and more difficult to use. This is because they can leave obvious over-lap marks. Solvent- and water-based stains are available ready mixed and are easier to apply.

1 Use a spirit-based (alcohol-based) stain mixed to match the colour of the furniture. For a small area like this, wrap a piece of cotton rag around one end of a dowel and use this to apply the stain to the new piece of wood. If staining a large area, use a brush to apply the stain. Continue until the colour is even, then leave to dry.

2 Check again that the stain is even. If necessary, add another layer, or draw in the grain with a fine brush (see p.362). When you are satisfied with the colour of the dried stain, charge a rubber with polish and apply a layer to the stain, and also to the rest of the bureau to blend in the stained area (see pp.356–7). Allow the polish to dry.

3 Cut back the polish with a rubber charged with a little methylated spirits (methyl alcohol). The new wood should now be indistinguishable from the old.

4 Use a soft brush to apply a thin coat of wax to the new wood, and the rest of the piece of furniture, to give a soft, even sheen. Leave to dry.

Above Now stained and polished, the new wood blends seamlessly with the old.

MODIFYING THE COLOUR

The room for which a table was initially commissioned will often not be the one in which it spends the majority of its life, and in the case of larger tables not all the original leaves will be used. An extra leaf may well be stored under a bed or in a cupboard, where it will keep its natural colour while the rest of the table will fade and mellow in colour. When the time comes to set the table up to its full size, it will be necessary to modify the colour and tone of the unused leaf to match the rest of the table.

This mahogany table shows how the two ends have been used together for most of the time – they have a warm, even colour and wax patination – but the middle leaf has had almost no use and remains much darker than the other leaves. The technique for lightening the darker section requires that the original polished finish be removed with a weak solution of paint stripper, after which the wood can be made paler with a solution of oxalic acid or bleach.

Materials	
• protective gloves	• oxalic acid
• weak paint stripper	• mutton cloth
• brush	• bleach
• flat-bladed knife	• acetic acid
• coarse wire (steel) wool	• dowel
• clean cotton rags	• rubber
• methylated spirits (methyl alcohol)	• polish
	• spirit- (alcohol-) based stain
	• fine wire wool
	• dark wax

1 Apply a weak solution of paint stripper with a brush in 30cm/12in squares. The reason for using a weak stripper is that it is required to remove only the top layers of polish and wax. Under no circumstance should it be allowed to bite into the wood.

2 Once the stripper has been applied, the polish will begin to glaze and congeal. At this point, use a flat-bladed knife to gently scrape away the dissolved polish and wax, taking great care not to mark the wood.

3 With coarse wire (steel) wool, remove any residue of polish and wax. The wire wool should simply be slid over the surface and not applied with any pressure, as this would cause unnecessary and unsightly damage.

4 Use a clean cotton rag to wipe methylated spirits (methyl alcohol) over the table top. This will neutralize any residue of the stripper. Make sure that you apply it evenly across the whole surface.

5 Having removed all the polish and wax, you now need to colour the wood to match the desired shade. The first method to try is to mix one part oxalic acid with ten parts hot water and apply the mixture with a pad of mutton cloth.

6 In this case, the oxalic acid was too weak to lighten the leaf to the desired tone, so you will need to try another method, this time using bleach.

7 To lighten the table further, apply bleach with a cloth. Wear gloves to protect your skin. Initially, treat the wood with a solution of one part bleach to three parts water. If this is unsuccessful, treat the wood with one part bleach to one part water.

8 When completed, neutralize the bleach by applying acetic acid using a cloth or a dowel with cloth wrapped around the end. The leaf is now ready to be polished and coloured to match the rest of the table.

9 Lay the bleached leaf beside one of the end leaves to see if the correct tone and colour cast have been obtained. Charge a rubber with polish and apply a thin layer to the lightened leaf to indicate its final colour.

10 If the colour and tone need further adjustment, mix a spirit-based (alcohol-based) stain to the colour required and apply it to the whole leaf or just localized areas, using a cloth.

Left After applying the coloured stain, you will need to add several rubbers of polish (see pp.356–7). Allow each layer of polish to sink in before applying the next. It is advisable to allow the last layer of polish to settle for a couple of days to ensure that the grain has been filled completely. After the top has hardened fully, cut it back lightly with fine wire wool, then apply a thin coat of dark wax using a cotton rag (see p.357). When cutting back and waxing, make sure that you work in the direction of the grain.

GRAINING

During the late 18th and early 19th centuries, rosewood was imported from India, South America and the West Indies for use in the manufacture of furniture. It was an expensive wood, and so only the finest pieces of furniture were made from solid rosewood; other pieces were made from beech, which was a hard-grained, easily workable, cheap native wood. The beech was "grained" with a paint finish to give the appearance of rosewood. Over time, the areas of graining wear away, revealing the beech underneath, as has happened with this Regency chair. In this case, it is necessary to simulate the rosewood graining while also giving it a patinated, antique look. The techniques for distressing are varied and include using smooth stones, fine wire (steel) wool and homemade tools. These should be practised and perfected before use.

Materials

- light brown spirit- (alcohol-) based stain
- fine brushes
- screwdriver
- rubber
- polish
- dark brown spirit-based stain
- wax
- cloth (cotton rag)

Above An area of the graining has worn away on the chair leg to reveal the beech wood underneath.

1 Apply a base coat of a light brown stain mixed to match the base colour of the rest of the chair (see p.369). Leave to dry. Charge a rubber with polish and apply a thin layer.

2 Apply a dark brown stain mixed to match the grain of the simulated rosewood, using a fine brush to replicate the pattern. If no residue of graining is left, use a piece of patinated rosewood veneer as a pattern.

3 When the graining is dry, distress the graining effect using a screwdriver, if necessary, to match the original. Give it another rubber of polish to seal in the effect, then wax the chair using a cloth.

Above The grained beech chair, on the right of the picture, now looks very similar to the solid rosewood chair on the left. Both these chairs are dining chairs, made c.1810.

GILDING

Water gilding requires great patience and an extremely delicate touch. Leaves of hand-beaten gold, beaten to a thickness of 0.025mm (0.001in) thick, are expensive, so it is wise to practise with metal leaf, which is much cheaper, until you are confident.

This 18th-century carved wood and gilt frame had been weakened by worm, which led to it becoming detached from its wire hooks and falling to the floor, causing considerable damage. Fortunately, most of the pieces had been kept together.

Materials

- animal glue
- two-part epoxy resin
- wood carving tools
- gesso and gesso kettle
- soft brushes
- fine-grade sandpaper
- bole
- size
- fine brush
- gold leaf
- suede pad
- blunt knife
- gilder's fitch or good-quality artist's brush
- agate

1 Place the frame on a flat surface and glue the separate parts together. Leave to dry.

2 Fill the missing areas with two-part epoxy resin. This useful substance offers strength as well as malleability. It will bond easily with the damaged parts.

3 After the resin has hardened, carve it to follow the line of the existing frame using normal wood carving tools.

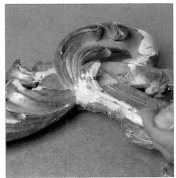

4 Heat a quantity of gesso in a gesso kettle to the consistency of double (heavy) cream. Apply it to the frame with a soft brush. Continue applying layers until you obtain the desired thickness. Leave to dry.

5 Shape the gesso with carving tools and cut in any detailing. It is always the gesso that is carved, rather than the wood, which is why many intricate mirrors with carved decoration appear quite ordinary when stripped back to the wood prior to regilding.

6 Give the gesso the lightest of sandings with very fine-grade sandpaper. The purpose of this is simply to remove any raised nibs and to smooth the sweeping curves.

7 Paint a thin layer of bole on to the gesso. Red bole is being used here to match the original bole colour of the mirror. Following the method used with the gesso, warm the bole and apply it with a soft dry brush. When dry, smooth lightly with fine-grade sandpaper.

8 Place a sheet of gold leaf on a suede pad edged with stiff card for protection, and peel off the backing. Take care when handling gold leaf, since even the lightest of draughts will blow it out of line.

9 Cut the gold leaf into a number of small sections with a flat-bladed, blunt knife; only the lightest of pressures is required. Note how the unused scraps (offcuts) of gold leaf are left at the back of the pad to be used for faulting (filling in any small areas).

10 Apply a coating of size to the frame with a fine brush. Apply it to small areas at a time, followed by the immediate application of the pre-cut gold leaf.

11 The leaf is so light that it can prove difficult to handle. One of the best techniques is simply to use static electricity. Rub a clean gilder's fitch or artist's brush against your skin to build up a little static.

12 With the fitch or brush charged, simply touch the bristles to the gold leaf to lift it from the pad and place it on the frame.

13 Lay the leaf on the sized area. The size will pull it down on to the various contours. Repeat this process until all the areas of bole have been covered. This requires patience, and rushing will affect the final finish.

14 After gilding a significant area, dust over with a large soft brush, called a mop. This will remove any loose and excess gilt, exposing any uncovered areas. Use the gilt scraps saved for faulting to fill these gaps.

15 With the frame now fully gilded, use an agate to burnish the surface. This will give an even finish and tone to the gilt throughout. Take care not to remove the delicate gilt surface.

Oil gilding

Oil gilding is a much simpler process than water gilding. After the gesso has been applied, the area to be gilded is painted with a special oil gilt size. The gold leaf is then laid directly from the sheet, held into place by its own backing. Oil gilding can even be used straight on to a wood surface. Unlike water gilding, the gilded surface is not burnished after application, so the carat of leaf used dictates the finish.

Left The fully restored frame is now ready to be fitted with its mirror plate. All evidence of the extensive damage has now been removed.

VENEERING

During the history of furniture making, the introduction of certain new techniques has radically altered the design and form of furniture. The skill of veneering, where thin layers of wood are laid on top of a different base wood, was introduced in the 17th century and this resulted in furniture taking on a much more flamboyant appearance. Woods that had previously been used in the solid could now be hand cut into thin sheets and laid to display the distinctive patterns of the wood, thereby greatly enhancing the look of furniture.

Highly decorative burrs and pollards, which had been too unstable to use in the solid, could now be cut and laid on to stable cores. It was indeed a giant step forward in the history of furniture construction.

The use of veneer in furniture construction became more popular during the latter part of the 17th century and the 18th century; prior to this it was used sparingly in decoration but more in a marquetry or parquetry form. Veneer was preferred over the solid during this period as it enabled a more decorative appearance to be achieved. For this reason it is common to find quarter-veneered tops or

bookmatch drawer fronts from this period. Indeed, during the latter part of the 18th century, it was usual to find expensive decorative veneer such as mahogany laid on top of an equally expensive, but plainer, mahogany core.

This reflects the philosophy of this time when the use of veneer was more about aesthetics than economy. The quality of an individual's furniture

was also seen to reflect the wealth of its owner and their position in society. However, by the 19th century, with the ability to cut wood mechanically, combined with the increasing demand for furniture by the merchant classes, the use of veneer enabled cheaper furniture to be made that could still be covered by the fashionable and expensive imported woods such as mahogany and satinwood.

Above A selection of old surface veneers.

Above A George III linen press veneered in figured mahogany throughout.

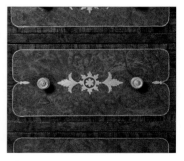

Above A Regency period drawer front veneered with figured rosewood and burr amboyna, and inlaid with brass decoration.

Above A late 17th-century bureau veneered in walnut rather than made from the solid.

Above A walnut bookmatch veneered end.

Removing veneer

On the whole, veneer does not need to be removed. Either it will be loose, in which case it can be heated and clamped back into position (see p.368) or it will be missing. In some instances, however, a previous repair may have to be removed because it was not done professionally. In the example here, the veneer patch is rectangular and can easily be seen. Had it been cut to follow the pattern of the grain, it would have blended in with the rest of the piece more successfully. The old piece of veneer must be removed completely before the new patch can be cut in.

Materials

- fine wire (steel) wool
- methylated spirits (methyl alcohol)
- metal rule
- craft (utility) knife
- masking tape
- chisel
- iron
- veneer
- PVA (white) glue
- clamping blocks
- G-clamps
- rubber
- polish

1 Wipe over the veneer patch with fine wire (steel) wool soaked in methylated spirits (methyl alcohol) until the polish comes off the patch. This allows you to see exactly where the patch meets the rest of the veneer.

2 Use a metal rule and a craft (utility) knife to score along the edges of the patch, making sure you cut all the way through the veneer.

3 Push a chisel under the veneer patch and place a hot iron on top. Lift and remove the veneer patch in sections, continuing until it is all gone. Be careful not to put the iron on any of the original veneer.

◀4 Select a veneer that has appropriate graining and pattern, and cut out a piece, following the pattern, that is slightly larger than the area to be patched.

▶5 Place the new veneer over the area to be patched and use a utility knife to cut a new patch to fit the shape. Glue it in place with PVA (white) glue, apply clamping blocks and leave to dry. Stain and colour the veneer patch to blend with the surrounding wood. Some graining may need to be added, too. Polish and wax.

Laying veneer sheets

Small areas of veneer are simple to glue and clamp into place; the difficulty is in selecting the correct veneer. Larger areas of veneer cannot be clamped; instead, they are sealed with a different glue and a veneer hammer, which is a rather complicated procedure. To veneer curved surfaces, a counter-core must be made, which allows the clamps to exert even pressure on the drying veneer. Corners and edges of veneer will often be missing or split after years of use.

Materials

- MDF (medium-density fiberboard)
- iron
- screwdriver
- paper
- clamping block
- G-clamps
- craft (utility) knife
- veneer
- PVA (white) glue
- ebony stringing
- masking tape
- rubber
- polish

Laying small areas of veneer

This bracket clock is veneered in Cuban mahogany. The veneer is loose, and parts of the veneer and the ebony stringing have been broken off and lost. It is not necessary to re-veneer the loose areas of veneer as they can simply be rebonded to the core.

2 Remove the base section, taking care not to lose the screws. Place a piece of paper on the upper side of the veneer, and a clamping block below, to prevent damaging the carcass. Clamp the hot MDF into place, then leave until cool.

3 Cut a piece of veneer slightly larger than the missing piece. Cut the damaged area to the size of the new piece, then glue the new veneer in place. Clamp it until the glue dries, using a clamping block.

Left A good match for the original veneer was found, making the repair to this clock completely invisible.

1 Veneer is secured with animal glue, which means that heat and pressure can often be enough to rebind the veneer. Heat a piece of MDF (medium-density fiberboard) on an iron for approximately 5 minutes.

4 Select a new length of ebony stringing (see p.373). Cut this to size, glue it in place and secure with masking tape. (Note that there is no need to soak the stringing because it does not have to be shaped.) Reattach the base. Charge a rubber with polish and apply a thin layer over the whole carcass (see pp.356–7).

Laying large areas of veneer

There is little call to lay new veneer in most antique furniture restoration, but in some circumstances, such as extreme fire or water damage or if large areas of veneer are missing, this may be needed. The tools used are almost identical to those utilized by cabinet-makers over the past 200 years.

Materials

- fine wood filler
- putty knife
- smooth toothing plane
- short, thick brush
- animal glue
- newspaper
- veneer
- veneer hammer
- cloth (cotton rag)
- flat piece of wood
- craft (utility) knife
- steel straightedge
- cabinet scraper
- medium fine-, fine- and very fine-grade sandpaper
- sanding block

1 First, prepare the base wood by filling any splits or dents with a fine wood filler. If these are not filled, they will show through the veneer when it is laid.

2 When the filler has hardened, level it using a smooth toothing plane. This will also key the surface for the veneer and adhesive.

3 Brush a size made of animal glue and hot water over the surface of the carcass. This will fill the grain and ensure that when the animal glue is applied prior to veneering, it will produce an even layer. Failure to do so can result in blisters in the veneer. Protect the rest of the carcass with newspaper.

4 Veneering half the surface at a time enables you to work while the glue is still malleable. Coat half the surface liberally with animal glue, then lay the veneer and use a veneer hammer with a firm pressure to expel all the excess glue. Dip the hammer into a mixture of glue and hot water to help it glide easily.

5 When half the surface is covered, wash off the surface of the veneer with a hot, wet cotton rag to remove any traces of animal glue.

6 Trim the excess veneer by placing a flat piece of wood against the edge and scoring around the shape of the carcass with a craft (utility) knife. The wood will prevent the veneer from splitting.

7 Repeat the veneering process on the other half. To obtain a perfect join, overlap the first piece of veneer with the second. Lay a steel straightedge over both pieces and cut through them with a craft knife.

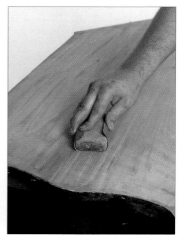

8 Lift away the trimmed strips from both sections of veneer, leaving a perfect join. Run the veneer hammer along this join to make sure the edges lie flat. Leave to dry overnight.

9 When the glue is dry, go over the newly veneered section with a cabinet scraper. This will level the veneer and flatten the grain, which will have become raised with the application of hot water.

10 Finally, use three grades of sandpaper (graduating all the time to the finest grade) wrapped around a sanding block to remove all scraper marks and prepare the veneer for polishing.

Laying curved veneer

On occasion, you may need to make or replace a missing veneered part for a piece of furniture that is shaped. For example, a moulding may have lost its veneer, or, as in this case, a piece of furniture has lost its cornice, so a replacement cornice (known as a core) needs to be made and then veneered to match.

Materials

- pine or mahogany
- band saw
- moulding plane
- veneer
- brush
- animal glue
- G-clamps
- craft (utility) knife
- curved cabinet scraper
- fine-grade sandpaper

1 Cut the core and also a counter-core, which follows the internal curve of the core or original moulding, out of pine or mahogany using a band saw or spoke shave. Shape both pieces with a moulding plane. Select a length of veneer that is wider than the core or moulding.

2 To make the veneer malleable so that it does not crack or split when applied, soak it in water until pliable. An old tin bathtub is often best for such a task, as it allows veneers of a good length to be soaked. Change the water if you plan to use different veneers, to prevent staining.

3 Remove the veneer from the bath and, while it is still wet and pliable, brush animal glue evenly over the core or moulding, and press the veneer firmly on to it.

4 Place the counter-core on top of the veneer and clamp it tightly. Make sure that an even pressure is applied throughout to ensure that no blisters result. Leave the veneer to dry overnight.

5 When the glue is dry, remove all but one of the clamps, but leave the counter-core in place while you trim off the excess veneer with a utility knife. The remaining clamp acts as a useful handle.

◀ 6 Remove the final clamp and the counter-core. Clean up the veneer with a curved cabinet scraper, applying an even pressure. The idea is to remove fine shavings and not to tear the grain.

▶ 7 Go over the veneer with fine-grade sandpaper. A section cut from the counter-core, which will fit into the shape of the moulding or core, makes a suitable sanding block for this purpose.

Replacing bandings

Decorative veneer inlays situated around the edges of tables, chests and cabinets are known as bandings. They are usually cut from the same veneer as the main body veneer, but across, rather than along, the grain to distinguish them from the body veneer. Their position makes bandings vulnerable to knocks, and they are often the first piece of veneer to break off. This table has lost part of its banding.

<table>
<tr><td colspan="2">Materials</td></tr>
<tr><td>• veneer</td><td>• fine-grade</td></tr>
<tr><td>• craft (utility)</td><td> sandpaper</td></tr>
<tr><td> knife</td><td>• spirit-</td></tr>
<tr><td>• dividers</td><td> (alcohol-)</td></tr>
<tr><td>• PVA (white)</td><td> based stain</td></tr>
<tr><td> glue</td><td>• clean cotton</td></tr>
<tr><td>• clamping</td><td> rag</td></tr>
<tr><td> blocks</td><td>• wooden</td></tr>
<tr><td>• G-clamps</td><td> dowel</td></tr>
<tr><td>• chisel</td><td>• rubber</td></tr>
<tr><td></td><td>• polish</td></tr>
</table>

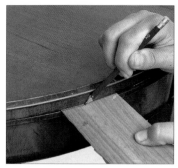

1 Cut out the chosen veneer with a craft knife into lengths of approximately 10cm/4in. If the table is curved, place a length of veneer under the edge or, in this case, the flap, and draw around the edge.

2 Scratch the width of the missing banding on to the veneer, using a pair of dividers. Remember to mark across, rather than along, the grain. Cut out the banding.

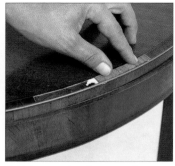

3 Make sure that the area to be veneered is clean before applying a thin layer of PVA (white) glue. Lay one piece of veneer on the glue and press it down. Clamp using G-clamps and blocks and leave for a few hours.

4 When the glue is dry and the bond secure, remove the clamps and blocks and level the veneer with a chisel. Take care not to damage the main body of veneer.

5 Repeat with the remaining veneer, then smooth with fine-grade sandpaper. The new banding should sit flush with the old and follow the curve of the table exactly.

Above Once it has been stained and polished (see p.359 and pp.356–7), the new banding should blend seamlessly with the old.

Replacing stringings

Very thin, string-like pieces of veneer, usually cut from boxwood, are also used as decorative veneer inlays. Stringings are often situated next to bandings, and are just as likely to be knocked, as was the case with this table, which has lost part of its stringing. For this project the stringing is soaked and applied wet as it needs to be malleable in order to bend around the curved shape of the table.

Materials

- craft (utility) knife
- stringing
- PVA (white) glue
- masking tape
- chisel
- fine-grade sandpaper
- spirit (alcohol-) based stain
- clean cotton rag
- wooden dowel
- rubber
- polish

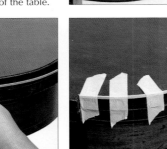

1 Using a craft (utility) knife, cut a length of stringing from a piece that matches the original in dimension and colour. Soak the stringing in some hot water to make it more malleable.

2 While the stringing is still wet, glue it in place with PVA (white) glue. Tape it down with masking tape and leave to dry.

3 When the stringing is dry, level the top and sides with a chisel. Take care not to damage the existing veneer.

4 Smooth the stringing with fine-grade sandpaper. Continue until the edges are blunted and the veneer is level.

Left Once stained and polished (see p.359 and pp.356–7), the new stringing is indistinguishable from the old.

Marquetry repairs

Intricate veneer inlay in the shape of flowers, leaves and other natural objects is known as marquetry. This table is Dutch in origin and was made c.1740. It is veneered in walnut with marquetry panels of box, sycamore and walnut laid on to an oak core. It is of good colour and patination, but there has been some shrinkage to the oak carcass, which in turn has damaged the marquetry panels. Closer inspection reveals that previous losses of veneer and marquetry have been disguised with coloured filler.

Materials

- fine wire (steel) wool
- small chisel
- tracing paper
- veneer
- fret saw
- PVA (white) glue
- masking tape
- fine brush
- spirit- (alcohol-) based stain
- rubber
- polish

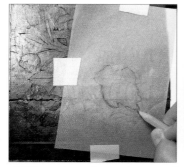

1 First, expose the old coloured-out parts by rubbing off the entire surface colour from the filler with fine wire (steel) wool.

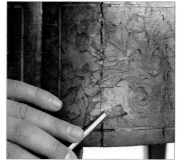

2 The areas of missing marquetry will now be visible. Remove the old filler with a small chisel, taking care not to dig into the core.

3 Determine the style and shape of the missing marquetry by looking for areas of marquetry that are undamaged. Trace their shapes carefully.

4 Offer up the tracings to the areas of missing marquetry and carefully position the copied patterns to ascertain which designs need to be cut.

5 Cut the veneer with care, using a fret saw. Once each piece is cut, stick it in place with PVA (white) glue, then tape it into position and leave to dry.

Above Once all the missing pieces of veneer have been replaced, the area needs to be stained and polished (see p.359 and pp.356–7). The table should then look as it did in 1740.

Parquetry repairs

Intricate veneer inlay in geometric shapes, such as diamonds and squares, is known as parquetry. It often utilizes differently coloured and grained veneer to give a three-dimensional effect. Some areas of the parquetry on this cabinet have worn away and must be replaced.

Materials

- veneer
- sliding bevel gauge
- craft (utility) knife
- small chisel
- PVA (white) glue
- masking tape
- small blade
- spirit- (alcohol-) based stain
- clean cotton rag
- wooden dowel
- rubber
- polish

1 Select a replacement veneer that has a similar grain and can be polished to the same colour as the existing veneer.

2 Cut the veneer to size using a sliding bevel gauge and a craft knife. This will make sure that the angles are correct so that you can achieve an exact fit.

3 Remove the damaged veneer with a small chisel, making sure that you remove complete shapes from damaged areas. Do not touch the surrounding veneer.

4 Glue the new pieces in place with PVA (white) glue and tape them down with masking tape. When the glue is dry, scrape the new pieces with a small blade until they lie flush with the other pieces.

Left Careful choice of veneer needs to be followed by expertly applied stain and polish (see p.359 and pp.356–7) to ensure that the restored diamond shapes echo the distinctive grain and patina of the original parquetry.

DISMANTLING AND REASSEMBLING CHAIRS

Learning how to dismantle and reassemble chairs is an important skill for the furniture restorer. One of the most common problems in chairs is loose joints, and the easiest way to rectify this problem is to dismantle the whole chair, reglue the joints and reassemble the chair. Other damage, such as to the frames and backs of chairs, may require a chair to be dismantled only partly before the restorer can start to put the problem right.

Removing upholstery

Upholstery often sustains the most damage and may need to be replaced, in which case it can be removed in the quickest possible way without regard for any damage that it may suffer. If, however, the upholstery is in good condition, it should be removed carefully so that it can be replaced once the frame has been repaired.

The upholstery on this single Regency dining chair is in good condition, but it must be removed so that the damage to the back can be repaired. A careful and methodical approach must be employed to ensure that the upholstery is not damaged and remains in a suitable condition to be reused, if wished.

Materials
• tack remover
• heavy mallet
• ripping chisel
• narrow, flat-bladed tool
• pincers
• craft (utility) knife

1 Place the chair upside down on a protected workbench (a blanket can be spread over it) and remove the tacks from the dust cover with a tack remover and heavy mallet. The latter is used because its weight will ensure that a gentle wrist action will knock out the tacks. Work along the grain, not across it, to avoid splitting the seat rail.

2 Decorative braid is often held in place by glue and a few gimp pins, as is the case here. Remove the pins with a ripping chisel, then pull the braid off. Alternatively, the braid may simply be glued on. If the chair is close-nailed, the nails can easily be knocked out with a tack remover and mallet.

3 Turn the chair on to its side to remove the top cover. Handle the fabric carefully because it may be refitted after the chair is repaired. Remove the upholstery tacks with a tack remover, as in step 1, and remove any staples by slipping a narrow, flat-bladed tool between the staples and frame to lift them, before pulling them out with pincers.

4 With the top cover removed, you can detach the various layers of material and stuffing from the seat. Do this with a tack remover and a heavy mallet. If necessary, remove each layer separately. You may need to use a utility knife to cut through some of the layers of upholstery.

5 Once you have removed all the tacks, lift away the top cover. Keep the horsehair and other stuffing materials safely together.

6 Finally, remove and discard the webbings. These will often be attached with the largest tacks found on the chair, which will require strong blows with the mallet. Make sure that the chair is secure on the bench; if possible, ask someone to hold it for you.

Knocking the chair apart

The majority of restoration techniques, regardless of the style or type of chair, will require the chair to be partially or completely dismantled. As the term "knocking apart" suggests, the chair will be taken to pieces with the aid of a mallet and/or hammer. This should be done with care and patience, however, to make sure that further damage is not caused in the process. The frame of this chair is in quite good condition, so care must be taken when knocking it apart to ensure that no damage is caused to the joints.

Materials	
• masking tape	• screwdriver
• pincers	• drill
• hardwood block	• wood drill bit
	• metal drill bit
• hammer	

1 First, label all the parts of the chair. With a single chair, the various components will be obvious. If more than one chair is being repaired at the same time, however, parts can easily be confused, causing a major problem when you try to reassemble them.

2 Check to see if the corner blocks have been nailed to the frame. If they have, remove the nails with pincers. Once the nails are removed, or if no nails were used, place a block of hardwood against each corner block in turn to protect it from bruising, and give a firm hammer blow. Remove the blocks.

3 Next, unscrew any metal brackets. These are often found where a chair has been broken and repaired in the past. While these solve a problem in the short term, at a later stage the repaired joint will work itself loose again.

4 Make a quick inspection of the chair to look for any tenon pegs and screws that may have been put through the mortise and tenon joints to strengthen them. If you find any, drill them out.

5 Knock the side seat rails apart from the back uprights. Lift the back clear of the workbench and apply a series of firm blows to the back near the joints, protecting the uprights with the hardwood block.

6 Follow the same process with the other seat-rail joints at the front of the chair. If some joints are very tight and cannot be knocked apart without causing damage, try the Tip (top right) or leave them as they are.

7 Finally, knock the back seat rail, back support and top rail away from the back upright. Note that for many chair repairs the knocking apart can stop before this stage, with the back left intact.

8 Once the chair is knocked apart, double-check that all the components are present before you begin restoration work.

Reassembling the chair

Once any necessary repair work has been undertaken, the chair can be reassembled. While chairs come in various styles, shapes and woods, the steps necessary to reassemble them remain fairly consistent. The process of gluing the chair joints together during reassembly will cure many problems, such as wobbly legs and creaking.

▶1 Clean all the joints using either a toothbrush and hot water, which will dissolve the animal glue, or, if this is not successful, a rasp or file. Be careful to remove only the old glue and not any of the wood itself, because any reduction in tenon thickness results in a sloppy joint.

Materials

• toothbrush	• sash clamps	• hardwood block
• rasp or file	• clamping blocks	• hammer
• PVA (white) glue	• gauge sticks	

2 Glue the front legs and seat rail
together and secure them with a
sash clamp and clamping blocks.
Check that the legs are parallel by
measuring the gap at the top and
bottom. Leave to dry overnight.

3 Glue the back uprights together,
making sure the back support is
inserted at the same time as the back
seat rail. As with the front legs, ensure
that the uprights are parallel. Clamp to
secure and leave to dry overnight.

4 Remove the sash clamps and fit the
side seat rails to hold the chair
together. Stand the chair on a flat
surface while doing this to ensure that
it sits level and does not rock. Apply
sash clamps.

5 Before the glue is dry, check that
the seat frame is square by
comparing both diagonals with
pointed gauge sticks held firmly
together. If any adjustment is
needed, loosen the clamps, ease the
joint(s) slightly, retighten the clamps,
then check again.

6 When the glue has dried, add the
corner blocks, tapping them lightly
into place and using a block of wood
to prevent bruising. Leave the sash
clamps in place while doing this to
make sure that the tapping does not
loosen the joint.

7 Now you can fit the back top rail.
This chair has sliding dovetails for
the joints, and so the top rail is fitted
last. In chairs where the back top rail
is mortised and tenoned, however, it
should be fitted when the two back
uprights are glued together.

8 Clamp the bowed back in place
under light pressure, using
clamping blocks to ensure that no
bruising occurs.

Left Once the
reassembled chair has
been re-upholstered,
it should last for years
before needing
further repair.

REPAIRING ARMS AND LEGS

The arms and legs of chairs are particularly vulnerable to damage and suffer all manner of problems. The most common of these is scuffing to the feet, which is inevitable and, in severe cases, can lead to the wearing away of the feet until eventually they must be cut off and replaced. Chairs are often not treated properly, with users leaning back on them too hard or balancing on the rear two legs, which puts tremendous strain on the structure, leading to failure of the joints or breakages of the frame. Even the worst damage can, however, be put right.

Restoring a scuffed foot

Everyday wear and tear takes its toll on most items of furniture, and chairs in particular. This claw and ball chair is more prone to scuffed feet than most because its feet are quite pronounced. Some of the scratches and dents on this foot are quite severe, but they are part of its history and do not need to be repaired. Sympathetic restoration should improve the condition of the item but care, as always, should be taken not to remove any existing colour and patination. The repairs to the surface should be blended in to match the existing finish.

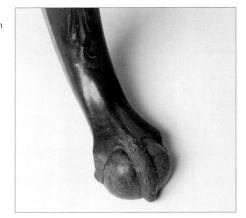

Materials

- fine-grade sandpaper
- brush
- spirit- (alcohol-) based stain
- rubber
- polish

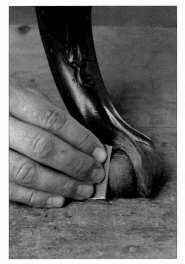

1 Place the chair on a workbench and go over the scuffed area with fine-grade sandpaper until you have removed the old polish and any other debris.

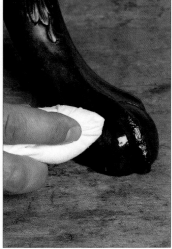

2 Mix some stain to the required colour and brush this over the foot, then use a rubber to polish the foot to match the rest of the chair (see pp.356–7).

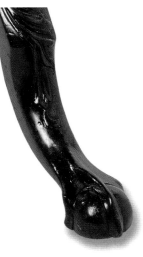

Above The restored foot has not been made to look brand new, which would make it stand out from the rest of the chair, but has simply had its colour and sheen restored.

Replacing a chewed arm

Some dogs and cats have a propensity for gnawing, chewing or sharpening their teeth on wooden furniture. Sometimes the damage inflicted is just a few scratches, but in other cases the furniture needs substantial rebuilding. This 18th-century Cuban mahogany child's rocking chair has had its arm and leg almost completely chewed off by the family dog. Before the arm and leg can be rebuilt, some of the damaged wood must be removed.

Materials

- Cuban mahogany
- PVA (white) glue
- sash clamp
- coping saw
- spokeshave
- fine-grade

- sandpaper
- brush
- spirit- (alcohol-) based stain
- rubber
- polish

Above The chewed-off arm.

1 Select appropriate replacement mahogany pieces and build up the rough shape of the arm in layers, using PVA (white) glue, and starting on the inside surface. Make the rebuilt arm slightly larger than the original.

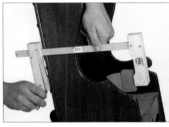

2 Glue a single block of mahogany to the outer surface, and a larger block to the front of this. Then clamp the rebuilt arm in position. Leave the sash clamp in position until the glue is dry.

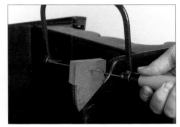

3 Remove the clamp and draw the shape of the arm on the new wood, slightly larger than the original. Cut along this line with a coping saw.

4 Shape the surface with a spokeshave, copying the contours of the other arm. Continue until you have an exact match. Repeat this process for the damaged leg.

5 Smooth both repairs with fine-grade sandpaper. Mix some stain to the required colour, brush this over the repairs, then polish to match the rest of the chair.

Above Once polished, the repairs become invisible, restoring the chair to its former state.

Repairing a cabriole leg

This 19th-century Victorian walnut balloon-back chair has a typical break to its leg. The curved shape of the cabriole leg, combined with the inherent weakness of walnut along the grain, means that this type of chair design is particularly vulnerable to damage, especially if misused.

Although this leg has a clean break, simply regluing it would not give it enough strength. Instead, a dowel must be inserted into holes drilled in both parts of the leg, which are then glued together to give a strong and lasting repair. The technique is quite straightforward, the most critical stage being the alignment and drilling of the dowel holes in the two broken pieces. Fortunately, there is a simple method of achieving this, using nothing more than a nail.

<table>
<tr><td>Materials</td></tr>
<tr><td>
• hammer
• 25mm (1in) nail
• snips or cutters
• pliers
• drill
• wood drill bits
• dowel
• thin chisel
• wood glue
• snap clamps
• fine-grade sandpaper
• rubber
• polish
</td></tr>
</table>

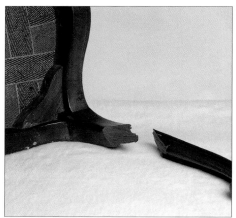

1 Place the chair upside down on a protected workbench. Hammer a 25mm/1in nail halfway into the centre of the upper section of the leg to provide a means of marking matching dowel hole positions on both pieces of the leg.

2 Cut the nail to a short, sharp point using a pair of snips or cutters.

3 The projecting piece of nail will now be used to mark the centre of the lower section of the leg.

4 Bring the two sections of the leg together and tap the lower section down so that the nail leaves an indentation on its broken surface. Remove the lower section and pull out the piece of nail with a pair of pliers.

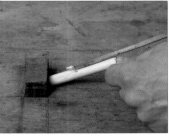

5 Drill a small pilot hole in both sections of the leg, using the indentations left by the nail as guides

6 Select a dowel that is about a third of the width of the leg and about 75mm/3in long. Use a drill bit of the same size as the dowel to drill holes about 38mm/1½in deep in both sections of the leg.

7 Rest the dowel against a block fixed to the workbench, and use a thin chisel to cut a narrow sliver along the length of the dowel. This will allow excess glue to escape.

◀ 8 Apply glue to both matching faces and the dowel, then insert the dowel into the upper section, tapping it down with a hammer if necessary, and bring the two parts together.

▶ 9 Make sure that the edges are flush, then clamp the leg sections together with snap clamps and leave the glue to dry.

10 Remove the clamps and stand the chair upright. Sandpaper the area of repair, then polish it so that it matches the rest of the chair (see pp.356–7).

Right Once polished, the repair should not be visible, while the strength of the chair leg will have been increased significantly.

Repairing a broken upright

This Georgian chair shows a common problem: the user has sat back perhaps a little too heavily and broken the chair at the weakest point, along the long grain, just above the seat level.
In this instance, a previous repair had been carried out and the break had followed the line of the old damage. This illustrates how make-shift repairs are only temporary measures. To create a more permanent repair, a new piece of wood must be inserted to enable the two parts of the broken upright to be secured properly.

Materials	
• white cardboard	• clamping blocks
• profile gauge	• spokeshave
• tenon saw	• sash clamps
• plane	• fine-grade sandpaper
• scissors	• fine brush
• mahogany	• stain
• band saw	• rubber
• PVA (white) glue	• polish
• G-clamps	

1 Place the chair on a protected workbench, remove the upholstery, then knock the chair apart. Place the undamaged upright on a large piece of white cardboard and use a profile gauge to trace its outline. This is the template (pattern) for the new piece of wood.

2 Now knock the back uprights apart from the stretcher, back seat rail, back support and back top rail.

Practical tip

When marking out a template on a shaped upright, a simple work-shop-made profile gauge is best. Join an upright to a face plate at right angles and drill a hole through that allows the refill from a ballpoint pen to be inserted.

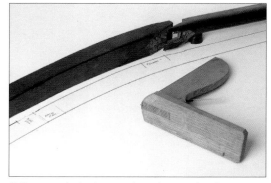

3 Compare the broken upright to the traced outline.

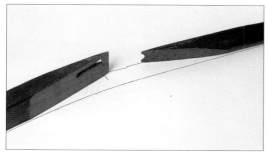

5 Cut out the cardboard template. Place it on a matching piece of mahogany, then mark the correct shape. Cut along this line with a band saw.

4 Cut away the damage with a tenon saw and plane the edges of the two parts flat. Lay the parts on the pattern in the correct position. The gap will indicate the size of the new part to be inserted.

6 Glue the matching piece of mahogany securely into position between the two pieces of the upright. Clamp it securely and leave to dry overnight – this will ensure a secure bond.

7 Form the correct shape with a spokeshave, using the undamaged upright as your guide. Cut three new mortises (see pp.392–3) in the upright to house the tenons of the side and back seat rails and the back support.

8 Reassemble the chair back and clamp until dry. Remove the clamps, then finish shaping the new wood with fine-grade sandpaper.

9 The final shape should now match the other upright exactly. Stain the replacement mahogany (see p.359) and polish the repairs to match the existing chair (see pp.356–7) before reassembling the whole chair. Replace the upholstery.

Right The new joint on the restored chair should be almost invisible.

Repairing a broken arm

Almost all arms on chairs have two points of fixing: one on a back upright, the other against a seat rail. Some are housed with a tenon or dovetail joint, while others may simply be placed flush and held with large screws. When faced with a damaged arm, as with all other restoration work, the first step is to examine the damage and ascertain the construction methods used in the piece. With this information, the correct procedure and techniques can then be determined.

The arm of this maple chair had become loose against both the seat rail and the back upright. This could have been caused by any number of events, including being dropped or knocked, or being picked up by the arms rather than by the seat. The arm must be removed and assessed before being reassembled.

Materials

- screwdriver
- hammer
- hardwood block
- chisel
- toothbrush
- PVA (white) glue
- G-clamp
- snap clamps
- clamping blocks

1 Place the chair on its side on a workbench, and loosen and remove the two large screws that hold the arm support to the side seat rail. The screws, which are fixed from the inside of the rail, are usually hidden by the drop-in upholstered seat. Keep the screws for reattaching the arm support.

2 Gently ease the arm tenon out of the mortise in the back upright, so that the whole arm structure is now detached from the chair. The dowel peg joint between the arm and arm support is also found to be loose. Place the arm on the workbench and tap off the joint using a block of hardwood and a hammer.

3 Remove any lumps of old glue from the joints using a sharp chisel, taking care not to mark any polished areas. If a crystalline residue is present, then an animal adhesive has been used; remove this with an old toothbrush and hot water. The water will soften and dissolve the glue, but make sure that it does not run and cause marks.

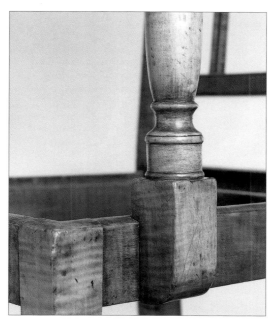

Left Once the glue has dried and the clamps have been removed, the chair should be as sturdy as when first made.

4 Check that all the joints are tight, then reglue them and reattach the arm and the support to each other and to the chair. Use a G-clamp to secure the support to the seat rail and snap clamps to secure the arm to the back upright and the arm to the arm support. Use clamping blocks at all clamping points; if the chair upright is bowed, you will need to pre-shape a clamping block to fit.

Removing a broken screw

If a screw has remained in a piece of furniture for many years, perhaps even hundreds of years, it may have become weak, and when you try to remove it, the shank may break. If this happens, there are three possible solutions. You may be able to make a new, temporary screw from the damaged one by cutting a new slot in the broken shank (see steps).

Alternatively, you could drill a hole, slightly larger than the screw shank, down the side of the screw, then tap it sideways into this hole with a screwdriver. This will allow you to remove it with a pair of long-nose (needlenose) pliers. You will have to plug the hole with a glued-in wooden dowel before reusing it.

Finally, you could simply drill out the screw with a metal drill bit of the same size, or slightly larger; but again you will have to plug the resulting hole in order to be able to reuse it.

1 If the shank of a screw breaks when you try to remove it, leaving a stub proud of the surface, cut a new slot in the end of the shank with a hacksaw.

2 Remove the screw simply by undoing it in the normal fashion. The metal will be weak, so use a screwdriver that fits snugly into the slot.

Reeding a turned chair leg

During the 18th century, reeded decoration on turned legs came into fashion. The legs were tapered, and so the reeding also had to taper from top to bottom, as well as being equally balanced around the leg. In order to do this work, a scratch box is used (see below). The scratch box has parallel sides and adjustable centre points at each end to allow a shaped reed cutter to be applied to the turned leg. In this instance, one leg from a Sheraton chair, c.1790, has been broken and lost, so a replacement is needed.

Materials

- callipers
- wood
- lathe
- turning tools
- dividers
- band saw or scraper
- rat-tail file
- scratch box
- try square
- back bent chisel
- cabinet scraper
- fine-grade sandpaper
- gouge
- fine brush
- stain
- rubber
- polish
- wax

Above A scratch box

◀ 1 Take the measurements for the template (pattern) leg from the original leg, using callipers for the circumference. Make sure that enough wood is left to allow for the reeds to be scratched. Turn the template leg on the lathe.

◀ 2 Using a pair of dividers, measure the width of the reed. When set, transfer the dividers to the template leg and mark divisions at the top of the leg corresponding to the original.

3 Now cut the reed cutter to the correct size and profile using an old band saw or scraper. As the blade will scrape and edge rather than cut it, make sure the edge is at a 90-degree angle to the side.

◀ 4 Fit the leg to the scratch box just below the height of the sides. To ensure that it is set parallel, measure the distance from the height of the sides both at the top and bottom of the leg with a try square.

▶ 5 Pass the cutter back and forth to scratch the reed into the leg. This should be done with an even pressure. When the reed is scratched, revolve the leg to the next division mark and scratch the next reed.

6 The scratch blade in the cutter will scratch a V shape. However, you can round it using a back bent chisel if you want a more rounded shape.

7 Use a cabinet scraper to clean the reed again. This will give a clean finish, as it is the same shape as the actual reeds. Then use fine-grade sandpaper with an overloe.

8 On certain reeded legs the top is not square but rounded. If you want to create this effect, use a gouge.

◀ 9 When finished, compare the new leg against the original to ensure that they are a good match. Note that enough wood is left at the top to allow a new mortise to be cut and joined to the seat rails.

Right The new leg can now be stained, polished and waxed (see pp.356–9), and any necessary distressing may be applied to make it match the patina of the other legs.

REPAIRING BACKS AND FRAMES

The most common fault found in chair frames is joint damage, such as broken mortise and tenon or dowel joints. Top rails are liable to break at the weak short grain at the end of each rail. Repairs can necessitate fairly major surgery on the broken parts, but the results can be very effective. Dowel joints are easiest to fix, since the broken dowels can simply be drilled out and replaced with new ones. Broken tenons, however, are more difficult, as their strength comes originally from being an integral part of the piece being joined. The answer is to replace the broken piece by gluing a wooden tongue into a slot cut in the frame piece.

Cutting in a tenon joint

The protruding piece of wood on a side seat rail is a tenon; the recess it slots into in a back upright is a mortise. This is the standard joint found on frame chairs, but on occasion the tenon can break. The tenon on this mahogany Regency chair has snapped off completely and been lost.

To make a repair, a new piece of wood must be cut to size and glued into a slot cut into the seat rail, before being shaped to fit snugly within the mortise. The mortise itself does not need repairing. When sanded and polished, the repair will not be noticeable.

Materials

- mortise gauge
- tenon saw
- mortise chisel
- heavy mallet
- mahogany
- PVA (white) glue
- clamping blocks
- G-clamp
- square rule
- spokeshave
- bench hook
- block plane
- fine brush
- stain

1 Knock the chair apart following steps 1–5 on pp.377–8. Set a mortise gauge to the width of the mortise in the upright, then run it over the broken end of the side seat rail and 10cm/4in down its underside.

2 Place the damaged side seat rail in a vice. Cut along the lines made by the mortise gauge with a tenon saw. It is important not to cut beyond the marks made by the mortise gauge.

3 Remove the mahogany from between the cut lines with a mortise chisel and a heavy mallet. It is important to cut to a reasonable depth in the rail to ensure that the new joint will be sufficiently strong.

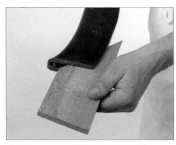

4 Cut a piece of mahogany to fit in the new slot in the side seat rail, allowing about 15cm/6in to protrude.

5 Apply PVA (white) glue to the new wood and insert it into the side seat rail. Clamp the side seat rail between two clamping blocks and leave to dry.

6 Remove the clamp and blocks. Place a square rule against the cut end of the side seat rail, draw a pencil line to mark out the upper end of the tenon. Repeat for the lower end and the top, to match the depth of the mortise.

7 Cut along the pencil lines with a tenon saw, then use a spokeshave to remove the excess wood from the bottom of the rail.

8 Place the side seat rail on a bench hook (see Tip below) and use a block plane to make the tenon the correct width. Check the fit of the tenon in the mortise repeatedly during this procedure to ensure a tight fit.

Left When the glue has dried, the clamps can be removed, and the underside of the tenon in the side seat rail stained to match the rest of the chair (see p.359). The new joint should last for many more years.

9 Once the tenon has been planed to fit exactly in the mortise, reassemble the chair (see pp.378–9) and leave to dry.

Practical tip

A bench hook comprises a board with a batten at each end, one of which butts against the edge of the bench top, while the other provides a stop for the workpiece to hold it securely. To make one, use a piece of 2.5cm/1in thick board, about 25cm/10in long and 17.5cm/7in wide. Cut two lengths of batten about 2.5cm/1in square and 12.5cm/5in long. Glue one of these flush with one end and the left-hand edge of the board. Turn the board over and glue the remaining batten to the other end, again flush with the left-hand edge.

REPLACING A MORTISE AND TENON JOINT

The mortise and tenon on this George III mahogany chair frame have both been damaged. An earlier repair was badly executed, so a new mortise and tenon will have to be cut and fitted. This involves cutting away the damaged wood, splicing in new pieces of similar material and forming the two halves of the joint. The result will be as strong as the original joint.

Materials

- tenon saw
- mahogany
- PVA (white) glue
- G-clamp
- spokeshave
- try square
- craft (utility) knife
- medium- and fine-grade sandpaper
- paring chisel
- drill
- wood drill bit
- mortise chisel
- carving tools
- mortise gauge

1 Knock the chair apart following steps 1–6 on pp.376–7, and place the side seat rail in a vice. Cut away the existing repair wood with a tenon saw to leave a flat surface for the new wood to adhere to.

2 Cut a piece of mahogany for a replacement tenon. Apply PVA (white) glue and attach the new piece to the seat rail. Clamp until dry, then shape the wood to follow the rail's curve with a spokeshave.

3 Using the undamaged side seat rail as a guide, transfer the measurements of the tenon on to the new wood with a try square and craft (utility) knife. Cut the tenon.

4 Smooth the new wood, including the newly cut tenon joint, with sandpaper.

5 Cut out the damaged wood and the old repair from the leg with a paring chisel, leaving a wedge-shaped cut-out. Shape a piece of new wood to fit this and glue it in place. Clamp until dry, then remove the clamp.

6 Remove the remains of the side seat rail tenon, which is lodged in the mortise joint, by first drilling access holes, then using a mortise chisel to clean out the remaining wood.

7 Place the leg in a vice and cut the new wood to size. Use carving tools to shape it to match the rest of the leg. Finish by sanding it smooth with medium-grade sandpaper.

8 You now need to cut a new mortise into the new wood. Use a mortise gauge to mark the correct width of the mortise and then a mortise chisel to remove the wood.

9 Smooth the joint with fine-grade sandpaper, then check that the tenon fits snugly into the mortise. Make any necessary final adjustments using sandpaper to ensure a perfect fit.

Above The restored mortise and tenon joint will have the strength of the original. The chair can now be reassembled.

DOWEL JOINT REPAIR

While the most common type of joint used in furniture construction during the 17th, 18th and 19th centuries was the mortise and tenon, by the mid-19th century, due to the increase of furniture production and the need for less time-consuming construction techniques, the dowel joint was being used in certain furniture manufacture. Although similar to the mortise and tenon joint in purpose, the dowel joint employs inset dowels to connect two pieces together. Like the mortise and tenon, however, it does, on occasion, break and have to be replaced.

The dowel joints of this mid-19th-century Victorian balloon-back chair had broken. An earlier repair between the frame and back upright, utilizing a metal bracket, was not successful, and the joint needed to be repaired properly. Once the upholstery had been removed and the chair knocked apart (see pp.376–8), the extent of the damage could be ascertained. The dowels in one joint had broken off and needed removing from the back upright, while the dowels in the other joint had been removed and covered with a mahogany patch; new holes would need to be drilled into this patch.

Materials

- drill
- wood drill bits
- tenon saw
- dowels
- PVA (white) glue
- hammer
- panel pins (brads)
- pincers
- sash clamps
- clamping blocks
- masking tape
- hand drill
- chisel
- rubber
- polish

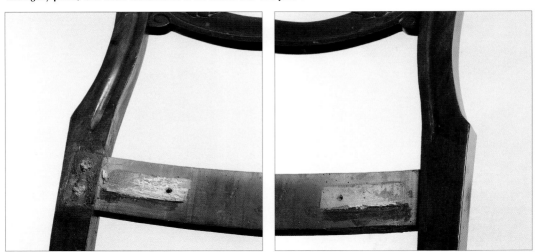

◀ 1 Place the left-hand upright in a vice and drill out the remaining dowel pieces. The auger bit used must be the same diameter as the dowels. Also drill out the remaining dowel pieces in the corresponding side seat rail, then cut and glue new lengths of dowel into these seat rail holes.

▶ 2 Turning now to the problem of the patched upright, place the other side seat rail in a vice. Fit a length of dowel into each of the two seat rail dowel joint holes. Do not glue them in, but cut them flush with the shoulder of the joint.

3 Hammer a panel pin (brad) into the centre of each of the dowel pieces (known as location pegs), and cut back the ends with pincers to leave sharp points standing proud of the surface.

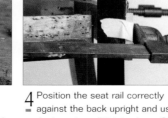

4 Position the seat rail correctly against the back upright and use a sash clamp to pull it into place. Clamp the other side seat rail to keep the frame square. Hold the clamping blocks in place with masking tape.

5 Release the clamps and remove the front and side seat rail structure. The location pins will have marked the correct positions of the new dowel holes in the mahogany patch.

6 Hand drill pilot holes into the pin marks, opening them up to the size of the dowels with an auger bit. Drill at an angle that is square to the back seat rail, so the shoulder of the joint pulls up flush with the upright.

7 Remove the location pegs by gripping the pins and pulling them out. Use the location pegs to determine the correct length of the new dowels required.

8 Cut and glue the new dowels into the joint, then cut channels into the dowels with a chisel. These grooves allow any excess glue to escape from the joint. Reassemble the chair (see pp.378–9).

Right After the glue has dried and the clamps have been removed, give the chair a rubber of polish (see pp.356–7). At this stage, it is ready to be re-upholstered (see pp.400–7). The joint is now as strong as it was when the chair was first constructed.

REPAIRING A BROKEN BACK

A common problem with chairs is that they can break along their top rails. This can be caused by a diner leaning back too hard or a chair being knocked over and the joints shattering. Many breakages of this type require extensive repair work.

In this instance, the top rail of a George III Cuban mahogany dining chair has become broken, and, unfortunately, one of the tenons was smashed beyond repair. An added complication was the fact that the chair retained its original horsehair upholstery, and it was considered wisest to leave the seat *in situ* during restoration. This meant that extra care had to be taken when making the repair.

Materials		
• masking tape	block	• flat-bladed
• tenon saw	• mortise gauge	knife
• Cuban	• chisels	• stopping wax
mahogany	• hammer	• brush
• coping saw	• nails	• stain
• PVA (white)	• spokeshave	• rubber
glue	• band clamps	• polish
• G-clamp	• fine-grade	
• clamping	sandpaper	

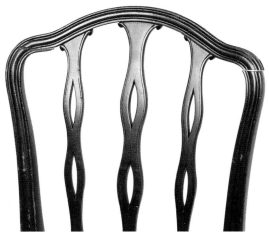

▶1 Remove the top rail and vertical back supports, which will all be joined by mortise and tenon joints. In this instance, the top rail split into three parts on removal. Label the different parts with masking tape (see p.377).

2 A new tenon must be cut to replace the smashed one, but first a section of mahogany must be let into the back upright. Line the vice with old baize and cut out the damaged section with a tenon saw.

3 Having removed the damaged section from the right-hand upright, select a suitable piece of matching Cuban mahogany. Holding it in position, draw the outline of the back upright on it. Cut along this line with a coping saw.

4 Glue the mahogany insert into place. Clamp it into position with a G-clamp and clamping blocks and allow the glue to set. This insert will form the new tenon joint.

5 Measure the tenon on the opposite side upright with a mortise gauge. Transcribe this dimension to the new wood.

6 Cut the new tenon with a tenon saw. Make it slightly wider than the scored lines so that you can pare it down later to produce a really tight and accurate fit.

7 Clean up the joint using a sharp paring chisel. Check the measurement repeatedly against the top rail mortise to ensure a tight fit.

8 The mortise on the left-hand side of the top rail has broken away. Glue back any large sections, pinning the joints together with nails for extra strength. Countersink the heads of the nails.

9 Replace the badly smashed piece from the top rail with sections of Cuban mahogany, trimming it roughly to shape with a chisel.

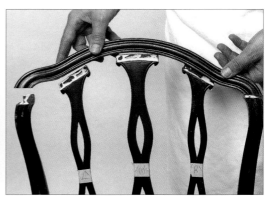

10 Continue shaping the new piece of wood on the top rail with a spokeshave, but do not shape the insert at the joint until the chair has been reassembled. This will allow it to be blended into the upright.

11 Reglue the vertical supports to the top rail and the back seat rail, then reglue the back uprights and top rail together. Note that the rail insert (right) has not yet been shaped.

◀ 12 Use nylon band clamps to apply pressure. These are made from nylon straps fitted with ratchets that allow an even pressure to be applied. Band clamps are ideal for gluing shaped chair backs. When the glue has dried, remove the clamps and shape the mahogany inserts to follow the line of the back upright and the top rail. Finish the repair by smoothing it with fine-grade sandpaper. Using a flat-bladed knife, fill the countersunk nail holes (see step 8) with stopping wax.

Right Stain (see p.359) and polish (see pp.356–7) the repairs to match the existing surface. By remaking the smashed parts of the joints, rather than simply gluing them back together, you will have restored the strength of the chair completely.

REPAIRING A TOP RAIL

The top rail of this 19th-century Regency mahogany chair has become loose due to a break in the stopped dovetail joint. It is old damage, and at some point a temporary repair had been made using a dowel to strengthen the joint, but this did not stop it breaking a second time. The joint now needs to be repaired properly. The process will involve splicing out the damaged areas from the upright and the top rail and remaking both parts of the joint.

Materials

- tenon saw
- Cuban mahogany
- plane
- PVA (white) glue
- G-clamp
- spokeshaves
- fine-grade sandpaper
- chisel
- sash clamp

1 First remove the damaged area of the upright using a tenon saw. Cut away an angled splice to ensure that the new joint will be strong and less noticeable.

2 Cut a suitable piece of Cuban mahogany roughly to size with a tenon saw. Plane one side flush and glue to the upright. Apply G-clamps overnight. When the joint is tight, roughly shape the new wood using a spokeshave.

3 Using a finer spokeshave, shape the new wood, carefully copying the profile of the intact upright. The repair should blend seamlessly with the original. Finish with fine sandpaper.

4 To repair the top rail, remove the damaged areas of wood with a sharp chisel. To make a good joint, ensure that the edges are clean and crisp.

5 Glue together the upright and top rail using PVA (white) glue. Apply sash clamps overnight to ensure a strong joint.

Above When the joint is tight, the new wood is stained to match the original wood and then polished.

UPHOLSTERY

The majority of antique seating furniture, ranging from stools to settees, will need to be upholstered in one form or another. The choice of fabric used will be a personal one, but you should always endeavour to match the style and method of upholstery to the relevant period, since the construction of the chair, stool or settee will reflect the original cabinet-maker's choice of upholstering. To alter this will not only spoil the aesthetics of the whole piece but can also devalue the chair. Also, for authenticity, use tacks rather than staples when reupholstering.

The earliest recorded mention of upholstery was during the 15th century. However, during this period it was the beds and state canopies that received lavish fabric treatments, with seating being confined in the main to squab or loose cushions. These chairs would have been filled with down or horsehair, but by the 16th century the X-frame chair was in use, often covered with velvet or silk damask.

Upholstery rapidly became more fashionable, and by the 18th century there were numerous types and styles of upholstery, ranging from the simple squab seat, to be used with a cane seat, to elaborate wing chairs, which were fully upholstered with only their show-wood legs showing.

The techniques and materials used can alter depending on the origin of the chair, but although modern materials are now available, traditional ones should be favoured whenever possible.

Left A Regency dining chair with a squab seat to protect the canework seat underneath

Right A George III dining chair with a drop-in seat

Right A George II dining chair with a stuff-over seat and close nail decoration

Above An elegant Queen Anne wing chair with fully upholstered back and arms and a down-filled loose cushion

Left A Regency bergère chair with deep-buttoned leather squab seat

Caning

Cane seating can be found in various patterns and styles, although the most common design found on antique furniture is the traditional six-way pattern shown here. Cane is actually rattan, which grows in tropical areas of the Far East, and to obtain the cane, strips are cut from the outside of the rattan, then reduced to various widths, which are classified on a scale of 0 to 6. This outer part of the rattan is used for seating, while the inner parts are employed for basketwork. The tools required are few, and it is very much a technique that requires patience and care. The most common examples of canework are chairs, stools and bed heads.

The method used in chairs is known as open caning, which describes the technique of interweaving long lengths of cane to form a strong, flexible platform on which a squab seat is usually placed. Prior to beginning work, remove all the old cane, including the pegs. The best method of doing this is to drill them out with a drill bit that is slightly smaller in diameter than the holes. Also make sure that the seat frame is tight, since caning a loose or rickety chair is pointless.

Practical tip

Although the cane can be worked dry, the task will be easier if it is soaked in water for a minute or two first and kept wrapped in a damp cloth to mellow while the seat is being worked. Do not make it too wet or keep it damp for too long, because either of these conditions will cause the cane to deteriorate.

Materials

- cane
- clean cotton rags
- rattan pegs
- shell bodkin
- secateurs (pruners)
- hammer
- stain or wax

1 The first stage, or first setting as it is known, is to thread damp cane (see Tip) through the holes from side to side. Hold the cane in place with a rattan peg, then pull the cane across the frame and thread it down through the opposite hole. After securing it with a temporary peg, thread the cane up through the adjacent hole from the underside and repeat the process.

2 Change direction and lay cane at right angles to the first setting, i.e. from front to back. This is the first weaving. Now thread a second row of cane through the same holes as the first setting, but slightly to the right to form a double-width band. This is the second setting.

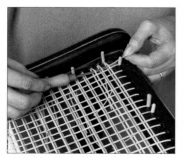

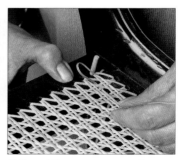

3 The second weaving, which involves laying a second strand of cane from front to back, differs from the first weaving in that this strand is woven over the second setting and under the first setting, which interlocks all four cane bands. Use a shell bodkin to help thread the cane through the various stages of weaving.

4 For the first diagonal weave, or first crossing as it is known, you need to thread cane over the settings and under the weavings, i.e. over the double cane bands set from side to side, and under those woven from front to back.

5 Repeat the process across the other diagonal. This second crossing involves weaving the cane under the settings and over the weavings. This is the opposite to the first crossing. The cane should slip neatly into the corners between the first weaving and the second setting.

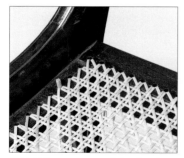

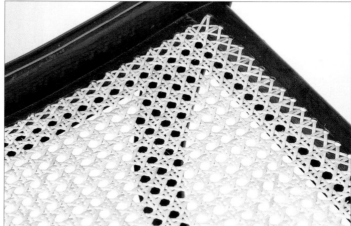

6 Hold the cane securely in place by inserting rattan pegs in the holes, cutting them flush with a pair of garden secateurs (pruners). No glue is used, you just hammer the pegs home with a gentle tap.

Beaded finish

Prior to 1850 a pegged finish (as shown above) was generally used. After this date a decorative beaded finish was favoured (see right). Always select the finish that fits with the period of the chair you are restoring.

Above When completed, the seat should exhibit an evenly woven geometric pattern that will give strength and flexibility. You can leave the cane in its natural state, but it is often better to apply some stained wax or a water-based stain (see pp.358 and 359).

UPHOLSTERING A STUFF-OVER SEAT

There are several ways to upholster a chair. The style and method employed will be dictated by the period and design of the chair, but the most common method in most 18th- and 19th-century furniture is that of over webbing. If carried out correctly, the chair will have an even, flat line that will be comfortable and durable and, most importantly, will show off the lines of the chair to their best effect.

Today, the staple gun is often used alongside the traditional tack and hammer in the upholstery workshop, but while the staple gun undoubtedly saves time, the tack and hammer are always the choice of the quality restoration workshop.

This chair will be upholstered using traditional methods and tools. Although you may already possess some of the tools – such as the mallet, pincers and scissors – the more unusual items will need seeking out from specialist tool suppliers and stores that stock furnishing materials. Alternatively, look out for traditional examples in car boot sales and second-hand stores.

Materials	
• webbing	• horsehair
• tacks	• calico
• hammer	• upholstery
• web stretcher	pins
• mallet	• skin wadding
• pincers	(batting)
• scissors	• top fabric
• hessian	• gimp pins
(burlap)	• braid finish
• twine	• bonding
• upholstery	adhesive
needles	• tack hammer

1 Fold over the ends of four lengths of webbing and tack them to the back of the chair frame at equal intervals. Stretch the webbing across to the front of the frame using a web stretcher, fold over the ends and tack them down. Repeat across the sides of the frame, interweaving the lengths of webbing as shown.

2 Cut a piece of hessian (burlap) slightly larger than the seat frame. Place it on top of the webbing, fold the edges over and tack it down to secure.

3 Stitch several lines of large, looping stitches around the edge of the hessian and across the centre using an upholstery needle. These loops will be used to keep the horsehair in place.

4 Starting from the middle of the seat and working outward, place handfuls of horsehair on the hessian and tease it under the twine loops to secure. Continue until the horsehair sits evenly.

◀ 5 Cut a second piece of hessian and drape it over the horsehair. Secure the hessian with temporary tacks along the chair frame. Stitch further twine loops through the seat with a long needle; these are used to pull the seating flat as well as to hold the horsehair in place.

▶ 6 Remove the temporary tacks with a mallet and tack lifter. Trim the hessian to size, then tack all the way around the seat, taking particular care at the corners. Mistakes at this stage will be very difficult to rectify later.

7 Stitch more ties through the seat, then use the long needle to apply a blind stitch just above the tack line, and also on the top edge, about 2.5cm/1in above the tack line. This begins the process of making the finished edge and will hold the horsehair in place for the next stage.

8 Use the ties to readjust the stuffing, flattening it as much as possible, then blind stitch around the top edges once more, just outside the existing stitches, paying special attention to the corners. When completed, the seat should be flat with the edges held firmly in place.

9 Place another layer of horsehair on the hessian and tease it to fit the dimensions of the seat exactly, producing a slightly domed shape.

◀ 10 Cover the horsehair with a piece of calico. Pull the calico tight and secure it with upholstery pins. The seat should be smooth and regular in shape.

▶ 11 Fold in the corners of the calico and cut to fit. Tack the calico in position and remove the upholstery pins.

12 Cut a piece of skin wadding (batting) to double the length of the seat, fold it in two and place it on the seat. This will prevent the coarse horsehair from coming through.

13 Lay the top cover on the wadding. Fit temporary tacks to the underside of the seat rails so that you can check that any pattern is aligned and the fabric is not overstretched.

14 Adjust the temporary tacks as necessary. Secure the fabric by hammering more tacks into the underside of the seat rails. Trim the corners and fold them away, making sure the folds are on the outside edge.

15 Use small gimp pins hammered in with a tack hammer to hold in the corners, if necessary. The top cover should look smooth and even.

Left The newly upholstered seat should enhance the overall design of the chair, be comfortable to sit on and, most importantly, last for many years.

16 Apply the braid finish with bonding adhesive and snip off any loose threads.

FINISHES

There are several ways of finishing the upholstery of a chair. These include applying attractive finishing techniques to the seat itself and adding various types of decorative edging around the seat rail. The latter have a practical purpose, too, since they are used to provide a neat finish to the edges of the top fabric.

Space nailing
This technique involves applying a braid with bonding adhesive, then hammering in large-headed nails at regular intervals. It is suitable for late 18th-century and Regency styles.

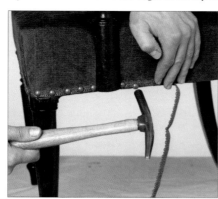

Close nailing
This technique, as the name suggests, involves forming a border of closely spaced nails tacked into the seat rail. It is suitable for tapestry fabrics and a mid-18th-century look.

Braid
There are numerous braids to choose from, in all colours, tones and styles. They are usually applied with bonding adhesive and can be employed with any suitable fabric.

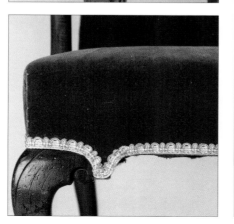

Rope and piping

Rope and piping finishes are used to emphasize the edges of cushions and seats. When used on upholstered seats they are known as "self piping" and give a sculptured look to a seat.

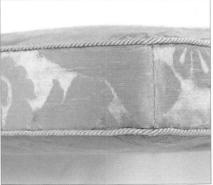

Floating buttons

The use of five floating buttons, combined with space nailing on a braid border, gives a smart, stylish finish. The technique of fitting the buttons is shown below.

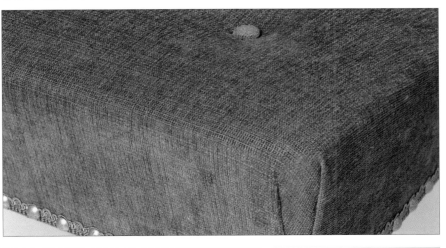

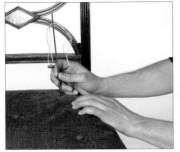

1 Pass some upholstery thread through a button, then use a long needle to pass the double threads down through the seat.

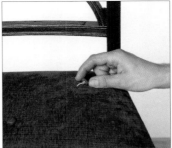

2 Guide the button into position while pulling the threads taut underneath. The button should form a gentle dip in the seat.

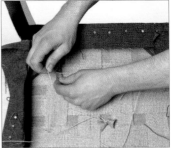

3 Tie off the threads from the underside of the seat, using a scrap (offcut) of webbing to spread the pressure. Repeat for the other four buttons.

RAYNHAM CHAIR

THE AGE OF THIS CHAIR WAS UNKNOWN when it was bought from an auction house. The material, Cuban mahogany, the style of the internal seat rails and the carving indicated that it was a mid-18th-century piece and almost identical to a number attributed to Thomas Chippendale or William Vile for the Marquess of Townsend at Raynham Hall, Norfolk. As such, it could be an important piece and would require sympathetic restoration to bring it back to its original condition. It needed a considerable amount of work to the frame to overcome the ravages of time, including the replacement of parts that were missing with new Cuban mahogany. However, with a great deal of patience and careful work, it was possible to re-create the beauty of the original craftsmanship.

Assessing the project

This chair was in need of comprehensive restoration. On removing the upholstery (which revealed original hay stuffing), it became clear that the seat frame was worm-eaten and loose, and new wood would be needed to strengthen it. Furthermore, the legs appeared to be too short for the height of the chair, and they were missing areas of carving. The feet looked as though they had been cut down and they did not have castors.

The seat frame

- loose
- worm-eaten wood

The feet

- wrong shape
- castors missing

The legs

- incorrect height
- areas of carving missing

Repairing the seat frame

The seat frame was found to be loose and, in areas, the rails were extensively damaged by woodworm. As with all restoration projects, it is important to keep as much of the original material as possible, so the seat frame must be knocked apart carefully and then restored sympathetically. The method used is to remove the core from the original wood and fill the space with a core of new wood. In this way, the strength of the chair can be restored with the new strong core, while the retained exterior of original wood helps to confirm the age of the piece. Chairs that have been completely rerailed can be substantially devalued.

Materials

- tack lifter
- hammer
- hardwood block
- masking tape
- circular saw
- beech
- PVA (white) glue
- clamping blocks
- G-clamps
- tenon saw
- fine brush
- spirit- (alcohol-) based stain

Left Woodworm damage

1 Remove the upholstery and set it aside (see pp.376–7). Note that the chair still has hay as part of its stuffing, indicating that it was last fully re-upholstered in the 19th century. With the upholstery removed, it could be seen that the seat rails were original throughout.

2 Use a tack lifter to free the ends of the now-revealed webbing and strip it away. The springs, which are stitched to the webbing, can be seen beneath the webbing.

3 Knock the chair apart completely (see pp.377–8 using a hammer and a hardwood block. The block ensures that an even pressure is applied and that no damage is caused to the mahogany surface.

◀ 4 Label the individual parts as you remove them. Although it would be difficult to confuse the pieces with just one chair, this could easily happen if there were more than one, so it is good workshop practice to label everything.

5 One of the seat rails has been radically attacked by woodworm and must have a new core inserted. Cut through the length of the seat rail using a circular saw, removing the inner core. Note that for the sake of clearer photography the safety guard has been removed.

▶ 6 Cut a central core from a piece of beech to the same dimensions as the one removed. The original face wood from the rail, which is quite damaged, will serve little more than a cosmetic role, so the beech insert, which will provide the strength, should be a good piece of wood, free from any knots or faults.

7 Glue the three lengths of wood together, with the beech (which will form the tenon) in the middle. Position some newspaper (to protect against leaking glue) and some clamping blocks, then clamp the three parts together and leave to dry. Cut a tenon joint (see p.391).

▶ 8 Although the other seat rails do not need new cores, they do have worm-damaged areas that need to be patched with new beech. It is important, however, to retain as much of the original seat rails as possible. Make sure that any joints that need to be restored still fit prior to the chair being reglued. Continue until all the seat frame damage is repaired, then stain the repairs to match the original wood.

Repairing the feet

Now that the seat frame has been repaired, attention can be given to the problem of the shortened legs. At some stage in their history, their length has been reduced by about 4cm/1½in, almost certainly because of damage. This gives the chair an unbalanced appearance. The answer is to glue mahogany blocks to the legs and to shape them to fit in with the overall design. Damaged areas of moulding around the bottom of the old legs are replaced with new wood, which is then carved and shaped to match the undamaged areas.

Materials

- tenon saw
- Cuban mahogany
- PVA (white) glue
- sash clamps
- clamping blocks
- G-clamps
- chisels
- spring clip
- fine-grade sandpaper
- craft (utility) knife

◄ 1 Cut four 4cm/1½in blocks of Cuban mahogany. Saw through the bottom of each of the existing feet to produce flat, square surfaces. Apply glue to the bottom of each foot, then, in the case of the front legs, clamp each block in place with a sash clamp.

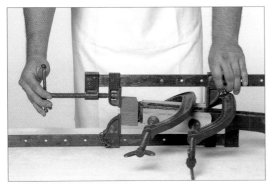

2 When clamping the back legs, you will need to compensate for their angle by adding clamping blocks to the sides of each leg with G-clamps. These will provide a purchase for the sash clamps that hold the new wood in place.

◄ 3 When the glue has dried, remove the clamps and start work on one foot by shaping the block with chisels so that it follow the lines of the original foot. Mark the indents carved on the original foot with a pencil.

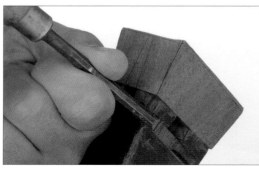

◄ 5 Cut small pieces of matching Cuban mahogany to size. Apply PVA (white) glue to the new wood and the existing foot, and press the new wood down firmly.

4 Cut any damaged areas of moulding on the foot flat and parallel with a chisel so that new wood can be glued on and later carved.

6 The replacement moulding covers a very small area, which means that a G-clamp is not suitable. The best method of holding this wood in place while the glue dries is to use a spring clip (see p.469).

7 When the glue has dried, remove the spring clip. Shape the moulding to match the undamaged areas on the other feet with a bevel-edged chisel.

►8 Finish off the shaping with fine-grade sandpaper. Repeat this process for the mouldings on the other feet.

◀ 10 Cut along the V-shapes in the foot with a tenon saw. Do not cut too deeply – about 1cm/⅜in should be enough.

9 Score along the pencil lines on the foot with a craft (utility) knife. This will act as a guide when sawing out the indentations.

11 Begin paring out the V-shape with a narrow chisel. Take care to follow the shape accurately, because any mistakes you make at this stage cannot be corrected.

12 Continue to pare out the V-shape until it matches the depth in the old foot. Try to achieve as smooth a finish as possible.

◀ 13 The restored feet should closely resemble the original ones. The shape of the new feet was determined by researching the various styles of the period in reference books. The feet will be stained and polished once the repairs on the legs have been completed.

Repairing the legs

The legs are worn, and in some areas the carving has been lost completely. Because carved detail can be quite delicate on furniture, it is vulnerable to knocks and scrapes. Over the years, little bits can be broken off. The solution is to glue on new blocks of wood and carve them to shape to reproduce the missing detail. The new wood then needs to be stained and polished to blend it into the original wood. The important requirement is to have some form of reference so that the carvings can be reproduced. Fortunately, in this case it was possible to copy the detail from one leg to another.

Materials		
• chisel	• fine brushes	• clean cotton
• tenon saw	• bichromate	rags
• Cuban	of potash	• rubber
mahogany	• polish	• methylated
• PVA (white)	• pumice	spirits (methyl
glue	powder	alcohol)
• carving tools		• wax

1 Trim the groundwork level using a sharp chisel. Cut a piece of straight-grained Cuban mahogany so that it is slightly bigger than the area to be carved, then glue it in place.

2 Using the surviving carving from one of the other legs as a guide, shape the new mahogany roughly to the correct profile with a chisel.

3 Following the design and, more importantly, the style of carving, recarve the missing parts. The skill of the carver in restoration work lies in being able to mimic the hand of the craftsman who originally carved the decoration.

◀ 4 The natural colour of mahogany is redder than is usually desired, so once the carving is complete, brush the new wood with bichromate of potash. This is a chemical stain that will react with the tannin in the wood to produce a more desirable brown.

5 Apply the first layers of polish in thin coats, using a fine brush. This will ensure that all parts of the carving will be polished.

6 Put some polish on a cotton rag and sprinkle some fine pumice powder on it, then use this to work the polish into the grain. This process is called fadding. Repeat until the grain is full.

◀ 7 Charge a rubber with polish for the final coats (see pp.356–7) and blend the new work with the existing surface on the legs. Use a cloth to give the original polish a clean using methylated spirits (methyl alcohol), then polish it to revive the surface. Follow this with a dark wax to finish (see p.358). Repeat this process for any other damaged legs.

Rebuilding the chair

Reassembling the chair frame is a straightforward process, but care must be taken to ensure that it is square.

Materials	
• chisel	• clamping blocks
• PVA (white) glue	• battens
	• gauge sticks
• sash clamps	• G-clamps

◀ 1 With the new feet glued on and shaped and the legs repaired, the chair can now be rebuilt. Begin by removing any lumps of old glue from the mortise and tenon joints with a chisel. Take care not to reduce the tenon size, as this will result in sloppy joints.

2 Glue the front legs and seat rail together and secure them with a sash clamp and clamping blocks. Check that the legs are spaced correctly by measuring them at top and bottom.

3 Repeat this process for the back legs, then glue the front and back assemblies to the side seat rails to form the seat frame. When clamping the seat frame together, stand the chair on a flat, level surface. Check that the side seat rails are at the same angle by placing a batten of the same size on each and then sighting across them. Their edges should be parallel if the rail angles are the same.

◀ 4 Check that the seat frame is square by measuring the diagonal dimensions with gauge sticks. You can make these from two lengths of wood with the ends cut to points. Hold the rods together so that the points touch diagonally opposing corners. Then, without allowing the rods to shift in your hand, position them between the other two corners. If both dimensions are the same, the seat frame is square. If any adjustment is needed, loosen the clamps, ease the joint(s) in question slightly, then retighten the clamps and check the diagonals again. Leave to dry.

◀ 5 Now glue together the four pieces of the chair back and secure them with sash clamps and clamping blocks. Check the frame for squareness using the gauge sticks. Leave to dry overnight.

6 Apply a generous amount of glue to the area where the back legs meet the seat back upright. This is a particularly fragile area that is easily damaged if the chair is mistreated.

7 Clamp the back legs and the seat back together, using a G-clamp and clamping blocks. Leave to dry overnight.

Fitting the castors

Castors were used on 18th-century furniture as a means to lift the pieces slightly and to give an impression of lightness. Their use for moving furniture was less important. This chair was missing the original castors, so suitable alternatives had to be sourced and fitted.

Materials

- castors
- drill
- wood drill bits
- chisel
- fine-grade sandpaper
- fine brushes
- stain
- polish

1 Try to find castors from a similar period; otherwise select good reproductions from a furniture restoration parts supplier.

2 Find the centre of the foot and drill a clearance hole for the castor spindle. Put the castor on the foot and draw around it. Make sure that the castor sits exactly in the centre.

3 Bore a hole with a diameter that matches the width of the castor base plate, making it almost as deep as the castor and base plate. The wheel should only just be visible when the castor is fitted.

4 Pare around the edge of the hole with a chisel. Continue until the hole is wide enough to accommodate the wheel.

5 Drill a hole for the castor spindle in the centre of the foot, matching the size as closely as possible.

◀ 6 Finish the recess by smoothing it with fine-grade sandpaper, then screw the castor in place. Repeat this process with the other three feet. Finally, use fine brushes to stain and polish the feet to match the rest of the chair.

▶ 7 When the feet have been polished, they can be distressed slightly so they are not so obviously new. The castor likewise can be toned down.

Fitting the brackets

This chair had curved brackets fitted between the seat rails and legs. These were secured originally with glue and dowels. The old dowels have been drilled out and the holes plugged, so the new ones have a secure fixing. The same method of fixing will be employed to refit them, requiring new holes to be drilled in the core wood and new mahogany dowels to be made to match the holes in the brackets.

Materials

- drill
- wood drill bit
- tenon saw
- mahogany
- hammer
- steel plate
- PVA (white) glue
- chisel
- fine-grade sandpaper

1 Hold the brackets in place and, using a closely matched bit, drill through the dowel holes into the legs and the new core wood or plugged dowel holes of the seat rails.

2 Cut strips of mahogany for the dowels. Hammer them through a hole in a steel plate to round them off and make them the correct diameter.

3 Glue the brackets in place, then knock the dowels through them into the seat rails and legs. Cut down the dowels with a tenon saw, then pare off the remainder with a sharp chisel. Sand them smooth with fine-grade sandpaper.

Right Once the chair has been re-upholstered (see pp.403–7) and polished (see pp.356–7), it will look as good as new and should last for another 250 years.

WINDSOR CHAIR

THIS 19TH-CENTURY WINDSOR CHAIR, made from beech and elm, had been found in a garage. Long forgotten and in a sorry state, it was in need of complete restoration. This required a variety of techniques, since there was a range of damage to be put right. Although such chairs are quite simple in appearance, they are still handsome pieces of furniture and it is worth making an effort to bring them back to their original condition. If the work is done correctly, the result will be a sturdy, good-looking chair that will give many years of service.

Assessing the project

The most obvious damage is that one arm had broken off. Upon further inspection, it was also discovered that the arm joints in the back upright and shaped seat had broken away and would need replacing. Moreover, the back legs had been reduced in height to give the chair a more reclined feel. This had, however, put an unequal strain on the other legs and stretchers, causing them to become loose. The back legs will therefore need to be removed and returned to their original height. Finally, the seat, unusually for a Windsor chair, had split, and will need to be glued and secured with butterfly keys.

The seat

split seat

The arm

• broken upright
• bobbin missing

The back legs

incorrect height

Repairing the seat

The split in the seat had probably been caused by a combination of misuse and climatic changes. Windsor chairs are very robust, and so splits in the seat are relatively uncommon. Fortunately, they are not difficult to repair. The application of glue and butterfly keys will produce a strong seat that will last for many more years to come. There is no need to match the wood of the seat for the butterfly keys; softwood will suffice, and it can be stained to blend in with the original material. You will need a router to cut the recesses for the keys, and, since the chair has a slightly curved surface, a routing guide to provide the router with an even surface to work on.

Materials

- tenon saw
- softwood
- router
- PVA (white) glue
- sash clamps
- clamping blocks
- plywood
- hammer
- nails
- plane
- water-based stain
- brush

1 Cut four butterfly keys from a piece of softwood (see p.484). Remove all the legs, which, due to their condition, should involve no more than simply easing them out. Turn the seat over. Set the stop depth on a router to slightly less than the thickness of the keys.

2 Glue the crack, then clamp the seat together using sash clamps and clamping blocks. Cut a plywood routing guide slightly larger than the butterfly keys. Nail this to the underside of the seat where the first key is to be inserted (the waist of each key sits on the crack).

3 Cut the remaining three recesses then glue all the butterflies into position. The crack is now secured.

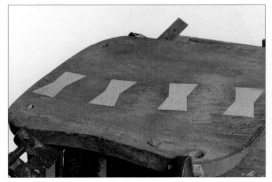

4 Allow the glue to dry. Plane the butterfly keys until they are level with the seat base, then remove the clamps.

5 Mix a water-based stain to match the wood colour then brush it over the keys. Once the top of the seat has been cleaned and waxed, the crack will be all but invisible.

Repairing the arm

The arm support had broken off at its base. It could not simply be reglued, as the joint would not be strong enough to hold it. A new section would therefore have to be made and fitted.

The bobbin linking the arm to the chair back had been broken off and lost, so a replacement would need to be turned on a lathe.

Repairing the support

The arm support was cylindrical in shape and tapered to a narrow point that fitted into a hole in the seat. This shape could not be turned on the lathe, but had to be formed by hand.

Materials

- drill
- wood drill bit
- beech
- tenon saw
- plane
- paring chisel
- PVA (white) glue
- snap clamp
- spokeshave
- fine-grade sandpaper
- hammer

◀ 1 Remove the broken part of the upright that still remains in the seat by drilling it out from the underside. Choose a drill bit that matches the diameter of the existing hole.

2 Plane the support at an angle and draw a
corresponding line on a piece of beech that is slightly
bigger than the support.

3 Cut the beech along the line. Plane the end of the longer
piece of beech until it is smooth and fits snugly against
the support.

4 Glue the support to the centre of the planed end of the
beech, and clamp it in position. Leave to dry then
remove the clamp.

5 Place the support in a vice and roughly shape the beech
with a spokeshave. Continue until it is cylindrical and
tapers to a size that will fit in the hole in the seat.

6 Smooth the support with sandpaper. Continue until it
matches the support on the other arm of the chair,
comparing the two often so that you do not remove too
much material.

◄ 7 Fit the
upright in
the chair seat.
Check its height
against the
upright on the
other side. If
necessary,
continue sanding
until the correct
height has been
reached.

8 With the suppot inserted in the seat, saw off the excess wood so that it protrudes slightly from the seat.

9 Place the arm support in a vice and use a saw to remove a narrow wedge, about 2.5cm/1in deep, from the bottom of the support.

◀ 10 Fit the support back into the seat and apply glue to the wedge-shaped slot. Cut a beech wedge that is marginally larger than the wedge cut out of the support, and hammer it into the slot. This will expand the end of the support, giving a tight joint. When the glue is dry, make the support flush with the underside of the seat using a plane or a paring chisel.

Turning a bobbin

To replace the missing arm bobbin, a new bobbin, with the same dimensions as the bobbin on the undamaged arm, must be turned. This requires skilful lathe work.

Materials	
• drill	• bench hook
• wood drill bits	• tenon saw
• beech	• PVA (white)
• lathe	glue
• turning tools	• sash clamps
• dividers	• clamping
• callipers	blocks
• very fine-grade	
sandpaper	

▶ 1 Drill out the remainder of the spigot that joined the original bobbin to the back upright. Use a drill bit that corresponds to the diameter of the original hole.

2 Turn a piece of beech to the approximate diameter of the bobbin on the other arm. It is always best to be cautious at this stage; if you over-turn the wood, you will have to start again.

3 Use a pair of dividers, set to the width of the existing bobbin, to mark the new bobbin's position on the rough-turned beech.

4 Use a paring chisel to cut into the wood on each side of the bobbin outline, in preparation for forming the spigots.

5 Continue turning the spigots until they approach the correct diameter, making frequent checks with callipers set to the size of the spigots on the existing bobbin.

◄ 6 Check that the diameter of the spigots is slightly larger than the spigot hole on the arm. This will ensure a good fit and make the joints stronger. Take care, though, that the larger size does not change the balance or proportions of the original piece.

7 Use an angled chisel to turn the bobbin to the correct shape. There is no easy way to do this except with patience and experience. If a mistake is made, the whole process has to be started again.

8 Having turned the bobbin, cut a series of shallow grooves into the two spigots with a turning chisel to give any excess glue somewhere to escape to when the joint is glued. (A joint with too much glue in, and no space for it to escape to, will split the surrounding wood.)

9 With correctly sharpened tools and the proper technique, there should be very little need for much cleaning up, but a final sanding with very fine-grade sandpaper will finish off the turned bobbin. Do not sand the two spigots.

10 Remove the length of beech from the lathe, hold it firmly on a bench hook and cut away the ends with a tenon saw. Make sure you leave enough spigot material to ensure a snug fit in both the back upright and the arm.

11 Use a drill to clean out the spigot hole in the arm. Use a drill bit that corresponds to the size of the new spigot.

12 Glue one spigot into the arm and the other into the back upright. The arm can now be glued to the new support and clamped until dry.

Repairing the legs

The back feet had been reduced in height, making the legs too short, so it is necessary to build them up to make the chair level again. They had been cut off at an angle, so it is not possible simply to glue on extra pieces without them being obvious. The best solution is to replace the whole foot section with a longer version, joining at the old ankle, so that the joint is cleverly disguised. The front original feet can act as a guide to both style and size.

Materials

- beech
- tenon saw
- steel rule
- drill
- wood drill bits
- lathe
- turning tools
- callipers
- fine-grade sandpaper
- bench hook
- centre finder
- PVA (white) glue
- sash clamps
- fine brush
- spirit- (alcohol-) based stain
- rubber
- polish
- clean cotton rag
- wax

◀ 1 Select a piece of beech to match the rest of the leg, and cut it to a suitable length and a width larger than the diameter of the foot. Mark the centre of the block on each end with a steel rule and drill a hole about 1cm/⅜in deep at each end.

▶ 2 Cut a shallow groove along a cross-mark at one end with a tenon saw. This drilled and grooved end will house the head stock of the lathe and the end with just the hole will house the tail stock. Both stocks are used to rotate the wood. Measure the existing foot with callipers.

3 Mount the beech in the lathe, then, using a large gouge, roughly turn the wood to the diameter of the widest part of the foot. Do not push the gouge too hard or at too acute an angle, as this could cause it to be "snatched" by the square edges of the wooden block.

4 Use the callipers to mark out the end of the foot and a turning chisel to cut a shallow groove. Then turn a spigot, which will be inserted into the leg.

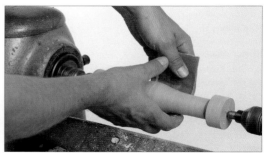

5 Mark a line from which the bulbous shape will be turned, then shape the foot using a skew chisel. Place the bevel against the wood and, after it has been raised and begun to cut, turn it with a smooth rolling action. This will give the required shape.

6 Finish off the shaped foot by gently applying fine-grade sandpaper to remove any tool marks. Cut the excess from the bottom and cut the spigot to the correct length.

7 Place the leg on a bench hook and cut off the shortened foot flush at the ankle. This will mean that the new foot will be attached at a natural joint line, disguising the fact that it is a later replacement.

8 Mark the centre of the leg using a centre finder. This is a useful tool that will enable you to determine the centre of any round item.

9 Drill out the centre of the leg to a diameter that matches the spigot at the top of the new foot. Make sure that the drill is held in line with the leg; it can be helpful to have someone watch you to make sure that the drill does not wander off line.

10 Glue the foot to the leg and use a sash clamp to apply pressure. By attaching the foot in this way, the strength of the joint will be as good as if the leg and foot had been turned from the same piece of wood. Leave to dry, then remove the clamp.

11 Make and attach another foot in the same way, then clean out all the leg and stretcher holes before gluing the joints and reassembling the chair legs and stretchers.

12 Mix a spirit- (alcohol-) based stain to match the original wood, then brush this over the two new feet.

13 Finally, charge a rubber with polish and apply a layer over both new feet (see pp.356–7). Then wax the entire chair so that the repairs blend in (see p.358).

Left The restored chair is as good as new and will now sit at the angle originally intended by the maker. The chair will require no further maintenance other than the occasional waxing.

DISMANTLING AND REASSEMBLING TABLES

Although tables come in many styles, their basic construction remains the same and the method required to knock them apart remains fairly consistent. The dismantling procedure must be followed in a logical step-by-step manner, and particular care must be taken to identify the types of joint employed. Failure to do so could result in smashed joints and unnecessary further damage. Once the table has been taken apart, you can inspect the components and carry out any necessary restoration or repair work before reassembling it.

Dismantling the table

This table is a George III, c.1800 drop-leaf Pembroke table made from Cuban mahogany. Over a period of time, its joints have become loose, but before any necessary repair work can be done, the table needs to be dismantled.

Materials

- chalk or masking tape
- screwdriver
- hammer
- hardwood block
- toothbrush
- rasp

Practical tip

If a screw is difficult to remove, fit the blade of an old screwdriver into the screw slot, tap the handle firmly with a hammer and tighten the screw slightly. This should break the bond, allowing the screw to be removed.

1 Label the various parts of the table, either with chalk or by applying marked masking tape, which will not mark the polish.

2 Turn the table upside down and lay it on a protected workbench. Remove all the screws from the frame, which will release the top.

3 Now unscrew any metal brackets that may have been added to the table in the past to strengthen any damaged joints.

◀ 4 Examine the construction of the joints to decide the best method of knocking apart without causing further damage.

◀ 5 Disassemble the various components, taking care not to cause structural damage to the joints. Failure to do so will result in smashed joints that will need to be restored prior to the table being reassembled. Use a hardwood block to prevent bruising by the hammer.

6 When separating the side frame from the legs, use the hardwood block again to guard against bruising by the hammer. Direct the blows as closely as possible to the actual joint.

7 Now knock the legs apart from the remaining frame, using the same technique and making sure you put a piece of hardwood between the hammer and the leg to prevent any damage.

8 Remove all traces of glue with a toothbrush and hot water. Where animal glues have crystallized, use a rasp to clean the joint. Take care not to file away any of the tenon, as this will result in a sloppy joint.

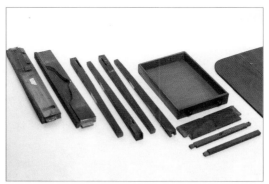

9 Carefully check the various parts of the table once it is dismantled, before carrying out any necessary restoration work.

Reassembling the table

When all the necessary restoration work has been carried out, the table can be reassembled. PVA (white) glue and animal glue are the best adhesives to use.

Materials

- PVA (white) or animal glue
- sash clamps
- clamping blocks
- hammer
- hardwood block
- masking tape
- drill
- flat-bottomed grain plug drill bit
- grain plug cutter
- mahogany
- chisel
- fine-grade sandpaper
- hand drill
- wood drill bit
- screwdriver
- screws
- flat-bladed knife
- stopping wax
- clean cotton rags
- methylated spirits (methyl alcohol)
- spirit- (alcohol-) based stain
- brush
- rubber
- polish
- wax

1 Rub the area around the scratch lightly with fine wire (steel) wool to remove the surface wax.

2 Now complete the table frame by gluing both pairs of legs together, using the bottom rail at the drawer end and the side frame at the other end. Stand the table on a flat, level surface to do this. Make sure that the frame is square by measuring across the diagonal corners. Clamp as before.

3 This top rail is secured by dovetail joints, so it should be glued back into position at this stage. Tap the dovetails into their recesses with a hammer and a hardwood block. If the rail had mortise and tenon joints, it should have been fitted at the same time as the bottom rail.

◀ 4 Before the glue has set, fit the drawer to ensure that the table is square. If the drawer sticks or rubs, you may need to make small adjustments. Leave the glue to dry overnight. When dry, remove the clamps.

▶ 5 Beneath the top, there was evidence that the previous screw fixings had been pulled out and the hinge moved to try to get a better purchase. Since the top will be reset in its original position, the old screw holes can be plugged.

6 Follow steps 1 and 2 on p.445 to enlarge the existing screw holes. Cut small plugs of wood to fill them, and then glue the plugs in place.

7 When the glue is dry, use a chisel to level the plugs off flush with the underside of the table, then sand them with fine-grade sandpaper. There is now a smooth surface for the screws to be set into.

8 Now turn the top upside down and put it on the protected workbench. Put the frame back in the correct position. Since the old holes have been plugged, drill pilot holes to locate the positions of the screws.

◄ 9 If you are using the old screws, screw them into the new holes. If you are using replacements, check that they are the right length and will not go through the table top and mark the surface.

►10 Using a flat-bladed knife, fill the screw holes made by the metal brackets removed earlier with stopping wax in a similar colour to the mahogany.

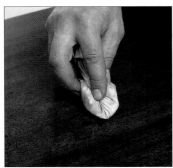

11 Stain the repairs to match the wood. Wash the surface off with methylated spirits (methyl alcohol). Charge a rubber with polish and revive the surface. Apply wax and buff the wood to a warm lustre.

Left Reassembled and polished, the table has been restored to its former glory and is ready to give many more years of service.

REPAIRING CARVING

Carving as a form of decoration on furniture has been in existence since medieval times, but by the 17th century its use was becoming more widespread.

When restoring or replacing carving, it is important to select a similar-grained piece of wood. It is often advisable to make an initial test cut with a carving tool to ensure that the wood is suitable to work with. This is because some wood will have a grain that is too "wild", which means that you may tear rather than cut the wood. Alternatively, the wood might be too soft, which could result in the wood simply crumbling when being carved and unable to keep a crisp edge.

Carving a damaged bracket

During the 17th and 18th centuries, carved and shaped legs had brackets, or ears as they are commonly referred to, that were applied separately rather than being part of the leg. As a result, if the animal glue perished, the bracket could become detached and even lost.

This table had lost a bracket from one of its swing legs, so the leg needs to be removed and a replacement bracket made. A profile of the carving on the other swing leg bracket needs to be taken so that it can be used as the basis for the new carved decoration, which can then be stained and polished to match the other legs.

Materials	
• tenon saw	• fine brushes
• Cuban mahogany	• bichromate of potash
• spokeshave	• polish
• animal glue	• pumice powder
• modelling clay	• clean cotton rags
• mallet	• rubber
• indelible ink	• colour
• marker pen	• fine wire (steel) wool
• carving tools	• wax
• screwdriver	• large soft brush

1 Cut a profile bracket out of Cuban mahogany and shape it with a spokeshave. It should be similar to the missing bracket but slightly larger to allow the carving to be undertaken, otherwise it will end up too small. Glue it into place.

2 To obtain the correct profile of the missing carving, lay a piece of modelling clay over the matching bracket on the other swing leg. Tap it lightly with a mallet, then gently peel it away.

3 Turn the clay over and use your thumb to cover the profile of the carving with indelible ink. Then lay it gently on the replacement bracket to leave the outline of the carving on the wood.

4 Remove the clay then thicken the outline with a marker pen, making sure the lines flow into the carving on the rest of the bracket.

◀ 5 Having established the outline of the carving, remove the groundwork using grounders. This technique, known as grounding out, establishes the depth of carving.

◀ 6 When the outline of the carving has been set, carve the detail into the relief, using either veiners or modellers. There should be no need to clean up the carving, as the razor sharpness of the tools should give a perfect finish.

7 Reattach both swing legs to the table and round off the sharp edges of the new bracket using the shank of a screwdriver or some similar tool.

8 In its natural state, mahogany is a red colour, but over the years it patinates to a brown tone. To mimic this colour, apply bichromate of potash, which, being a chemical stain, reacts with the tannin in the wood to turn the natural red tone into a more suitable brown.

9 Apply the polish with a brush, painting it on evenly. The idea is just to fill the grain, so do not use too much, otherwise streaks and runs may occur.

10 Put some polish on a cotton rag and sprinkle some fine pumice powder on it. Use this to work the polish into the grain. Do not round over the edges or break through highlights to reveal wood.

11 With the grain filled, use a rubber to apply further polish mixed with some colour until the bracket tone blends in with the leg and matches the original bracket (see pp.356–7).

Right After the bracket has been polished and waxed, it will look original. It is worth noting the amount of distressing on the bracket you have taken a profile from and trying to mirror it on the replacement. However, be careful not to overdo this and give the bracket a "fake" look.

12 After the polish has hardened, cut it back with fine wire (steel) wool, then wax the bracket (see p.358).

Carving small pieces

The previous technique covered replacing a completely missing carved section, piece or bracket; on occasion, however, you may need to replace only small pieces of carving. The method or technique used for this is different to that of replacing a complete section, because your aim is to fill in the small areas that are missing with pieces of wood, and then to carve them to match the original. The pieces cannot be carved and then glued into place, as the detailed carving needs to be flowing and the replacements undetectable. This carved foliate bracket has many sections of leaf and vine missing.

Materials

- mahogany
- fine-bladed fret saw
- animal glue
- carving tools
- fine brushes
- stain
- polish

1 Hold a new piece of mahogany against one of the missing areas and roughly sketch out the profile in pencil.

2 Use a fine-bladed fret saw to cut the wood to the approximate size. Repeat steps 1 and 2 for all the other missing pieces.

◄ 3 Glue the pieces into place and leave them to dry. Draw in the outlines of the missing pieces to give a guide for carving, although the majority of the work will be done by eye.

► 4 After roughing out the outlines, carve the chosen shapes and patterns. Use tools that are razor sharp, otherwise the new pieces may break off. Should this happen, glue them back into position. Finally, add the details, matching the original carver's style.

Above When completed, the newly carved areas should be stained and polished to match the rest of the bracket. The highly carved surface demands that a fine brush be used for both techniques.

REPAIRING TOPS

The top is subject to more general wear and tear than other areas of a table. Scratches, dents and stains are commonplace, and methods of restoring tables with these problems are covered earlier in the book (see pp.344–75). Other common problems that can occur with table tops are warping, splitting and damaged decorative edges. By using the correct restoration techniques, however, it is possible to make good all of these defects and to bring a damaged top back to the condition it was in when the table was made.

Restoring a damaged table edge

This Cuban mahogany Georgian tripod table is missing a section of its decorative edge. A new piece of wood needs to be cut, glued in place and shaped to fit, before being stained and polished to match the table top. This technique can be used on all moulded edges, including pie-crust tops.

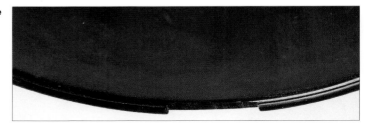

Materials

- screwdriver
- mahogany
- jigsaw (saber saw)
- tenon saw
- chisel
- PVA (white) glue
- spring clip
- plane
- carving tool
- spokeshave
- fine-grade sandpaper
- brush
- stain
- rubber
- polish

1 Remove the table top from the frame by undoing all the screws (see p.430). Turn the table top upside down and lay it on a protected surface. Put a piece of mahogany, slightly thicker than the decorative edging, underneath the top, and draw around the edge with a pencil. Slide the mahogany farther out by an amount slightly greater than the width of the decorative edging, and draw another curved line.

2 Cut the mahogany along the pencil lines using a jigsaw (saber saw), then turn the table top right side up again. Cut through the damaged edging on either side of the missing area with a tenon saw.

3 Remove the damaged wood underneath the missing edging with a chisel. Continue working until you have a flat, level surface.

4 Check that the piece of mahogany fits in the allotted space. Apply PVA (white) glue and secure it with a spring clip (see p.469). Leave it to dry, then remove the spring clip.

5 Plane the mahogany down until it is level with the rest of the edging. Make small strokes to avoid damaging the table top.

6 The inner ledge on the table must be shaped with a suitable carving tool. Again, avoid damaging the polished mahogany.

7 Use a spokeshave to shape the curve along the edge of the top. It is easier to obtain a more delicate shape with a spokeshave than a plane.

8 Smooth the top of the restored area with fine-grade sandpaper. Fold a small piece of the sandpaper in half and hold it with your thumb and forefinger for accuracy.

Above Once the detailed shape of the edging has been formed with sandpaper, stain (see p.359) and polish (see pp.356–7) the repaired edging so that it is invisible.

Repairing a rule joint

The rule joint is commonly found on drop-leaf tables. It allows for a leaf to be raised and supported along its length. On occasion, it can become damaged, as shown here, where part of the rule joint has broken away, allowing the hinge to be seen from the top. This could have been caused by the leaf having been raised too high, putting too much pressure on the hinge and joint.

Materials

- tenon saw
- mahogany
- PVA (white) glue
- spring clip
- chisel
- fine-grade sandpaper
- fine brush
- stain

1 Trim away the damaged area of moulding with a tenon saw. Cutting the ends at angles will help to disguise the repair when it is finally polished.

2 Cut a piece of mahogany to the length of the gap and a little wider, and glue it in place. Clamp it using a spring clip (see p.469), which is ideal for this type of small repair, and leave to dry. Remove the clip.

3 Shape the wood with a chisel and fine-grade sandpaper so that it continues the lines of the existing wood, otherwise the flap may not open properly. Stain it to match the existing moulding.

Drilling out damaged screws

The photograph shows a very common problem: after the screws had been put into this card-table hinge, their heads were filed flat to remove the slots. The flap of this table needed routing out, which meant that the screw heads had to be drilled out so that both hinges could be removed.

Materials

- centre punch
- hammer
- drill
- metal drill bit
- screwdriver
- long-nose (needlenose)
- pliers
- Cuban mahogany
- PVA (white) glue
- chisel

1 First hammer a centre punch into each screw head as accurately as possible.

2 Drill out the heads of the screws taking care not to drill the actual holes in the hinges any larger than they already are. This will leave countersunk holes, which will be filled by the replacement screws when the hinges are refitted.

3 Using a small screwdriver, carefully ease the hinges clear, being careful not to bend the flaps of the hinges out of shape.

4 Removing the hinges will expose the shanks of the screws, which will still be embedded in the table edge. Drill small holes on each side of, and as close as possible to, the embedded screw shanks.

5 To remove the screws, insert a pair of long-nose (needlenose) pliers into the freshly drilled holes, grip the shank of each screw in turn and pull it out.

◄ 6 The holes must be filled before new screws can be inserted. Cut wedges of Cuban mahogany and glue them into the holes. Trim them flush with a chisel when dry.

Right Once the table has been repaired, the hinges can be refitted.

Repairing fretwork

The illustration shows the damaged open-fret gallery from a Georgian silver table, 1760. The silver table, as the name suggests, would stand in the drawing room and have the silver tea service placed upon it. Such tables were designed to be elegant and often had open-fret galleries, made from three layers of veneer for strength.

The gallery on this silver table has been damaged and small areas have broken away and been lost. As much as possible of the damaged fretwork will be glued back into place, and the missing areas within this will be filled with pieces from a new section of gallery made specially for the purpose.

Materials

- bonding adhesive
- paper
- wood block
- clamping blocks
- G-clamps
- Cuban mahogany
- band saw
- toothing plane
- cascamite glue
- pigment
- brushes
- hammer
- veneer pins (tacks)
- pincers
- plane
- drill
- wood drill bit
- fine-bladed fret saw
- paring chisel
- tweezers
- fine file
- spirit- (alcohol-) based stain
- polish

1 The first step in the restoration process is to put back as much of the damaged work as possible, gluing it into place with bonding adhesive. The quick-drying nature of this glue allows the gallery to be held in the correct position while the glue sets.

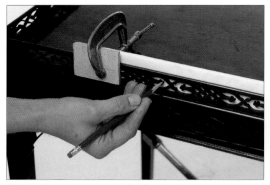

2 To make a new section of gallery for the repairs, wrap a piece of paper around a long block of wood and then use G-clamps and some clamping blocks to hold it against a section of gallery that matches the damaged area. Draw the outline of the fretwork very carefully. Release the clamps and blocks and remove the piece of paper.

3 Cut three lengths of Cuban mahogany with a band saw, roughly the length of the damaged fret area, and, using a toothing plane, plane one side only of two lengths and both sides of the third length. This will aid the purchase of the mahogany when the three layers are glued together.

4 Cut one length into pieces of the same length as the width of the remaining two lengths. These will be the inner core pieces that will give strength to this new section.

5 Cascamite glue, while suited to this job, could show as a white line on this gallery, so add a small quantity of pigment to the powder prior to mixing it with water.

6 Coat the planed side of one length of mahogany with cascamite glue then place the short pieces on top to form a second layer. Coat these short pieces with glue.

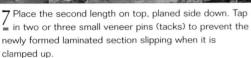

7 Place the second length on top, planed side down. Tap in two or three small veneer pins (tacks) to prevent the newly formed laminated section slipping when it is clamped up.

8 Place paper strips on either side of the section then put clamping blocks in place. The paper will ensure that any excess glue does not bind the two together. Clamp the section under pressure and leave to dry. The pressure must be even along the whole length.

9 Remove the clamps and blocks, then pull out the veneer pins with pincers. Failure to remove the pins could result in damage to the fret saw when the fret is being cut.

10 Place the gallery in a vice and plane the long edges level with a jack plane.

11 With the laminated section now ready, glue the paper template (pattern) made in step 2 on to it.

12 Drill holes in each area that needs to be fretted out. This will allow the fret saw blade to be put into position.

13 Using a fine fret blade, cut out the open fret, following the design. Work slowly and take great care not to spoil the work already done. Scrape off the remains of the template.

14 Before restoring the glued fretwork, cut any splintered breaks flush using a sharp paring chisel. To protect the fragile fret, place a block of supporting wood behind it.

15 Cut out the sections from the new fret needed to fill the gaps with a fret saw, and carefully insert and glue them in place.

16 Use a fine file to smooth the edges flush where the old and new pieces join, taking care not to alter the open-fretted shape.

17 Repeat until all the damage is repaired. Finally, stain and polish the new portions of fret to match the existing gallery.

Right With the fretwork restored, stained and polished, this silver table can once again be returned to the drawing room of the large country house from where it came.

Filling screw holes

Over the years, a piece of furniture may be subjected to a number of repairs that relied on brackets or reinforcing plates being screwed on. During restoration, these will be removed, leaving the screw holes behind. Fortunately, it is easy to fill these holes with wooden plugs.

Materials

- masking tape
- drill
- flat-bottomed grain plug drill bit
- grain plug cutter
- wood
- PVA (white) glue
- chisel
- fine-grade sandpaper
- brush
- stain

1 Mark the required drilling depth on the flat-bottomed grain plug drill bit with some masking tape (see Tip), then drill a hole larger than the old screw hole.

2 Use a grain plug cutter to cut a plug from matching wood, making it slightly longer than the hole's depth. Glue it into the hole.

3 When the glue has dried, pare off the projecting portion of the plug with a sharp chisel, then sand it smooth.

Above The finished repair is now ready to be stained.

Practical tip

If a drilled hole must not penetrate all the way through a piece of wood, it is vital to know how far you can drill before this will happen. First ascertain the required depth of the hole by holding the drill bit against the edge of the wood, then mark this level on the drill bit with a piece of masking tape. When drilling into the wood, stop as soon as the masking tape touches the surface. The hole will then remain invisible from the other side.

Correcting a warped card table

A dry level of humidity is the most common cause of warping. The flaps of veneered card tables, and other types of flap-over or drop-leaf table, are more prone to warping than frame tables for two reasons. First, they are usually relatively thin (for ease of handling), and second, they are free-standing, secured to the base only by their hinges.

The flap of this mahogany card table is significantly warped. Fortunately, the veneer has not split, which means that the core material can be removed from the baize-covered side, and then replaced with a new, flat MDF (medium-density fiberboard) interior. Finally, a new baize cover can be added without disturbing the veneered upper surface.

Materials

- flat-bladed knife
- screwdriver
- 5cm/2in masking tape
- padded packaging
- clean cotton rag
- iron
- board
- scraper
- marking gauge
- chipboard (particle board)
- saw
- softwood
- drill
- wood drill bit
- chipboard screws
- MDF (medium-density fiberboard)
- router
- gouge
- smoothing plane
- jigsaw (saber saw)
- fine-grade sandpaper
- PVA (white) glue
- large pieces of wood
- G-clamps
- rubber
- shellac polish
- wood filler
- baize
- craft (utility) knife
- tooling wheel

1 Lever the edge of the baize away from the table with a flat-bladed knife. Grip the baize firmly with both hands and pull it off with one continuous movement. Unscrew the hinges linking the flap to the table.

2 Place the flap, veneer side up, on a protected workbench. Cover the surface with strips of masking tape. This will hold together the veneer, banding and stringing on this side until a new core is inserted.

3 Cut a semicircle of padded packaging to fit the flap. Secure it over the veneered side with masking tape for extra protection. Turn the flap over so that the stripped side is uppermost.

4 Immerse a cotton rag in a bowl of water, then lay it over part of the banding. Place a hot iron on the damp rag and press down for a few seconds, then remove the iron and rag. The steam will soften the glue holding the banding on to the core. Take care not to scorch the banding.

5 Slide a flat-bladed knife under the banding while the glue is still malleable, and lift a section of it from the flap. The stringing should be removed at the same time. Continue steaming and lifting sections of the banding and stringing until all of it has been removed.

6 Tape the pieces of the banding and stringing together on to a board in the same positions that they occupied on the table. This will ensure that they can be replaced in the correct order.

7 Scrape any remaining baize from the flap with a scraper. In this case, evidence of a previous, and unsuccessful, restoration can now be seen. This method involved removing strips of wood from the warped upper layer, flattening the table, then replacing them with new wood.

8 Scribe a line around the edge of the flap, just inside the banding's position, with a marking gauge. Turn the flap over, remove the padded packaging, then turn it back again. Removing the packaging will allow the flap to lie completely flat.

9 Place the flap on a piece of chipboard (particle board) and press it flat with both hands. Place holding blocks (see Tip) at regular intervals around the edge.

Practical tip

To hold a table flap securely while working on it, you will need to make several holding blocks, which can be screwed down over the table flap on to a chipboard (particle board) base. Make each block 5–7.5cm/2–3in long from softwood that is at least 12mm/½in thicker than the flap. Cut a rebate (rabbet) along the length of each block to the depth of the flap, producing an L-shaped end profile. Drill two screw holes in each block. Place the flap on the chipboard base and clamp the edges down by screwing the blocks to the base, using chipboard screws (see right).

10 Select a suitable thickness of MDF (medium-density fiberboard) for the core. Remove sections of the flap to this depth, leaving borders to support the router.

11 Cut away the supporting border with a gouge. Take great care not to cut too deeply because you risk damaging the veneer from the underside.

12 Level the surface with the iron from a smoothing plane, continuing until it is completely smooth.

13 Place the flap on the MDF and draw around the outline. Remove the flap and cut along this line with a jigsaw (saber saw).

14 Mark another line on the MDF that approximately matches the width of the banding, and cut along this line. Check that the MDF core fits the cut-out area of the flap, sanding it to fit.

15 Spread PVA (white) glue over the cut-out area of the flap, then insert the MDF. Place the flap between two pieces of wood and use G-clamps to apply even pressure. Leave to dry.

◄ 16 Remove the clamps and wood, turn the flap over, remove the masking tape from the veneered side. Place the flap, veneered side down, on a protected workbench. Apply PVA glue to the edge of the flap and replace the pieces of banding and stringing.

► 17 Reattach the flap to the table and lightly polish the banding with shellac polish. This will remove any traces of watermarks that may have occurred when it was being steamed off.

18 Scrape any remaining baize from the rest of the table with a scraper and then use the scraper to fill any damage with wood filler. Protect the banding and stringing by covering them with masking tape.

19 Cut a piece of baize about 7.5cm/3in larger all around than the table and flap. Apply glue to the surface and lay the baize on top. Working from the centre, push the baize outward to remove any creases.

20 Cut the baize with a utility knife so that it lies flush with the inner edge of the banding. Take care to cut in an even line and not to cut the banding. Leave to dry. Remove the protective masking tape.

◄ 21 Seal the baize by heating a tooling wheel on a hotplate and then running it around the edge of the baize. Apply a firm, even pressure from start to finish.

Below MDF (medium-density fiberboard) does not warp easily so there should be little or no risk of this card table warping again.

Practical tip

If a surface is warped only slightly, it may be best to leave it as it is. To assess the extent of a warped surface, hold a long ruler alongside it. As a guide, if you can fit your little finger between the ruler and the surface, restoration is required.

Repairing a split pedestal table

Splits to table tops occur either along the grain of the wood or, if the top is made from glued boards, along the joints. Splits along the grain should be secured with butterfly keys (see p.484), but splits along the joints can simply be reglued and clamped.

The top of this mahogany pedestal table is made from two pieces of wood. The original glue that held them together has perished, allowing the pieces to separate and a gap to appear. The task of regluing is a relatively simple procedure – most of the work involved in this instance lies in dismantling and reassembling the table.

Materials

• screwdriver	• hammer
• chalk	• hardwood
• flat-bladed	block
knife	• mahogany
• drill	• grain plug
• flat-bottomed	cutter
grain plug	• fine brush
drill bit	• stain
• chisel	• rubber
• plane	• polish
• PVA (white)	• clean cotton
glue	rag
• sash clamps	• wax
• clamping	
blocks	

1 Place the table upside down on a protected workbench, and unscrew the column and legs from the bearers. Mark the position of each separate section of the table top with chalk.

2 Remove the decorative mahogany plugs that cover the steel screw heads on the rim, lifting them out with a flat-bladed knife. Place these in a labelled container for safe keeping (see Practical tip).

3 Unscrew each of the screws on the rim, remove them and place them in the container. Lift the rim from the underside of the table top and place it to one side.

Practical tip

Small fittings and fixtures are easy to lose, and if you are working on more than one piece of furniture, you may waste time trying to attach the fitting from one piece of furniture to another piece. To prevent this from happening, always store small parts from a single item of furniture – such as plugs, screws, hinges and knobs – together in a labelled container, such as a glass jar, a can or a box with a lid. Keep them on your workbench for easy access.

4 Drill out the wooden plugs that cover the screws in the bearers with a flat-bottomed grain plug drill bit, but stop short of the heads of the screws. Remove any remaining wood above the screw heads with a chisel.

5 Loosen the screws on the bearers with a screwdriver, remove them, and put them in the container. Lift the bearers from the top and place them to one side.

6 Set a plane to the shallowest cut possible and go over the mating edges of the top once or twice. Apply PVA (white) glue and clamp the pieces together. Tap down raised edges with a hammer and a hardwood block.

7 Cut new plugs from a piece of mahogany using a grain plug cutter. Taper one end of each plug with a chisel, making small grooves down the length at the same time.

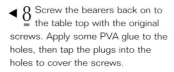

◀ 8 Screw the bearers back on to the table top with the original screws. Apply some PVA glue to the holes, then tap the plugs into the holes to cover the screws.

▶ 9 Pare the plugs down with a chisel until they are flush with the bearers. Avoid scratching the bearers as far as possible.

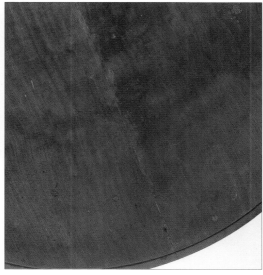

Left The gap between the sections of the top has gone. This technique is quick and simple, and produces a very satisfying result.

10 Mix a water- or spirit- (alcohol-) based stain to match the bearers and apply with a brush. When the stain is dry, attach the column and legs. Charge a rubber with polish and apply a light layer to the table top (see pp.356–7), then add a wax finish (see p.358).

DROP-LEAF TABLE

DURING THE EARLY 18TH CENTURY, the drop-leaf table became a favoured type of dining table. This design allowed the table to be stored with its flaps down when not in use, thus saving space. Nowadays, such tables are still extremely popular, and are particularly practical in modern homes where space may be at a premium. Unfortunately, like so many other items of antique furniture, drop-leaf tables may have led hard lives and may now suffer from all manner of ills, ranging from stained and discoloured tops to severe damage to the structure.

Assessing the project

This George II table, constructed in c.1745, is made from dense red walnut, and its distinctive moulded pad-foot design suggests that it is Irish in origin. It has sustained a sprung glue line in a panel on the flap, which reveals a previous dowel-joint repair. There is also veneer and bracket damage to the carcass, several pieces of one of the feet are missing, and one of the swing legs has broken off and been lost, so needs to be replaced.

The top

- split top, previously repaired with dowels
- watermarks and scratches

The legs

- foot broken
- one swing leg missing

The carcass

- veneer missing
- damaged shoulder
- broken brackets

Repairing the top

Damp caused the glue joining two sections of the table top to perish, producing a split. This revealed an earlier dowel-joint repair. As the dowels were in good condition, they can be incorporated into the new repair. The table top is also marred with various marks and scratches, so the surface needs to be revived thoroughly.

Materials

- screwdriver
- chalk
- pliers
- plane
- PVA (white) glue
- sash clamps
- long clamping blocks

1 Place the table upside down on a protected workbench. Remove the fixing screws and put the frame and legs aside. Now the frame is off, the pivoted gates and the remaining swing leg can be lifted clear.

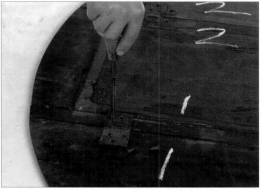

2 Unscrew the flap hinges from the main section of the table top. Mark the underside of the top with chalk so that you can tell which flap belongs on which side. Remove the dowels with pliers.

3 Place the main section of the top in a vice and plane the split side of the wood until smooth. Do not take off too much wood, as this will reduce the width of the table. Repeat for the other split side.

4 Apply PVA (white) glue along both split edges, replace the dowels and secure with sash clamps and long clamping blocks. Leave to dry, then remove the clamps.

Repairing the carcass

The framework of the table is in good order and does not need to be knocked apart and reglued. There are, however, missing areas of veneer and two brackets that have fallen off and need refitting. One of the shoulders is also damaged. Due to the untouched patination of the piece, only old surface breaker veneer is used for repairs.

Refixing the brackets

One of the brackets had broken cleanly off and needed gluing back in place. A second bracket had also fallen off, due to damage at the point where it joined the table leg. This meant that the shoulder needed to be repaired before the bracket could be refixed in place.

Materials

- toothbrush
- PVA (white) glue
- spring clips
- tenon saw
- red walnut
- plane
- G-clamp
- clamping blocks
- gouges
- fine-grade sandpaper

◄ 1 Remove the old glue from both the brackets that have fallen off using a toothbrush and hot water. Refit the bracket that sits under the missing veneer patch using PVA (white) glue. Use spring clips (see p.469) to hold the bracket in place while the glue dries

◄ 2 Turning now to the leg with the damaged shoulder, use a fine tenon saw to cut away a small section to allow for an inset patch to be applied. Cut a new section from a piece of red walnut.

► 3 Glue and clamp the new piece of wood in place. When it is dry, plane it flush with the shoulder. There is now a level surface to which the bracket can be reattached.

4 Glue the original bracket back into place, sandwiching the new wood between the leg and the bracket. Clamp until dry. Using a shaped gouge, pare away the excess wood to give a smooth, flowing repair.

5 With a smaller, rounded gouge, carve the moulded edge to the bracket, so that the repair is unnoticeable.

6 Finally, finish the repair by using fine-grade sandpaper to remove any rough edges. Take care not to mark the polished areas.

Replacing the veneer

Parts of the decorative veneer on the base have become detached and been lost after the animal glue has perished. The veneer must be replaced with matching old surface veneer.

Materials

- old veneers
- toothing plane
- craft (utility) knife
- PVA (white)
- glue
- clamping blocks
- G-clamps
- fine-grade sandpaper

◀ 1 Select a few possible replacement veneers for the missing patch on the frame, and hold them by the table to see which provides the best match to the original, paying attention to grain and colour.

◀ 2 Before laying the new piece of veneer, remove all traces of the old animal glue with the iron from a toothing plane. Scrape away only the residue of old glue without altering the actual groundwork.

◀ 3 Trim the veneer to roughly the correct size and glue it into position. Make sure that the veneer is laid with the grain pattern running in the correct direction, otherwise the repair will be all too obvious.

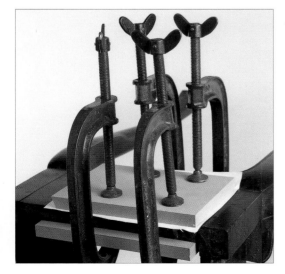

◀ 4 Place some paper on top of the veneer and then put clamping blocks on either side of the damaged frame. Clamp securely with G-clamps and leave to dry. Remove the clamps and blocks.

5 Hold one of the clamping blocks at an angle against the front of the frame to form a cutting base. Use a craft (utility) knife to trim the veneer, following the outline of the carcass, then sand the edge.

Repairing the legs

This table is unusual because it has two different styles of leg. The four fixed corner legs are cabriole with shaped lozenge feet. One of these feet has been damaged and needs to be rebuilt. The other two legs, which are swing legs, are turned club legs with small pad feet. They are attached to the frame by swing gates, which support the table flap when it is lifted. One of these swing legs in now missing and a replacement must be made to match the remaining leg.

Turning a new leg

Legs on tables seldom break into pieces, but if they do sustain substantial structural damage, they must be replaced, as it is important that they are extremely robust and strong. One of the swing legs on this red walnut drop-leaf table had been removed, then misplaced, so a new leg needs to be turned and fitted.

Materials	
• red walnut	• callipers
• steel straightedge	• turning tools
• tenon saw	• dividers
• drill	• fine-grade
• wood drill bit	sandpaper
• lathe	

1 Cut a piece of red walnut slightly larger than the final size of the leg. Mark the centre of each end of the block by drawing two diagonal lines with a steel straightedge. Cut a shallow groove along one of the lines at one end with a tenon saw.

2 Drill a hole in the centre of each end, about 1cm/⅜in deep. The tail stock of the lathe will be housed in the end with just the hole, and the head stock will sit in the end with the groove and hole.

3 Secure the block of walnut in the lathe and make a shallow cut with a tenon saw where the turned area will finish and the square section will begin.

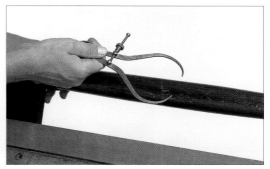

4 Use callipers to measure the widest part of the other swing leg so that you can turn the new leg to the correct size.

5 Turn the wood until you achieve the required diameter. Check the size of the new leg frequently with the callipers so that you do not inadvertantly remove too much wood.

6 Use dividers to transcribe the various dimensions of the decorative foot area from the other swing leg.

7 Turn the decorative parts of the leg with a very small gouge. Always remove less wood than you think you should, at first, and take measurements regularly from the existing leg.

8 Once you have turned the leg to the correct shape, use fine-grade sandpaper to finish off and smooth it. Remove the leg from the lathe and cut it to shape.

Cutting the mortise

The newly turned leg now needs to have a mortise cut into the square section that was left at the top. The leg can then be attached to the tenon on the gate.

Materials

- try square
- craft (utility) knife
- mortise gauge
- G-clamp
- clamping blocks
- mortise chisel
- cardboard
- tenon saw
- PVA (white) glue
- sash clamp
- fine-grade sandpaper
- bichromate of potash
- fine brushes
- water-based stain
- rubber
- shellac polish
- screwdriver

1 Detach the other swing leg from its gate and place the new leg side by side with it. Using a try square and a craft (utility) knife, mark across the shoulder lines.

2 Set a mortise gauge to match the width of the tenon on the swing gate that belonged to the missing leg.

3 Mark the correct position of the mortise between the scribed shoulder lines on the new leg.

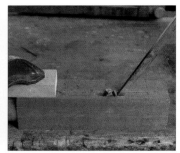

4 Clamp the leg securely to the workbench, using a clamping block to stop any possible bruising to the leg, and cut out the mortise with a mortise chisel of a suitable size.

5 Take a cardboard template (pattern) of the top of the other swing leg, then mark out this shape on the top of the new leg. Cut away the unwanted wood with a tenon saw.

6 Apply PVA (white) glue to the end of the original tenon and insert it into the newly cut mortise. Clamp the joint under pressure using a sash clamp and clamping blocks. Leave the joint to dry then remove the clamp and blocks.

7 Sand the top of the leg with fine-grade sandpaper, wetting the wood in between sandings to raise the grain. The benefit of this is that the grain will not be raised when a water-based stain is applied.

8 Apply a thin layer of bichromate of potash to the entire new leg. This will change the reddish tone of the walnut to a more suitable brown.

9 After selecting and mixing a suitable water-based stain, apply this to the leg to match the other swing leg.

10 Charge a rubber with shellac polish and apply it to the leg. Distress the leg to match the other swing leg.

Repairing a foot

One of the pad feet has various broken and missing parts, which, due to their damaged edges, cannot simply be reglued, and so must be replaced. A template (pattern) must be taken of an undamaged foot, so that the extent of the repairs can be determined and the new pieces of wood cut to size.

Materials

• profile gauge	• coping saw
• mount card (stock)	• rasp
	• carving tools
• red walnut	• bichromate of
• tenon saw	potash
• PVA (white) glue	• fine brushes
	• polish
• spring clips	• clean cotton
• craft (utility) knife	rag
	• fine pumice
• block plane	powder

◀ 1 Draw the outline of an undamaged foot using a profile gauge (see p.384) on a piece of stiff mount card (stock). This will be used as a template (pattern) to repair the damaged foot.

▶ 2 Place the damaged foot on the template and mark along the broken edges. This will indicate what shape and size the new pieces of red walnut need to be. Cut the pieces of walnut to a suitable size to fill the gaps. Glue them into place one piece at a time so that you build up the profile. This gives extra strength.

3 Using a tenon saw, trim the excess wood away, but remember that the foot has yet to be shaped, so allow enough extra thickness for the shaping to be done.

4 To get the profile of the undamaged foot's chamfer, make a second template, this time of the bottom of the complete foot. Cut it out and place it on the bottom of the foot being restored and mark the outline.

5 Using a small block plane, follow the mark on the bottom of the foot to obtain the correct chamfer. Remember to work with the grain and not across it, as this would result in the wood tearing.

◀ 6 Use a coping saw to create the shape of the actual pad foot. The coping saw allows an angled cut to be made, which helps to shape the foot.

▶ 7 Use a rasp to shape the desired profile. Do not to go too far, because there is still a raised lozenge foot to be carved.

8 By cross-referencing to an undamaged foot and by following the line of the raised decoration on the original leg, sculpt the moulding on the restored foot.

9 Give the new wood a thin coat of bichromate of potash – a chemical stain that will react with the tannin of the wood and change the walnut's natural red tone to a more suitable brown.

10 Brush on a thin layer of polish to fill the grain of the walnut. Put some polish on a cotton rag and sprinkle some fine pumice powder on it. Use this to work the polish into the grain, blending the old and new surfaces.

Reassembling and polishing

With all the structural work now complete, the restored table can be reassembled. The old screws will be used again and as all parts were labelled prior to disassembling, and the correct position of the top marked, this should be a fairly straightforward process.

Materials

- screwdriver
- methylated spirits (methyl alcohol)
- clean cotton rags
- fine brush
- stain
- rubber
- polish
- wax

1 Turn the table top upside down and place it on a protected workbench to avoid any unnecessary scratches or marks. Screw the frame and legs back in place, as well as the gates for the two swing legs, using the original screws.

2 Put some methylated spirits (methyl alcohol) on a cotton rag and cut back the surface, taking care to remove as little of the original surface as possible. Attend to any surface scratches or marks (see pp.344–9).

3 Stain the repairs (see p.359). Polish the table (see pp.356–7) and when it has hardened, wax and burnish it (p.358).

Above The restored table, with its brackets refitted, missing veneer replaced, foot repaired, a new swing leg attached and the surface revived and polished, can be fully enjoyed and appreciated once again.

DISMANTLING AND REBUILDING CHESTS

It is unusual to have to dismantle a chest of drawers, but you may have to do this when a chest has become very loose or when a side or top has been badly damaged and must be removed from the chest in order to be repaired.

The techniques required and steps taken are equally applicable for the majority of carcass furniture, such as bureaus, bookcases or tallboys. The main consideration is to examine the construction of the piece closely prior to commencement to make sure that no unnecessary damage is caused to either the constituent parts or joints during the dismantling process. All polished areas should be laid on a protective surface and any hammer blows or pressure to dismantle joints should be applied next to joints to ensure that no unnecessary splintering occurs.

Dismantling the chest

This George III chest, 1760, has become loose and a split has appeared in the top. It is a typical example of 18th-century carcass construction, and closer examination shows that there are no through dovetails that have been veneered over, and no nails or screws have been added to give strength at a later date. Before any work can be done, the chest must be dismantled.

Materials

- chalk
- hardwood lengths and blocks
- nails
- hammers
- mallet
- wide chisel
- flat-bladed knife

1 The back of the chest consists of a number of boards. Their location should be marked before removal; a suitable method is to mark them with chalk lines, as shown here.

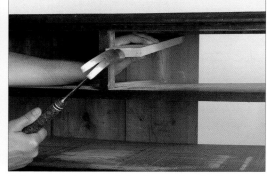

2 Remove the backboards by placing a length of hardwood against the location of the holding nails and tapping it with a hammer. Make sure that only the areas nailed are struck, to avoid unnecessary splintering of the boards.

3 Remove the kickers, which help to make the drawers run level, as well as the wedges, which hold the dust boards in place, by using a mallet to tap a wide chisel between each board and kicker.

5 Remove the dust boards from the long drawers by knocking them out either backward or forward (depending on the construction of the chest). Place a hardwood block between the board and hammer to avoid any unnecessary damage to the wood.

7 Having removed the dust boards from the long drawers, there still remains the frame from the two short drawers, which is jointed with the twin drawer centre stile. In this case the joint is a through tenon, and therefore the stile and frame must be knocked apart.

4 Remove both facing strips, which cover the rebates (rabbets) for the dust boards along the front edges, by sliding a flat-bladed knife along the glue line. Use a hammer to help the knife move down each facing edge.

6 As well as being nailed together, the top and side joints are given extra strength by glue blocks. Remove these by placing a chisel behind each block in turn and giving it a sharp blow with a mallet. The glue line holding the blocks should come away easily.

►8 Remove the top from the sides using a hammer and hardwood block as for the backboards. Slide out the remaining dust board. Now lift the remainder of the carcass clear of the workbench with the aid of a helper and place it the right way up.

◀ **9** Now dismantle the sides, which are dovetailed into the base, using a hammer and hardwood block, as before. Tap the base while lifting one side clear, then repeat for the other side.

▼ **10** The chest is now dismantled. The feet have not been removed to prevent further damage to the chest of drawers.

Reassembling the chest

When the necessary repairs have been made (in this case, the table had developed a split top, which needed gluing together), the chest of drawers can be rebuilt.

Materials

• toothbrush	• clamping	• masking tape
• PVA (white)	blocks	• nails
glue	• snap clamps	• animal glue
• clean cotton	• gauge sticks	• rubber
rags	• hammer	• polish
• sash clamps	• length of	• wax
	hardwood	

1 Remove traces of the old animal glue using an old toothbrush and hot water. The water will soften the glue and enable it to be removed without any damage to the actual joints.

◀ 2 Apply only a small amount of PVA (white) glue to the joints between the sides and bottom, then refit the sides and the drawer frame. Wipe away any excess glue with a cotton rag immediately. Apply sash clamps and a snap clamp.

3 Before the glue sets, fit a drawer to check that the drawer frame is square, and check the carcass for squareness using gauge sticks.

◀ 5 Glue the top back on and clamp it securely into place with snap clamps and sash clamps. Refit the old glue blocks using animal glue. Leave to dry. Also reglue the facing strips, holding them in position with masking tape while they dry.

4 Slide the long dust boards back into position, then gently tap the kickers and wedges back into place using a length of hardwood to guard against unnecessary bruising.

◀ 6 Finally, nail the backboards back into place, remembering to match up the chalk lines to ensure the correct positioning.

Right With the chest reassembled, any surfaces that need it can be revived, polished and waxed, and any missing handles replaced.

REPAIRING CARCASSES AND TOPS

Traditionally, carcasses are very strong and rarely suffer serious structural damage in normal use. Exceptions occur when changes in humidity cause carcasses and tops to crack, heavy doors put undue strain on hinges, and plinths and feet become scuffed and damaged. None of these problems is insurmountable, provided the correct repair and restoration techniques are employed, and the results can be very pleasing.

Repairing a split top

Changes in humidity can cause chest tops to split in exactly the same way that table tops split. If a split occurs along the line where two pieces of wood are joined, they can simply be reglued and clamped to secure. If a split occurs away from a natural join, the top must be repaired with butterfly keys.

This c.1845 pine chest of drawers, veneered in Cuban mahogany, has a split top, due to the pine core shrinking away from the mahogany until the resulting tension caused the core to split apart. The mouldings must be removed, the split must be separated and reglued and then re-secured with butterfly keys, glued into cut-outs routed into the underside of the top.

Above right
The split in the top.

Materials

• hammer	• chisel
• hardwood block	• jack plane
• flat-bladed knife	• water-based stain
• tenon saw	• fine brushes
• PVA (white) glue	• cabinet scraper
• sash clamps	• fine-grade sandpaper
• clamping blocks	• rubber
• softwood	• polish
• deep-throated clamps	• stopping wax
• cardboard	• spirit- (alcohol-) based stain
• craft (utility) knife	• clean cotton rag
• router	• wax

1 Remove the top from the carcass using a hammer and hardwood block and place it upside down on a protected workbench. Blocks of wood had been glued to the underside in a previous attempt to repair the split. Remove these now with a flat-bladed knife, then turn the top over.

2 Carefully cut the mahogany long-grain mouldings that pass the end of the split from the pine core with a tenon saw. The mouldings have not split, and so they can be removed intact and reglued later (see step 5). Apply PVA (white) glue along the split in the top.

3 Clamp the width of the top together using sash clamps and clamping blocks. Place a piece of paper, then a piece of softwood, along the length of the split, then secure both with deep-throated clamps to make sure the two parts of the top remain level. Leave to dry.

4 Cut butterfly keys from pine and rout matching holes along the underside of the split (see p.484). Glue in the keys and plane them down until flush with the underside. Stain the keys to match the top.

5 Turn the top over and work along the split with a cabinet scraper to remove any loose veneer. Take great care to scrape only along the split, to avoid damaging the rest of the veneer. Reglue any un-split mouldings.

6 Smooth the area along the split by rubbing with fine-grade sandpaper. Avoid sanding too wide an area around the split.

7 Charge a rubber with polish and apply a layer to the split area to conceal any tiny missing areas of veneer (see pp.356–7). The split will now be almost invisible.

8 Select a stopping wax to match the colour and tone of the veneer. Fill the small areas of missing veneer with the wax, using a flat-bladed knife.

9 Mix a spirit- (alcohol-) based stain to match the colour and tone of the veneer, and apply it to the sanded and polished area. This will blend the two pieces together and help to mask the joint.

10 Put the top back on. Treat the entire top with a wax chosen to match the colour and tone of the veneer. Take care not to rub too hard on the split area, because you risk removing the applied colour and wax.

Left Now stained and waxed, the split is almost invisible. With the inset butterfly keys on the underside securing the joint, no further restoration should be necessary.

Replacing a bracket foot

The bracket foot was introduced during the early 18th century and remained basically unchanged in its construction through the rest of the century. When replacing a single missing foot, you can copy one of the remaining feet, but if all the feet are missing you will need to seek advice from an expert in this field to determine the correct shape and style required. This chest of drawers is missing one of its mahogany feet, although some of the glue blocks remain.

Materials

- cardboard
- craft (utility) knife
- mahogany
- coping saw or band saw
- jack plane
- mitre box
- scotch glue
- spring clips
- softwood
- rasp
- chisel
- screwdriver
- rubber
- polish
- fine brush
- stain

1 Make a cardboard template (pattern) of one of the remaining feet and mark this outline twice on the selected old surface mahogany, once for each side of the foot.

2 Cut out both pieces of the foot by hand with a coping saw or by machine with a band saw. Plane the joining mitres with a jack plane, ideally using a mitre box.

3 Attach both parts of the foot to the carcass and each other with scotch glue. Rub each part back and forth a few times to create suction between the foot and carcass, then apply pressure with spring clips.

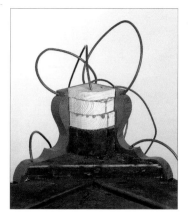

◀ 4 Cut new glue blocks from softwood. With the clips still in place, glue these blocks, into position and secure them with more spring clips. Leave them slightly proud of the foot so that they can be trimmed flush later. This will help to distribute the weight.

5 If the foot parts were cut with a band saw, use a rasp to remove the blade marks that will have been left. Note the wear patterns on the opposite original foot and try to mirror them.

6 Trim the glue blocks flush with a chisel or plane. Round over all the sharp edges with the shank of a screwdriver. This mimics the natural process of years of waxing and handling. Also, if a clean piece of mahogany has been used to make the foot, add a few knocks to match the existing feet.

Left Polish the exterior of the foot, and stain the interior and the glue blocks. The new foot now matches the carcass in grain, colour and finish. The wear and patination also match the other feet on the chest, and no casual observer should be able to spot the replacement.

Spring clips

There are numerous types of clamp designed to help in the restoration of antique furniture. One of the most versatile, used for difficult and awkward clamping, is the spring clip. This is home-made from old upholstery springs, and is ideal for applying pressure or simply holding small pieces of wood or furniture in place.

◀ 1 Choose a large old upholstery spring; this will allow you to make several clips of different sizes. The spring steel will keep its shape and will apply considerable pressure when pulled apart.

2 Using a bench grinder, cut through the tensile-steel spring at two points to form a circular clip, the two ends of which should meet. When pulled apart, the natural curve of the spring should give the necessary pressure to hold any parts together.

3 Grind a point on each end of the clip. These points will make sure that the clip remains in place when it is being used.

4 When completed, the clip can be used for a variety of awkward clamping tasks. To keep the tension, push the two end points until they overlap, then pull them apart and place them in the required holding position.

REPAIRING DRAWERS

Prior to the late 17th century, the majority of drawers would have run on rebated (rabbeted) side drawer runners. After this time, the runners were fitted on the bottom of the drawer. Due to their constant action, drawer stops and drawer runners are sometimes worn away. A sure sign that they need to be replaced is when a drawer begins to stick. Failure to attend to this can, in extreme cases, make the chest unusable.

Replacing cock beading

Cock beading is the name given to the moulding that runs around the edge of inset drawers. This decorative feature, which was introduced during the early 18th century, also protects the edge of applied veneers from flaking and splitting. Sometimes the beading can become loose or broken due to being snagged. On this drawer, part of the beading had become detached and lost and another part was damaged.

Materials

- paring chisel
- mahogany
- craft (utility) knife
- PVA (white) glue
- spring clips
- block plane
- fine-grade sandpaper
- fine brush
- stain
- rubber
- polish

1 Using a paring chisel, remove the damaged area of cock beading. Select a piece of mahogany for the new beading.

2 Cut 45-degree mitres with a sharp craft (utility) knife at either end of the new cock beading. Glue it in place with PVA (white) glue and hold it with spring clips (see p.469).

3 Cut a piece of cock beading to replace the missing beading. Cut 45-degree mitres at both ends, then secure the piece as in step 2.

4 When the glue is dry, use a block plane to remove any excess wood so that the beading is flush with the side of the drawer.

5 As the cock beading will almost certainly have a rounded edge this can be first shaped using a small paring chisel and followed by papering with fine-grade sandpaper.

Above The new cock beading should be stained and polished to match the existing beading, with efforts made to match any light distressing on the original.

Replacing drawer runners

The drawer runners on this drawer have been completely worn away in places. Further damage has been done by the carcass drawer stops, which have grooved trenches into the drawer bottom. The damaged runners must be removed and replaced with new ones.

Materials

- flat-bladed knife
- hammer
- smoothing plane
- beech or mahogany
- tenon saw
- PVA (white) glue
- snap clamps
- toothbrush
- plane
- chisel

1 If the runners are glued to the sides and bottom, tap a flat-bladed knife slid between the runner and the side to break the joint.

2 Remove the damaged runners from the bottom by sliding the knife underneath and gently tapping it with the hammer.

3 Use the iron from a smoothing plane to remove any traces of old and perished glue.

4 Choose a similar wood to the old runners (usually beech or mahogany) and cut some runners to the same width and length as the old ones, but deeper to allow for planing at a later stage. Glue them into place.

5 Hold the new runners firmly in place with snap clamps and leave to dry. Remove any excess glue using a toothbrush and water.

6 This drawer also had runners attached to the exterior of the drawer sides, and these too had become worn. Remove and replace these with new ones, as before, gluing them to the replacement bottom runners.

◄ 7 When dry, plane the runners to the correct depth to enable the drawer to sit evenly in the carcass. This is very much a case of trial and error, but take care not to plane the runners too thin, or the drawer will sit unevenly.

► 8 The final touch is to cut an angled mitre at the back of each runner. This will help the drawer to run smoothly as well as preventing snagging.

◀ 9 Use a sharp chisel to cut a bevel at the back of each mitred runner. This will make removing the drawer and inserting it back into the carcass much easier.

Right With its new runners in place, the drawer will slide smoothly and freely.

Replacing drawer stops

Drawer stops are designed to prevent a drawer from sliding in too far, and ensure that all the drawers line up correctly when closed. Stops are normally fitted so that they come into contact with the back of the drawer front, although they may be placed at the back of the drawer. If the runners wear, the stops may also become worn. In this case, the stops had worn away to expose their fixing nails, which had gouged the drawer bottoms.

Materials

- flat-bladed knife
- hammer
- pincers
- tenon saw
- wood blocks
- PVA (white) glue
- pins (tacks)

1 Using a flat-bladed knife and a hammer, gently tap the knife between the worn stops and the carcass, and lift the stops away.

3 Insert one of the drawers into the carcass. Pulling the drawer forward slightly, measure the gap between the drawer bottom and the carcass. Cut a block of wood to a thickness that will be less than this measurement, to ensure that it does not interfere with the smooth running of the drawer, then cut it into two squares of suitable size. Repeat for the other drawers.

2 When the stops have been removed, they may leave behind the fixing nails. Remove these with a pair of pincers.

4 Glue the new drawer stops to the carcass, setting them slightly forward of the original positions. Before the glue has dried, insert both drawers, carefully aligning them with the front of the chest. This will push the blocks into their correct positions. Leave the glue to dry before removing the drawers. If extra strength is required, drive a few pins (tacks) through the stops.

Cutting a dovetail joint

The dovetail joint was one of the most common types of joint used in the construction of furniture in the 18th and 19th centuries. In the main, it was used when two flat sections overlapped each other and a strong, secure joint was required, such as in carcass, plinth, drawer and cornice construction. Small dovetails can be difficult to cut, and the skill of the cabinet-maker is demonstrated by the quality of his dovetails.

This drawer, which dates from 1780, has lost one of its sides, but fortunately the interior parts used to house the ink bottles have survived. Before work starts, the drawer must be dismantled by gently tapping it apart using a cabinet hammer and a block of protective hardwood. The drawer dovetails are finer than normal so care must be taken not to damage them during the dismantling process. The drawer was made from Cuban mahogany, and a piece of matching wood must be found for the new side. Once the new dovetail joints have been cut, the drawer can be reassembled.

Materials	
• Cuban mahogany	• chisel
• tenon saw	• mallet
• marking gauge	• hammer
• craft (utility) knife	• hardwood blocks
• fine dovetail saw	• mortise gauge
• G-clamp	• narrow chisel or router
• clamping blocks	• PVA (white) glue

1 Dismantle the drawer. Find a matching piece of mahogany for the new side. If the colour is slightly different, it can be stained to match at a later stage, but it is important that the grain is the same. Cut it to the same size as the existing drawer side.

2 Measure the length of the dovetail pins on the existing drawer side, then mark them out on both ends of the new side using a marking gauge.

3 Hold the front of the drawer against the corresponding end of the new side transfer the pin lines with a craft (utility) knife. Repeat with the back, holding it against the other end of the new side.

4 Place the side in a vice with the marked lines held vertical. Using a fine dovetail saw, cut along the waste side of the marked lines. This will help to achieve good tight joints.

5 Clamp the side to a flat piece of wood and use a sharp chisel and a mallet to cut halfway through the top of the waste wood. Turn the side over and cut through from the other side. This will ensure a clean cut.

6 Some drawer bottoms are nailed in place, but this one is housed in a groove. Mark this groove on the new side with a mortise gauge set to the thickness of the bottom.

7 Cut the new groove for the drawer bottom with a narrow chisel or a router.

8 Tap the dovetail joint gently together with a small hammer and a hardwood block. The joint should be tight with no gaps. If necessary, make small adjustments by paring the wood with a craft knife.

Left The drawer can now be reassembled and the internal parts glued back into place.

Cutting a dovetail housing

1 Lay the newly cut dovetail pins against the end grain of the corresponding piece of wood. Mark the outline of the pins clearly with a utility knife.

2 Measure the depth of the pins with a marking gauge, then score a line across the wood. Use a dovetail saw to cut on the waste side of the marked lines for a good fit, using the scored line as a depth guide.

3 Bring the two parts of the joint together. It should be tight with no gaps. Apply a small amount of glue, then remake the joint. Before it sets, check that the drawer is square by using gauge sticks (see p.416).

Repairing a split drawer bottom

During the 18th and 19th centuries, drawer bottoms were made up from a number of pieces. They were then either slotted into grooved drawer sides or nailed flush. Due to the fact that wood will shrink across its grain, it is not uncommon to find that the original glue line has come away with the shrinkage of the various sections of a drawer bottom, leaving gaps. This drawer has an unsightly gap, so the bottom must be removed and the gap reglued before the drawer can be reassembled.

Materials

- chalk
- stiff-bladed knife
- hammer
- smoothing plane
- PVA (white) glue
- sash clamps
- clamping blocks
- nails
- clean cotton rag

1 Mark the underside of the various pieces of the drawer bottom with chalk before removing them. This shows which way around the boards should be and also how the parts join together.

2 The bottom slides into grooves on the drawer sides but is nailed to the drawer back, and the nails have been punched below the surface. To remove them, insert a stiff-bladed knife between the wood and the back, then tap it with a hammer to cut through the nails.

3 Remove the bottom pieces and clean off the old glue with the iron from a smoothing plane. Replace the bottom pieces in the correct order, applying a small amount of PVA (white) glue along the glue lines.

4 Clamp the bottom pieces together with a sash clamp and clamping blocks, and nail the back piece to the drawer back at the same time. Finally, wipe off any excess glue and chalk marks with a clean cotton rag.

Right Once restored, the drawer bottom will be gap-free, giving an aesthetically more pleasing appearance.

REPAIRING DOORS

The doors in pieces of furniture can suffer from a number of problems, some of which are easier to put right than others. Broken glass is common in glazed doors, while doors of all types can stick in their openings or become distorted. As with other types of furniture, any carved detail or mouldings may be damaged over the years, while the hardware (hinges, catches and locks) can also give trouble.

Repairing a glazed door

From the late 17th century onward, glass was introduced into furniture construction. It was hand blown and rolled into very thin sheets. During both the 18th and 19th centuries, the style of the glazing bars, or astragals, found in bookcase and cabinet doors varied greatly, but the actual method of securing the glass remained fairly constant.

This door is from a mid-18th-century bookcase. One of the smaller panes has been cracked and so needs to be replaced. Once the glass has been removed, a new pane must be inserted. This will be held in place with plaster rather than putty. Once dry, the plaster can be stained to match the original putty. There are various sources for suitable glass (see Selecting glass, p.478).

Materials

- iron
- chisel
- glass
- methylated spirits (methyl alcohol)
- fine wire (steel) wool
- felt-tipped pen
- diamond-tipped glass cutter
- steel straightedge
- plaster
- ochre
- flat-bladed knife
- fine brush
- water-based stain

1 First, remove the original mid-18th century putty. Do this by heating the putty with an iron to soften it.

2 When the putty is soft, begin to pare it away with a sharp chisel.

3 Remove all the old putty from the back of the astragal with the chisel, making sure not to cut into the wood supports, since this would weaken the construction of the door.

4 When the putty has been removed, carefully lift out the broken pieces of glass (you may wish to wear protective gloves for this job). If the glass is antique and hand blown, do not discard any pieces of a reasonable size, but store them carefully for a possible later use.

5 Period hand-blown glass was often not flat but uneven in texture, so it was bedded on to a putty base to counter any movement. This was the case in this door, so pare away the bedding putty as well.

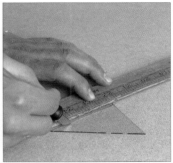

6 Clean your selected piece of glass using methylated spirits (methyl alcohol) and fine wire (steel) wool, and check that it matches the existing glass in both colour and type.

7 Place the glass over the astragal and mark out the shape with a felt-tipped pen.

8 Using a diamond-tipped glass cutter, scribe along the marked line and cut the glass to size and shape.

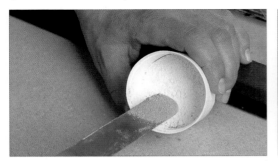

9 Putty was used to hold the original glass in this door, and you could use putty to fix the new pane, but it takes several days to harden fully. A better choice is plaster, which hardens in minutes and can be pre-coloured. Mix the plaster with a small quantity of ochre before stirring in the water.

10 The glass will not be completely flat, so apply a small layer of plaster with a flat-bladed knife to act as a levelling base.

11 Press the glass gently into position on the wet plaster.

12 Apply more plaster with the knife and shape it into a bevel.

13 While the plaster is still malleable, trim away the excess with a chisel.

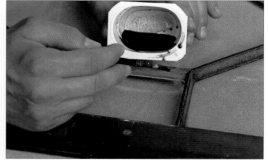

14 When the plaster is dry, stain it with a water-based stain mixed to match the colour of the original putty.

15 Apply a darker stain on top of the coloured plaster to try to mimic the patina of the original putty. This should blend the repaired glazed panel to match the others.

Right As the restored pane is of a matching glass and was fitted properly, it is undetectable from the original when viewed from the exterior.

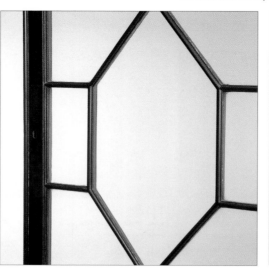

Selecting glass

It is always preferable to use an old piece of glass to replace glass lost from antique furniture, as new glass will stand out. While certain specialist glass manufacturers still supply old-style glass, the best sources are old picture frames and stocks collected from previous repairs, which can be cut down to the required size.

Repairing a sliding tambour

Sliding tambours were introduced in the 18th century. Their construction method is simple: lengths of wood are bonded to a cloth backing, which can be slid back and forth around a curve. Several lengths of wood have become loose on this 18th-century Dutch cabinet, and closer inspection revealed that a previous repair was causing the problem. The tambour must be detached from the cabinet, the pieces of wood removed from the old backing and reglued to a new linen cloth.

Materials

- masking tape
- flat-bladed knife
- long-shanked screwdriver
- smoothing plane
- Irish linen
- PVA (white) glue

1 The tambour is held in place only through tension, so, once the frieze at the top has been removed, pulling the top of the frieze should release it. Alternatively, the back of the cabinet may have to be removed.

2 Lay the tambour face up on a flat surface. Secure the lengths of wood with 5cm/2in strips of masking tape, laid at right angles to the strips, at 10cm/4in intervals.

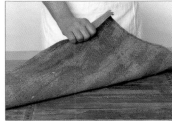

3 Turn the tambour over. Lift up a corner of the backing material with a flat-bladed knife, then pull it away and discard it.

4 Some metal strips from an earlier repair were revealed. These would have held the tambour together, but would have been too stiff to allow it to run freely. Use a long-shanked screwdriver to remove these strips. Scrape away any remains of glue with the iron from a smoothing plane.

5 Cut a piece of Irish linen to match the height and width of the tambour. Coat the back of the tambour with glue, then smooth the linen over the surface, making sure that there are no air bubbles or wrinkles. Leave to dry. Remove the masking tape and test the flexibility of the tambour by manipulating it into a curved shape, then refit it.

Above The restored sliding tambour, with its decorative parquetry frieze replaced, now operates smoothly in the cabinet.

Refitting a door

The door on this 18th-century wall cupboard has dropped due to wear on the pin hinge. This has resulted in the door no longer sitting square in the frame, and a gap can be seen at the top. The two alternatives are to have the hinge remade or to pack up the bottom of the door, which is an easier and quicker method.

Materials

- flat-bladed knife
- hammer
- tenon saw
- wood
- hand drill
- fine brush
- stain

1 Due to the construction of the cabinet, the hinges have been attached with hand-made clout nails rather than screws. Ease the nails out gently by tapping a flat-bladed knife in behind the hinge.

2 Fold the detached part of the hinge forward to reveal the housing. Cut a thin packing piece of wood to size and trim to fit in the recess of the housing. This will counteract the dropping of the hinge.

3 Drill pilot holes into the packing piece (see p.488). These will make sure that the original clout nails, which will be weakened by their age, will not shear off when they are refitted. Stain the packing piece to match the surrounding wood.

Left With the packing piece in place and the hinge replaced, the door once again sits squarely in its frame.

Correcting a minor twist

Doors come in many styles and designs, but one theme that is common to all doors is that they can warp, twist or bind due to climatic change. In extreme cases, the door may need to be completely remade, with the core wood being replaced. In most cases, however, there are a number of steps that can be taken to help alleviate the problem. The door on this mid-18th-century bookcase has twisted slightly and no longer closes flush against the opposite door. Since the problem is fairly minimal, a technique known as half and half (half packing/half paring) will be employed to correct the twist.

Materials

- screwdriver
- tenon saw
- wood
- hand drill
- wood drill bit
- chisel

1 Unscrew both hinges from the carcass and remove the bookcase door. Keep the original screws safely.

2 Cut a small packing piece of wood to fit in the bottom hinge recess. This will push the bottom of the door out slightly. Drill pilot holes for the screws and refit the hinge.

◀ 3 Pare down the top hinge recess slightly then refit the hinge. This will pull the top part of the door nearer to being flush with the opposite side. Both the packing and paring have an element of trial and error about them, so make small changes at a time and refit the door regularly to make sure that a correct balance is obtained. Note that the packed and pared areas do not need staining because they are completely covered by the refitted hinges.

Right With the corrective work undertaken, the door is once again able to close flush against the opposite side.

19TH-CENTURY DESK

WHEN THIS DESK WAS originally purchased, its age was unknown. It was not immediately apparent, therefore, whether or not it was worth carrying out restoration. After some investigation and upon close examination, however, it was discovered to be a 19th-century English oak-veneered writing desk, and, despite the generally distressed condition of the piece, it was indeed worth restoring to its former glory.

Assessing the project

The desk is damaged in several areas, particularly the top, the drawers and the carcass, with areas of veneer missing in some places. An initial assessment was made of each problem in order to decide in which order to proceed. The final decision was to split the restoration work into three sections – first the top, then the drawers and finally the carcass – after which the whole desk would be polished and cleaned.

The top

- split wood
- torn and worn leather

The carcass

- damage to frame supports
- splits to pedestal
- missing veneer on plinth corners

The drawers

- damaged runners
- missing knobs

Repairing the desk top

The wood of the desk top needs extensive restoration, but the leather is too badly damaged to be saved and so must be replaced. The first stage is to secure the splits in the wood from underneath using butterfly keys. Then the splits in the top surface should be filled, planed and polished, and finally some new leather applied.

Securing the splits

Although the splits in the desk top appear dramatic, they require one of the more straightforward repairs, using softwood butterfly keys that are inset and glued underneath the top at right angles to the split. These keys secure the split and so prevent any further movement.

Materials

• screwdriver	• toothing plane	• craft (utility) knife	• jack plane
• long pole	• cardboard	• router	• fine brush
• G-clamp	• softwood	• chisel	• water-based
• clamping block	• tenon saw	• PVA glue	stain or ochre

1 Remove the top drawers and lift the desk top and frame off the pedestals. Prise a corner of the leather free and wrap it around a long pole. Pull the leather gently away while rolling the pole toward you.

2 Remove the second piece of leather in the same way. As the leather is removed, you can assess the extent of the damage to the top. In this case, the splits in the top go right through the wood.

3 Secure the top to the workbench with a G-clamp and clamping block, then run a toothing plane over the wood to remove any old glue or pieces of leather.

4 To clean the edges, remove the iron from the toothing plane and scrape it along the surface, parallel to the polished edge, until no traces of old glue or leather remain.

5 Remove the clamp and turn the top over. In this instance, a previous owner had tried, unsuccessfully, to restore the desk top by screwing a wooden panel over the split. This has to be removed.

6 Detach the frame from the top by removing the recessed screws, known as pocket screws, with a screwdriver. This will provide complete access to the desk top. Set the frame aside for later repairs.

7 Make a cardboard template for the butterfly keys (see right). Mark out as many keys as you need on a piece of softwood and cut them out with a tenon saw.

Butterfly keys

Butterfly keys are dovetail-shaped blocks of wood that are inset at right-angles to a split, thus preventing the split from opening up further. They should be made from a soft-wood, such as pine, and their size and number depend upon the size of the split and the depth of the wood. In the case of a split that cannot be closed up, the keys will secure the surface in its current position. If the split can be glued and clamped (such as the Windsor chair, p.420), the keys will secure the glued join.

8 Place a butterfly key over one end of the first split, about 13cm/5in from the edge of the desk top, with the waist of the key directly over the split. Mark out the position of the key with a utility (craft) knife.

9 Cut an angled back chamfer around the key outline with the craft knife. This will prevent the edge from splintering when it is routed.

10 Set the depth stop on a router to slightly less than the thickness of the key, then cut out the marked key shape.

11 Use a sharp chisel to straighten the edges of the cuts. It is important to match the recess exactly to the shape of the key to ensure a snug fit. Continue cutting shapes at 23cm/9in intervals along all the splits.

12 Apply a thin coat of glue to each recess and press in a key. When they are dry, plane the keys level with the surface of the desk top using a jack plane.

13 Use a water-based stain or ochre that matches the colour of the wood to tint the keys. Although the underside of the desk top will not be seen, this is a finishing touch that should always be made.

Preparing the top

Any cracks or dents in the upper surface of the desk top will show through the leather, as the construction of the desk top made it simply impossible to glue the top together. Therefore, they must be filled and the top smoothed down. A two-part wood filler can be applied to smaller cracks, but larger splits also require filling with thin strips of wood. The veneer around the edge of the upper surface requires some patching, and must be cleaned and polished before the leather is applied.

Materials

- softwood
- tenon saw
- PVA (white) glue
- hammer
- chisel
- two-part wood filler
- putty knife
- smoothing plane
- veneer patch
- fine wire (steel) wool
- methylated spirits (methyl alcohol)
- rubber
- polish

1 Cut strips of softwood to the correct width and length to fit the larger splits snugly. Apply a generous amount of PVA (white) glue to the splits.

2 Put each sliver of wood over its split and set it in place by lightly tapping it down with a hammer. Wipe away the excess. Leave to dry.

3 Use a sharp chisel to pare away any excess wood. Continue until each insert is flush with the desk top.

4 Apply a two-part wood filler to all cracks and knot holes with a putty knife, packing the filler in well. Leave to dry.

5 Plane the surface with a smoothing plane to smooth off the filler and to produce a surface to which the leather can adhere.

6 Patch the damaged areas of veneer banding on the edge of the top, making sure the grain and figure match (see p.493).

7 Lightly rub the veneered edge with fine wire (steel) wool to remove any top wax and loose dirt. Always work in the direction of the grain, otherwise you will leave scratches.

8 Moisten the wire wool with methylated spirits (methyl alcohol) and lightly rub the veneered edge again. This will give a surface to which the new polish can adhere.

9 Charge a rubber with polish and apply a layer to the veneered edge to enhance the grain and colour of the veneer. A final polish will be applied when the desk is reassembled.

Leathering the top

The value of the desk demands that a best-quality piece of hide should be selected and purchased from a tannery. Prior to cutting it, examine it for scars, scratches and stretch marks, all of which will be emphasized when coloured and polished). Time taken at this stage will ensure that the finished result complements the rest of the restoration work undertaken.

Materials

- large brush
- PVA (white) glue
- leather
- "bone"
- craft (utility) knife
- clean cotton rags
- leather sealant
- water-based stain
- tooling wheel
- pressurized spray gun
- cellulose lacquer
- dividers
- roll of gold leaf
- steel rule
- decorative pattern wheel
- stamp
- wax (optional)

1 Spread PVA (white) glue evenly over the wood, making sure it covers the whole area, especially up to the edges. Lay the new piece of leather down on the desk top, making sure it covers the whole area.

2 With the aid of a tool known as a "bone", flatten out any blisters and uneven areas, working from the centre outward. Use the edge of the "bone" to make sure the leather is pushed into the corners.

3 Use a sharp craft (utility) knife to cut away the excess leather, taking care that the cut is accurate and no gaps are left. Use the edge of the veneer banding as a cutting guide.

4 When the leather is dry, wipe the surface with a leather sealant, applied with a cotton rag. This will make sure that the leather dyes will give an even covering and not become blotchy.

5 Apply a water-based stain with a cloth in a circular motion and gradually build the colour to the desired intensity. Avoid the veneer banding around the edge.

6 Heat a tooling wheel to create a decorative border. Apply even pressure and, once the wheel is rolling, do not stop until you reach the end of the leather.

7 With the leather fitted, coloured and sealed, the next stage is to lacquer it. To make sure the lacquer will not mark the veneer, mask it off (wrap it) with paper.

8 Using a pressurized spray gun, apply an even coat of cellulose lacquer. If necessary, apply a second coat once the first has dried. Lacquering gives a protective layer to the leather as well as locking in the colour and stopping it bleeding out.

9 When the lacquer has dried, and the paper has been removed, decide on a decorative border. There are many styles and patterns to choose from, but it is a good idea to seek advice on what would be suitable. Use dividers to decide the best proportions.

10 Lay a roll of gold leaf in place and put a steel rule on top, then run the tooling wheel along the leaf. Keep the pressure even and ensure the wheel is at spitting heat: if too hot, it will burn through the gilt, and if too cold, the gilt will not stick to the leather.

11 Apply a more decorative pattern wheel inset inside the original single line, working freehand. Carefully peel the gold leaf away.

12 Join the corners using a stamp, which again has been heated to spitting heat. This gives a neat appearance and completes the process. The top can now be sealed with a coat of wax or another thin layer of lacquer.

13 Finally, using a craft knife, carefully lift off any excess areas of gilt and tidy up the finish. Obtaining a perfectly straight and even line, like many restoration techniques, takes many years of practice.

Repairing the drawers

All the drawers are suffering from worn runners, which cause the drawers to sit unevenly and to stick. Two of the drawers are also missing knobs, which need replacing, and there are several patches of chipped and missing veneer to be restored.

Replacing the runners

Drawer runners are often attached to the drawer bottoms, and are designed to allow the drawer to run smoothly and evenly in the carcass. In this case they are attached to the drawer sides, so the drawer will have to be dismantled before work can begin. Remove the plinths first; these will be repaired at a later stage.

Materials

- masking tape
- marker pen
- stiff-bladed knife
- hammer
- hardwood block
- circular saw
- mahogany
- PVA (white) glue
- snap clamps
- flat piece of wood
- plane
- gauge sticks
- small pins (tacks)
- G-clamps

1 Remove the drawers from the pedestals and place them on the workbench. Label each part of each drawer in a way that identifies not only which drawer it belongs to but also its position within that drawer.

2 Starting with the first drawer, slide the bottom out of the frame. You may need to remove small pins in order to be able to do this (see p.475, step 2). Put the drawer bottom to one side.

3 Stand the drawer up and place a hardwood block on the inside of one of the sides. Gently knock the block with a hammer until the dovetail joints loosen and the pieces come apart.

4 Using a circular saw with the fence set, cut a small amount from the drawer runner. This is to provide a parallel edge for the new wood to attach to. Note that the guard has been removed for the photograph.

5 Cut a straight strip of matching mahogany to the same length as, but marginally deeper than, the drawer side and glue it to the freshly cut edge of the runner. Apply snap clamps and leave to dry.

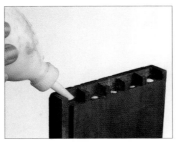

6 Place a flat length of wood between the drawer side and the workbench, then clamp them both securely to the bench. Plane the edge of the runner flush with the drawer side. Repeat steps 2–6 for all the other worn drawer runners.

7 Now all the drawers can be reassembled. Apply only a small amount of PVA (white) glue to the inside of the dovetails on the drawer backs and fronts, as the tightness of the joints will hold them together.

8 Immediately after applying the glue, tap the dovetail joints together using a hammer and a block of wood. Apply only light pressure to avoid unnecessary damage to the delicate dovetail pins.

9 Use gauge sticks to check that each drawer is square (see p.416). Do this straight after gluing, so any minor adjustments can be made.

10 When the glue has set, slide each of the drawer bottoms back in place, and secure them with three or four small pins (tacks).

Pre-drilling a nail hole

When hammering a small pin (tack) or clout nail into a hardwood, you may find that it can bend or shear off. An easy remedy is to pre-drill the hole at a slightly smaller diameter than the nail (a pilot hole).

◄ 11 Clamp a hardwood block at the back of the workbench to keep each drawer securely in place, then plane the runners so that they fit into the desk and run smoothly.

Replacing the knobs

The desk retains its original oak wooden knobs, although a number have become detached and are now missing. Using an original as a template (pattern), copies must be turned to match.

Materials

- callipers
- oak
- lathe
- turning tools
- paring tool
- dividers
- skew chisel
- very fine-
- grade sandpaper
- spirit- (alcohol-) based stain
- fine brush
- rubber
- polish

1 Take a measurement from an original knob using a pair of callipers, and use this to determine the diameter of the new knob. Prepare a piece of oak for the lathe (see p.427), then turn it to the correct diameter.

2 Mark out the depth of the knob using a paring tool, then remove it from the lathe and pare it away from the rest of the wood. Replace the knob into a lathe chuck.

3 Turn the shape of the wooden knob, constantly comparing its shape and size to the original using dividers.

4 With the proportions already determined, turn the final shape, using a skew chisel to create the domed shape of the knob.

◀ 6 The completed replacement knob should be identical to the original. Repeat this procedure to make as many knobs as are needed. Stain and polish them to match the other knobs, before fitting them in place.

5 Finish off the knob by lightly sanding it while it is still rotating in the lathe. Take care during this process that you do not alter the shape of the knob.

Repairing the carcass

The drawer runners have worn deep grooves in the frame; one of the pedestals has a large split in the back due to shrinkage; and both plinths are missing sections of veneer and have sustained damage to the core wood. The frame supports for the drawer runners will be repaired with new pieces of wood, while the split will be glued and clamped. Damaged core wood on the plinths will be replaced and the veneer patched.

Repairing the drawer supports

The action of opening and shutting the top drawers over many years has resulted in deep grooves being worn into the frame supports. This damage must be repaired, as otherwise the frame will continue to be worn away until it breaks in two.

Materials

- screwdriver or pincers
- hardwood block
- hammer
- circular saw
- softwood
- PVA (white) glue
- jack plane
- sash clamps
- clamping blocks
- nails

1 Place the frame on the workbench and remove the screw or nail that secures each end of a support to the frame. Place a piece of hardwood over the support and gently knock the support out using blows from a hammer.

2 Make two parallel cuts down the centre with a circular saw. Reset the saw and turn the support on to its side. Making sure the depth is set correctly, run the support over the saw to remove the worn parts. Note that the guard should always be in place.

3 Using the circular saw, cut two fillets of softwood to replace the worn parts of wood that have been removed, and glue them into position.

4 Plane the new wood flush with the original. The inserts will allow the replaced drawer runners to run on a level surface. Repeat for the other damaged support.

5 Glue the restored frame supports back into position and clamp until dry. Hammer nails into each end while the supports are still firmly clamped.

Repairing the pedestal

Shrinkage has caused a crack to
develop from the top to the bottom of
the back panel of one of the
pedestals. The panel is attached to the
sides by dovetail joints, which have
been veneered over. To leave the
dovetails and veneer intact, the back
is scribed down each side and only
the broken sections removed. Once
the crack is repaired, the split is
glued and clamped in place and a
fillet is added to fill the gap.

Materials

- marking
  gauge
- circular
  saw
- stiff-bladed
  knife
- hammer
- iron
- oak
- PVA (white)
  glue
- sash clamps
- G-clamps
- clamping
  blocks
- plane
- nails
- veneer

1 Place the pedestal on the workbench
and scribe along both edges of the
back with a marking gauge. Cut along
the lines with a circular saw to free the
broken sections.

2 Cut through the fastening rails
with a stiff-bladed knife and
hammer, then prise the broken
sections off the pedestal. Turn the
pedestal on to its front.

3 Remove the thin strip of veneer
left between the right-hand edge
and the scribing line by placing a hot
iron on it to soften the glue and
prising it away.

◀ 4 Before
mending the
split, cut a fillet of
oak to compensate
for the back being
narrower now than
it was. Apply glue
to both sides of
the split and also to
the fillet, and glue
this to the right-
hand edge of the
back. Clamp the
pieces together,
using sash and
G-clamps and
clamping blocks.
Leave to dry.

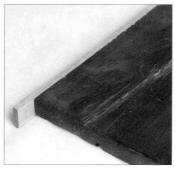

5 Trim the fillet and plane it to the
correct width. Glue the new back
into place and nail it at top and
bottom. Apply a strip of veneer to
cover the fillet and bare edge.

Restoring damaged wood and veneer

Sections of veneer are missing from the corners of the plinths, after years of being kicked and knocked, and the core wood on to which the veneer was laid is also damaged. The core wood needs to be rebuilt, and the veneer patched and polished to restore the piece. This is a relatively straightforward task but it is important that the new core wood is cut and fitted correctly before the more cosmetic veneer can be applied.

Materials

- snap clamp
- try square
- craft (utility) knife
- router
- wood
- tenon saw
- bench hook
- PVA (white) glue
- masking tape
- small block
- plane
- veneer
- scotch glue
- cabinet scraper
- fine-grade sandpaper
- sanding block

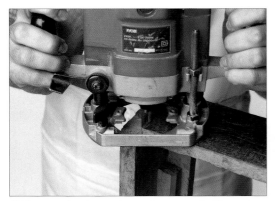

1 Place one of the plinths on the workbench. Clamp it firmly to the bench using a snap clamp, or fix it into the vice.

2 Score a line close to one of the damaged sections of veneer and core wood, using a try square and a craft (utility) knife.

3 Cut away the damaged area of core wood with a router. Repeat this procedure on each of the damaged corners, removing the wood and veneer if necessary, or just the veneer if the core wood is undamaged.

4 Cut replacement pieces of core wood from a suitable wood using a tenon saw and bench hook.

5 Glue the replacement patches into place using PVA (white) glue.

6 Apply strips of masking tape, pulled tight, to secure each patch as it sets. Make sure that all the edges are square, to achieve a firm joint.

7 Plane each new section of wood with a small block plane. Continue until there is enough depth to allow for a replacement piece of veneer.

8 Select a piece of oak veneer that matches the original. Cut it to size. Apply scotch glue to the new wood and tape the veneer firmly into place. Leave to dry.

9 Using a cabinet scraper, level the veneer patch to match the original veneer. Trim off any excess using a sharp utility knife.

10 Sand the veneer with fine-grade sandpaper and a sanding block. Repeat steps 1–10 for the other plinth.

11 Note the importance of choosing new wood that matches the original grain of the existing veneer.

Reassembling and polishing

With all the carcass repairs completed and the surface cleaned and revived, the desk can now be reassembled. This will involve replacing the knobs after they have been coloured and stained to match the originals, and may include servicing the locks.

Materials

- screwdriver
- brush
- stain
- ground
- pumice
- soft clean cotton rag
- polish

1 Reattach the plinths to the pedestals using the original screws. If you have carefully labelled the fittings when the carcass was dismantled you can ensure that they are put back on the right pedestal.

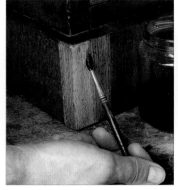

2 Stain any replacement veneer or moulding to match the original finish before polishing.

3 After filling the grain with ground pumice and polish, polish the new patches of wood until they match the rest of the desk (see pp.356–7).

Left The restored and reassembled desk is ready once again to be used. Treated with care, it should not need further attention for several generations.

United Kingdom

Axminster Power Tool Centre
Chard Street
Axminster
Devon EX13 5HU
Tel: 01297 33656
Power tools supplier

Black and Decker and Dewalt
210 Bath Road
Slough
Berkshire SL1 3YD
Tel: 01753 567055
Power tools supplier

Blumson Fine Timber
36–38 River Road
Barking
Essex IG11 0DN
Tel: 020 8594 5175
Timber (lumber) suppliers

Chestergate Wood Supplies Ltd.
Porron Street
Portwood, Stockport
Greater Manchester SK1 2JD
Timber (lumber) suppliers

Colour Centre
Offord Road
London N1
Tel: 020 7609 116
Paints and DIY equipment supplier

Crown Fasteners and Fixings Ltd.
Watermill House
Restmor Way, Hackridge
Surrey SM6 7AH
Tel: 020 8773 3993
Hardware supplier

Dewalt
210 Bath Road
Slough
Berkshire SL1 3YD
Tel: 01753 567055
Power tools supplier

Foxell and James
Farringdon Road
London EC1M 3JB
Tel: 020 7405 0152
*Wax, oil, varnish, and finishing
products.*

FR Shadbolt & Sons Ltd.
North Circular Road
South Chingford
London E4 8PZ
Tel: 020 8527 6441
Veneer suppliers

Heward and Dean
Grove Park Road
London N15 4SP
Tel: 020 8800 3447
Tool supplier

HSS Power Tools
25 Willow Lane
Mitcham
Surrey CR4 4TS
Tel: 020 8260 3100

James Latham
Leeside Wharf
Mount Pleasant Hill
Clapton E5
Tel: 020 8806 3333
Timber suppliers

John Boddy's Wood and Tool Store
Riverside Sawmills
Boroughbridge
North Yorkshire YO51 9LJ
Tel: 01423 322370
e-mail: info@john-boddy-timber.ltd.uk
Timber (lumber) suppliers

Machin Bros. Ltd.
79 Sceptre Road
Bethnal Green
London E2 0JU
Tel: 020 7790 3575
Veneer suppliers

North Wales Timber Ltd.
Industrial Estate
Pinfold Lane
Buckley
Flintshire CH7 3PL
Timber (lumber) suppliers

Plasplugs Ltd.
Wetmore Road
Burton-on-Trent
Staffordshire DE14 1SD
Tel: 01283 530303
www.plasplugs.com
Tiling tools, fixings and fasteners

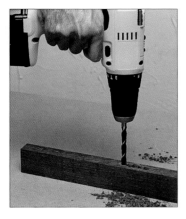

Record Tools Ltd.
Parkway Works
Kettlebridge Road
Sheffield S9 3BL
Tel: 0114 244 9066
Hand tools supplier

Ronseal Limited
Thorncliffe Park
Chapeltown
Sheffield S35 2YP
Tel: 0114 246 7171
www.ronseal.co.uk
Ronseal, Colron, Thompson's products

Spear & Jackson
Neill Tools Ltd.
Atlas Way
Atlas North
Sheffield S4 7QQ
Tel: 0114 261 4242
Tools supplier

Stanley Tools UK Ltd.
Beighton Road East
Drakehouse
Sheffield S20 7JZ
Tel: 0114 276 8888
Tools supplier

Vitrex Ltd.
Everest Road
Lytham St. Annes
Lancashire
FY8 3AZ
Tel: 01253 789180

West and Heaton Timber Ltd.
4 North Back Lane
Bridlington
East Yorkshire YO16 5BA
Timber (lumber) suppliers

Winther Browne & Co.
Nobel Road
Eley Estate
Edmonton
London N18 3DX
Tel: 020 8803 3434
Fine wood carvings and mouldings

Woodfit Ltd.
Kem Mill
Whittle-le-Woods
Chorley
Lancashire PR6 7EA
Tel: 01257 266421
Furniture fittings supplier

Y Goldburg & Sons
3–5 Waterloo Road
Uxbridge
Middlesex UB8 2QX
Tel: 01895 253491
Timber (lumber) suppliers

United States
California Redwood Association
405 Enfrente Drive
Suite 200
Novato, CA 94949
Tel: (415) 382-0662
Fax: (415) 382-8531
www.calredwood.org

Colonial Hardwoods Inc.
7953 Cameron Brown Ct.
Springfield, VA 22153
Tel: (703) 451-9217
www.colonialhardwoods@rica.com

Compton Lumber & Hardware Inc.
P.O. Box 84972
Seattle, WA 98124-6272
Tel: (206) 623-5010
www.comptonlbr.com

Constantine's
2050 Eastchester Road
Bronx, New York NY 10461
Tel: (718) 792-1600
www.constantines.com

The Cutting Edge, Inc.
7123 Southwest Freeway
Houston, TX 77074
Tel: (981) 9228
www.cuttingedgetools.com

Diamond Machining Technology Inc.
85 Hayes Memorial Drive
Malborough, MA 01752
Tel: (800) 666-4368
Fax: (508) 485-3924
www.dmtsharp.com
Woodworking tool supplier

North Atlantic Timber Corporation
South Road
Chilmark, MA 0235
Tel: (508) 696-8939
Fax: (508) 696-8232
www.northatlantictimber.com

Northern Tool and Equipment
Corporate Headquarters
2800 Southcross Drive West
Burnsville, MN 55306
Tel: (800) 533-5545
www.northerntool.com

Southern Pine Council
P.O. Box 641700
Kenner
Louisiana, 70064-1700
Tel: (504) 443-4464
Fax: (504) 443-6612
www.SouthernPine.com

Talarico Hardwoods
Route 3, Box 3268
Mohnton, PA 19540

Tropical Exotic Hardwoods of Latin America
2579 State Street
Carlsbad, CA 92008-1624
Tel: (760) 434-3030
Fax: (760) 434-5423
www.anexotichardwood.com

Viking Woodcrafts Inc.
1317 8th Street SE
Waseca, MN 56093
Tel: (507) 835 8043
www.vikingwoodcrafts.com

Australia
Anagote Timbers
144 Renwick Street
Marrickville
New South Wales 2204
Tel: 02 9558 8444

BBC Hardware Stores
Hardware House
For details of your nearest store
in either of the above two chains,
contact (02) 9876 0888.

Bunnings Warehouse
For details of your nearest store
contact (03) 9607 0777.

Lazarides Timber Agencies
PO Box 440, Ferny Hills
Queensland 4055
Tel: 07 3851 1400

Mitre 10
For details of your nearest store
contact (03) 9703 4200.

Thrifty-Link Hardware
See you local state directory for
your nearest store.

Trend Timbers Pty Ltd.
Cunneen Street, McGraths Hill
New South Wales 2756
Tel: 02 4577 5277

The Wood Works
8 Railway Road, Meadowbank
New South Wales 2114
Tel: 02 9807 7244

Veneers
37 Alexandra Road
East Ringwood
Victoria 3135
Tel: 03 9870 8733

Useful addresses

United Kingdom
The Association of Noise Consultants
6 Trap Road
Guilden Morden
Hertfordshire SG8 0JE
Tel: 01763 852958
www.association-of-noise-
consultants.co.uk

British Antique Furniture Restorers' Association
BAFRA Head Office
The Old Rectory
Warmwell
Dorchester
Dorset DT2 8HQ
Tel: 01305 854822
Fax: 01305 852104
www.bafra.org.uk

British Cement Association
Century House
Telford Avenue
Berkshire RG45 6YS
Tel: 01344 762676
www.bca.org.uk

British Wood Preserving and Damp-proofing Association
1 Gleneagles House
Vernon Gate, South Street
Derby DE1 1UP
Tel: 01332 225100
www.bwpda.co.uk

British Woodturners' Association
Treetops
78 St. Mark's Avenue
Salisbury
Wiltshire SP1 3DW
Tel: 01722 328032
Fax: 01722 333558

Conservatory Association/Glass and Glazing Federation
44–48 Borough High Street
London SE1 1XB
Tel: 01480 458278
www.ggf.org.uk

Energy Saving Trust
21 Dartmouth Street
London SW1H 9BT
Tel: 08457 277200
www.est.org.uk

Forest Stewardship Council
FSC UK Working Group
Unit D, Station Building
Llanidloes SY18 6EB, Wales
Tel: 01686 413916
Fax: 01686 412176
www.fsc-uk.demon.co.uk

Home Energy Efficiency Scheme
Eaga Partnership
2nd Floor, Eldon Court
Eldon Square
Newcastle-upon-Tyne NE1 7HA
Tel: 0800 316 6011

The Institute of Electrical Engineers
2 Savoy Place
London WC2R 0BL
Tel: 020 7240 1871
www.iee.org.uk

The Institute of Plumbing
64 Station Lane
Hornchurch
Essex RM12 6NB
Tel: 01708 472791
www.plumbers.org.uk

Kitchen Specialists Association
12 Top Barn Business Centre
Holt Heath
Worcester WR6 6NH
Tel: 01905 726066
www.ksa.co.uk

Laminated Glass Information Centre
299 Oxford Street
London W1R 1LA
020 7499 1720
www.martex.co.uk/prca/condor

National Association of Loft Insulation Contractors and National Cavity Insulation Association
PO Box 12
Hazlemere
Surrey GU27 3AH
Tel: 01428 654011
theceed@computer.com

National Fireplace Association
6th Floor
The McLaren Building
35 Dale End
Birmingham B4 7LN
Tel: 0121 200 1310

RIBA (Royal Institute of Chartered Architects)
66 Portland Place
London W1B 1AD
Tel: 020 7580 5533
www.architecture.com

SALVO (Directory of Salvage Yards)
PO Box 333
Cornhill on Tweed
Northumberland TD12 4YJ
Tel: 01890 820333
www.salvo.co.uk

Timber Research and Development Association Technology Ltd
Stocking Lane
Hughenden Valley
High Wycombe
Buckinghamshire HP14 4ND
Tel: 01494 563091
Fax: 01494 565487
www.tradatechnology.co.uk

United States
Forests Forever
973 Market Street, Suite 450
San Francisco, CA 94103
Tel: (415) 974-3636
Fax: (415) 974-3664
www.forestsforever.org

Timber Reclamation International
3011 Killarny Drive
Cary, Illinois 60013
Tel: (847) 516-3804
Fax: (847) 516-2313

GLOSSARY

Some of the less familiar woodworking terms encountered in this book are
listed here. Turn to the sections on tools and wood for more information on
tools and materials.

animal glue Also known as scotch glue and traditionally used from the 17th century onwards.

astragals Glazing bars on cabinet furniture, forming a geometric pattern.

bain-marie A pot containing hot water in which another container, holding animal glue, gesso or bole, for example, can be gently heated.

banding Decorative inlays of veneer that are used for aesthetic effect. They can be either long-grained or cross-grained and on earlier pieces can be joined to give a chevron effect, known as herringbone.

bare-faced A type of tenon joint where the shoulder is formed on only one face of the tenon.

batten A length of timber (lumber), usually square in section, for joining or strengthening.

baulk A squared log from which smaller sections of timber (lumber) are converted in the sawmill.

bench hook A portable stop, often home-made, which fits over the edge of a bench for steadying the workpiece.

bevel The angled edge or end of a piece of wood – measured and marked with a bevel gauge.

biscuit A small flat lozenge-shaped dowel for edge or corner jointing – fitted with a biscuit jointer.

blister A bubble that forms on a surface when part of the veneer has become detached from its core.

blooming The name given to the white marks left on a polished surface that has been water-damaged or chilled.

bole A clay-like substance that is used in the gilding process.

botanical name The Latin name that uniquely identifies the genus and species of timber (lumber).

boulle Also known as buhl, this is the use of fine brass inlay inset into tortoiseshell or ebony backgrounds.

bracket foot A square foot which might have a shaped profile on the inside. The foot most commonly used during the 18th century.

breaker A piece or a collection of pieces of furniture used in the restoration of another item of furniture.

burr (burl) The part of a tree with twisted and complex grain formation, prized for its decorative appearance.

bun feet A ball type of foot favoured during the 17th century and replaced by the bracket foot in the 18th century.

butterfly key A butterfly-shaped piece of wood used to secure and hold splits. It is inset into a piece so that the grain runs at right angles to the main wood. Also known as a dovetail key.

carcass The actual framework of any construction or piece of furniture, such as a cabinet or shelving unit.

cascamite A glue used when forming laminates or shape work. It is very strong but also brittle.

chamfer To remove the sharp corner of a section of wood and produce a smooth bevelled edge. *(vb & n)*

chuck The adjustable jaws of a power drill or hand brace.

clearance hole A hole drilled through a panel to allow clearance for the shank of a wood screw.

cock beading Thin strips of decorative beading often found around drawer fronts.

colour The tone or shade that wood develops over time.

conservation To maintain a piece by undertaking as little work as possible so as not to alter its present or original form (see restoration).

conversion A method of cutting timber (lumber) from the baulk to produce boards for woodworking.

core The moulded shape on to which veneer or mouldings are applied.

cornice The top of a carcass piece of furniture often decorated with dental mouldings, cross bandings or a pediment.

counterbore A cylindrical hole at the top of the clearance hole to recess the head of a screw below the surface.

cross-dowel A threaded metal rod inserted across the grain of a wooden member to receive a connecting bolt.

cross-grain mouldings Wood applied to a softwood backing and planed to a moulded profile, applied to a carcass for aesthetic reasons. Introduced during the 17th century, they are more decorative than long-grain mouldings.

Cuban mahogany Mahogany imported from Cuba during the 18th and 19th centuries and the preferred wood for quality furniture. It is densely grained and red in tone when first polished.

cutting gauge A tool fitted with a small blade that is used across the grain to cut a groove. Often used prior to fitting boxwood lines.

de-nibbing The removal of dust that has combined with polish to form small raised nibs on a surface after polishing. This is done by lightly using fine wire wool in the direction of the grain. The surface is then waxed.

density The relative weight of a substance, expressed as kg per cubic metre, or pounds per cubic foot.

dental mouldings Small rectangular pieces applied to a cornice and resembling square teeth. Popular during the mid-18th century.

dovetail saw A fine-bladed saw used for cutting accurate and delicate dovetails.

dowel A cylindrical length of wood used for connecting a joint, sometimes fluted to allow good adhesion.

face and edge marks Pencil marks to identify the square and straight edges of a length of wood before working it.

escutcheon The brassware used in conjunction with locks for both aesthetic and protective reasons.

fading/fad Filling the grain in wood with a mixture of polish and pumice powder. The cloth with which it is applied is known as a fad.

fire gilding   A mixture of gold and mercury applied to a metal base and heated until the mercury evaporates and binds the gold to the metal. Favoured during the 18th century; used on the mounts and handles of the finest pieces.

flute   A semicircular groove in a piece of wood; also, the description of the cutting tool to produce it.

follower (fence)   A circular fitting for the base of a router used to follow the curved edge of a template.

French curve   A kidney-shaped scraper used on concave curves.

French polishing   Using shellac polish, which is usually applied with a linen and wadding (batting) rubber.

fret   A lattice-like decoration, in which open fret is pierced and blind fret is applied to a solid background.

gauge sticks   Two lengths of stick which are held together and used to check the equal diagonal measure of a frame to ensure it is square.

gesso   A plaster-like substance that is used in the gilding process.

graining   Using surface stains and colours to mimic the grain of a solid piece of wood. Favoured during the early 19th century.

growth rings   Layers of annual growth in the tree, clearly visible in cross section.

hardwood   Wood from broad-leaved trees, usually harder and more close-grained than coniferous softwoods, ideal for fine finishing or joinery.

haunch   A shortened section of a tenon, formed at the outside edge of a joint to prevent twisting.

heartwood (core)   The inner part of the tree below the sapwood layer, yielding the most usable timber (lumber).

hockey stick (corner bead)   A moulding used to trim the edges of a panel, with a J-shaped section in the profile of a hockey-stick to produce a finished edge.

Honduras mahogany   Mahogany imported from Honduras during the 18th and 19th centuries and favoured for carcass construction.

horn   The end of frame member in a door or panel, which projects past the mortise for added strength.

housing   A grooved joint, square in section, which receives the end of another component.

jig   A woodworking aid for controlling the tool or locating the workpiece, for added safety or accuracy.

kickers   Strips of wood applied to the inside carcass of a chest, running along the top of the drawer linings, to stop the drawers tipping forward when extended.

kiln-dried   Seasoned timber (lumber) that has been dried in the kiln to a low moisture content of approximately 10%.

laminate   A thin layer of wood or other material, used for forming curves or building up a decorative surface. (vb & n)

liming wax   Finishing wax that imparts a delicate white colour to the grain of the wood, especially oak.

linings   The name given to the sides and often the bottom of a drawer.

long-grain mouldings   Mouldings planed from one length of wood along the grain and applied to a carcass for aesthetic or structural reasons.

MDF — Medium-density fibreboard – all-purpose sheet material, available in a range of thicknesses with a smooth sanded surface, suitable for home woodworking projects of all kinds.

marquetry — Inlays of decorative scenes. Two parts of a piece of furniture that started life separately but have now been brought together. Such an example would be a bureau bookcase in which both halves would have started life with another part.

mitre — Halving the angle of a corner joint where two members intersect: in a right angle, two 45 degree angles. *(vb & n)*

moisture content — A measure of how dry a sample of wood may be – low moisture content means the wood is stable and well-seasoned.

mortise — The hollow housing part of a mortise and tenon joint, which is the most widely used joint in furniture construction.

mortise gauge — A marking tool that has a small steel point and is used along the grain to mark the shoulders of a mortise.

moulding — Decorative profiled edge of a length of wood, formed either by hand or with machine tools.

movement — The tendency of wood to shrink or expand with the changing atmospheric conditions of its surroundings.

nominal — The size of a section of timber after sawing, before machining further to an exact dimension.

overloe — A shaped block used in conjunction with sandpaper.

pare (shave) — To remove thin layers of wood by hand with a flat chisel blade.

parquetry — Inlays of geometric patterns.

patera — A round or oval, raised decoration often found on cornices or the tops of legs. Can also be used in veneer form.

patination — This refers to the build up of waxes, natural greases and dust that over numerous years combines to form a desirable finish on a surface.

pediment — Found on top of a carcass and, depending on the period, can be arched, broken-arched or swan-necked in shape.

piecrust — The name used to describe the shape of a top usually applying to a tripod table. The top, as the name suggests, looks like the top of a pinched pastry pie top.

pilot hole — A hole drilled to receive the threaded end of a wood screw, to assist location and prevent the wood from splitting.

plinth (kick) — A raised base of a cupboard or floor unit, usually detachable.

prepared — Describes planed timber (lumber) with smooth faces and square edges.

profile — Any shape produced from a square blank of timber (lumber).

profile cutter — A special cutter fitted to a router, used to follow a template for reproducing a particular profile.

PVA glue — Polyvinylacetate glue, also known as white glue. Ideal for day to day use.

rail — The upper or lower horizontal member in a door or panel.

rebate (rabbet) — To cut a rectangular, stepped recess along the edge of a section of wood. *(vb & n)*

reeded decoration — A raised decoration of parallel, tapering lines, usually found on chair and table legs.

relish A cutaway section of a tenon joint to avoid the edge or corner of a frame, and thus avoid weakening the joint.

restoration To undertaken any necessary work to return a piece as near as possible to its original form but retaining its integrity (see conservation).

revive a surface The action of attending to any minor damage or surface oxidation of a polished surface while not repolishing the whole top.

rubber Wadding (batting) wrapped in linen, which is used to apply shellac polish.

runners The strips of wood attached to the bottom or sides of a drawer on which the drawer will run. Sometimes also found as part of the carcass.

sapwood The outer layer of the tree, just below the bark; softer and more perishable than heartwood.

scratch box A workshop-made tool that allows parallel reeds to be scratched on a leg (see reeded decoration).

scribe To mark or shape the end of a section of wood to fit around a moulding or profile for a neat joint. *(vb & n)*

shooting board (stop) A home-made jig used with a bench plane to square the end or the edges of a length of wood.

shorts/short ends (cuts) Shorter lengths of wood as sold by a timber (lumber) yard, often suitable for home woodworking projects at lower cost.

shellac Polish that is obtained from the shellac beetle.

shoulder The edge of a tenon joint that mates with the surface of another component, keeping it square.

skiver Leather taken from sheep. Not as good quality as cow hide.

softwood Relatively inexpensive, general-purpose timber, from pine or other coniferous trees.

sole plate The smooth base plate of a plane, which makes contact with the wood when in use.

splay feet A shaped bracket foot that is splayed in profile. Favoured during the late 18th century.

spring clip A workshop-made cramping device made from upholstery springs. Ideal for securing awkward shapes.

stains Usually bought in powder form and mixed with water, spirit or oil depending on the intended use.

stretcher Part of a wooden frame, usually between two rails, to maintain a fixed distance between them.

stringing Thin lines of inlay, usually made of ebony or box, which were used for both aesthetic reasons and as protective edges.

TCT Tungsten-carbide tipped: better quality but more expensive cutters and sawblades.

template A pattern, usually of wood, which is used as a guide to form complex shapes or to create repetitive, accurate work.

tenon The protruding part of a mortise and tenon joint, which is the most widely used joint in furniture construction.

twist When wood bows in two directions.

veneer Very thin slices of wood for high quality decorative work.

wane The uneven edge of a board, where the outside edges of the tree have not been cut away during conversion.

warp When a piece of wood has bowed along its length or width.

INDEX

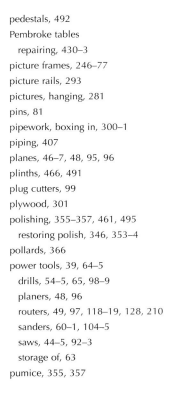

ACKNOWLEDGEMENTS

The publisher would like to thank the following individuals and suppliers for loaning equipment and their help with photography.

Bob Cleveland
111 Stillingfleet Road
London SW13 9AF
Tel: 020 8748 9726
For the loan of the rocking horse, and for the carving demonstration.

Liz Boddy
John Boddy's Wood and Tool Store
For the loan of images.

Justin Browne
Winther Browne & Co.
Fine Wood Carvings & Mouldings
For the loan of mouldings.

Andrew Gillmore
For making the three-legged chair and computer cupboard projects.

Mr. Mark Blewitt
c/o The National Federation of Roofing Contractors

Burlington Slate Limited
Cavendish House
Kirkby-in-Furness
Cumbria LA17 7UN
Tel: 01229 889661

Canonbury Art Shop
266 Upper Street
London N1
Tel: 020 7226 4652

Chromacolor by Perstorp
Perstorp Customer Hotline
Tel: 01325 303303
For the loan of the worksurface (page 200).

Colour Centre
(see Suppliers)

John Bruch
Woodfit
For the loan of fixtures and fittings.

David Cropp
Rentokil Initial plc
East Grinstead
West Sussex RH19 2JY
Tel: 01342 830220
http://www.rentokil-initial.com/photos
Dewalt
For the loan of power tools.

Egg
36 Kinnerton Street
London SW1Z 8ES
Tel: 020 7235 9315
For the loan of ceramics (page 174 and 186).

Eternit Building Materials

Fothergills
79 Salmon Lane
Limehouse
London E14 7NA
Tel: 020 7790 7774
For the loan of the music case and scarf (page 226).

Farbo Nairn Ltd.
PO Box 1
Kircaldy
Fife KY1 2SB
Tel: 01592 643777
For the loan of kitchen flooring (page 238).

Drew Geldart
Spear & Jackson
Neill Tools Ltd.
For the loan of tools.

Gill Wing Cookshop
190 Upper Street
Islington
London N1 1RQ
Tel: 020 7226 5392
For the loan of kitchen products.

Grahams Hi Fi
Canonbury Yard
190a New North Road
London N1 7BS
Tel: 020 7226 5500
http://www.grahams.co.uk
For the loan of the stereo system (page 158).

Heward and Dean (BD) Ltd
(see Suppliers)

Hunter Plastics Limited
Nathan Way
London SE28 0AE
Tel: 020 8855 9851

Marcus Jervis Hughes
Y Goldburg & Sons
(Timber Importers).

Marley Roofing Products

Paul Machin
Machin Bros. Ltd.
For the loan of veneers.

Plasplugs Ltd.

Sandtex
Julie Coleman
ICAS Public Relations
19 Garrick Street
London WC2E 9BB
Tel: 020 7632 2424

Spear & Jackson
For the loan of saws.

Stanley UK Tools Ltd.
For the loan of tools.

Alan Stiles
Axminster Power Tool Centre
Chard Street
Axminster
Devon EX13 5HU
For the loan of tools and images.

Glyn Storey
William Marples
Record Tools. Ltd.
For the loan of chisels.

Suzanna Tabor
FR Shadbolt & Sons
For the loan of veneers.

Thompson's
Pure PR
PO Box 1430
Sheffield S11 7XH
Tel: 0114 230 9112

The Tool Shop
97 Lower Marsh
London SE1
Tel: 020 7207 2077
For the loan of tools.

Vallance Adhesive and Sealant Range
Stransky Thompson PR
Denton House
40–44 Wicklow Street
London WC1X 9HL
Vin Vara

Vitrex Limited

Volume
21 St. Alban's Place
London N1 0NX
Tel: 020 7359 0224
For the loan of the glass table (page 182) and wooden table (page 232).

Mr Wright
Blumsom Timber Centre
For helping with photography.

Yale Security Products UK Limited
Wood Street
Willenhall
West Midlands
WV13 1LA
Tel: 01902 366911

The publisher would also like to thank the following people for designing projects in this book:

Victoria Brown for Decorative Moulding Frame p252–3. Stephanie Harvey for the Frame Restoration p276–7. Alison Jenkins for the Pressed Flowerhead Frame pp254–5. Rian Kanduth for the Multi-window Frame p268–9, Reclaimed Timber Frame p272–3. Mary Maguire for the Deep Box Frame p258–9. Dorothy Wood for Cutting and Joining a Frame p248–9, Creating a Rebate p250–1, Halving Joint Frame p256–7, Cross-over Frame p264–5, Jigsaw Puzzle Frame p266–7.

Thanks to the following for individual projects: Ofer Acoo, Deborah Alexander, Michael Ball, Amanda Blunden, Esther Burt, Gill Clement, Louise Gardam, Jill and David Hancock, Rachel Howard Marshall, Terry Moore, Jack Moxley; Oliver Moxley, Deborah Schneebeli-Morrell, Debbie Siniska, Karen Triffitt and Josephine Whitfield.

Picture acknowledgements
DIY Photo Library p28br; p29br; p134bl; p136tr, br; 318–19 all; 320–1 all. Forest Life Picture Library pp6tr, bl; 10tr, 11tl, b; 21cl. Imagebank p14b. Liz and John Boddy p14tr; 15tr, br; 18c. Ian Durrant p135, 137br. John Freeman: 108–9, 302–3.

Thanks to the following photographers: Steve Dalton, Nicki Dowey, Rodney Forte, Michelle Garrett, Rose Jones, Debbie Patterson, Spike Powell, Graham Rae, Steve Tanner, Adrian Taylor, Lucy Tizard, Peter Williams and Polly Wreford.

The publisher would also like to thank FSC for allowing the reproduction of their logo on page 20; Graham Bruford at Forests Forever for permission to reproduce text on page 21; Ian Durrant for his help on woodturning and permission to reproduce the image on pages 135 and 137bl; to Tony McMullen for permission to use images on page 135tr, cr; to Anthony Bryant for permission to use images on page 134tr, 137bl, tr and to Kenneth Wilson for permission to use the image on page 138bl.